ada

For the Love of Cornwall

Brenda

For the Love of Cornwall

The Life and Times of
Brenda Wootton
Cornwall's First Lady
of Song

Brenda For The Love Of Cornwall
by Sue Ellery-Hill

First published in 2018
by TBC

Back cover photo: © Damian Dawes;
[Brenda's Bardic name, Gwylan Gwavas, means Newlyn Seagull]
Front cover photo: taken during a concert in the Palais des Papes at Avignon.

A catalogue card for this book is available from the British Library.

Paperback ISBN: 978-1-9996788-6-9

Publication support
TJ INK
tjink.co.uk

Printed and bound in Great Britain by TJ International, Padstow, Cornwall

With fond and grateful memories of

Richard Gendall

"Gelvinak"... Curlew

1924 – 2017

Thanks for all the music, Richard

We will sing you for

all the long years to come

Gen covyon caradow ha grasek a

Richard Gendall

"Gelvinak"... Curlew

1924 – 2017

Meur ras dhis rag oll an ilow, Richard.

Nei a vedn gana dha ganow

rag oll an bledhydnyow hir a dheu.

Contents

Foreword

I'd been dreading this for over 30 years – long before Brenda died, I had an inkling that at some point I would be compelled to write her story… a daunting prospect which, until recently, I didn't want to contemplate. I always had this uncomfortable feeling that there was something nefarious, nepotistic, about potentially earning a crust from the exploits of such a close family member – might people feel I was cashing in on her achievements, on her memory, when I so obviously lack her talents? Was I too close to the subject – would I lay myself open to accusations of partisanship? Now she's been gone for over 20 years – is that time enough to write about her dispassionately, to do her life story justice? We shall see…

The title, by the way, was chosen to reflect Brenda's attitude to her life. I did not want to write a book solely about her singing career – and pretty much everything she was involved in was to do with her love for Cornwall.

Writing a book about your mother would never be easy – and writing a book about Brenda, a larger than life character known to so many, yet not known so well… is challenging, exciting and terrifying, all in one. And apologies from the start if you begin to feel this is an autobiography – it is not intended as such, but it is difficult to leave yourself out of your mother's story. If Brenda was Cornwall's Ambassador for Song, maybe I can be an Ambassador for Brenda.

I'll give it a go.

Introduction
by Mike Sagar-Fenton

Brenda Wootton has rightly become a legend, her place in any list of Cornish cultural icons – especially female icons – unchallenged. At the height of her powers she was without question the most famous Cornish woman in the world, and probably still is.

It was her fate that other countries – France, Belgium, Spain, Germany, Canada, Australia – fell under her spell more readily than her own. Something in the mainstream English character could not see further than a large middle-aged Cornish housewife, almost a figure of fun, and failed to respond to her incredible musical talent and equally magical stage presence. And in Cornwall she was simply Brenda from Penzance, one of us, doing rather well overseas. Unknown to us she could regularly fill the most prestigious halls in capitals all over Europe, meet and perform with the major stars of the day, shake hands with presidents and royalty, and conquer all she met with her music and supercharged personality.

She however never forgot her roots. On the contrary, she made a point of putting Cornwall and its heritage front and centre of all her recordings and performances, fulfilling a self-made promise to include some items in the Cornish language at every concert she played. It was commonplace for sophisticated French audiences to be seduced into joining in the choruses of "Little Eyes" or for a Barcelona audience to be regaled with the glories of Jelberts' Ice Cream. But she was no faux-rural comic turn. She could switch an audience in a moment from such homely visions to entrancement as her sweet pure voice pierced the heart of their emotions.

A proper biography of Brenda is well overdue. Others have tried to encapsulate such a wide-ranging story, pin down her complex and extraordinary character, but all have failed, myself included. I'm now so grateful that we did, because only Sue, her daughter, has the full story, the memory, the detail, and the courage to tell it as it was. Sue was long in denial that she had the talent to write this book, but the blood-line of engaging conversational story-telling, passed down from Brenda, her grandfather Angus and who knows how many other generations, runs sweet and true in her. It is a terrific story, beautifully and movingly told, and will give pleasure to the thousands who fell under Brenda's spell and thousands more who were never lucky enough to know her.

Where She Came From

A Newlyn Maid...

There's a sense of poignancy about one of Brenda's most popular and beautiful songs, 'Silver Net'. Written by fellow Cornish Bard Richard Gendall, it describes the writer's wish to throw a silver net over Cornwall, to prevent its young people being driven away from their homeland to find work. The song could have been written about her own parents.

It is a fact that irked Brenda more than somewhat.

Brenda Ellery was born in Willesden in north-west London, on February 10th 1928. It was always a great mystery to me – why did Lena and Angus, her Cornish born and bred parents, then living in Newlyn, just happen to be up in London briefly at the time of Brenda's birth? It was a thorn in her side when she grew old enough to think about it, and not something she wanted widely known, but there is little point in denying it now – and it's a classic conundrum for that hoary old chestnut 'what makes a true Cornishman (or woman)'. When asked, she would say she, yes, she *was* born in London – but she was 'Made in Cornwall'... "My mother said I was in such a hurry to be born there was no time to get me back to Cornwall... but I was made there, and no mistake!"

But that doesn't quite ring true... It's taken a lot of digging, but I now have a much clearer picture of what was happening around the time of Brenda's birth. According to her Aunt Marjorie – only 3 years older than Brenda, and hence a playmate when they were children – the young couple could not find work in Cornwall, so in the Spring of 1927 they travelled to London in search of gainful employment. Angus found work as a jobbing builder, and Lena, an experienced cook, found a job in Willesden 'in service' at a big house, hard work which required her to carry each course up several flights of stairs. But it is likely they knew Lena was pregnant when they left – and this could indeed have been a contributory reason for the move. So by the summer of 1927, with Lena pregnant and unwed, the situation needed remedying swiftly. The decision was taken to marry in London, have the baby, wait a few months, and then return to Cornwall.

The wedding took place in St Andrew's, Willesden, on 3rd September 1927, with Angus's sister Doris named as one of the witnesses. Lena's parents Bartle and Lena senior were also living or staying in Willesden at the time, so this may have been their incentive to move – although it can only have been for a short while, so maybe they were just up in London for the wedding. It is unlikely that many more relatives would have been able to make the long journey from Cornwall for the event, so the family probably felt cheated of the chance to enjoy a good wedding – significantly, there are no group wedding photos. Once Brenda was born, I suspect the newly-weds chose to stay in Willesden for a few more months to draw attention away from the suspiciously narrow five-month gap between their wedding in September and Brenda's birth in February. In those days, that sort of thing mattered. She was baptised on 15th April 1928, at St Andrews Church, Kingsbury, and named after another sister of Angus's.

It is likely that a pregnant Lena would not have been permitted to give birth in their lodgings at 4 Vicarage Way, Ealing. So Brenda was born in what had been, until only a few years earlier, Willesden Workhouse. The name change in 1921 to Park Royal Hospital seems initially to have been largely cosmetic – certainly Brenda's birth certificate bears the birth address of Twyford Lodge, Acton Lane, Ealing, a fictitious address which had been used on the birth certificates of babies born there for many years previously as a euphemism for Willesden Workhouse – presumably in an attempt to alleviate the stigma for children born at the site. The deception was obviously still felt necessary in 1928, so it seems little else had changed.

Angus and Lena in their finery - possibly for their wedding in 1927

For Brenda, her birth in exile meant a lifelong feeling that she had to justify herself as a Cornishwoman – even if no-one else knew. Perhaps this contributed to her passion to take Cornwall with her everywhere she went... She never lied about it, but she tried not to draw attention to her birth details, saying she 'had a Newlyn childhood', and was a 'Newlyn maid' – which she was. Even today, I sometimes have to answer accusations from internet trolls, absurdly claiming that Brenda had no right to call herself a Cornishwoman – even that she was a Cockney (she was *not* born within the sound of Bow Bells). As Professor Charles Thomas so memorably commented in his erudite lecture 'The Importance of Being Cornish in Cornwall'[1]: "...if a cat has kittens in the oven, this doesn't make them into pasties." Moving on...

Brenda has said she was just six months old when they came back home to live – first in Ludgvan, then in 1 Vine Cottages, Boase Street, Newlyn, a small fisherman's cottage tucked away in Newlyn's tiny back lanes, a home of which she had many happy memories. The cottage features in a well-known Victorian sepia photograph, of which she did a painting, many years later. At the time Brenda lived there, the old vine still grew outside her bedroom window, and still produced grapes – she even took some to school to show her teacher, Miss Myra Trembath.

She once described her parents' origins as a mixed marriage: Angus – Penzance and church, and Lena – Newlyn and chapel. I think Lena won out there.

There is much I have to say about Angus, as he was such a huge influence on Brenda, and on me. He was born in Penzance in 1905, and I've traced his Cornish Ellery ancestry back to 1399, east of Wadebridge and around St

Brenda's childnood home – 1 Vine Cottage, Boase Street, Newlyn, from a painting by Brenda of an old photograph

[1] *'The Importance of Being Cornish in Cornwall', Professor Charles Thomas, 1973; Inaugural Lecture, Institute of Cornish Studies*

Columb. (Interestingly, I believe John Ellery, one of the famous Ringers of Egloshayle, subject of a song much sung by Brenda in the 1970s, is an ancestor.) Angus was a signwriter and painter by trade, and he carried the tools of his trade around the district on an old handcart – pulled, as you might guess, by hand. He was most well-known for painting pub signs – a favourite occupation of his, as he was good for a pint in practically every pub in the district as a result. (One of his signs can still be seen, out the back of the Turk's Head in Chapel Street, Penzance, signed.)

In his usual entrepreneurial style, in the 1940s and '50s he made plaster of Paris moulds for a series of small wall plaques to sell to the landlords, to be sold on in the pubs – there was one for every pub sign he painted, and he paid Brenda sixpence a go for hand-painting them. I still have several of them displayed in my bathroom. As a young woman, Brenda even used to help him with painting his pub signs: the 'Lion & Lamb' at Ashton, 'The Slip' and the 'Prince Charles', she remembered.

Other 'sure-fire hot sellers' were his little posy or spill pots – Shippams meat paste glass jars encased in cement, and studded with beach pebbles to look like a cairn of stones, mounted on a slate roof tile. He made a little 4-branched crossroads sign from strips of metal and constructed a hand-painted signpost which stuck out of the top of each one. The one I managed to keep, appropriately, recorded the signpost on the crossroads below the house at Newmill which would be bought by Brenda many years later, and which she passed by every day.

'Angus Ellery & Son', outside his New Street studio, painting a sign for the Mermaid pub on the Scilly Isles

Angus took an old garage and studio in Abbey Mews off New Street in Penzance, and here he painted his pub signs, smoked his Woodbines, made his 'creations' and did his oil paintings. One wall of the studio was all small glass panes, looking down on the yard below, and another was covered in tiered ranks of grubby, wooden cubicle shelves – each filled with treasures a young girl could spend days exploring: baccy tins full of buttons or beads, fascinating bits of wood, or old tools, or long-ago collected beach stones or shells, tins with packs of old cigarette cards, or old family photos. The stone steps leading up to the studio were worn smooth and deeply concave with the tread of feet over generations; the smell of oil paint takes me straight back there today. As well as his commissioned signboards, trade names and pub signs, he also painted local scenes in oils to resell. Almost uniquely, for I have never seen another artist use the same technique, he sketched out his design and then built up the details with plaster of Paris, moulded with an old palette knife. He favoured landscape or harbour scenes, so boats, hedges and trees, usually with the Mount in the distance, stood out in relief, painted in a loose impressionistic style in natural colours. His favourite scene was 'The Mount from Gulval Lanes', and he often quipped he charged 'sixpence a colour' for his paintings – but he was a natural artist, and it was always a great sadness to me that he was never acknowledged as such by the notoriously cliquey local art scene.

A few of his paintings *were* included in an exhibition titled 'Unknown Artists', held in Newlyn in June 1939, to raise funds for West Cornwall Hospital (plus ça change, eh? Eighty years on and it still needs help...). The Cornishman reported: "There are several interesting contributions from A Ellery of Newlyn. Mr Ellery shows 'Trevaylor' (one of the pleasantest landscapes in the show), 'Newlyn Silhouette' and 'Mousehole' (both after Garnier), 'Sonning-on-Thames', 'Up the Creeps' and 'St Ives Harbour'."[2] His brother Bill also had paintings in that exhibition.

Sometime in the 1950s two young photographers, Peter Watson-Wood and Mike Courtney, set up a small business enterprise at Land's End, which was not then the slick tourist trap it is today. They erected a signpost with channels in the boards to slot in letters and numbers, and offered to take photographs of anyone wishing to record their visit with a reference to their home town and its distance from Land's End. They later went on to form Courtwood Film Services

---

[2] *The Cornishman Newspaper , June 29th 1939*

in Penzance. So this provided another string to Angus's bow: for some years, he kept them supplied with the hand-painted letters and numerals – one of his little 'sidelines', and the inspiration for his miniature Signpost posy pots sold later at Tremaen Craft Market.

Brenda's school and work colleague Marjorie Phillips recalls "Mr Ellery was very talented... when they lived in Boase Street (Vine Cottage) he used the now vacant shop as a workshop, and every Christmas he produced an assembly line of toys. My mother used to send me down to order them for Christmas presents, and they were so well made, they lasted years and my own children played with them. One year it was quarry lorries, another year, biplanes with propellers, another year, battleships. He used to make wheels from cotton reels until he found a supplier". Brenda said she and Peter used to help him paint the wheels, although they hated it, and got 1d each for them. Angus – the original up-cycler!

They lived comfortably enough, with economies. Necessity is the mother of invention...Angus's beat-up old car, when he finally acquired one, was an Austin 7 he called Bessy; it only managed to stay viable on the road in a rainstorm by virtue of the piece of string tied to the single, top-hung, windscreen wiper, it being the role of whoever was in the passenger seat to yank it regularly back and forth to clear the screen of water. Angus would coax Bessy up hills with cries of encouragement, urging her forward... 'Come on old girl... you can do it...' ...his passengers rocking back and forth in their efforts to help.

Brenda aged 5 in a studio portrait

In the late 1950s, Lena and Angus occasionally took in some visitors in a bed and breakfast capacity... quite ambitious, as they only had a little three-bedroomed cottage. Writing to her sister Marjorie in Canada, Lena says "I have had just four separate couples to stay this summer, and a honeymoon couple booked in September – just enough to give me a nice holiday..."

I remember with great fondness Christmas presents Angus made for me: a doll's cot, a doll's house, a bagatelle board, and even a roulette wheel. As a grandfather, and I imagine as a father to Brenda and Peter, he was a delight. Brenda remembers he always knew where to find the best watercress beds, tiddybottles (wild red fuschia flowers which produced honey-sweet juice when sucked) and soursobs (wood sorrel), both sometimes eaten by children – few sweeties in wartime!

> "He always made us May whistles and would take us to see Fairy Groves. He'd say to us, 'Just because you haven't seen a fairy, don't mean to say there aren't any there. You see that stone ball there? Well, every Mid-Summer's Eve it d'get off and dance...' – and you just had to believe him."[3]

He loved to play games with me – Shops, when we would raid Lena's pantry and line up the contents on the 'counter', with their brass crinoline lady bell as the shop's doorbell – "Yes, modom, and how can I help you today?"... He would drag down Lena's best Chapel hats off the wardrobe for me to dress up in, or take me on winkling or shrimping expeditions in Newlyn Harbour.

He told me stories that I believed for years, that cows that were born on the side of a hill had two legs shorter than the others, or that the pennies he mysteriously 'discovered' under a stone in an old hedge at Paul had been put there by the fairies. If we had 'boy's legs and shoulders' for tea (boiled eggs and 'soldiers'), it was always drummed into me that I *must* break a hole in the bottom of each eggshell when I was done, or risk the shells being used as boats by the witches, who would then be able to sail out and sink the ships of the sailors... and don't *ever* eat the very first blackberry you pick each year, throw it away – the witches have peed on it. (I still do that. Those witches are a damn nuisance.) Oh – and new shoes must never be placed on the table, on peril of ... something perilous, perhaps. He was a trickster – a Cornish 'Loki'... he once 'doctored' a full toilet roll, and wrote something wickedly humorous on every sheet, before rolling it up again and hanging it in the loo, a thunder-box in the back yard, at Daniel Place.

He had his own language and turn of phrase – if something was very agreeable or he approved of it, he would describe it as 'very adjacent...', and he would speak in posh tones of 'pay-shows' for patios,

---

[3] *'Cornish Life', Vol 6 No 2*

or 'gaze-bows' for gazebos. Penwith's answer to Mrs Malaprop, he was also adept at spoonerisms, eggcorns and neologisms, and general daftness. One of his favourite rhymes was "Dan, Dan, dirty old man, washed his face in a frying pan, combed his hair with the leg of a chair, and died with a toothache in his ear". Other much-loved sayings included: "Hark Hark! The silent bell!"... and (loudly, with emphasis), "We're the boys who make no noise!! Ooh! Aah! Ooh aah aah!"... and 'What's yours is mine, and what's mine's me own...'.

If he was particularly proud of himself, he'd yell "Lightning Bryce Strikes Again!!" In recent years I've discovered that Lightning Bryce was an early Hollywood silent screen cowboy character played by actor Jack Hoxie – likely to have been seen by the young Angus in the Gaiety Cinema in Newlyn – and that, presumably, was his trademark cry. A few years ago, for Christmas, Chris presented me with a sepia copy of a Lightning Bryce film poster, which I treasure. And more (sorry, can't stop now, the spirit's moved me): on getting ready to go out somewhere, said briskly: "Here are we, 'fore the storm!", (no idea...), and as conversation lapsed suddenly when the food appeared on the table and all present started eating: "All your best friends died sudden?" (always a risky one, just in case it hit the mark...). One of my favourite Angus-isms: "I don't care how much money you make, you can't eat more than four-pennorth of chips at a sitting".

Brenda developed her own sayings, possibly learned at her father's knee: when asking what you would like to eat, she was known to proffer "...liver and bits fried in a teapot", and if she was asked what she'd like as a present, it was often "ten tall dancing boys in short shirts". If anything was ever lost in our house, she advised it was likely to be found "...up St Just under the clock" (which has turned out to be almost true, as all my worldly goods are now very close to that location). But it was obviously a family trait, broad dialect and nonsense humour being the norm in our family at that time. Aunt Bessie, for example, (two Greats, to me, but always fully as irreverent as Angus), provided some class sayings: "She dawn think no small taties of 'erself'", "She d'think 'er ass is dipp't in diments!" and "Fine git fella, but la!! No bottim!" You can read many more in 'Pantomime Stew' – I could write a book...

William Henry, Angus's father, had several strings to his bow: he was a groundsman for the bowling club, a horse trader, an ostler for the Bolithos at Ponsandane, and a livery stable manager for the Queen's Hotel on the Prom, for whom he was responsible for collecting visitors from the station on his horse and carriage and delivering them to the hotel. The hotel's coach-house and stable, Queen's Garage, was in the centre of Daniel Place, where Angus and Lena ended up buying a house – it later became Bunny Asendorf's garage, and is now a tasteful mews.

William Henry 'Leatherass' Ellery at far right, with all his family in Queen's garage; his wife Margaret is front left, Angus is beside him

He met his future wife Margaret Clarke at the Queens when she came down from Inverness to work there as a Chambermaid in the late 19th century. He wore the ostler's trademark leather patches on his trousers, which earned him the sobriquet Leatherass Ellery – likely also with a nod to his stern personality. A gruff and dour man, he reputedly loved his horses better than any person – they were kept in a stable in the Queens coach-house, and he claimed they would 'do their business' on a shovel to help him out...

But despite his severe reputation, he was highly regarded by many. Leatherass for Brenda was 'Dada' – a bald fat man with gout, confined to his bed in his last years – he died when she was 4, but he did love his granddaughter Brenda, calling her his 'goldeneyes', and his 'chylies'. She often told the tale of an encounter in St Just, many years after Dada's passing: while working as a telephonist in Penzance, she was sent for a spell to work in the St Just Telephone Exchange in Fore Street, as it was then. Walking back to the Square to catch the bus home one day, strolling confidently in her fancy high heels, wearing a tight white sweater, and sporting a Veronica Lake bob, she met an old red-faced farmer coming out of the Star Inn. He addressed her thus: "Well – I dawn knaw who 'ee are my cock, but you must be some relation to dear ol' Leatherass Ellery".

Brenda was mortified – she remembered her Dada as a grizzly old man in bed, and there she was thinking she looked the height of glamour; but the old man felt he had paid her a compliment – he had nothing but respect for Leatherass. "The man who could charm horses and who'd never tasted beer", Brenda wrote of him.

There is a fascinating archive photo of Leatherass with all of his children around him, signing the Census Return on his kitchen table in 1911, which was published in the newspaper of the day – to publicise the importance of this task for everyone.

Lena Ellen Rowe, Brenda's mum, was born at Paul near Newlyn in 1906, and her ancestors, mostly agricultural workers, seem to be based in the Crowan, Praze, St Hilary, Rosudgeon areas by around the 18th century. As a young woman, Lena had been 'in service', and was a classic homemaker – she baked, scrubbed, cleaned and knitted happily, fondly scolding Angus now and then for his wicked humour and roguish ways. She washed her clothes by hand in the copper with a 'dolly' and Reckitts Blue, used a washboard, and wore a perm, twinsets and pearls and pleated skirts. When son Peter went away to college, she filled a huge trunk with all the things she'd knitted or baked for him.

Four generations of Rowes: Great Granfer 'Gacky' Tommy Nicholls, Granny Lena Ellen Rowe, mum Lena Ellen Ellery and baby Brenda

Her parents, Bartle Rowe and Lena Ellen Nicholls, lived at Roskilly – I can just remember them – and the matriarchal line next goes back to Thomas Nicholls and Elizabeth Ferris... or Great Granfer 'Gacky' Nicholls and Granny Bessy, to Brenda. They died when she was 2-3 years old – and you can see her on his knee in the Four Generations photo.

They lived in Foundry Lane in Newlyn. Gacky liked to look 'tanto' – smart and spruce – justifiably earning the sobriquet 'Dandy' Nicholls, as a lad. He had a fine set of whiskers, and his exuberant beard was a source of some pride. So proud was he of a new pair of boots, that to keep them dry and clean he once walked home in the pouring rain in his socks. He was the only member of the family to earn his living as a fisherman, and can be seen in Douglas Williams' book, 'Mounts Bay' on page 90, one of a group of fishermen (and *not* from Porthleven, as claimed by Dougie Williams, according to my Great Uncle Willie!).

Brenda says that when grandchildren came calling, Gacky would whisper to Bessie –"Got a a'pney, 'ave ee dear? I've nawthen for the dear childern" then pass on the coin, with "There my lover – tha's from Granfer!" Brenda wrote: "Granny Bessy was his Queen, Very staunch up the Wesley'n"...

While she was doing her Sunday Best programme on Radio Cornwall, Brenda received a letter from a Miss Josephine Pender, who remembered working with Lena as a young woman. She says she and a friend used to...

> "...leave home in the dark at 7am to walk from Mousehole, and stop to pick up Lena and her sister Katie from Newlyn, to start work at 8am in the knitting factory at the bottom of Queen Street in Penzance. While at work, Lena and Florrie Rogers were always singing and joking – and you, Brenda, always remind me of her. Then Bessie (Lena's aunt) joined the group, and of course Saturdays she started coming to our place, fishing for Frank Praed, but after a while that season finished, and she cast her net to Wherrytown and ended up there. Katie also caught Dickie Humphreys at Mousehole... and of course Lena, your dear mum, ended up where she started, in Newlyn with Angus – your dad was her first and last, bless her..."

Brenda's brother Peter was born, in Newlyn, four years after her in April 1932 – and she always adored him. They attended the Newlyn

Brenda with younger brother Peter

Board School on Paul Hill, and she went on to Penzance County School for Girls (later Penzance Girls' Grammar), he the Boys County School – but despite passing her final Matriculation with top marks, she was not able to go on to college, unlike Peter, who attended Bath Academy of Art at Corsham from 1953-56. She was awarded the Oxford School Certificate in seven subjects: Geography, Domestic Science, English Language, English Literature, French, Maths and Art – at which she was 'very good'. Peter left the County School aged 16 with 6 'O' levels. He initially joined his father in the sign-painting business and attended Penzance Art School for 5 years, before going up to Corsham. In those days, it was assumed the son of the family would need to be the breadwinner, and hence, if money was tight, it was he who warranted the extra expense of further education. In May 1947, Lena and Angus moved into 4 Daniel Place near the Promenade in Penzance, where they were to stay almost for evermore, and where I was born.

Brenda as a schoolgirl at Newlyn Board School at the top of Paul Hill is remembered by her friend Marjorie Phillips as a 'rosy-cheeked girl with dark hair and a fringe'. Of their time at the Penzance County School, where Brenda started in 1939, she says "I thought her a very brainy girl but she was also very mischievous, and was always losing house points, sometimes as many as 10 in a term – which was detrimental to our house, Pydar, as at the end of the school year, a cup was awarded to the house with the most points – so she was often reprimanded by the house captain, Audrey Richards". I read in her Report Book that she was mostly regarded as an intelligent and lively pupil, but I loved the comment from her composition teacher in 1944: "A gallant bravado of style does not hide ignorance and lack of study". Interestingly, Music was not taught.

Brenda at Newlyn Board School in the 1930s

Brenda says she enjoyed her time at both Newlyn Board School and the Girls' County School… "I was always around the top 6 or 7, but I never really bothered about it. The only thing I used to get a bawling out for was P.E., but the teacher was kind and wrote 'She tries!' on my report. I was a champion swimmer, but not interested in team games."[4] (Unsurprising – Brenda was ever a leader, rarely a team player.)

Another school-friend that Brenda remained in touch with throughout her life was Beryl Richards. I had a lovely letter from her a few years ago, in which she described her first memories of Brenda. She says:

> "I first met Brenda at Newlyn Board School, Scholarship Year. I'd moved from St Just, taken the exam at Madron, then heard the results at Newlyn. A few days after the declaration of war, we set out to walk, gas masks on our shoulders, towards Penzance, and the great adventure of a new school!
>
> "In spite of the troubles of 1939-44, we enjoyed it all and were taught by a remarkable, dedicated group of staff. They coped so well with everything thrown at them, from the rationing of school dinners, to the arrival of evacuees from Devonport, a whole school of *boys*!"

What was life like for the young Brenda? Steeped in tradition, and surrounded by love and laughter, I think. She says she was raised

---

[4] *'Cornish Life', Vol 6 No 2*

"on a basinful of chapel and a bucket-load of superstition".[5] Her parents, Lena and Angus, both came from large families, so there were Aunts, Uncles and cousins a-plenty within visiting distance. And Lena, always the glue that kept the extended family together, wrote letters and visited every one she could, especially the elderly or the sick, 'keeping things going'. She never visited without taking 'a little something' – homemade cake, flowers, cream – and of course Brenda and Peter would have gone with her. All of this became learned behaviour for the young Brenda, and a habit she never grew out of. Several of the cousins lived in or near the Newlyn area – in fact, at that time, the 1920s-40s, the inhabitants of the entire row of seven square, castellated flat-topped houses at Roskilly (twixt Newlyn and Mousehole) were all relatives of Brenda. It was fondly known as Skilly Gap.

Just over the hill behind the steep gardens of these houses was Penlee Quarry, so they all had reinforced concrete roofs and wire mesh on the windows, to reduce the risk of blast damage from the daily explosions that took place at midday. Lena's brother Tom worked in the quarry, and his son, my cousin Malcolm, permanently damaged an eye there as a child, playing with a detonator. Brenda's maternal grandparents, Bartle and Lena Ellen, lived at number 1, closest to Newlyn, and various other Aunts and Uncles filled the rest – and Brenda and Peter, with cousins Barbara, Rena, Olive and others, spent most of their free time playing on Skilly beach, below the houses.

Brenda and family on Skilly beach – with cousins Barbara, Pauline, Rena, Olive and boyfriend Willy, brother Peter, her Aunt Marjorie, and father Angus – Brenda holds a boat Angus has made

[5] *Interview in Cornishman Newspaper 10/12/1992*

As a young girl Brenda became a strong swimmer, and often won prizes in local competitions. She took part in the annual long-distance swim from Newlyn to Penzance... "That was before it became a race, when we did it for fun. Skilly beach was my pool, and though I didn't know it then, swimming set me up with the lungs and legs I needed in later life." [6]

In August 1943, a report appeared in the Cornishman newspaper that on Perranuthnoe beach, a Mr Hope, 'a non-swimmer, had been swept away by a strong current. Two girl members of the Penzance Youth Centre, Brenda Ellery and Jean Thomas, rushed to his assistance and succeeded in bringing Mr Hope ashore in an unconscious condition'. It was reported that two girls had got into difficulties, and that Mr Hope, recently out of hospital and advised against going in the water, rushed to their aid. They got out safely, but he was left floundering. Brenda dived in and swam out to him, grabbing the struggling man to bring him to shore – he apparently thumped her with his wild thrashing, and she thought she might have to knock him out, but Jean came to her aid, and together they managed it. Mr Jones survived, and the girls, it was said, "should be commended for their plucky action".

It is likely that Brenda's brother Peter was also a member of the Penzance Youth Centre – he was certainly a member of Newlyn Scout Group, under the auspices of lifelong Scouter Ben Maddern, as were his pals Clary Ash, Chuck (Frank) Ruhrmund, and Biscuits (Peter Lawton). Peter and Biscuits went on to become Scout leaders themselves.

Beach babe Brenda with friends Beryl Richards and Cynthia Tripp at Porthcurno

Brenda often described herself as 'forthright and foolish', with a habit of going into things 'feet first'. She had a cussed independence, and strong evidence of a trait she sometimes accused me of: '...like a St Just man... don't knaw and wain't be told'... an attitude she maintained stolidly throughout her life.

---

[6] *Interview in Cornishman Newspaper 10/12/1992*

As a teenager, she loved to swim out and around the Low Lee Buoy (a quarter of a mile) and also around Mousehole Island – both quite a distance, and a practice strictly forbidden by her parents. She recalled one day on the return leg, hearing splashing around her – and was terrified to find herself swimming in the midst of a school of porpoises, who were gleefully swooping below, beside and above her as she fought for the shore... which she regained safely, if breathless and panicked.

The families met often – there were many regular local events which inspired home visits or drew them out: the traditional Good Friday walk to Lamorna (where her parents first 'walked out' as it was euphemistically called – more like kayeeking, I believe, if truth be told), Feast Days and Chapel Sunday School Tea Treats, May Horns (with home-made May whistles cut from hawthorn twigs), Allentide in October (when Allen Apples were exchanged), Bonfire night, Tom Bawcock's Eve in Mousehole, Carol singing everywhere at Christmas and Guize dancing, and of course the local annual Carnivals – Angus's forte. He organised and built outrageous carnival floats every year, usually on the lorry over in Newlyn Quarry, or tinkering in Bunny Asendorf's garage in Daniel Place. He used every family member and friend he could as characters, and expected to win First Prize – which he often did.

Some of Angus's complex carnival floats from the late 1940s and 1950s

We've found press cuttings from the Cornishman archives stating that he won first prizes at Penzance, Hayle and Marazion Carnivals in 1947, (the first year the carnivals had been held since 1938, due to the war) 1948 and 1950 – so he obviously took his amazing creations to several other carnivals around the district.

Here is the report from the Cornishman in 1947:

> "The London Palladium Crazy Gang never staged anything more crazy than a first-prize-winning exhibit in Newlyn's Carnival on Saturday, 'House To Let – When Finished'. All through the procession of the carnival along the main streets of Newlyn and Penzance, they mixed their mortar, laid their bricks, but never achieved their purpose – humorous commentary on what some people feel to be the national effort."[7]

Living so close to such a magical coastline, Brenda and her family and friends took full advantage... there were outings to the beach at every opportunity, often just prompted by 'shall'us go down Prom?', but also many a planned day out to Sennen Cove or Porthcurno on the bus.

And the beach parties and picnics – fondly remembered by those of us still able to do so... huge numbers – 30, 40 or more – all family, all contributing something to the feast, down at Marazion or on Prom Beach, Carbis Bay, or Skilly for the day (can you spot Brenda and John?). I cannot imagine the amount of organisation involved, getting all those relations to turn up at the same time, in the days when social media wasn't even a thing; it must have been down to Lena.

One of the legendary family picnics, at Marazion, 1950s

[7] *Cornishman, 1947*

And it was Angus – clown, fool, silver-tongued devil, the raconteur with the ready wit and the gift of the gab – that started the family tradition of writing bad poetry (porchery, we called it, rhymes with debauchery – examples follow) for every birthday, wedding or anniversary... and Brenda took up the porchery habit – a tradition still upheld by me today.

One of Brenda's teachers at the Girls' County School, Gladys Tranter – fondly known as 'Trants' by her ex-pupils – writing in her book on the school, 'The Human Spring'[8], remembered a poem Brenda had written during her school days about wartime austerity: "When eating bread, Please think with care, And eat more home-grown, Pomme-de-terre". Brenda kept in touch with Trants, and many years later, visited her at the small holiday bungalow she owned near the slipway on Bryher Island on Scillies, and, with school-friend Beryl Richards, had tea in the sunshine. Miss Tranter and Miss Hannah Greenwood were two of the Grammar School's longest-serving teachers, and had each taught both Brenda and me, thirty years apart.

Brenda with Penzance Girls' Grammar School friends, clockwise: Beryl Richards, teacher Hannah Greenwood, Elizabeth Langford, teacher Gladys Tranter, Stella Sherrat (May), Doreen Turner (Hillier), Doris Fowler 1984

Here's a birthday poem Brenda wrote for Beryl Richards, who was fond of cycling...

Whether you ride your bloomin' bike,
Whether you run or whether you hike,

[8] *'The Human Spring', Gladys Tranter, publ. by Penzance Girls' Grammar School (1980)*

To see you arrive is just what we like...
No matter which way you travel, too,
I'll still be eight days older than you!

Peter also took to porchery. He and his pal Chuck Ruhrmund wrote porchery to each other at every birthday for years – always on the same card, sent back and forth between them with extra pieces of paper sellotaped in place, each accusing the other of their abject meanness in refusing to buy a new card; when the original card was lost, they were forced to invest in a new one, and the correspondence continued.

More formal family occasions involved parlour games or party pieces – everyone had to contribute something to the proceedings. But in those pre-TV days, an evening around the piano or playing games was, in any case, a regular event. Lena always played the piano ('Daisy, Daisy', 'Moonlight Bay', 'Underneath the Arches', 'Just like the ivy on the old garden wall'... and 'Lily of Laguna' – which I still sing to my young granddaughters, Lily and Lena Luscombe, today!), and Angus told 'yarns'. And oh – what yarns... Angus's story-telling was legendary. He had the natural skill of the old Celtic droll-tellers, and his maxim was always 'What you don'knaw, make'en up'... a rule that stood Brenda in good stead, as she inherited his gift of the gab.

I always looked forward to my bedtime stories, when I would hear of the latest exploits of Gian' Googoo and Little Jack. He'd tell them to the grown-ups too, and he'd have everyone crying with laughter – and all completely made up out of Angus's own head. Gian' (Giant) Googoo and his pal Little Jack got into all sorts of scrapes, and spoke broad Cornish dialect. In 1964, Brenda's Aunt Marjorie and her family having emigrated to Canada, it was decided to record a tape to send to them for Christmas, and several family members gathered in Brenda and John's front room for the purpose. John was in charge of the technology – scary for some of the older family members – and recording onto a cassette. Lena played the piano, various carols were sung, with great emotion, my cousin Joyce and I sang Silent Night, and Angus told some yarns – including a bona fide Gian' Googoo story. Brenda was so thrilled when she rediscovered a copy of this tape many years later, and I have transcribed all Angus's yarns from that tape – including Gian' Googoo – for the 'Pantomime Stew' book.

At family gatherings, the children, too, were expected to perform: little dances, recitations, monologues – and in Brenda's case, of course – singing. Her first party pieces were probably along the lines of 'Jesus wants me for a sunbeam', and 'Every little girl would like to be, the fairy on the Christmas tree' (which she later performed, with great spirit, in one of her pantos). Brenda recalled: "I was told to stand at the end of the front room to sing for Aunt Liza, Uncle Johnny and Grandma. I'd sing something like 'Jesus loves me, this I know...', and mother would say 'Shoulders back... sing out. I can't hear all the words...' But it taught me not to be ashamed of performing." (Despite the difficulties of wartime, Brenda's first recorded dramatic performance was in Tolstoy's 'What Men Live By', playing Matryona in a production by Penzance Youth Centre Drama Group "to aid Russia", in 1943, aged 15.)

Her renditions caused sufficient interest that she was soon singing in the chapel choir. She has said that Mr Irving Thomas, the tough choirmaster of the Newlyn Centenary Chapel Choir where she first sang in public, instilled in her the importance of thorough rehearsal, and gave her some great advice: "If you can't hear the voices on either side of you, you're singing too loud!". When the family moved to Penzance, she joined the choir at the Wesleyan Chapel. And there were influences too from the powerful oratory of the local ministers "as dramatic as any Shakespearean ham, who, as well as enlightenment, provided real entertainment for the children of Newlyn".[9]

Singing was very much a part of Brenda's young life – at each and every house visited around Christmas-time, the doorbell was rung, and the party launched into at least one carol, with full harmonies, and kept going till the end, while those visited stood on their doorstep and joined in, regardless of the weather. No-one dreamt of going indoors until the song was finished.

Lena died just before Brenda's life-changing encounter with folk music, so never saw her performing in that role. She did, however, see her in her pantomimes... from a letter she wrote to her sister Marjorie, then in Canada, in 1959, she says "We went to Sennen to see the panto last evening, 'Abou Hassan' – a first class show, our Susan and three other little girls did some excellent dancing, and Brenda has all the confidence in the world, she sang and danced

[9] *'80 From the Eighties', Martin Val Baker*

with the crowd, and her size doesn't embarrass her one bit, which is a blessing. They have had a very good write up in the paper, so you will probably see it in the Cornishman. She wrote it, did scenery, costumes, songs, the lot, and they all think she is wonderful down there, they all enjoy working with her..."

Here is Brenda, in an interview with She Magazine in December 1980, talking about her singing:

> "Harmony singing does seem to be inborn in the Cornish and the Welsh. It comes from chapel you see – all the family were in chapel choirs... well, you think of that, with four-part singing all the time, so the tenors naturally sing tenor. I'll never forget my brother, when he was first going to grown-up chapel, not Sunday School, sitting next to mum, pulling her skirt and saying 'Mum, you're singing the wrong tune!', because she was singing alto, and he was very embarrassed. So there's probably just an echo, an unconscious thing from the time you're a baby.
>
> "I can remember arriving at Grandma's house one evening. We had winter coats on, and I was about 7 then – and as we got to the open door (she lived over at Roskilly at the time, right beside the sea), wind's blowing in, you know – and she give us all a kiss, and then, whether there was something on the radio, I don't know, but I can remember Grandad pitching in with 'Sweet is Thy Name, My God My King'. Deep harmony, they call that, and if anybody pitched it, before we even thought of it, we're all pitching in. And we kids knew better than to make any fuss to take our coats off, we had to stand there and wait while the grown-ups made music – 'strike sound' they call it."

I have transcribed the whole interview with Leonard Pearcey for She Magazine in the Appendix, as I think it explains much of Brenda's attitude to music.

Sometime in 1938, a report appeared in the Cornishman about a successful charity concert put on in Penzance 'To Help China', which probably referred to the sufferings of the Chinese after the Massacre of Nanking in 1937. The 10-year old Brenda is mentioned: "A particularly favourable impression was created by Miss Brenda Ellery, whose delightfully sweet voice was heard to its fullest advantage when she sang 'Tell Your Troubles to the Breeze' and 'Beneath the Lights of Home'".

And where did that delightfully sweet voice come from? Lena sang, but slightly tremulously, and Angus's musical renditions were much more strident. So – who knows. Out of the blue... But for sure, her stage presence, the ability to charm, entrance, and woo an audience, the easy confidence and camaraderie of her dialogue, whether face to face, over the radio, or in the spotlight of a vast concert hall – without a doubt, that came from Angus.

And these days – how much has changed. How little I see of any of my cousins – the Aunts and Uncles are mostly gone before now in any case, but it is not common to have such large families, or for those that do exist to search each other out, living as they often do at much greater distances. We have established global links now far more readily than local familial ones – though I have rediscovered many relations on social media in recent years!

But for young Brenda, the family was all, the traditions sacrosanct, the music inspiring, the love tangible, and the land, the granite land, was under her feet. She ate homemade Cornish pasties, Cornish mackerel, and 'eavy cake, she swam in Cornish seas, she listened to Cornish legends and stories, she sang in Cornish Wesleyan Chapels and attended Cornish festivals, she heard and spoke Cornish dialect every day.

That's where she came from – Cornwall.

T'was Guy Fawkes night at Skilly Gap, and weren't the kids excited!
Ma's and Pa's that place were at to see the bonfire lighted...
Gathered round the Mousehole bus they stood there in their thousands
Waiting for the Guy and 'Gus around those flat-topped housens
Marjorie Rowe, now she was there, and so was Barbara Payne,
Uncle George was drinking beer so we did just the same,
At last the Guy was put on top and fireworks got ready,
A p'liceman tried to put a stop, but kids said 'Shut it, Freddy...'

(A fragment of a longer epic, by Angus Ellery – 'Gus is Angus)

Brenda – The Teen Years

The film with that title would have been a racy affair indeed. The teenage Brenda was a very glamorous and vigorously active socialite, constantly on the prowl for 'the One', and bored to tears without plentiful romantic encounters.

From the age of 16 in 1944 until she met John Wootton two years later, Brenda welcomed the visiting wartime troops with open arms, and seemingly in multiples. In amongst the occasionally purple prose of the hundreds of passionate love letters exchanged almost daily between Brenda and John (1948-49), I discovered a sheaf of earlier mail in different hands, from a number of Armed Forces beaux all declaring their love – some seemingly concurrently.

Brenda's diaries from those years reveal countless attempts at finding romance, with hints at moments of passion with assorted potential mates, mostly from the Armed Forces, who would then have the effrontery to get themselves posted away. But once the war was over, the ready supply of potential suitors soon dried up. Comments like "Quiet week – too damn quiet. I want something exciting to do" and "What a life. Fed up again... no men, no nothing... just work", are sprinkled throughout – by early February she's had enough: "Deadly life I'm leading – fed up to the gills – oh for a man to love me!"

There had been many willing to try their chances...Ralf, American Red Cross, Aug 44; Bruno R, USS Adonis, Plymouth, Aug/Sep 44, Jan 45; John, Oct 44; Johnny, Nov 44; Andy, London, Jan 45; Dean, American, May 45; Gene, Germany Aug 45; Johnny M, Guantanamo Bay, Oct 45; Sepin, Dec 45; Zaneck, Polish Naval Barracks, Devonport Dec 45; Ken, Canadian Navy, Jun/Jul 46; Phil, London, Nov 46; Bob, RAF Sennen, Jan 47; Mal, HMS Helmsdale; Jan B, Polish Navy; Gerald B S, American Air Force... and these are just the ones whose letters I've found...

But family was still – and always – important. The cousins, aunts, uncles spent far more time socialising than I think happens today. Lena went out of her way to keep in touch with and informed about, everyone.

Work at Penzance Telephone Exchange

After leaving school in 1944, Brenda was appointed to work in the Penzance Manual Telephone Exchange in New Street, along with school-friend Marjorie Phillips – she was also quick to join the Post Office Choir. Marjorie remembered their initial duties included menial tasks such as ticket duties, preparing tea rotas and collecting Union subs, before being allowed, in January 1947, to do 'proper' work as telephone operators. Sometimes they were sent to help at other telephone exchanges to fill in for holidays and sickness. Brenda made many good friends in the telephone exchange, in particular Alice Raisin (later Shears) and schoolmate Stella Sherratt (later May).

Marjorie says the girls there used to love to hear Brenda singing at work: "she would imitate Deanna Durbin, who was our favourite singer at that time." She remembers that after the war, she and Brenda volunteered to go to an Agricultural Camp in Hersham in Surrey. The Post Office allowed them 2 weeks with pay if they volunteered, "...and of course, anything away from home was seized on, especially as the war had curtailed our travelling around Britain." The girls caught the Cornish Riviera to Paddington, and Brenda, who had been to London before on visits to her Aunt Kate, led the novice traveller Marjorie through the subway system to Esher, where they were due to be collected. The lorry never showed, and again Brenda took the initiative and phoned for help.

They arrived in a field with two segregated rows of bell tents, a tented cookhouse and dining hall, and a brick built washroom with cold showers. The cook reluctantly prepared them a meal of tinned pilchards and salad, which Brenda wolfed down, but Marjorie says she was not keen. The work was back-breaking, picking beans or peas by hand, which apparently Brenda did well – making full use of the cold showers on her return, with 'awful screams'. In their spare time they visited Walton-on-Thames by bus, walked into Hersham village for Sunday lunch or snacks in the cafe, and on one occasion both went to visit Brenda's Auntie Kate in Islington.

At the end of their fortnight, they travelled back down to Cornwall on the train with Aunt Kate and family who were going home on holiday, and who had managed to save just one seat in the carriage for the girls. Brenda offered it to Marjorie, who promptly fell asleep. When she woke and looked out in the corridor, Brenda was sprawled across the suitcases, fast asleep, but with a firm grip on her handbag.

Marjorie says Brenda was very talented, making 'pottery' brooches (most likely, plaster of paris, which Angus used in his paintings – he didn't have a kiln) which she brought in to sell to the other girls in the telephone exchange "...as we didn't have much jewellery, other than Cornish Stone, which was very expensive. They were oval, and moulded either with a beautiful woman in costume or sometimes a head with a turban and huge earrings". (Interesting – probably from Angus's Turk's Head pub sign – I wish I'd seen one!) Marjorie remembers Mrs Ellery as being a very easy person to get along with... and that every Saturday they had fish and chips from Jimmy Veale's chip shop in South Place Folly, near to Daniel Place.

"A man to love me..."

By 1948, Brenda was still having weekly choir rehearsals, enjoyed swimming, knitting and sewing, and was going to the cinema two or three times a week with friends such as Beryl and Cynthia. Her open friendly nature in the telephone exchange ensured her popularity, and she was soon made 'Social Secretary' – a post she probably relished, as it provided her with fresh opportunities to find 'the One', following the departure of the Armed Forces from Penwith. She arranged a joint dinner and dance with the men from Skewjack, the listening post at RAF Sennen – whose corresponding Social Secretary was a pleasant and handsome young lad called John Wootton. Brenda was a popular and very attractive girl and, as we've seen, had already had many boyfriends. She hadn't been backwards in coming forward when the American soldiers arrived during WWII – but it was John who was to capture her heart. Unfortunately, her first meeting with John isn't recorded, as she gives up keeping her diary around that time – too busy doing other things, presumably.

'Johnny' Wootton had also had quite a few girlfriends in his home territory of Wolverhampton, where he had lived prior to the war and his Cornish posting. His father, George Edward Wootton, was the gardener for both the Wolverhampton Boys and Girls Grammar Schools, and amazingly he grew all the fresh fruit and vegetables for the school canteens – they actually lived in a cottage in the school grounds. John was a Radio Telecommunications Technician for the RAF during the war, and was stationed in Ceylon, and, I'm very glad to say, never saw active service – though he did, years later, receive the standard War Medal.

Handsome young RAF Technician, John Wootton

In contrast to the horrors of the war raging elsewhere, John's diary from the war years reveals a life of comparative calm and ordered routine in Ceylon. There were frequent visits to the cinema and occasional mentions of his work, but almost every day he records writing letters to a variety of girlfriends.

Brenda, too, enjoyed the movies as a young girl... she has said "the cinema was very important in my young life. It was in the Gaiety Cinema in Newlyn that I had my first 'grown-up' date, when I was 14 years old. He bought me chocolates, and ate most of them himself..."

The glamorous Brenda and her fiancée, John Wootton

Brenda became engaged to John Wootton on her 20th birthday, 10th February 1948 – in her diary, she records visiting the Gaiety again: "Saw 'Ideal Husband' – not as good as mine..." she commented, anticipating her forthcoming wedding. The sheer volume of the correspondence between the young couple at that time was monumental... I still have over 100 apiece of their passionate daily tomes, covering the few months in 1948 and '49 when John still had to work out his job in Wolverhampton both before and after the wedding, whilst Brenda remained in Daniel Place with Lena and Angus.

They were married in the Alexandra Road Methodist Church in Penzance on 3rd July that year, and honeymooned for a week in Stratford-on-Avon.

Initially, John went back up to Wolverhampton alone, and was later joined by Brenda, and for a short while the young couple lived on the Grammar School site with John's father George. Brenda found him somewhat curmudgeonly, so she was pleased to make the move back down to Cornwall in June 1949 – just in time for a momentous event. In November 1949 I was born, upstairs in Daniel Place in Penzance, with no midwife, but none the worse for that. (I too, am pleased that Brenda chose to return to Cornwall at that time – most likely remembering her own regretted 'accident of birth'!) For that first year back home in Cornwall, like so many young couples, Brenda and John lived with her parents, Lena and Angus, in 4 Daniel Place.

Brenda and John's wedding, with cousin Jackie Rowe and his wife Pat, and Angus and Lena, 1948

When browsing through Father's Log Book from his earliest days as a 'Radio Ham', I was touched to see that there were a couple of occasions in the first year of their married life when Brenda was making some of the written entries... it appears the young bride was permitted to enter the inner sanctum of The Shed, and join in the fun! Well, the wheel soon come off that, as they say...

Sennen

Sennen – the first and last parish in Britain – straggles along the last few miles of road in the country before Land's End. It has three distinct and fairly self-explanatory areas. Residents were identified by their location, and at different times we classed as all of them. Churchtowners live anywhere in the region of the Church down towards Land's End, Covers live down in the Cove itself, and Overhillers live on top of the Cove and back along the A30.

Churchtowners – Atlantic Breezes

John started work at Skewjack near Sennen in September 1949, and by October 1950 they managed to rent a large rambling house close to his job, down near Land's End – Atlantic Breezes – a woefully understated euphemism for the reality – where we lived for just over a year. It was the last house on the left before Land's End, and my only memory of it is the field below the house, bordered with trees, which always seemed to be filled with anemones.

Baby Susan's first word, apparently, was 'book', and as a baby, I'm told I was fond of 'reading' the Radio Times upside-down. Brenda and John, like many other newly-weds, struggled to make ends meet, and over the next few years Brenda taught herself all the money-saving tips she could – making jams and preserves, ends-to-middling sheets, making her own teatowels and pillowcases, and designing and making her own clothes – all practices she continued throughout her life, when she could. Recycling is not a new idea!

Covers – Beachfield

In November 1951 we moved down to Beachfield, a large granite house in the centre of the Cove, and instantly upgraded from being 'Churchtowners' to 'Covers' (bottom of the cove = top of the tree). This was a close-knit community – of necessity, really, cut off from the rest of the world as it was by that daunting Sennen Cove hill – many's the time the Sennen bus had to offload passengers partway, leaving them to walk up the steepest stretch to climb back on again at the top. Community and village life centred around the lifeboat, the Cove's unifying force. The Sennen lifeboat house dominates the Cove, and then as now the Sennen family names of Angove, Hutchens, Pascoe, Pender, George, Oliver, Nicholas and Shannon, from that day to this, dominated the crew list – and all their children were my school-friends. Peter's son Adam, now a local GP, has been officially serving as 'crew' for some years, as the Lifeboat's Honorary Medical Adviser.

Our house Beachfield was centre front right by the sea, and appropriately named, as originally the house stood opposite what had once been tiny fields between the road and the shoreline, used to grow violets and anemones, some housing little wooden shacks – which I do remember, though the fields are long since washed into the sea and now replaced by a strong seawall.

Next door lived someone I only ever heard referred to as Mare Trare – I'm guessing now her name was Mary Trenary. She was an old lady I dimly remember wearing the long dark skirt and white pinny of the Victorian Cornish granny. I was a little frightened of her, and only ever saw briefly into her house down a long dark passage with coloured lights at the end – a stained glass window probably. A few doors to the other side lived Marjorie Thomas and her family; I was great friends with the daughter Katherine, who had a big sister called Wendy, and Marjorie attended Sennen WI, as, of course, did Brenda, later. There were many friendships forged there, and many a WI member was persuaded to take part in the village pantomimes – Betty George and Mrs Maitland I remember particularly as unlikely harem girls in diaphanous trousers.

There was a little grocers shop down opposite the Lifeboat House – now a lovely café – and next door to it, a knitting shop, which I recall as being owned by the delightfully-named Marigold – or did I dream that? The bus from Penzance called quite regularly, and a large space between the houses on the front was kept vacant as

Sennen Cove in the 1950s – is that me? ©Francis Frith

the bus turning space, as is still the case today. Some years ago, Chris gave me a framed copy of a wonderful Francis Frith photograph taken in the Cove in the mid-1950s. I'm convinced the little girl making her way to the shop is me...

For me – for any child – Sennen Cove was an idyllic place to live. Every day, rain or shine, I was down on the beach, eyes down, 'wet ass, no fish', squatting in rockpools, leaping over or scrambling among the boulders finding treasures, paddling in the foamy waves, building 'dens' in nooks and crannies, damming the stream at Vellandreath or cartwheeling down the sand dunes. Brenda used to bring me down a sandwich and some home-made lemonade to keep me going. I couldn't have wished for a better childhood. I learned to swim off the lifeboat slip in the harbour, learned to love the wildlife, the wild winter waves, and the people. Getting to Sunday School up that hill was a bit of a challenge, especially on cold wintry days, but it was a small price to pay – Susan Pender (now Midwinter) remembers tackling the climb with me. Despite living quite a way from 'town', I still spent a lot of time with my lovely grandparents in Penzance, where I was Angus's 'queen of the roses'...

Sue in Lena's back yard in Daniel Place, with Brenda

Churchtowners once more – Treeve Moor

In early 1954 we moved again, back up the hill to Treeve Moor, almost the last house before Land's End on the right – a wonderful big old granite house with barn and a small plot of land, rented from a lovely couple, Bod & Dick Trenary. Bod was actually Mrs E Trenary who taught at Sennen School for many years (she'd left before I started there), and it's good to report the house is still in the family. There was no electricity, so John set about teaching himself how to make a wind-powered generator – and there was certainly plenty of that natural resource at Land's End. In the winter storms the wind moaned and howled around the house like a crazed wild animal, searching out crevices and cracks – but we were safe and warm in the parlour with a blazing fire and basking in the gentle golden glow of the tilly lamps, softly hissing... the eerie sound of that wind still makes me feel safe and comforted today.

There was a well in the garden, useful if the pipes froze, next to which was an old piece of corrugated iron sheeting which was often home to a family of slowworms – while a huge conch shell beside the front door was the domain of a big old toad. There was a cold scullery to the left of the front door with a large marble slab for preparing fish and a zinc-screened meat safe, and in the kitchen on the right was an original Cornish range. It needed regular black-leading and was messy to operate, but Brenda took full advantage, 'firing up the slab' and producing some of the tastiest pasties I ever remember. As a toddler, I was washed in front of it in the old tin bath.

Treeve Moor was home to some of my earliest memories, including some much-loved yet inexpensive toys – the family's economies spread to presents for me, but they were none-the-less adored. One such was Bruno the huge bear... all four foot of him. Father bought him for 6d in the Church jumble sale, and I was still snuggling in bed beside him in my teenage years, using his flattened straw-filled belly as an extra pillow. I remember waking early one Christmas morning in great excitement to spy some strange shapes hanging on the end of my bed – a pair of string puppets, a man and a woman, made for me by Brenda and John; Father had made the bodies out of old cotton reels and dowelling, and Brenda made their clothes – I was thrilled with them. And I still treasure a slightly ragged little black and white panda bear bought for me as a christening present by Peter.

Frugality was the watchword. There were various money-making schemes attempted. For a few years, Brenda and John took in Royal Marine Commandoes, stationed at Land's End for cliff-climbing exercises. I remember Happy Days and Chalky White were regulars – and one of them, Dan Allen, bet Brenda she could not make a pasty so big that he wouldn't be able to finish it. She could barely fit it in the slab, but she won.

Brenda and John with Commando Dan Allen and pasty at Treeve Moor

The Commandoes were also very amenable to helping out with the preparations on November 5th – building a huge bonfire for us, as well as supplying some very spectacular and unorthodox rockets – illegally of course. I was very popular among my friends on Bonfire Night that year.

Another scheme, which ultimately failed dismally, was keeping geese. It had been suggested as a great ruse – geese cost hardly anything to feed, and produced wonderful eggs which could be eaten and the spares sold, they were advised – quite apart from the bonus of a proper goose at Christmas. So Brenda and John eagerly acquired a small gaggle of around half a dozen. John had to go to some effort to build a suitably-sized pen, and then a house for shelter – hoppers were needed, and they simply refused to eat household scraps, so food had to be bought. The biggest and feistiest of the gaggle was Tallulah – and not only was she unapproachable without risk of attack, she was also a great escape artist. No matter how high John raised the fence, she somehow managed to fly over it and had to be chased and caught. In the end, a howling storm one night brought the pen down, and the geese fled, never to be seen again. Not even a goose for Christmas, that year...

So, let's look at...

Food in the '50s...

Fish were prepared in the cold scullery on the marble slab. Living in the fishing village of Sennen had its benefits, and fresh fish was a cheap and nutritious food that was relished, often straight off the boats; the local fishermen would often hawk their wares door-to-door, especially for regular customers. Soused mackerel, marinated or pickled in vinegar and spices, was popular, but more often, mackerel just fried in butter was a quick and very tasty option. As Brenda explained in her song, 'Thunder and Lightning': "Now take a mackerel out the sea, 'Oh, souse it!' they all say... My cock just put 'en in the pan and fry 'en straight away!" If money was tight and the fish weren't biting, perhaps it would be the salty 'toerag' – dried salt cod that needed soaking at least overnight to withdraw as much of the salt as possible. My favourite was a wing of ray "...a sweet bit of fish – boiled taties and butter d'make a rich dish!" (all from 'A Cornish Alphabet'), and with the added bonus of the white meat being easily removed from the bones. If Angus and I had been on a recent winkling expedition, there'd be a saucer of boiled winkles with a little vinegar and salt, a slice of thin bread and butter – and a pin, of course.

Meat was usually a bit more expensive, but if they were feeling flush, under-roast was always popular, and raw fry as well – Cornish recipes which can be found in many good regional cookbooks. Cheaper cuts prevailed; Angus's favourite was pigs' trotters, John favoured tripe. Pasties were also an economical and of course much-loved meal, although very labour-intensive – the best meat for pasties is the cheaper cut of marbled skirt, as it makes for a juicier filling, and Brenda often used flaky pastry. Lena taught Brenda well, and we always looked forward to pasty day – in fact, Brenda always said you had to let the family know in the morning if you were making pasties that day, as the anticipation was part of the enjoyment. Each person's pasty would be marked with their initial on one corner in pastry, so if you couldn't eat it all at one go, as was usually the case, the saved corner would still be identifiable later.

This poem she wrote many years later:

P is for the Pastry – not too rich, to start,
A's the way make it, for it truly is an Art,
S is for the Skirt beef, which provides the ansum juice,
T is for the Turnip, so tender, rich and loose,
Y is You who eat it – the best meal in the world,
I salute the Cornish pasty, under Cornish flag unfurled!

The essential drink to accompany a pasty, by the way, is always a cup of hot sweet tea.

While we're on pasties, I must just mention a chap from over Newlyn (as told to me by Angus)... Joe Perry had a hare lip, and consequently a bit of a speech impediment. His missus made him a pasty for his dinner every day... but one day he was horrified to come home to find she'd decided to ring the changes and made him stew. "Sthnew??" he cried... "I dawn want no bleddy sthnew... pathties I work fer – an' pathties I sh'll 'ave...!" Oh, and not forgetting the poor widower Brenda met, forced to make his own pasties once his wife had gone, trying to close his pasty with safety pins because he couldn't manage the crimping properly.

Any left-over pastry was filled with jam and made into a jam pasty for pudding. Other artery-clogging desserts we often enjoyed: cheap and filling steam puddings like Spotted Dick with custard, Yorkshire puddings with treacle, or treacle tart, blackberry and fruit tarts of course, or maybe junket, with Cornish clotted cream, which she sometimes made herself – a long but rewarding process which involved scalding the milk in a wide shallow pan and eventually skimming off the thick, luscious cream. Brenda also made excellent home-made lemonade, from a recipe of Lena's.

Any sudden glut of fruit or vegetables was always put to good use – pickled, or made into jams, fruit tarts or chutneys – and glass jars were never thrown away. The WI provided invaluable information for impoverished housewives on pickling, bottling and preserving – no fridges or freezers – or plastic! – in those days. And every year without fail, come September would be the blackberrying. We'd all go out searching, and having found a likely picking ground, usually field hedges, country lanes or clifftops, we'd each chose our own spot and 'cooty down' and guard it jealously while we picked it clean, with the warning call "Cooty cooty eye-oh – anybody come round here get a black eye-oh!"

Years later, she wrote a poem – serious, for once – about blackberry picking at Lamorna, which began...

'Last September we lined the willow basket
With rusty, curled bracken
Filled it to the brim with the best berries –
No scroff – cooty, cooty eyehole...'

No fast foods or heavily processed foods then... we collected fresh wild watercress from clear, clean streams, wild mushrooms from the fields, eggs came from a local farm, and Brenda and John grew what they could in the wind-battered garden – they even had a go at home-made wines... gorse, elderflower and parsnip I remember – all-in-all, I think our diet was pretty healthy.

When Father was working nights at Skewjack, Brenda would sometimes suggest our 'special treat' tea: egg banjos followed by banana sandwiches... this was our 'fast food'. An egg banjo is basically a fried egg sandwich, and I suspect it had more to do with Brenda not wanting to get involved in major cooking, but to me, it was our 'snuggling in front of the fire' secret comfort food. I don't remember Brenda making much saffron cake, possibly because saffron itself is devilishly expensive, although Lena did from time to time – but 'eavy cake was a staple, made with plain, not self-raising flour. And the ultimate wicked sweet treat was, of course, thunder and lightning: a thick slice of fresh bread drizzled with treacle (actually golden syrup, which makes the bread slightly crispy – although many will argue the cream should go on first, it is personal choice really), and smothered in a thick coating of clotted cream. I'm drooling...

Apart from cooking, Brenda found plenty down at Land's End to keep her busy. Her first adult attempt at oil painting, a hobby she enjoyed all her life, was made at Treeve Moor... unsurprising given that both her father and brother were artists. It was obviously in the blood. Brenda and John took full advantage of the wonderful countryside, the cliffs and the beaches, and walks and picnics happened

Picnic outing with Sue and friend Joy Whent – and painting in progress

whenever possible, which at least countered the nutritious eating, somewhat. The picnics often took on something of an epic quality – as well as all the food and drink (fizzy lemonade tablets and bottles of water) and the usual paraphernalia – rugs, umbrellas, beach gear – there was often Brenda's paintbox, easel, boards and brushes as well. She loved to paint 'en plein air', outdoors – and many of these early paintings made it onto the wall in her front room, which became a gallery of happy events that I still keep up on my front room wall today – each one a fond memory of a blissful childhood outing.

After the 'annus horribilis' of 1994, when both Brenda and John died, I discovered, on clearing the paintings from the wall, that years after the event she had written a short paragraph on the back of each one of those 'picnic' paintings describing the day: what the weather had been like, anything of interest that had happened etc. One such was a painting of an old barn on Kerrow Farm at the foot of Chapel Carn Brea near Land's End Airfield at St Just. Not sure how we managed to access the site to drag the picnic there, but I remember the day – as a big old sow ambled up to watch her while she worked, and tried to eat the paints. You remember things like that. The barn is still there, unchanged, and I see it regularly.

Brenda's first 'adult' painting, done at Treeve Moor in 1955

Her paintings done in the 1950s and 1960s have a natural quality that I love. Like Angus, her style was impressionist, and her particular interests were sun on granite walls and old barns. She loved the warmth and solidity, the history they held. This was her comment about her 'first adult painting' of a gateway at Treeve Moor:

> *"My first adult painting. All around Treeve Moor was drystone walling – the sun would set through the stones. We could hear the rocket of Longships sounding through the fog. The winds could reach 130 mph. Oil lamps – cook on the slab – carry water. We were very happy here. BW"*

In those days we never had a car, and John rode to work on his old motorbike, which, as it did have a sidecar, at least meant that me and the picnic gear could be carried short distances, with Brenda riding pillion.

As the years passed she became very involved with the local community – village activities she says she was active in include "church, chapel, WI, council, drama, life-saving and bed and breakfast". At Christmas time, we joined forces with others and walked round the farmsteads for miles around, carol singing, usually fundraising for the Sennen Drama Group or some other local cause. Electricity didn't come to Sennen until 1933, and street lights were still few and far between in the 1950s, so the locals were used to traipsing round in the dark – but John made improvised candle lanterns out of tin cans on bamboo poles for everyone to carry, which served the purpose admirably.

In 1954 I started at Sennen School, a wonderful establishment that thrives today. Then, the headmistress lived on site, and there were just 2 classes, with playgrounds and a large playing field at the back. My favourite memory of the school: the nature table and nature rambles down the country lanes, and Brer Rabbit reading books; my least favourite: sports day and the egg and spoon and sack races – oh, and the pickled adder in a jar (useful, though, to know what to avoid on the country walks! Always stamp heavily when walking along cliff paths... scares them off). Beside the school the old flooded quarry – still there today – was a favourite spot for tadpole hunts. As I was nearly 5 at that first term, I was one of the older children in that class – by the following year, as a 'precocious reader', I'd been moved up a year (...though I was *not* precocious at sums...)

At my first school medical it was recognised that I had some health problems, and before too long I was diagnosed with what was then called a hole in the heart. Normally such problems are detected at birth, as the newborn is a 'blue baby' – but apparently I was not sufficiently blue for anyone to notice. It was actually a hole in the aorta, the main valve leading into the heart, which meant that half of my blood was not being re-oxygenated. I needed a specialist heart operation, and at the time Brenda and John were told that the nearest specialist was in London, that I might have to wait for 2 years, and the chances of a successful outcome were 50:50... but without the operation, I was unlikely to make it past my teens. This was a very traumatic time for them – not me so much, as I had no idea of the gravity of the situation, and was little affected at the time – the main issue being I got out of breath and tired easily (still do – I'm obviously in my second childhood).

Eventually, they were told a specialist surgeon had moved to Bristol, and there would be a 6-month wait – then a specialist moved to Cornwall, and within short order, at age 6, I was sent to the delightfully placed Tehidy Hospital in Camborne – long since closed. The operation, the first of its kind in the West Country, was a great success – obviously, as I write this over 60 years later – and the recovery period was 6 weeks. Needless to say, I have ever since been thankful for my reprieve, for the skill of the surgeons and nurses, and for the blessing of the NHS. Long may it survive, against the current outrageous odds. I had a great time – my chief memory of the whole event was that I got lots of nice presents, and the only unpleasant bit was having the stitches out – oh, and getting my kit off in front of the doctor at my annual checkups, as I approached puberty. With great consideration, for young girls they entered the chest cavity at the side, rather than down the centre front, which was apparently the preferred option for boys – so I acquired an impressive scar running around the shoulder blade down to right under the arm, with no embarrassing impact on my future décolletage.

It was many years later that Brenda told me she had had several miscarriages while living at Sennen – at least 3, I believe (she told me 5, Father later remembered only 3 – but then, he wasn't experiencing them). This certainly contributed to her weight gain. Apparently, her stomach muscles had collapsed when I was born, and she was unable to maintain a pregnancy after that, although she kept trying. On one of these occasions (all of which I was blissfully unaware of at the time), while I was in Tehidy recovering from my heart operation, Father set out from Sennen on his motorbike and sidecar to visit both me in Tehidy and Brenda in Treliske Hospitals, following yet another miscarriage – and came off his bike at Buryas Bridge, which then had a low stone wall beside a narrowing of the road over the stream. He ended up in West Cornwall Hospital with a smashed ankle – so all three of us were in different Cornish hospitals at the same time. God bless the NHS.

Susan as Sennen Fairy Queen, with her Fairy King, Ronald Angove, and attendant

Around this time I was appointed Fairy Queen at Sennen Carnival – a huge honour! My Fairy King was Ronald Angove, the son of milkman Josie Angove. I've always suspected that my Royal appointment was the result of a sympathy vote...

Over'illers – 18 Atlantic Crescent

From Treeve Moor, in early 1956 we moved up to 18 Atlantic Crescent – the new estate on the top of the hill, and became Over'illers – easier for both my walk to school and John's drive to work. We had a lion-maned black and white cat called Moppet, and briefly, a wild hedgehog in the kitchen and an orphaned wild rabbit in an elaborate hutch John built in the garden, which sadly it never lived to enjoy for long. I came a cropper on my tricycle here, and subsequently, like Brenda, never owned or rode a bike. My friends and I (Joy and Chrissy Whent, Bernard Rhodda, Ronald Angove) made a secret den in the long grass opposite the houses, where a large rectangular hole had been dug exposing an oblong table-sized granite boulder. The hole was covered in a corrugated metal sheet, and we enjoyed hiding beneath it, illicitly taking down candle stubs and matches to hold secret meetings crouching in the mouldy earth. More new houses were being built at the back, and they seemed to have been left half-built for ever – this was a good place for playing 'house'. The main source of fun, and days out with picnics for all of us, was straight down Sunny Corner Lane to the dunes of Vellandreath, at the far end of Sennen beach.

Every so often an old man in a black coat would come knocking at the door, carrying a huge lidded box at the front supported by a strong strap around his shoulders. He was a pedlar, selling all manner of small household items: sewing notions, buttons, zips, shoelaces, cleaning materials, scissors, kitchen equipment and more. Brenda was always pleased to see him, and always bought something from him. I was amazed at what he would bring out of his box – and he always had a little something to give to the children; a little plastic animal, some pretty ribbons, and always something special at Christmas, like a tree ornament. He was quite diffident, but very friendly and would chat happily to anyone. I only recently discovered he was the same much-loved local character, Cloggy, or Albert, Mellor – who I remembered later, as being well-known throughout West Cornwall for playing his barrel organ, one of two he owned, in towns and at events, wherever people gathered. He wore clogs, naturally, and originally had had a real monkey on his barrel organ, but apparently gave it up when it bit him, and substituted a toy one. He was the last itinerant organ grinder working in the West Country, and had a definite 'summer tour', even visiting the Scillies; he died in 1985.

Brenda and Jean Hards paddling in Sennen Harbour

Particular friends for many years – such that I knew them as Auntie and Uncle, though they weren't related – were Jean and Nicky Hards, who lived at Porthcurno. Nicky fished out of Sennen, and the couple had two daughters who became good friends – Gloria and Colleen. The elder, Gloria, was about my age and we often stayed over in each other's houses (secretly listening to Radio Luxembourg under the bedcovers), had joint bonfires on Guy Fawkes' night, and visited frequently at Christmas and throughout the year. Nicky was a taciturn man, his serious expression enlivened sometimes with a warm chuckle. Jean I remember especially for her soft low Mousehole burr, and her frequent... "Awww, the dear'ob'm...".

I mourn for the evenings of home-made entertainment which kept us amused at Jean and Nicky's, and elsewhere. Nobody seems to play games any more, not proper games – and they were such an important part of my childhood. These weren't so much 'boughten' games, but more usually devised by Brenda or gleaned from old games books. At family parties, we would have team games – the Drawing Game (no skill required), where each team had to guess (without the other hearing) the meaning of a scribbled drawing (no words!) from their teammate who had to stay dumb, and just gesticulated wildly to convey his current 'object' – a rubber band maybe, or the Queen's left ear, or the pith of an orange. Not easy, and inevitably, hilarious. I remember a game which required three of the party – Peter, say, and two others, consulting secretly, then presenting themselves in front of the audience: "Three jolly workmen come to see for work"... Audience: "What can you do?"... Peter et al: "All sorts and everything, just the same as you"... and then followed some sort of 'dumb crambo' type of mime where the object was for the watchers to guess their jobs. Another drawing game involved holding a blank sheet of paper on a book on top of your head, and following instructions to draw on it, blindly, a house, then a fence, then a tree in the garden, then a path, then windows and a door – and falling about laughing at the results. Then Charades maybe, a homemade Beetle Game, a race to reassemble mismatched newspapers, or making hats with newspaper and a few pins – and for the children, feeding each other cornflakes while blindfolded and wearing a pinny round the neck. Making up porchery often featured; here's an example from Angus, written at Jean and Nicky's about Jan Yeates who was with us that night: "I wish I was a little fly, I'd fly from place to place; I'd land on top of Yeates's head, and wee-wee down his face".

Even good board games seem to be dying out – Cluedo and Careers were our favourites. The TV and the internet may be wondrous things, but they have a lot to answer for.

During a recent visit to Cornwall Record Office in Truro, researching this book, I was astonished to discover an anecdote of Brenda from this period which was complete news to me. It's 1955, and Brenda, mother of a young child and a full-time homemaker, is living on Atlantic Crescent, a small estate at the top of Sennen. She knows she has a good singing voice, but apart from a couple of public performances when she was a schoolgirl or in the Chapel choir, she has never stood in front of an audience to sing solo as an adult. Her self-image is likely at an all-time low – since giving birth five years ago, she has ballooned from the glamorous young woman who paraded down the street in heels, head held high, into a frumpy dumpy housewife. She is good at her role though, and as well as looking after young Susan, spends her days cooking, cleaning, doing housework and listening to the wireless.

The Lands End WI had decided to put on a play – a first for them – and for some reason had selected Hans Christian Andersen's story of the Emperor and the Nightingale – an odd choice, as they could find no member with the singing skill to play the role of the Real Nightingale. The play was cast – all but the Real Nightingale. No one could think of any member suitable to play the part. One day the producer, Bill Maitland, is walking close to the open window of his near neighbour, Brenda Wootton, and overhears her singing along to the BBC Housewives' Choice. He is struck at once by the purity of her voice, and realises his search for a Real Nightingale is over.

However, it takes some persuasion to get Brenda to perform – according to the annals of Land's End WI (from whose 'The Story of Our WI' this account was taken) she only agrees, as the play they have selected does not need her to stand on the stage in front of an audience, something she is apparently 'loath to do' – the sweet voice of the Nightingale in the play is only heard through an open window.

> "We played to a packed Church Hall, and after the final curtain, the audience insisted on the Real Nightingale taking a curtain call, which she did to ecstatic applause. As a result of this performance, Mrs Brenda Wootton became a member of the Lands End WI, and also a founder member of the Sennen Drama Group." [10]

---

[10] *From Land's End WI's 'The Story of Our WI', Cornwall Record Office*

I am struck by this account for several reasons – it sounds almost apocryphal, but from the authenticity of the source, and the fact that I never heard this story from Brenda, it is very likely true. The WI were looking for a vehicle for their Ladies Choir, to put on performances and dances to entertain the old people to whom they supplied Meals on Wheels. The role of the 'Real Nightingale' could have been tailor-made for Brenda – and this seems like such a serendipitous, life-changing and iconic moment – it draws her out into the public gaze for the first time, and it is particularly strange to me as I've never heard it before. It seems now that this performance and enforced public appearance was the trigger which brought back her self-confidence, and set her on the path which brought her ultimately to the stages and the spotlights of Paris. But this wasn't the last time that Brenda was reluctant to enter the spotlight... although once that first applause at the Count House died away, she had by then been hooked.

We made many good friends as Churchtowners, Covers and Over'illers – the families of Joy and Chrissie Whent, Sally Ellis, Laura Hutchens, Bernard Rhodda, Leslie Trewern, Marjorie Thomas – the Shannons, the Maitlands, the Penders, the Angoves, the Georges. Being one of the first on the street to get a TV – small and square, with a grainy black and white picture – certainly helped with my popularity amongst my peers, at least. Peter did a wonderful sketch of Sally and me watching TV in the front room here.

Peter's pen and ink sketch of Susan and Sally Ellis watching TV in Atlantic Crescent

Sennen Drama Group & Madron Players

At Sennen, Brenda began what became a life-long love of the stage... following on from her 'outing' on stage with the WI, she and John, with others, were founder members of the Sennen Drama Group in November 1956, which met regularly in the little Church Hall. Both Brenda and John were on the group's committee and executive committee, which met up in member's houses, and the group soon acquired quite a large membership. They held regular play-readings and produced 1 and 3 Act Plays, and then decided to put on a pantomime; they opened it up to the members to propose a story and plot, and Brenda's, 'The Golden Goose', was accepted – so she began to write the scripts. John was named as Stage Manager and Props, and Brenda as Scenery Painter, but she soon widened her scope. The pantos became an annual event, and many local families were involved in some way – most of them petrified at their first attempt at treading the boards. Brenda says she and John were also involved in the inauguration of the Minack Theatre Society around this time.

There was a gaggle of Jackson lads whose family ran the store up 'overhill', opposite Zacky Nicholas' garage. One of them, Bobby, had a joke to say on stage, which he thought so funny, whilst he was at the same time so nervous, it caused him to stammer and stutter wildly... "I d'live in a rude hut" he had to say – "Oh yes, and why is it called a rude hut?" was the feed line... "Well, you should... you should... (hysterical giggles)... you should see... aww, heck... you should see (more hysteria)... you should see the writin'... you should see the writin' on the walls!!" he finally spluttered out. Mike Sagar-Fenton revived another memory of Bobby for me: "I remember well the Sennen postman with the stutter. He had a not-very-funny line 'I had a girl once, she was 36-24-36, but that was just the shape of her head.' It came out as 'I 'ad a girl wonce, aaaaand she was ah ah thirty-six ah twenny four an' thththirty-six...' (and then all in a rush) '...but-that-was-just-

Brenda in 'Abou Hassan', flanked by Betty George and Laura Hosken, as village gossips, the Mesdames Omar, Hassan and Hafiz 1959 [© belongs to Sennen Drama Group, no longer in existence; documents held at Cornwall Record Office, ref: X684/24]

'Abou Hassan', the full cast, in Sennen Church Hall (see previous footnote)

the-shape-of-her-'ead-mind..." No-one caught the joke of course, but for the cast, it was the highlight of every show."

Brenda's involvement with the pantomimes was total. As soon as one finished she'd begin researching the next – she collected jokes from newspapers and joke books throughout the year, and made use of local characters, incidents and events. I still have some of the fabulous antique books of fairy stories she amassed, looking for a story she could adapt to suit Sennen and its folk. After The Golden Goose, came Abou Hassan, Grisleybeard and The Shoes That Were Danced To Pieces... and The Rolling Stones of Plouhinec – performed in 1964 with the Playgoers Theatre Group in Penzance, of which more later (there are full details in the Appendix). At the initial meeting, she would ask who would like to have a go, and always tried to include roles for everyone who wanted to participate. She arranged the publicity and the tours – they actually toured the local village and church halls with some of the pantos, carrying the flats, costumes and props with them, sometimes across muddy fields, for one night stands. There are records of pantos being taken to Pendeen Sunday School and St Just British Legion, to St Buryan, Paul, and Ludgvan Village Halls, to the Playgoers Theatre in Penzance, and even to the Cheshire Homes at Marazion. She was heavily involved in all of them – generally, she wrote the scripts, made the costumes, did the makeup, produced, directed and acted. John made the props, built the flats, did the lighting, and acted. Painting the scenery flats was a joyful communal affair, enriched by the 'pantomime stew', the stewpot bubbling away on an old primus in the hall, filled with everything contributed by everyone there, meat, veg, tinned stuff – whatever.

Mike Sagar-Fenton recalls:

> "Brenda even danced, and I remember a song called "You bring out the savage in me". Originally this was a big boastful tribal number, and in the middle she did a tribal-type dance with Vera. The tempo was quite fast and the dance quite demanding so in rehearsal they found themselves completely out of breath, not to say knackered when it came to the final chorus "...You'll find out how wild I can be! For you bring out the savage in me!" Instead of booming it out they literally tottered through it, wheezing – which was of course so funny they kept it in for every performance."

Brenda and Donald performing with the Choughs

Some of Brenda's lifelong friendships were forged from her Amdram involvement; Vera Round, also a Chough, wife of Arnold, who lived at Marazion, did a wondrous parody of Joyce Grenfell, and had a wicked sense of humour. She was known to me as 'Auntie Vee', and came from Bolton, and was often heard to say 'I could'a been a film star if it wasn't for me faaace...'. Vera loved dancing, a pastime she pursued throughout her life, but her fall from grace was forgetting to wear her knickers one evening for one high-kicking performance. There was Doris Wernhard, a British Drama League Adjudicator who, as an Elocution Teacher at West Cornwall Girls School in Penzance, also took me for private Speech lessons. Mike Sagar-Fenton, who I first remember as a young lad playing the drums for the panto, also wrote songs and worked with Brenda as a guitarist later in life... and then there was the inimitable and incorrigible Donald Jarvis. Donald lived at Sennen with his mum, his auntie and his uncle in a large house on the edge of the Atlantic Crescent estate. He worked for BEA at Land's End airport and at Penzance Heliport at Eastern Green. He was an excellent cook and a brilliant raconteur – particularly in Cornish dialogue, although his accent when you met him was more languid upper-class lovie, with his 'Dahhling!! How div*ine* to see you!!' He was so laid back he famously fell asleep onstage during one Revue show they did together. All will crop up again in Brenda's story...

One theatre group Brenda also often worked with in the late 1950s/60s was Madron Players. Leading lights Francis Monk (Vicar of Madron) and Mary Laity (the dear of 'er) appeared in several plays and pantomimes, but Brenda also took the company through a couple of British Drama League Festivals, reaching the semi-finals with 'The Mayor of Torontal'. This involved moving the entire company, costumes, props, makeup and scenery by coach to Leamington Spa for the event (very exciting, despite the 10-hour coach journey – I went along as 'props girl').

Brenda remembers her association with the various local groups in Madron: "My first contact with Madron Players was when the County Drama Adviser, John Trelease, asked me to produce 'The Smugglers of Sennen' by Cornish Bard Molly Bartlett' (also, she later recalled it as the first time she had sung 'Lamorna' in public). Madron Players shared several members with Madron WI and Madron Young Farmers, (she remembers Ivor Staines, Harry Scrase, Tom Pollard and Leonard Eddy), and WI member Vida Pengelly, after some persuading from Brenda, 'proved a fine actress', as did the young Mary Laity, heavily pregnant with Treve (who many years later was to build Brenda's house at Newmill). One very enthusiastic member of both the WI and Madron Players was Lady of the Manor, Wilmay Le Grice of Trereife – for whom the older residents of the village still tugged their forelock.

Says Brenda,

> "I recall lovely fetes at Trereife Manor, donkey rides on the front lawn, wildflower competitions, Wilmay's gooseberry tarts in the kitchen, Baby Shows upstairs... I was given free rein of the Manor, looking for props and furniture for many of the plays and shows. Upstairs in the attic, covered in dust and cobwebs, were priceless pieces of antique furniture... we borrowed some 19th-century French bedroom chairs for the 'Mayor of Torontal' (Madron Players' entry for the British Drama League Competition), and they were heaved into the back of Peter Ley's lorry – which broke down 5 times on the way back from Leamington Spa."

> "We were given the Freedom of the City of Leamington Spa, which basically meant we could borrow a library book or play tennis... but we didn't have time to do a thing, other than the play competition. I was so scared we'd win, and have to go on to Belfast for the Great Britain BDL Finals – the whole of Madron, it seemed, had raised cash and looked after children to enable us to go to the Semis! As it was, we came just 1 point behind the winners, so honour was satisfied."

> "The children of Madron's Daniel School (named for the same benefactor as Daniel Place in Penzance, interestingly) were very lucky in their teacher Francis Monk – but they couldn't believe their eyes when they saw 'Sir' and 'the Missus' (Mrs Le Grice) in the Feast Concert, dressed in exotic Arabian costumes (Wilmay's included baggy translucent harem pants) and wolfing down a whole banana each during a performance of the comedy play 'Carpet Slippers'."

Other productions got to the quarter-finals in Truro City Hall – and here Doris Wernhard, JP, reigned, as one of the Chief Adjudicators. She was a remarkable woman – tall, with a chest like a ship in full sail, and a birds' nest of fiery henna-red hair perched wispily atop slate grey sides. She lived with her husband Stephen, a German Jew, in a green-painted 'clapboard' bungalow in Mawnan Smith.

Brenda had tried to interest me, as do so many eager mothers, in the piano lessons in Sennen – a dead loss – and the ballet lessons, at Miss O'Mingay's Dancing School in Penrose Terrace in Penzance – another non-starter. When Brenda mentioned this to her friend Doris, she suggested I undertake speech lessons with her, at her room in West Cornwall Girls School in Penzance, where she was then teaching elocution – not to get rid of my Cornish accent (although that was one of the end results), but because I gabbled so fast, it was difficult to make out what I was saying. I loved it, and passed all my LAMDA Speech medals through to gold – despite being too 'sibilant' – so Doris did some good. Amongst other things, we ran the gamut of speech exercises, from "round and round the rugged rock the ragged rascal ran", to "Which witch had the wen on her hand when we met them, and you asked them whether we would have fine weather?" (delivered in 'received pronunciation' with aspirated h's, a style now mostly out-moded). Doris often said to me: "You'll never forget this, Susan. Whenever you have to stand up in public and give a speech, or attend an interview, or act on the stage – you'll remember what you learned here today." And she was right... a little hovering Doris bubble appears in my mind on every such occasion...

When one of my speech exams loomed, I and one or two other girls in the same plight would be invited to stay with Doris at her home in Mawnan Smith, for a few days of intensive training. Sally Trelease was one, daughter of County Drama Adviser John Trelease, who was also working to restore the Cornish lugger Barnabas for the Cornish Maritime Trust, and featured in one of Brenda's TV shows for Westward.

Brenda interviewing John Trelease on board the lugger Barnabas

Doris was obsessed with Siamese cats. Not only did she have half a dozen living and breathing specimens, but every surface in every room in her house – tables, shelves, picture rails with shelves, cupboards, sideboards – was covered in ceramic or glass representations of them, including several of those giant-sized coloured brandy glasses with secreted mice, with their attendant cats hanging on the edge, frozen in pursuit. In between speech training sessions, we picked hazelnuts from her trees, marvelled at the aviary with 80 noisy budgies in the garden, or went down to the creek below the house to paddle and laze.

Mike Sagar-Fenton tells a delicious story of Doris: apparently she was appalled when some children in one class she was called upon to take kept using the 'f' word in their general speech. So, "I can't fucking do it, Miss", one would say. "Why must you *do* this?" she asked, mystified... "*why* do you preface everything you say with this word, fucking?" "Well, everyone does it nowadays, Miss", was the general consensus. "Oh, I see..." she replied, still mystified. She resolved to put this to the test. On her return home, she called out to her husband, with her immaculate diction: "Hello, Stephen, I'm fucking home... I'm going to have a fucking cup of tea, and a fucking sit down now – I'm fucking tired..."

Stephen looked up at her, horrified. "Don't you ever do that to me again..." he growled.

Brenda also did a few productions with the CRDF – the Cornwall Religious Drama Fellowship – in the 1950s, appearing in plays at the Minack Theatre with them, and also at the City Hall in Truro. I remember particularly 'Noah'. Noah was played by a guy called Ted Miller, and Mrs Noah was a sweet little lady called Mrs Kliskey – others involved included Colin Stephenson and Vera Round. This is especially memorable for me as Ted's daughter got the part of a lamb in Noah, and I didn't – she had a congenital problem with her hand, and we were in the same room together at Tehidy Hospital throughout my convalescence there. There was also the West Cornwall Theatre Company – and several of the leading characters from both these theatre groups went on to form the Playgoers Theatre Club in Penzance around 1960.

Skewjack

John's workplace, and the reason for our living in Sennen, was a mile or two out of the village on the Porthcurno Road. Royal Air Force Sennen was built on the site of Skewjack Farm by the RAF in 1940 as the RAF Regiment Barracks for the greater Chainhome Station CH17. After they were married, for a few months Brenda and John lived with his father in Wolverhampton, Brenda later moving back in with Lena & Angus until such time as John could find work in Cornwall... but in June 1949, with Brenda pregnant,

John applied for a job at Skewjack, and in September he began work as Radio Mechanic Class 1 at No 428 Signals Unit, RAF Sennen.

He worked there throughout the 1950s, becoming a Radio Telecommunications Technical Officer Grade III, and his responsibilities, as far as I'm aware, involved monitoring and identifying whatever flew overhead, and keeping the machinery in good order. There were usually two men on duty, and it was shift work, allowing the station to be manned at all times.

John 'busy working' at Skewjack

The site had a couple of 360' high Link Aerial radar masts, which, along with all the other machinery, required regular maintenance. On August 4th 1968 John and his mate Charlie Jollow set off to clean the machinery at the top of the tower – a regular task – and as usual, Charlie switched off the machinery at the bottom of the mast. John began the hair-raising climb to the top, and Charlie went back to the hut to carry on with the cleaning. From experience, John knew that by the time he reached the top, the motor drive would have had time to slow down and stop. Maybe he climbed a little quicker that day… as on this occasion, on reaching the top, he removed the canvas cover and the inspection panel, and reached inside the awkward space with the rag in his hand to begin the cleaning – but the heavy gears hadn't quite finished rotating, and were on their last turn. His rag was caught and his hand pulled into the works, severing one fingertip and smashing several others. He was trapped 360 feet up in the air, precariously balanced on a small metal platform, losing blood and in great pain – and his co-worker, the hard-of-hearing Charlie Jollow, was in the Nissen hut a little way away.

He screamed for Charlie, who thankfully appeared a few minutes later and climbed the mast, but even with John's feeble attempts to help unbolt the mechanism, they couldn't release his hand. Charlie had to leave John there to climb down to phone for help, and eventually John's boss Mr Bradley arrived, and between the three of them, all at the top of the tower, they at last managed to release John. He later said he couldn't remember much about it... he knew he couldn't faint, as he would likely have slipped and could have fallen and lost his hand, or worse. Amazingly, he then managed to climb back down the tower, and was taken to Penzance Hospital in Mr Bradley's car, and eventually to Treliske Hospital around 40 miles away. He arrived there some 4 hours after the accident, at last received his first pain-killing injection, and his hand was operated on. I dread to think what he must have gone through.

The 360' aerial radar mast at Skewjack

By the time Brenda and I got up to Treliske, a few hours later, he was white as a sheet and still in shock. Thankfully, apart from losing the tip of his forefinger (which gave him endless amusement later pretending to pick his nose), his other fingers all healed, though they bore scars, and he was not seriously disabled.

John was also a member of the ROC – the Royal Observer Corp – and Raynet, the Radio Amateurs Emergency Network, and sometimes went on training exercises with a Civil Defence theme, usually incorporating all the different services, military and civil. He took part in a few of these, often 2-day affairs involving many volunteers, some grotesquely 'wounded', playing out a nightmare scenario of nuclear or other attack or natural disaster.

Some years after we left Sennen, he had the opportunity to go up to the Shetland Islands on an aircraft recognition refresher course. He was put in the nose of a Shackleton aircraft and taken up on a routine training flight – the weather was none too clear, I believe. Some time into the flight, he spotted another aircraft seemingly on a collision course with his own plane, and fearing that his pilot hadn't seen this potential danger, alerted him. The pilot, a rather well-spoken RAF chappie, responded briskly with "Oh, good show, Nose!" Father gleefully told us this story on his return home, and forever after we were able to taunt him for all his small achievements with cries of "Good show, Nose!" – particularly when he was pretending to pick it with his shortened forefinger.

Penzance – 4 Leskinnick Street

In September 1959, Brenda and John moved from Sennen to Leskinnick Street in Penzance, just up from the train station. I'm not sure of the reasons for the move at that time – I know John resigned from the ROC in March 1969 ('personal problems' were mentioned, mysteriously) and from Skewjack at the beginning of January in 1970, so I imagine he must have been commuting from Penzance to Sennen throughout the 1960s. The site remained an RAF base only for another couple of years, and by the early 1970s it had become a Surf Village, with bar and disco – of dubious repute!

Number 4 Leskinnick Street, just up from the station in Penzance, had once been a Temperance Hotel – but its great virtue as far as Angus was concerned was that it was within crawling distance of no less than 7 pubs. Brenda wanted a name for their new house, and as she had come from the Newlyn Coombe area, and John from Badger Dingle near Wolverhampton, they chose the name Coombe Dingle. It was years later before she discovered they'd christened their house 'Valley Valley'. Donald took to calling her the Duchess of Dingle Dangle, and amazingly his letters written to her with this name, addressed just to 'The Duchess of Dingle Dangle, Penzance', were usually successfully delivered.

Angus did something similar when sending a Christmas card to Brenda's cousin Barbara and husband Ron in Canterbury in 1973. Beneath a franking stamp which read: 'Remember to use the Post Code!', the envelope was addressed to 'Ron Coleman Esq, Post Office Enquiries, (also singer in opera), c/o Post Office, Canterbury.' The message inside read: "Happy Christmas to Ron, Barbara and family – If you don't get this, send it back, Love Angus and Vera." Obviously, it was received safely...

Whatever the reason for the move, after leaving Skewjack, John began work at Rediffusion in Penzance for a guy called Marshall, electrical work which mainly involved installing, maintaining and servicing TVs, intercoms and sound systems. I started at my new school, St Mary's C of E at Redinnick near the Prom... almost certainly chosen for its proximity to Angus and Lena in Daniel Place rather than for any religious convictions. I remember spending many happy hours staying at 'Gran and Grandad's'. In the mornings I would climb into bed between them, and Angus would bring us all up a cup of tea and some biscuits. He taught me how to pour my tea into the saucer a bit at a time to cool it if it was too hot, and how to dunk my biscuits so they wouldn't break too soon... and Gran would scold "Awww, Angus... you're teaching the child bad ways!"

Brenda, Sue, Angus & Lena at Leskinnick Street

Years later I found a couple of scribbled notes from those days which I treasure – this from Angus: "Gacky gone bylows... nicobles-hyou..." (Grandad gone to bed – good night, god bless you); and from Lena: "Dear Susan, eat the rice pudding, there's cake in the tin, don't forget to do your homework, love Gran"... with below, from Angus: "Not unless you want to, my Queen...". He was a natural subversive, bless him.

Every week Grandad (as I knew him – he later became Gacky to my cousins Adam and Jonathan), took me to Millie's newsagents shop across the road from Daniel Place to South Place Folly to get my comics. Initially, this would have been the Beano or Dandy (Angus was a great fan of Desperate Dan), later Judy or Bunty – and six-pennorth of sweets: Five Boys chocolate perhaps, or Black Jacks, or liquorice sherbet. When I got back with my 'nicies', he'd get down on all fours by my knee, hands up like paws, tongue lolling, bum wagging... "I'll be your little doggy! You feed me, alright?" – I fell for it every time. Lena and Angus used to love babysitting, but he hated missing his pint, so he was prone to standing in his doorway in Daniel Place with an old enamel jug and a few coins, looking for a likely passer-by he could hijack, to ask him if he wouldn't mind dropping in to the nearest pub and getting them to fill up his jug for him, and bringing it back. Sometimes his ruse even worked...

When I got a little older and sheepishly returned from a date with a young boyfriend, Angus surprised us attempting a first kiss on the doorstep with the ruthlessly cheerful comment "Bring en in, trot 'en up and down a bit, less 'ave a good look at 'en..." – surely a killer strike for any fledgeling relationship.

On the move to Penzance, I was 9, with 2 years to go before I passed my 11+ exam and went up to the Girls' Grammar School... and became, as we were cruelly taunted by those who had ostensibly 'failed' and would be going to Lescudjack or elsewhere, a 'Grammersow' (Cornish for a woodlouse).

The Playgoers Little Theatre

Once again, in Penzance Brenda's amdram instincts came to the fore, and she became involved with a new theatre company just starting up above the library in Morrab Road, in the old Science Reading Room – the Playgoers Little Theatre. The prime mover behind this I remember as a small and feisty lady called Gwenny Wood – although there were many others involved – not least Gay Sagar-Fenton, (mother of Michael), Colin Stephenson, Vera Round and Donald Jarvis again, Wilfred and Amy Tinsdale, and Betty Barnard from Marazion. I remember there being vigorous efforts from a small and energetic army of volunteers transforming the bare rooms into a proper little theatre with a stage.

There were various plays and pantos staged in the Little Theatre, and variety-style revues I remember particularly. By way of example... Brenda and natural comic Ray Clulow performed a very simple and hilarious sketch called John and Marsha... Brenda stood to the front stage left, and Ray to the right, and each had a household paintbrush and a tin of paint (something colourful) flanking a door placed centre stage. They held a conversation between two young lovers, with full dramatic inflexions, and running the whole gamut of their relationship from coy innocence through lusty passion and finally to chilly animosity, using only the words 'John' and 'Marsha' alternately, and punctuating each spoken name with a dab of paint on the door. It was brilliantly done.

The Playgoers put on a production at the Minack every year from 1960 to 1969, and in 1962, the recently formed Young Playgoers staged 'The Young Elizabeth' at the Minack; they also took the play to north Germany as part of an exchange.

Members of the Young Playgoers at a barbecue in a flooded quarry, early 1960s; Brenda, John and Sue are on the right

The Reference Library took over the Little Theatre room in 1970, and the Playgoers ceased to be – but before long the old Wesleyan Chapel in Parade Street was acquired, with the help of a loan from Gay Sagar-Fenton, and became the Acorn Theatre, which is still operating successfully today. The names of all those movers and shakers responsible at the time of the move were, until recently, recorded on the side of a window on the right of the main theatre room.

Here are Mike Sagar-Fenton's memories of his first encounter with Brenda and her pantomimes:

"I'm 18 years old, which puts it at 1964. I've been to the Playgoers Theatre in Morrab Road with my Mum and I'm allowed to drive the car back to where we live in Praa Sands. We've been to a not especially inspired variety evening – what used to be called 'socials' – consisting of various people doing their party pieces. I'd noticed Brenda of course, though I've forgotten what songs (from the shows?) she sang. But anyway Mother offered Brenda a lift home. It was only to the bottom of Penzance but Brenda didn't like walking through town, especially after dark.

"The first thing I noticed about her, shamefully, was her weight, the way the car canted to her side when she got in. It was for everyone, I think, the thing they had to get past before they saw the real person, this great big fat body, its sheer physical impact, so at odds with the sprite within. But she was lively and funny and dead keen, like me, on drama.

"Soon afterwards I was invited to be in one of the famous pantomimes. Who was I, Selim or some other small part, but I still remember we were:

"Out in Egypt, down beside the Nile, dirty old Arabs doing things in style,
A camel too we have here for you, a fine romance and song and dance and rhyme,
You ain't lived until you've seen it, oh, oh , what a pantomime..."

"We weren't too politically correct back in those days, were we... I think this must have been 'Abou Hassan'...

"Stealing the show, of course, were Del Johnson and Ray Clulow, two brilliant and irrepressible comics, plus the sterner fun of Vera, possibly Donald as well, and not least Brenda herself, front and centre as ever. You, Sue, were in it too [*yes, I remember – a harem girl – my white school knickers showed up through my diaphanous harem pants*]. I don't think we toured that one.

"I played the drums on a crappy old drum-set, and having assessed my acting skills fairly accurately she asked me to get together with Christine Monk, her pianist, and put some oomph behind the dozens of songs she managed to squeeze into every pantomime. They were such a gorgeous rag-bag, classics, standards, joke-songs, show songs, a few pop songs and other obscure and often beautifully tuneful numbers. We toured a lot – back to Sennen, Pendeen, St Just, Porthcurno, Ludgvan, and every other church hall that would have us."

Brenda with Mike Sagar-Fenton at Tredinnick Stack

Having established a clear interest, and with plenty of experience and expertise to hand, Brenda even started giving occasional Drama training workshops and Day Schools for interested groups, with small dramatic exercises to be undertaken, illustrating many of the different aspects of stagecraft: choice of play, mood and characterisation, make-up and costume, and more.

The Choughs

From the sketches and the pantos sprang a theatrical gem – The Choughs. Vera Round, Donald Jarvis, Jan (John) Yeates and Brenda were the performers, and Christine Monk (wife of Francis Monk, Vicar of Madron and member of Madron Players), played the piano; Mike Sagar-Fenton sometimes joined them on drums, and others occasionally sat in – George Watts, was it? From the mid-1960s and over the next 10 years, The Choughs appeared anywhere and everywhere: Old Peoples' Homes, Hospitals, WIs, Charity events... performing a wide range of material from Victorian Music Hall, to popular songs from the 30s and 40s, to sketches and monologues. Brenda wrote a lot of the sketches herself, filling out old jokes and silly stories with fully rounded characters. I don't ever remember them getting any payment for it – petrol, maybe.

Brenda in the kitchen with Donald and Vera of The Choughs

One enduring favourite, performed with the Choughs (and later over many years in the folk clubs) was the 'Cornish Alphabet'. She wrote it one sunny afternoon when we were having a picnic down on the cliffs at Pendeen, near Levant Mine. She had a long list of possibilities, and as I was with her, she occasionally tried out her efforts on me. I quibbled about one – "J is for Janner, that's our Cousin Jack, you give 'ee some cheek, and ee'll give 'ee wan back... ". Surely that should be '...ee'll give 'ee *some* back...', I argued; but Brenda insisted on the 'wan'. She later wrote other versions for special occasions or places: the Newlyn Alphabet, and the Saltash Alphabet, for her huge fans at Ashtorre Rock, the Waterside Community Centre beside the bridge there.

Another gem, which became a firm favourite for many years and through several configurations of performers, was 'Flames' – un-performable now, following 9/11 and Grenfell Towers. Other skits included 'Obadiah' (see 'Pantomime Stew'), 'The Shimmymatic' (about a washing machine salesman), 'The Driving Lesson', and 'Honeybun' from South Pacific – a spoof version: "Six hundred and one, pounds of fun, that's my little honeybun... Get a load of honey-bun toni-ight... " with both Brenda and Donald bundled up in old coats and with blacked-out teeth, dressed as a couple of ancient smelly tramps, and singing in a particularly slow and fractured way, stopping occasionally to pick their noses, or do a lumbering shuffling dance. "I'm speaking of my, sweetie-pie – only 60 inches wide – every inch is packed with dyna-mi-ite... ('boom' says Brenda, grinning toothily, and punching the air with a loose fist)... Her hips are wide and waggly (she demonstrates), her hair is grey and straggly, and when she bakes... her pies and cakes... she makes... them all caggly"...

At our wedding in October 2016, husband Chris and myself steeled ourselves to perform this as our 'wedding dance', with huge and tatty overcoats hiding our wedding gear, and an old hat pulled down over my flower tiara (we decided against the blacked-out teeth). It's the only time I've ever been tempted to perform one of Brenda's numbers in public – though I must say the reception we received was damn near rapturous.

Jan Yeates was a drama enthusiast and natural comedian from Willesden in London and the youngest of the four, with a warm personality and an irreverent sense of humour. Christened John, it was Brenda who chose to call him by the Cornish variant Jan – to save confusion, once again, with all the Johns amongst her close acquaintances. He had friends who also became ours: Russ Hedges, an artist who later worked on the cover of the 'More Singing' Count House album, and David Beschi, another amdram fan as well as a very talented jazz musician – Mike Sagar-Fenton remembers re-hearsing jazz piano and drums with him. In the mid-60s David and

Brenda became involved with a touring repertory company, Fabian Theatrical Productions, who were putting on a series of shows in the old Pavilion Theatre on Penzance Promenade throughout the summer. I remember shows such as The Boyfriend and Salad Days, and the Brian Rix Whitehall farce Dry Rot, in which Brenda had a small (!) part as a large policewoman, Sergeant Fire. They couldn't find a policewoman's costume the right size, but were eventually able to borrow TV comedienne Hattie Jaques' costume for her, who luckily had once played the same role. The British comic actor, Arthur English (later of 'Are You Being Served' and 'Dad's Army' fame), was a guest in this production. 'Doing rep' was cruelly unforgiving for actors and all concerned (I'm sure it still is), performing 6 nights a week for months, with just one day in between to prepare for next week's play. Subsequently in 1965 David was inveigled into joining Brenda's panto 'The Stones of Plouhinec' with Sennen Drama Group.

David Beschi's only other claim to fame that I can recall, was his taking pity on me one day and giving me half a crown to buy a pathetic grey kitten I had seen in the pet shop around the corner (by a strange quirk of fate, the shop was originally owned by Gay Sagar-Fenton, I now discover). Having been sent for fish and chips in Adelaide Street, I'd fallen for the runt of the litter in the pet shop window next door, and begged Brenda for the asking price of 2/6. David proffered the money, and I rushed back to buy him. He

Brenda and John with Beschus at Leskinnick Street

became known as Beschus after his saviour, and was well known to all visitors at our house for a surprising number of years for his thin reedy cry and his kinky skinny tail – caused by a close shave with a car. His insistent cries every morning regularly prompted my dad John to beg him to "go out and play with the lorries"... (but he didn't mean it really). David, I discover, is now a successful artist living in Australia.

Coombe Dingle B&B

Not long after the move from Sennen, around 1960, Brenda decided to set up a Bed & Breakfast business. Leskinnick Street was ideally situated for such trade, as it was almost the first B&B seen by visitors arriving by train; indeed, the notion may well have prompted the move to Penzance. Coombe Dingle had four bedrooms, and in order to maximise its B&B potential, Brenda turned one of the two front rooms into their bedroom, releasing three bedrooms for visitors, with me in the fourth, and the other front room as Breakfast Room/Lounge. Before I left for school in the mornings, it was my job to lay the tables for any visitors. Breakfast was most definitely a 'full English', and could include tinned grapefruit, toast, and cereal, followed by sausage, bacon and eggs with mushrooms, tomatoes and a fried slice, or poached, scrambled or boiled eggs as preferred. The cost, for bed *and* breakfast, was 12/6 pppn... about 62 pence, and probably equivalent to about £20-30 in today's money – still amazingly cheap!

Some of the families who came down as visitors became firm friends and returned regularly. I am still in touch with Susie Cooper – nicknamed Susie Coo (who was my age, hence I became Susie Woo), who came down with her parents, Joyce and Jimmy Cooper from Plaistow in East London, and we also spent many happy days out with Hilda and Arthur Weaver from 'Ull (Hull), looking for obscure sites further up in Cornwall for picnics. On one

Brenda, John and Sue by B&B sign, Leskinnick Street

hot and sunny day in the pertinently named Flushing, opposite Falmouth, Father had left Brenda, Hilda and Arthur and me in the car to go and get us ice creams. When he climbed back in the passenger seat, a persistent wasp followed him in, and to Father's horror, thought the quickest way to the treasure was up Father's trouser leg. John jumped out the car door and promptly dropped his trousers and his ice cream to the floor, in double quick time. There is never a camera handy when you need one...

One of the events we sometimes visited was Culdrose Air Day. One year in the early '60s, John was surprised to receive a phone call on the day following his visit, to tell him he'd won the raffle prize at the Air Day. Well, that's nice, he said – what was the prize? It turned out to be a 9' fibreglass dinghy with an outboard motor. He was flabbergasted, but apparently, other enthusiasts were outraged – they'd spent pounds on buying up tickets to win this coveted prize – John had bought just one ticket for 2/6p, and didn't even know what the prize was. Well – major adjustments were called for – his old work van had a heavy-duty roof-rack added to carry the boat, and his rented garage in Mabbots Yard behind Leskinnick Street had an elaborate pulley system set up so the boat could be lifted off the van and up into the ceiling of the garage. The small SeaBee outboard motor fitted in the back of the van – along with all our picnic gear, blankets, folding chairs, emergency equipment, fuel for the engine, maps, swimming gear, and yes, usually Brenda's paints... and me.

John steering the dinghy in Mount's Bay

Oh, the glorious days we had on the Fal and the Helford rivers. The little dinghy, loaded up with all that stuff, a teenager, and two – let's face it, substantial – adults, sat about 6" above the water – no way was John going to risk it on the open ocean... although if the weather was really kind he did take it out in Mount's Bay once or twice.

The effort involved in getting us and all our gear up to the estuaries on the south coast was huge, but so worth it. Not least because Brenda, by now a very large lady, had not been able to indulge her love of sea swimming for many years, feeling deeply self-conscious about appearing in public in a swimming costume... I'm not even sure, in those unenlightened days, that such a garment was available in her size. As it was, with the help of the little dinghy, we could pootle up the sides of the Fal or the Helford estuaries, find a little beach inaccessible from land, and claim it for our very own. Here Brenda was so relaxed and happy – swimming in her petticoat to her heart's content. Sometimes Hilda and Arthur joined us, or Peter and Mary, with baby Adam in his own little life jacket – but extra passengers necessitated two trips of course.

There were a couple of other opportunities for Brenda to enjoy getting in the water. One of John's best friends was Les Torrance, a broadly-accented Scotsman prone to kilt-wearing, who lived with his wife Pat in a house in Rose Valley in Morvah. They'd built a swimming pool beside their house, well fenced off from prying eyes, and here Brenda and John had the freedom to go skinny-dipping, and to eat their breakfast from the side of the pool. (After Pat sadly died, too young, Les married Margaret and moved to St Buryan.) There was also a rocky natural swimming pool called the Muzzons, just past Nanjizal Beach en route to Land's End, and down a precipitous stony track. I shall never get down there again, even if I knew exactly where it was – but Brenda must have managed to get her painting stuff down there in 1960, as I still have the memory preserved in oils. Here is the comment Brenda added to the back of her painting:

> *"This deep pool is difficult to find even from the cliff path. Seawards of Diamond Horse, below the west shank of Carn Les Boel, deep enough to stand up to your neck in. The rock formations here look like some ancient temple, and the lovely granite colour, so warm and cream. I climbed inside three huge boulders to paint this at the right angle – not the best place to have the scats! Must have climbed out half a dozen times! I can still see Susan splashing in this clear, clear water."*

Angus, Lena and the budgie come to stay after the Great Ash Wednesday Storm

On 7th March 1962, west Cornwall suffered particularly badly from the 'Great Ash Wednesday Storm' – much of the promenade was torn up and many buildings lost. Lena and Angus, living in 4 Daniel Place just back from the prom – and crucially, slightly downhill from it – were flooded out, with the water rising perilously close to their electric box beneath the front room windows. Angus carried Lena out on his shoulders, she carrying the budgie in its cage, and for a few weeks they came to stay with us while their house was restored and repaired. As you can see, all got out safely...

Tremaen Pottery

In early 1964 Lena, Brenda's mum, had a stroke, and came to live with us in Leskinnick Street to recuperate as she needed care, and Angus still needed to work. Taking in her over-flowing bowl of porridge for her breakfast one June morning, I found her on the floor, her lips blue. Carefully I carried the porridge back to the kitchen, and managed not to spill a drop, before breaking the news to mother. Funny what you remember... Despite all that Brenda could do, it was too late. Peter, married now with a young son, Adam, and living in Welwyn Garden City, came home for the funeral with wife Mary, then pregnant with Jonathan.

Peter had studied Fine Art at Bath College of Art in Corsham, but his first job was teaching pottery at a secondary school in Welwyn, where he'd worked from 1956. Following Lena's death, Peter decided to follow his dream, and phoned both Brenda and Angus with a proposition to help him start up his own studio pottery in Cornwall. They each agreed to put in £100 – and with that £300 start-up funding, in January 1965 Tremaen Pottery was born. Tremaen, meaning 'three stones' in Cornish, was to represent the three founding directors: Peter, Angus and Brenda – and Peter designed a suitable 3-legged Lanyon Quoit style logo for the new business.

The first premises was an old barn in a field at Marazion – 'The Barn', Morlands, Marazion – rented from Tommy Cattran. Despite their interest in art, Angus and Brenda had never created anything in clay, so Peter's first job was to teach them the basics of pottery... creating, moulding, decorating, glazing and firing. Soon he took on his first trainee, Bunty Duffin, from Camborne, so the workforce grew to four.

Peter, Brenda, Angus and Bunty at Tremaen's barn at Marazion

Experimenting with ideas for things to create. Peter began with vases, but soon moved on to what became his trademark range: lamp bases. He initially worked from thrown shapes, but increasingly took to creating plaster moulds, adapting the natural forms of wave-washed beach stones – in particular, the lovely egg-shaped stones found in Cot Valley at St Just (since protected by the National Trust and now illegal to remove!).

Tremaen Pottery became very successful, and it wasn't long before they outgrew the barn at Marazion (now long since vanished under a bungalow estate opposite the main beach car park). In 1967 Tremaen moved to a net loft – 'Mullion Stores' – above Stevenson's garage in the corner of Newlyn harbour, beside the slip, rented for £200 pa. Larger kilns were installed, and part of the loft was converted into a small showroom at the head of the stairs. Angus was in charge of the showroom, and enthusiastically made his own 'specials' to sell there cheaply as well as the official Tremaen lines.

Peter selecting stones at Cot Valley, later transformed into lampbases, as displayed on the Tremaen Pottery signboard at Newlyn

Bunty Duffin was a key worker there; she had a strong Camborne accent, and Peter delighted in taking the mickey out of her comments on the 'auringe qworry lawries' – the lorries that passed regularly from Newlyn Quarry just up the road... and often greeted her with 'Bunty Duffin, dawn knaw nawthen...'. Fortunately, Bunty took it all in good part, and she became his most valued worker, staying with Peter for many years; she is now married and living in Australia. I worked there in my holidays from college, and as a workspace, to sit at the workbench at the loft window and gaze over Newlyn harbour held a special magic for me (I did do some work as well, from time to time).

As the fortunes of the pottery improved, the workforce grew to a dozen and more, and at different times and in no particular order, included the following (courtesy of Bunty Davies, as she later became, and apologies to any I've missed!):

Ian McCloud, Roger Walker (used to work at Arch Pottery at St Ives, made goblin-shaped mugs), Alan (also made mugs, flared shape with low handle), Charman ('a cheeky little redhead'!), Sue Penrose (who eventually bought Tremaen's second property in Newlyn, Zimmerman's Barn), Heather from Sancreed, Mary Tregurtha, Geraldine Silcock, Lesley Grist (did she later marry St Buryan blacksmith Trevor Male?), Jackie, Alex – and, once again, Mike Sagar-Fenton. Peter took to giving all the regular shapes local place-names – Bowjey, Jizal, Mayon, Zennor, Mulfra and so on – and Michael tells me he was known for his heavy Perrans. As he explains, "I made the mistake at the beginning of rolling out clay on a bendy piece of ply instead of a firm counter, with the result that the clay thickened in the middle, not noticed until Peter picked them out of the kiln – thereafter known as my heavy Perrans...".

Mike remembers potter John Buchanan from Halsetown coming over to throw mugs: "He was lightning fast... I had to pug (prepare the clay) and weigh up his clay balls, called 'cannon' balls after him (as in Bu-cannon). He later inherited the name – though not to his face."

Brenda's role in the pottery was a varied one. She was able to multi-task, and could lead any new staff through the whole process: wedging and rolling out the heavy slabs of clay like pastry, cutting and placing in moulds – formed as a clean half of the finished shape, pressing into place, sponging smooth and slicing off the excess with a cheese-wire, placing on the drying racks, tipping the halves out when leather-dry, scoring the edges, 'gluing' the two halves together with slip and finishing off the joins smoothly. Once the lamp was complete, a hole was cut in the bases during the finishing stage, leaving a space large enough for a hand to go through, and they were then replaced on the racks to dry again ready for their first biscuit firing.

Once biscuit fired, the blank pieces were decorated. All the design work was done by Peter, at least initially, and all designs went through a series of decorating processes: some moulds were formed with a relief-moulded pattern or shape already, so the slab of clay, like pastry, took the same form in reverse; for others, the flat clay slab was first impressed with objects pressed into it with a rolling pin to give it texture before being laid face down in the mould, such as pieces of crumpled sacking or hessian, or stems and seed-heads of dried cow parsley – other bases were left plain, to be hand-painted with abstract designs in coloured slips, oxides or glazes, or sometimes all three.

The hand-painting was a more specialist task, and was often, but not always, done by Peter. Bunty painted many of the stylised fish designs on the dishes, and Brenda too, and a few selected others were also taught the finer points. The oxides burned strong colours into the designs, the slip gave a wash of softer colour, often dripped from a spoon over the pot at different angles or painted as a recognisable design – of boats, for example – and the all-covering glazes were sometimes sprayed on, or the pot dipped neck first into a glaze bucket, the other colours burning through the glaze on the finished item; wax resist was also used occasionally. Once the firing and decorating were complete it was necessary to attach a cable and plug – for this Angus devised a long stick with a tapered end which could hold a screw fitting to fasten to a lamp-holder, and could then be pushed up from the base into a pre-cut hole in the neck of the pot and glued in place. The final stage was glueing felt and card onto the base, covering the hole.

Peter decorating a pot – note one of Angus's Turks Head pub signs on the toilet wall behind (the toilet, as 'The Throne', was painted gold)

Mike Sagar-Fenton told me some of his memories of working in Tremaen Pottery:

> "It really was a family firm – Peter in charge, Brenda doing her thing in the back corner, Angus doing his electrical things when not chatting, telling jokes or telling stories of Gian' GooGoo to the two boys, Mary coming in to do the books. On the slave benches, I worked alongside Bunty, Jackie and Alex pugging away, rolling out my (heavy) Perrans, with cocoa at eleven every morning, pasties every Friday, and various other traditions. Very happy times."

Angus's role included the electrical fitting of the finished lamps, the displays in the showroom and other practical work. He obviously also saw staff morale as part of his work, telling yarns, cracking jokes, and once a year encouraging all the staff to stick a pin in the list of Derby runners. Mike continued: "I have to put in here about Angus's phone call to order pasties one Friday. He was asked for more detail than usual – 'you like them nice golden brown Angus – or a little bit darker? And not too much tate?' Eventually, he said 'You're taking an awful lot of trouble about a few pasties aren't you?' to which the answer came 'Well we don't often get asked for them.

This is Harveys crab-meat here!'. Angus had dialled the wrong number and whoever it was had recognised his voice at once. The best part was that Angus came off the phone laughing so much it took us five minutes to get the story out of him."

Year on year, Peter worked on creating new designs – lamp bases were always the meat, but there were many other smaller pieces added to the range – ashtrays, bowls, mugs, pendants – even door-knobs, light pulls, and pipe, pen and toothbrush holders.

A Tremaen catalogue from the mid-1970s

Most of the vases and dishes were based on pebble shapes, found on the local beaches, but the shape of one very successful oblong dish with two fish painted in oxides came from an old red plastic fruit bowl Peter had found. The designs for the lamp bases could loosely be categorised as natural, sculptural or figural, and have been usefully displayed as such on the excellent www.tremaen.com, a website created by avid Tremaen fan Tom Richards. The rarest, a one-off prototype which never went into production, and which only came to light recently (no pun intended), was a huge standard lamp made from a column of four conjoined Zennor lamp bases.

In March 1969 the Cornishman newspaper published an article about the 'blossoming local industry' of Tremaen Pottery, and the 'expanding markets' enabling the pottery to 'export to England' (I particularly like that phrase) two-thirds of their production to 'departmental stores in London' and 'boutique-type shops' in England and Wales. Already lamps had been sold abroad to Sweden and Italy.

Tremaen Craft Market entrance behind the Humphry Davy statue, with Brenda and her cousin Barbara

Eventually, in 1971, it was decided to take on the lease of a shop in Penzance, to tap into the lucrative tourist market. This was the peak time for interest in Cornish studio pottery, and Tremaen was fast becoming one of the 'big three', along with Celtic Pottery and Troika Pottery – all managed by friends and associates of Peter's – and with a location which really couldn't be more central, Tremaen Craft Market opened beneath and behind the Humphry Davy statue in Market Jew Street.

The premises in the basement of Lloyd's Bank had once been the town lock-up, and the original brick cells in the entrance passage and at the back of the shop were still in place. Display and storage units were built, an office and store-room were created at the back, with the rear cells becoming staff toilets, stock was purchased, shop assistants were employed, local papers were notified and the shop was launched. Brenda left the pottery and became the manager of the shop, but the overall planning was still managed by the three directors, with Peter splitting his time between pottery and shop.

Princess Anne visiting Tremaen Pottery at Newlyn, with Penzance Mayor, Councillor Doctor W J Turney

A further boost to Tremaen's fortunes came on 8th May 1972, when Princess Anne, visiting Newlyn as part of a Royal tour of Cornwall, made an official visit to Tremaen Pottery. Peter designed a special lamp base, the 'Lanyon', as a Royal gift for her.

Peter's ethos from the beginning was for the shop to act as a showcase for Cornish products, principally studio pottery, and the shop carried examples of the work of dozens of different local craftsmen and women. Celtic and Troika potteries were represented in abundance of course, but there was also pottery from Lamorna, Mousehole, Marazion and Pendeen, Leach-trained potters such as Nic Harrison, Scott Marshall, Alan Brough, Kernewek Pottery, Carn Pottery at Nancledra, Tremar at Liskeard, Anthony & Christiane Richards at Crowlas, the delightful small clay creatures of Biddy Picard and Linnea Lehtonen, work by Eric Leaper, John Vasey, and numerous others. The shop also sold craft jewellery and textiles, toys, glassware, fishermen's smocks – any craft item made in Cornwall, and books covering every aspect of life in Cornwall.

Brenda standing in front of the lamp display in the shop

An aside – following the recent sad death of former potter Julian Greenwood Penny, I must just add this comment. I only met him for the first time a few months ago, and we had a fascinating conversation. He remembered Peter with great affection – and is the only person ever to greet me with 'Ah, the green-haired lady – I was told it was Brenda's daughter, but it's not Brenda's daughter – it's John's daughter, and Peter's niece'! He worked for both Troika and Celtic at different times, sister potteries to Tremaen, and recalled a shared trip to Torquay Trade Fair one year, where the three potteries each had trade stands displaying their wares. Maggie Fisher and Ev Stevens from Celtic, Leslie Illsley and Julian from Troika, and Peter and Brenda from Tremaen, had shared the use of a dilapidated holiday cottage near Torquay for the event, which lasted several days, to save costs. They shared also the daily commute to and from the Trade Fair to the cottage, which was way out in the country and down a tortuous and very bumpy lane. Peter, driving his beat up old van, hurtled down the track at speed, with all four passengers thrown about in the back. When they stopped at the bottom, Brenda, in the front passenger seat, beamed happily if a little breathlessly – "Well! That was fun!' she said, 'almost orgasmic!!' – at which, Peter turned the van around and hurtled back up and down the track again...

Julian also told us of John (Mr Woottie), doing the electrics for Celtic Pottery... firing kilns daily is a very costly business, and apparently he managed to rig up some bypass to the system which enabled Celtic to access economy tariff electricity during the day-time as well as at night – which worked wonderfully, but had to be 'put to rights' whenever SWEB were due to come and read the meter. The ruse was never discovered – naughty Mr Wootie.

Eventually, realising perhaps that being 'made in Cornwall' is not necessarily a guarantee of top quality or design – or, to be more realistic, top sales – Peter became less purist and widened his range to include popular selling lines from elsewhere, including shells and jewellery from the Middle East and the Philippines, courtesy of friend Keith Hall, who ran the Shell Shop in the harbour (still there, now run by Keith's son). Large ranges of cards and postcards, tea-towels, scarves, bags, decorative tins, and even mid-century modern Scandinavian designed kitchenware and Portuguese rustic glassware were added, and the shop became more of a high-class gift shop. However local studio pottery was always a priority and a top seller, and given pride of place. The benchmark for how well the shop was doing could be gauged from the number of coffee sets sold in a week, a top week in the summer months showing sales of up to 20.In 1969, Peter also took a unit in the newly-opened Sloop Craft Market in St Ives for a while.

Interrupting the chronological narrative flow to include all of Tremaen's history in one hit...

In 1974, Brenda called me into the shop one day to ask me a crucial question: was I willing to take over the management of the shop, as she wanted to leave to pursue her professional singing career. I was stunned. My relationship with Brenda had been somewhat stormy on occasions, throughout my teenage years and after, and I was amazed and gladdened to realise that, despite my lack of experience and my proven ability to screw up now and then, she actually believed me to be capable of running the family business of Tremaen Craft Market. I accepted without a second thought – my teaching career following my return to Cornwall had never got beyond random supply work, and this opportunity was heaven-sent, in my eyes.

I loved running the shop. Peter was quite a demanding boss, and I didn't always meet his high standards of performance, but generally speaking, we worked well together, most likely because of course he was still spending part of his working week in the pottery. Peter was actually a real fun guy to spend time with, having a terrific sense of humour and boundless energy – he had a lot of Angus's easy charm. I loved selecting and ordering the stock, dealing with customers, and re-doing the displays, although Peter often did a lot of that himself, and I thoroughly enjoyed attending the annual trade fairs with him, to the NEC in Birmingham, or to Torquay or Harrogate, where he would sometimes be both buying and selling. I did *not* enjoy having to discipline staff, and on one occasion having to sack one particularly garrulous lady. But my confidence and self-esteem improved, my ability to organise and manage was enhanced, my love of pottery, fine design and art grew, and all contributed to having a profound and positive influence on my future life.

The large oblong shop was on two levels, the left-hand side inside the door raised as a platform up a few steps. Peter had designed large storage boxes on castors to be pulled out from under the counters, but behind that the area beneath the platform was really just a dark and empty inaccessible space. One summer the staff reported finding a few large cockroaches in some of the drawers, and when three were discovered having a party in one of our Portuguese wine glasses on a shelf in the stockroom, we realised we had a problem. We called in the Council pest control fellas, and had to close the shop down for a weekend while the entire place was fumigated. It turned out the cockroaches had been procreating with a will beneath the platform, and when I turned up to open the shop on the Monday morning, I found a nightmare scene... I could barely push open the shop doors for the press of chitinous bodies littering the floor inside. Thousands – millions, it seemed to me – of dead and dying cockroaches lying on their backs, certainly millions of little legs waving feebly in the half-light. I rushed out again to the nearest shop and borrowed a large broom, and we swept up every single one.

We were instructed by the Council to keep the bodies in a box until they all stopped moving (ugh), and then to let them know so that the carnage could be inspected by their operatives. Every day for a week or more I had to walk past this horror, checking to see if any life still remained in the grotesque carcasses, which it did, for a distressingly long time.

This unpleasant incident aside, working in the shop was usually great fun – there was a lot of camaraderie with the staff, and when I was married in 1975, one of the 'shop maids', Karen, kindly prepared much of the food for the reception. I remember Tristan Hole, a wonderful character who had been a flapper in her younger days, and her son Mike Carr; there was Florence, my sister-in-law, and the efficient and charming Marjorie, who went on to work for Celtic Pottery's Maggie Fisher in her Mounts Bay Trading shop in Causewayhead for years, and Peter's mother-in-law, Mary's mum Gladys Guy. The calmly efficient Mr Barratt came in every week to do the books. And there was Joyce, a lovely mumsy lady – who joined me a few years later, handcuffed to the radiators in the kitchen of Bolitho Maternity Home in Penzance, in a massive 4-month occupation and protest squat attempting, but sadly failing, to prevent its closure.

Christmas was an especially wonderful time. Tremaen Craft Market – as with all the town's shops – was decorated and brightly lit, the main street hung with decorations and the huge tree, usually just outside our front door. In the days before Christmas, there would often be a band or a choir outside the shop as well, as it was one of their main performance areas... and we would all stop what we were doing and stand in the doorway to join in with the carols. Mulled wine and hot mince pies were out the back in the stock room for any friends or family who came visiting. And I would hunt through the town for the very first 'sols' as a present for Brenda; we both adored the blissfully fragrant narcissus Soleil D'Or from the Isles of Scilly, which in those days only appeared a day or so before Christmas. Now you can buy them as early as October...

Brenda with Auntie Ellen, Peter, Donald, French agent Olivier's wife, and the roadie Dominique, in the stockroom in Tremaen's at Christmas

Christmas drinks for the pottery staff in the Yacht, with cousins Barbara Coleman and Mary Gendall

So Brenda went on the road… but she continued her duties as a Director of the business, and any decision-making still involved all three partners. One major decision relating to the pottery which involved a heavy financial commitment was the purchase of an old barn in Newlyn Coombe. By this stage Peter had designed attractive packaging boxes for posting the bases together with the bought-in hessian shades which were sold with them; the lampshades side of the business was run as a separate operation under the business name 'Angus'. And with orders coming in for lamp-bases from Heals and Liberty in London, and orders from overseas, Peter wanted to expand. Zimmerman's Barn, tucked down in the Newlyn Coombe valley behind St Peter's Rectory, seemed ideal, and much work and expense was involved in adapting it to fit the pottery's needs. Mike Sagar-Fenton recalls that Peter originally turned down offers of orders from Liberty in London, "despite the cachet – he said they'd take his whole output, he'd lose all his local customers, and in a year they'd choose someone else. Very wise...". According to Julian Greenwood Penny, it was just such a devastating move by Heals that proved the final death knell for Troika – fashions change, sometimes very suddenly.

After Lena died in 1963, Angus coped on his own for a few years, but it was not his natural state. In 1966 he married Vera Bending, a widow living in Penzance, and moved in with her and her feisty Jack Russell to her house in Chyandour. Vera cooked and cleaned and looked after him, for which I will always be grateful, but it can't be said she ever got on well with the rest of the family. At least he had care and company in his final years.

In April 1975, when I was working in the office at Tremaen Craft Market, I got a phone call from Peter with the most heart-breaking news. Angus had been on holiday with Vera in Torquay, and walking on the promenade in the sunshine, had suddenly dropped down dead. He was found lying on his back and smiling at the sky. God, I loved that man. I was totally grief-stricken – we all were – but really – what a way to go. He certainly had style.

In 1977 I left the shop to have my first baby, Davy Arthur Ellery Luscombe, and largely lost touch with developments. Ultimately the big orders dried up, and Zimmerman's Barn became an expensive luxury. It was eventually sold to one of the ex-pottery workers, Sue Penrose, for conversion to a private house. The peak period for Cornish studio pottery had passed, and Tremaen Pottery closed in 1988.

Years later, I took husband Chris to show him the pottery site in Newlyn – with permission from the chaps downstairs in Stevenson's garage. Then just full of debris and garage bits, it was a sad sight – but one of the men very kindly ferreted about in the office and gave me a champagne cork, inscribed and given to him by Peter on the day of closure, as he'd brought a bottle down that day to share with the men, to commemorate the end of an era. Lovely gesture...

Tremaens, the shop (as it was renamed) closed in 1995 – and sadly Peter, who had planned so much for his retirement... painting, walking the dog, travel... died of prostate cancer within a year – a cruel ending to his plans, and a poor reward for a lifetime of dedication to his craft.

But I'll finish with Tremaens on a more cheerful note, with one more Angus story from Mike Sagar-Fenton:

> "Peter had helped put up the Newlyn Christmas lights, and was very cross when some naughty young boys threw stones and smashed some of them. They were spotted and sent to Peter to decide their punishment. He took on full school-teacher mode and made them do odd dirty jobs around the pottery all one Saturday morning, hanging their heads now and looking very small, Peter very stern. Angus came up to me quietly as Peter was barking at them and said in my ear 'I couldn't be hard like that, could you? I'd be more likely to give 'em sixpence and tell 'em to do it again…'"

Peter and Brenda in Tremaen Pottery at Newlyn

Peter & Mary

Despite appearances to the contrary, Peter and Mary did have a life outside of Tremaens, and a very busy one. He met his future wife Mary Walsh in Hertfordshire, following his move there to teach after leaving Corsham. Mary had trained as a teacher, and became a respected headmistress at both Tolcarne School at Newlyn and Bodriggy School at Hayle. Peter was an accomplished artist in his own right, as well as a potter, and enjoyed painting in any medium; in his youth he had copied Angus's traditional sculptured style, but his time at Bath Academy of Art at Corsham awoke a latent talent that was superbly modernist and abstract – his paintings of the reflections of boats in Newlyn harbour are some of the finest I've seen. His drawings for the cover of Brenda's 'Pipers Folk' album are a typical, if more graphic, example, and he produced several similar screen-prints at the time, which I still have.

Peter's painting of boats in Newlyn Harbour

His lifelong friend, the Cornishman's reporter on the local arts scene, Frank Ruhrmund, said this in his obituary of Peter:

> '[...at Corsham]... he was taught by, and became friends with, such well-known artists of the period as Peter Lanyon and Bryan Winter... For more than 30 years he was a member and sometime Chairman of the Management Committee of Newlyn Art Gallery – a period of service equalled only by the doyen of the Newlyn School, Stanhope A Forbes... For several years he also embraced education, serving as a Governor of Mount's Bay School and Penwith Sixth Form College.'[11]

Wearing my LibDem County Councillor hat, I served on the Newlyn Orion Gallery Committee with Peter when he was Chair, during his final years, and it was a lovely opportunity to spend some time with him. He was as sharp and witty as ever. As well as his other community work, Peter was active every year in maintaining the Christmas lights in the area, and in ensuring the continued success of the Alternative Tom Bawcock's Eve carol singing in pubs in Nancledra, and subsequently, Penzance.

Peter and Mary often went on holidays to the Greek islands, where Peter was able to indulge his artistic skills to the full. There were always dogs, usually daft red setters, one of whom was so famous

---

[11] *Western Morning News, December 10th 1996, Frank Ruhrmund*

for getting himself lost and then found, he would just take himself off to the police station straight away, and cut out the middle-man – the dog of the moment accompanying Peter on his regular long walks around cliffs and countryside. The couple were naturally very involved in the local arts scene, and moved in elevated artistic circles… and their house on Laregan Hill in Penzance was an architectural gem: built as a folly by a wealthy businessman in the early years of the 20th century, it had some wonderful Arts & Craft Movement touches… hand-cut polished wood parquet flooring in the over-large hall, Newlyn Copper finger-plates on all the doors, and a round castle-like turret in one corner of the building.

Of their two sons, my cousins – Adam, born in Welwyn Garden City in 1961, is now a successful GP in Praze-an-Beeble in West Cornwall and a Director of Kernow Health, and Jonathan (1964, also Welwyn born) founded his own very successful graphic design business in 1998, Browns Design in Bermondsey in London. Since her retirement and Peter's death, Mary has moved into Penzance, to a lovely house right beside Morrab Gardens, and in recent years has served as Chair of the Morrab Library.

Peter and Mary with Adam

Brenda's daughter

It is one thing to give a chronological account of the events in Brenda's life, but it is quite another to describe living with Brenda as her daughter during my formative years. As adolescence started to bite, I found myself frequently at odds with her view of how I should behave – a plight probably experienced by most teenage girls. She was a strong-willed character, and I often fell foul of her temper. She could be both an unstoppable force and an immovable object simultaneously. Here are a couple of examples which are burned into my memory...

I had a friend during my early years at the Grammar School called Sarah L. Her parents were separated, and her father was an artist, and Brenda was quite the reactionary in those days, which might explain why a daughter of such 'Bohemian' parents may not have appealed to her as a suitable friend for her daughter. I was forbidden from going to St Ives, a potentially dangerous territory riddled with beatniks apparently (hence the attraction of course), but Sarah and I devised a plan. Occasionally I would tell them I was going to see my friend Denise in Marazion (a safer prospect) and primed Denise that if Brenda or John should phone asking for me, she was to say I was down on the beach or some such inaccessible place. So Sarah and I would catch the bus to St Ives, stroll down to the Sugar & Spice café above the harbour, sit and drink hot chocolate and eat chocolate gateau, and gaze at the (definitely prohibited) beatniks; at the appropriate time we would catch the bus back to Penzance, and all would be well. It really was that innocent...

Inevitably I suppose, disaster struck. One evening, aged maybe 12 or 13, I missed the bus from St Ives that was supposed to arrive in Penzance at the same time as the last bus from Marazion. With trembling heart, I called home from the public phone box in St Ives. Father answered the phone. In those days, there were still operators in the local telephone exchanges, so before I had a chance to speak, a tinny voice on the line warbled brightly "St Ives exchange calling..."

A slight pause, then Father's voice: "Susan? Is that you? Where are you!?"

I knew not what to say. "Marazion?" I tried feebly. "Get home! Get back here now!" he barked. My ploy hadn't worked, obviously. All the way back on the next bus from St Ives I quaked with fear; I knew I was done for. As I crept up the road from the station, I saw

Brenda planted like an oak tree outside our front gate. Her arms were folded high on her chest, and she was holding a rolling pin. "Get in!!" she yelled, "Get up those stairs!!" She followed me closely as I snuck through the door, and slammed the front door behind her so hard that both Tremaen pottery doorknobs fell off and smashed on the floor. Somewhere between the front door and the bedroom she'd swapped the rolling pin for a ruler, mercifully, and she set about belabouring me with it. It was one of only two times that she ever hit me, and both occasions were for lying. Lying was by far the worst crime – now, as a parent, I can see where she was coming from, but then – well, it just hurt. Logic didn't come into it.

It seems Sarah & I weren't alone in finding the 'beatniks' fascinating in the early '60s... Jonathon Coudrille has commented "Beatniks came to St Ives in quantity and were hugely unpopular with the town elders but immensely attractive to youngsters like myself... Beatniks were political, they were intellectual, they were sexy, they were cool. We all aspired to beatnik chic... that was the style of the day."[12] And the beatnik invasion was just the vanguard of the coming folk revival movement of course, which was to impact Brenda so profoundly.

Another major conflict happened when I was 16. Jan Yeates, he of Choughs fame, and I, had developed a serious – and secret, of course – passion for each other. He was 10 years older than me, and a friend of the family to boot, so I knew there was little point in asking for parental approval. We wrote impassioned love poetry to each other – mine liberally decorated with bits of cut up lacy paper doily on coloured heart-shaped paper and suchlike. That Good Friday, I hatched a cunning plan to visit Jan in his flat opposite the church in St Just. Every Good Friday my friends and I walked to Lamorna – as did most everyone I knew – a local tradition that had been in place for aeons probably. I primed my friends who I knew were going: if you see my parents, or they stop and ask you where I am, tell them I went by the cliff route with some others, rather than by road.

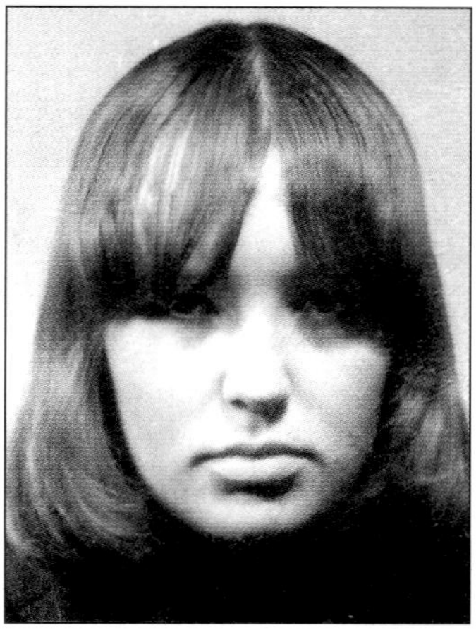

A moody teenage Susan, photographed by Jan Yeates

[12] *'Folk in Cornwall', Rupert White*

Off I went on the bus to my tryst with Jan in St Just, and after a highly eventful day, returned home to find Brenda seated in the kitchen, ice cold with rage, brandishing in front of her on the kitchen table all my carefully hidden love letters and photos to and from Jan (innocent ones, of course – no questionable selfies in those days). She and Father *had* decided to drive to Lamorna, *had* met my friends on the road, and had been unconvinced by their story. On her return home, having smelled a rat, she searched high and low in my messy bedroom until she discovered my hidden cache.

She demanded – with menaces – that Jan and I cease our outrageous relationship this instant, threatened to burn every piece of the evidence in the Rayburn, and then proceeded to make good her threats. For once, I yelled back. I accused her of having an ego the size of a house and warned her to back off. To be honest, that's about where my memory fizzles out, and I'm happy to say it must have ended relatively favourably, as Jan and I did become 'official' for a while. Until I went off to college – but that's another story...

One more rueful incident: I was allowed to have a teenage party one night when Brenda and John were elsewhere. Of course, we had illicit booze, though probably mostly just beer and some cheap wine (I don't think we'd heard of drugs in those days). But in the back kitchen was a rather strange thing: the sink was full of oozing red clay my Father had dug up from an archaeological site and was drying out, in an attempt to see if he could make a clay pot from it. One rather over-dramatic girl, acting more drunk than she probably was, freaked out totally, and started screaming and smearing herself with the mud, yelling about blood, and ran out in the street causing a proper ruckus. We had to get her parents to come and collect her. It did not go down well with Brenda – or with John, whose stock of native red clay had been severely interfered with and spread all over the kitchen.

I think the greatest hardship in having a mother like Brenda was my feeling of total inadequacy. At that age when girls want to prove to themselves and everyone else how hot they are, how talented, funny, witty and wise, I felt like I was on a total road to nowhere. Every potential beau I spotted was gazing adoringly at my mother singing her heart out on stage. She baked pasties and cakes like a dream. She painted and created pictures, wrote and directed plays and pantomimes, and made friends easily. She had an amazing ability to create her own sewing patterns and made all of her own long flowing robes (she looked with scorn on my broken bra straps held together with safety pins, and described my pathetic attempts at sewing repairs as using "a red-hot needle and a burning thread...").

Whenever I was introduced to anyone, by anyone, I was always 'Brenda's daughter'. Never 'Brenda and John's daughter' – and Brenda was never 'Sue's mum'... not until many, many years later. Come to that, John was always 'Brenda's husband', too. I developed a stock response to the stock question I was always – *always* – asked, by new acquaintances: "Do you sing like your mother?" My answer was always "No, but I clap well...". No, I didn't, and don't, sing like my mother. No way could I hope to compete, or even compare, with her for singing, sewing, cooking, painting, acting, making people laugh or cry, or good old general charisma. Even her large size didn't stop her from oozing charm and seduction from every pore if there was an appreciative audience within range. So I sort of stopped trying. (Having said that, there is now some comparison to be borne in our comparative sizes, and many have said to me in recent years "You look *so* like your mum!". Facially, certainly, I know I do – I recognise the same expressions, and lines around the mouth, the same set of the eyes. But I find I really don't mind... And I also have Lena's nose – and her mole!)

So – I had a massive chip on my shoulder. Doesn't every teenager? And don't they think that they're the only one who is treated so harshly? And the untidiness and general squalor of my bedroom, the smelliness of my gang of boy friends who littered her front room regularly ('the great unwashed' she called them), my 'attitude' problems and wilfulness – these were all sources of great annoyance to her. Resentment on both sides festered gently, and it was probably a relief to both of us when I went up to London to Philippa Fawcett Teacher Training College in Streatham in 1968. (Jan Yeates broke his heart, but I wasn't ready then to make any promises to 'stay true'.)

I was so homesick during that first 6 months away, living in college digs, not yet knowing anyone. But I was cheered by letters from home – from Brenda, from Dad, and especially from Angus. In one, Angus recounted an incident that occurred outside the pottery:

> "Some to-do over Newlyn last week... imagine 30 fellows outside the pottery, arguing the toss, then starting to fight, strikers and blacklegs, five in hospital, black eyes and broken ribs, while I egged them on with joyous shouts of acclamation, much to your

> Ma's disgust (she being busy in the showroom at the time with customers)... I think our side won."

And here's an extract from a letter from Brenda and John – fixing the old toilet:

> "Daddy and Mary have spent the day in the toilet together, fitting a new pipe on the cistern... however, they held spanners and things together... Daddy said Mary was very 'flushed', I noticed he had a dead-'pan' expression, anyhow they had a 'swinging' time, and the cistern looks very snug once more..." and John adds: "As Confucius say, 'swinging chain denote warm seat'. Mrs Overcoat [the cleaner] is tackling your bedroom in 19 easy stages... so far, the mats have been lifted and the floor cleaned... 85 woodworm, 12 spiders and 3 ants died of shock. Two mice threatened to leave home..."

Gradually I gained enough confidence to get out and enjoy the London scene, and occasionally made it to some great parties, and some folk clubs to see old friends: Ralph McTell at the Half Moon in Putney, Wizz Jones, Pete Stanley and Mike Silver at the Troubadour in Soho, or whoever was playing in The Crypt at St Martins-in-the-Fields. I even saw the Stones in Hyde Park...

Sue and her class in Smallwood Junior School, Tooting 1972

After completing my Teacher Training course in 1971 – more by accident than design... it was not a vocation – I got a job teaching at Smallwood Junior School in Tooting. Teaching jobs in Cornwall, where I really wanted to be, were few and far between. Eventually, after 2 years in Tooting, I got a supply teaching job back home, with unsatisfactorily random stints in various local schools.

Three years absence up in 'the smoke', even with extended college summer and Christmas breaks, did make the heart grow somewhat fonder in relation to Brenda – but it was on my return in 1973 when the game changed totally. Every mother's worst nightmare you would think is when her daughter gets herself unintentionally pregnant after a one-night stand. I was sharing a flat in Wellington Terrace in Penzance, and when I got the positive result – by phone, taken on the public call box outside Tremaen Craft Market – I can remember wishing the ground would open up and swallow me. I had to go into her office in the shop and tell her the news. I expected that life as I knew it would be over. I just knew I had nothing to hope for anymore.

And of course, she astonished me. Something was threatening her daughter, and nothing would stand in the way of her getting it sorted out – whichever way I wanted it to go. She summoned the offending youth to a meeting, just the three of us, and questioned both of us in depth. There were no recriminations, no yelling, no pressure to take any particular course of action. When she was completely satisfied that neither of us wanted or was prepared to deal with a baby, she made some phone calls, and within 2 days I was on the train to a clinic in Ealing. It was not pleasant, and many years later I beat myself up about it soundly, but for then, the nightmare was over. This would not be a decision I would make today, with an older and hopefully wiser brain, but then, she saved me, and I found a new respect and affection for her which had been lost for some time. I remembered then, something that I'd forgotten. When a vindictive English teacher (Miss Furness – she never liked me!) had demanded I should not be allowed to take English A level as she was determined I wasn't good enough, Brenda had stormed up to the headmistress, Miss Milton's office, and fought, verbally at least, and successfully, for my right to take it. Brenda could be fierce in protection of her own (...yes, I passed).

Within a year, she was offering me the position of Shop Manager, to run the family business. Can you wonder at my sense of amazement and disbelief, that she could think me adequate to the task, after our history of the previous few years?

And by that time, too, she had been running a folk club for a while, and her reactionary attitudes had long since mellowed – she was far more tolerant of the differences in people, in their lifestyles and their views. Brenda had changed, and I had grown up some too, so gradually, over time, the chip disappeared, and I became proud to be Brenda's daughter. She wasn't always an easy person to deal with – every guitarist she ever had will testify to that – but there were huge benefits in knowing her too. Watching her years later, standing in the spotlight and singing like a bird in that voice of pure silver to huge French audiences in a darkened auditorium, all of whom were in love with her, and silent, reverent as only the utterly devoted can be – who would not be proud?

That was my ma up there...

Brenda and Sue at Trewellard Meadery

Where She Went To

The history of the 'Folk Scene' in Cornwall is quite well documented – and Rupert White's recent book 'Folk in Cornwall'[13] covers all the permutations of the clubs, the groups and the artists very well... so I am only describing here those aspects of it that impinged on Brenda's progress towards her future career.

West Cornwall in the early '60s, with the advent of the beatnik culture, had become a melting pot of musical styles. What later became known as the Folk Revival was underway. New eclectic sounds – new to us at any rate – were being heard, enjoyed and learned. Skiffle, beat, rock'n'roll, jazz and blues, even the ultra-traditional folk music, were being explored, merged, developed, thrilling the youngsters, and new clubs opened, responding to that need.

The Count House

I was 14 in 1964 when a report appeared in the Cornishman newspaper about an unlikely new music venue opening on the cliffs near Pendeen. Brenda decided to check whether this would be a suitable club for her daughter to visit, so all three of us went along.

The Count House Folk Music Club was set up by John Ian Todd, his wife Judi, and John Wood, and was initially planned as a cabaret club. Ian didn't really have his finger on the pulse so much as the zeitgeist impacting on him. He couldn't really find anyone too interested in cabaret, but the artists available played folk – so, folk it was.

The club opened in June in an old 'counting house' belonging to the Botallack Mine – set amongst the stark granite mine ruins and old arsenic tunnels, with the iconic Crowns Mine stacks holding out against the waves at the foot of the cliffs and zawns. Perched on the cliffs and miles from the nearest sizable town of Penzance, the site was indeed an unlikely one for a new club. The large oblong barn-like room was painted white over the rough stone, and the high ceiling and the walls were draped in black fishing nets. The

---

[13] *'Folk in Cornwall', Rupert White, Antenna Publications*

seating was old oak pews from the old chapel at Trewellard that had closed down (and has been the Trewellard Meadery ever since), and upturned barrels and planks.

It was rudimentary. There was an Elsan toilet and a small coffee bar, and a low wooden platform at the far end served as the stage.

The original resident singers were one John the Fish and Tell Mann, and a couple of clean-cut young schoolteachers, Mel and Miles. The very first record, an EP called Folk Music at the Count House, featured both duos, and it was produced in October 1964. (Endearingly, the phone number for the early Count House was St Just 8...)

Anyway – we loved the club. More to the point, Brenda loved it, and so we started to come regularly, Brenda joining in from the audience with some of the songs she already knew – and inevitably, her voice, heard above the audience, soon drew attention.

Jack King, who became a great friend and lives in Australia, remembered:

> "I was lucky enough to be there on the first night that Brenda turned up at the Count House, and like so many of us was astonished at the amazing harmonies that suddenly started ringing out from the audience. As we all know it wasn't too many evenings later before she was up on stage and, with John the Fish, forging the beginnings of a great musical relationship. In those days I was just a teenager either camping down in Kenidjack valley or sleeping in the railway carriages overnight in Penzance railway station after my shifts in the Wimpy bar. Innocent days, but the beginnings of my introduction to the fabulous folk music that was to come. As you know the Wooties' house became a wonderful centre for a veritable Who's Who of the folk world. It was an inspiration that played no small part in my later joining the BBC where I was lucky enough to be able to invite them onto my folk shows and was very honoured to be asked to write the sleeve notes for 'Crowdy Crawn'."

Mike Sagar-Fenton recalls, "Ian Todd once told me that when they'd spotted where the harmonies in the audience were coming from, they asked Brenda to get up on stage and sing – but she wouldn't do that... would she just stand up in the front? No... then would she just stand up and sing from where she was sitting? ... A star was born..."

John the Fish and Tell Mann at the Count House

Des Hannigan was one of the main residents in those early days, together with John the Fish – his memories cast a slightly different light. He says his responsibilities were to "marshal, cajole and then dispose of, the stream of itinerant performers who queued up for a chance… During Brenda's first appearance on stage as one of the resident team, she said to me… 'I don't think you should put so many of these itinerants on…' She was probably right, but *she* had been an itinerant for several weeks past, albeit a strikingly talented one. I think I saw the writing – or singing – on the wall, then… there was only going to be one bright shining star…" He comments that he was a particular fan of the singers Vicki Hughes and Jill Johnson "…both of whom appealed to me more than did Brenda. I was never shy of saying so, and it didn't always go down well before that splendid Brenda glower." I knew that glower well.

Despite Des's reservations, he says he was "hugely fond" of Brenda, and remembers clearly "her kindness, her Cornishness, and her unflinching determination". He describes Brenda and husband John as being "protective of me, and very kind…dragooning…" him into recording the "threadbare clutch of songs" he had written onto a tape in their front room, which he thinks may have been sent to Cecil Sharp House – "depository of every wailing folk song in the book". He is being unkind to himself – Des has always been a fine performer, and is a superb writer.

The Count House – Des Hannigan with 'Handshake'

Des remembers his first night at the Count House, when he got up and sang 2 or 3 Scottish folk songs... "and they thought this was the real thing, a proper folk singer, finger in both ears and everything...".

Other regular residents in that first couple of years were Ronald Handfield-Jones, aka Handshake ("a terrific 12-string man and a student at Camborne School of Mines" says Des), the Four-Fifths Jug Band from Helston, a group of talented and enthusiastic lads who stayed the course for some years, and Terry Kemp and Alec Shaw...

Brenda's first song, with John the Fish as impromptu accompanist, was Lamorna, which was to become a trademark number she sang throughout her musical career. ('Lamorna' was first publicly performed by her as part of a production with Madron Players, 'The Smugglers of Sennen', in 1961).

Once she had become a resident singer at the club, she quickly learned a much wider repertoire of songs from the other residents and visiting guests. One performer she admired greatly was Nadia Cattouse. Born in British Honduras and based in Britain since the 1950s, she taught Brenda several songs, including the haunting 'Port Mahon'. But the range of influences was wide – from bluegrass and country singer Bill Clifton to Irish folk performer Steve Benbow, or jazz, blues or pop, Brenda cherry-picked whatever appealed to her, which turned out to be a pretty eclectic mix.

Brenda and Fish on stage at the Count House in the mid-1960s

In November 1965, a second private record was produced – a full-length album this time, entitled 'More Singing at the Count House', and featuring John the Fish, Mel & Miles, Des and Brenda. (Tell Mann had moved on by then to open his own club, the Tell-a-Tale, in Penzance.) Des recalls:

> "I remember us recording the LP with affection. I think that only about 100 copies were produced. They sold out in no time, and there were rumours of a copy being sold in Bristol for as much as a fiver, only a month later – and for much more even now. Ian Todd was furious with himself for not producing more. A teenage Angela Rippon came down to do a piece about the record for the Western Morning News. The record's cover was a joy: picture by David Wills and the whole designed by Russ Hedges and Ian, whose wee dog, Kega, staged the HMV impersonation... People today still refuse to believe it's me in the photograph. I cherish that photo – all that 'big hair'... Brenda lit up that record, in truth."

Here are Mike Sagar-Fenton's memories of the early years of the Count House:

> "By the mid-1960s some of us had formed a little folk cult. Our home was the snug in the Turk's Head (under the genial eye of landlord Peter Byrne) where we'd gather every Saturday and sing. Only a few of us could play then – Piglet (Philip Rowley), Tim Knight and above all the near-mystical figure of John The Fish, bearded, solitary, almost a tramp but full of brilliant American songs none of us knew, learned at the knee of Doc Watson and Rambling Jack Elliot, just one step removed from Woody Guthrie himself. He was always on hand in any of our parties, sitting in a corner on his own, playing and singing. We'd already cut our teeth on the early records of Baez and Dylan and warmed to the politics as well as the singing. Before that I'd been into jazz rather than pop music and flirted with the Beatnik culture, so innocent with its love of dark cellars, long hair, long jumpers (preferably black), cigarettes (preferably French) and COFFEE! WINE! JOSS STICKS! Wow.
>
> "When the Count House opened, supposedly as a night-club, we simply followed the music out there, a ready-made audience which gave the would-be night-club entrepreneur Ian Todd such a shock and forced him to change his venue to a folk club instead. John had teamed up with Tell Mann, a builder, as a powerful folk duo, and they became club residents.

"Brenda and I were good friends by then and I had learned a few songs on the autoharp, mostly Baez classics. I called in to Coombe Dingle whenever I was home, often finding Brenda writing her next panto, and she asked me a lot about folk music and the folk scene. I taught her a few songs by ear, including my own setting of Kipling's 'Harp Song' which she loved. I doted in turn on her record collection of jazz singers. We had a lot in common. I was the lucky boy with the use of a car so I could get to the Count House easily, often with a carful of friends and hitchers, a familiar journey (I'm now living in Newlyn) up the St Just Road, into the fog on Newbridge Hill, off to Pendeen, down to Trewellard and along to the ridiculously remote mine building where scores of people gathered, first at weekends, then on week-nights, then half the night, then all night, just to drink coffee and coca cola and listen to and sing songs. It was a true phenomenon.

"I was away a lot and back home at intervals so I don't really remember when Brenda began performing at the Count House. I remember her singing harmonies from the audience – audible on the Count house EP – but then John, after his stint with Tell, would call her up for a couple of numbers. She certainly had courage. I can see her standing there, her hands clenching and unclenching while John took his time and started up his intro. She was twice the age of most of the audience, a different generation, a big lady, singing songs in an idiom she had only just learned. I never heard anyone titter, but they must have wondered what on earth was coming. Fish was, however, the ideal foil for her early work. His accompaniments were spare, grounded on bass with little embellishment, leaving oceans of room for the singer to fill.

"And when Brenda started singing, the room stopped breathing.

"Perhaps they expected a low growl from such a body – and when she sang jazz Brenda could deliver that too – but no-one could have anticipated the undecorated purity of her tone, the warmth of her expression or her extraordinary range. The song '500 miles' – the slow version, not the Proclaimers' stomp – was a prime example. The audience knew their stuff and were aware that it featured a challenging octave jump. Singers approached it with caution, careful to start low enough to make that upward slide without falling off. But Brenda began where most singers stopped, right up there, and the audience tensed, waiting for the car-crash that was bound to happen. But when the moment came she pitched an effortless and full octave rise into the stratosphere, up to the stars, a full clean note of such quality that the audience, I swear, rose vertically from their seats.

"She was soon a fixture. Fish continued to sing with Tell, not just in the Count House but in gigs around the district, and they made a good driving sound. They always ended a Count House evening with an unaccompanied 'Wild Mountain Thyme' with full audience chorus. Brenda joined in with everything she could. She had an almost supernatural ability to find a part, a line of her own, not always the highest line though she had such an amazing register, sometimes low, often tricky close harmonies, and always pitch-perfect. Her sessions with Fish grew more regular, longer, gradually taking over the central 'residents' performance. Tell split and started his own club in Penzance's Chapel Street. Brenda and John were the show.

"I carried on writing for her, and once when John was away she sang a short set to the accompaniment of nothing but my drums. The fame of the Count House spread throughout the folk world. It certainly was unique. Most clubs were in town pubs, but the Cornish circuit consisted mainly of the Folk Cottage, a derelict barn in the dark countryside near the hamlet of Mitchell, and the cliff-side Count House. Singers doing their summer busking thing flocked to it, of various qualities including very, very good, and with such a faithful audience it was worth booking guest singers too. Soon a gig there was the highlight of any singer's tour. The audience was almost as impressive as the venue, full of good singers and knowledgeable folk fans. I remember once Alex Campbell came and began to sing his song 'So Long'. He started in a quiet world-weary voice but when the chorus came the audience boomed back 'So Long' so loud and sweet that he almost fell off the stage. Fish had been singing it for weeks.

"Brenda's fame grew with the club. She was still in demand for concerts and socials but nothing else had the same buzz or the connection with a younger generation. It was intoxicating. We wondered how she would go down elsewhere..."

For Brenda, with her life-long love of singing and music, the new music at the folk club, together with the attention and adoration she was getting from audiences at home and away, was a heady wine, and she embraced this exciting new experience with open arms. New, firm, friendships were forged – many to last for years. She heard and learned so much new material, tested and expanded her own boundaries, visited new places, often – the opportunities seemed endless. The attractions of amateur dramatics and painting paled in comparison, and, despite the demands of her work role in Tremaen Pottery – which she also relished – the music held her fast.

In more recent years, the Count House has changed much from the rough and ready era when we knew it best. Here is the former stage area, as it was at the 'last gasp' of folk in the building, Michael Chapman's last concert there in 2016 – with a happily nostalgic crew of Mike Sagar-Fenton, Des Hannigan, John the Fish, Jack King, and Michael Chapman.

The 'stage' at the Count House as it was in 2016, with some of the old stagers, 50 years on...

John the Fish

Peter John Langford was born in 1935 and grew up in North London, and developed an early interest in Skiffle, often visiting the Skiffle Club, later to become Les Cousins. Sometime around 1960, John came down to Cornwall at the instigation of a mate, and between three of them, bought a boat, with a view to fishing for a living. "Our attempts at fishing kept Newlyn amused for months," he says, but they did eventually make a go of it – and of course it resulted in his long-standing stage name, John the Fish.

He and some friends then signed up to crew on a boat called the Falcon – an enterprise that ultimately failed. One of his crew-mates, Tim Knight, played in a group called Ricky & the Layabouts, and introduced John to Tell Mann, a country and western singer. (Another crew-mate, Mike Carr, has already been mentioned as the son of Tristan Hole, one of the assistants in Tremaen Craft Market.) John and Tell worked out a few numbers, and they sometimes played in the bar of the Turks Head in Chapel Street in Penzance, where they were seen by Ian Todd and John Wood, and asked to perform at their new venture, the Count House. John jumped at the chance.

By the time Brenda got up on the stage at the Count House, John had given up fishing with a view to making his living from music. So he was quite receptive to becoming Brenda's official accompanist, and at the prompting of visiting guest, Scotsman Alex Atterson, they began a series of tours to folk clubs and festivals around the country, eventually performing together for 6 years.

Brenda's repertoire was very limited at the start – John recalls: "We would look around for songs. We would share songs. I had a wealth of songs and songbooks, and she would learn things from other people when they came down. Brenda's interest in Cornish folk came later. We were still mainly doing bits of jazz and blues, and English and American folk."[14]

Alex Atterson, Brenda and Fish

Fish has led a varied career since, including performing with the Dandy Cloggers, and making and selling the leather clogs in Truro's Pannier Market. For many years he presented a weekly folk music programme on Radio Cornwall called Fish on Folk; he eventually gave up performing a few years ago.

[14] *'Folk in Cornwall', Rupert White*

Fish and Carrie at their wedding, July 1970 – and John Langford today – better preserved than most of us!

To everyone's delight, Fish married Carrie in July 1970. They acquired famed folkie dog Cain, and soon had daughter Tabitha. Tragedy struck with their second child, son Merrick, who was a victim of Cot Death, resulting in Carrie developing a life-long involvement with the SIDS charity (Sudden Infant Death Syndrome, now renamed The Lullaby Trust). Thankfully, they were luckier with their second daughter Hannah. The experience of the unwanted religiosity of Merrick's funeral led John into an interest in the Humanist Society. He trained as a Humanist Celebrant, and now often takes baby naming ceremonies, weddings and funerals for those wanting an alternative to a religious event.

Fish toured with Brenda all over the UK, and accompanied her on her first trip to the Lorient Festival in Brittany in 1971, where they were on the same bill with legendary Breton performer Alain Stivell, the Dubliners, Robin and Barry Dransfield and Martin Carthy. He made three LPs with Brenda for Sentinel Music, and following a Reunion Concert in Redruth in the late 1980s, a cassette produced by Chough Tapes and called 'So Long', in aid of the SIDS charity. The folkies of Cornwall regard him with huge affection, as a sort of elder statesman of the folk music scene in the region; he was recently described by folk stalwart Mic McCreadie as'Supreme Commander of the Folk Armies of the South West'. He rarely performs nowadays, but still lives near Truro with his wife Carrie, and they are now happy first-time grandparents. Following a successful heart bypass in 2013, John enjoys regular walks and cycling with Carrie, and still keeps in touch with the local music scene.

Michael Chapman

In the summer of 1966, a scruffy young lad appeared who couldn't afford the entry fee to the club. He offered to play guitar instead, and Des Hannigan having given him the 'just the one number please' routine, fell over himself signalling for Michael to keep going after that first song. Of course, he did, and is still going now, over 50 years later. July 2016 marked Michael's Jubilee – his 50th year of performing at the Count House. What were those first songs? I remember Train & the River, and Green Onions – but perhaps that was another night.

He's been a part of my life ever since, and is still one of my greatest mates.

Michael Chapman's first night at the Count House

His memory of that night is:

> "It was pissing down with rain, I had no money to go in and just enough petrol to get me back to Bolton the next morning, which was Plan A. I just wanted to get out of the rain and so I said to them that I didn't have enough money to get in but I'd play guitar for half an hour because it was a folk club. At the end of the night the guy asked me what I was doing for the rest of the summer, because they needed another resident. The deal was that, at the end of the week, you got a share of what they took at the door. I got more than I was getting for running a department in a college of further education! So I thought, I like this –

> lie on the beach all day, play a bit of guitar for an hour a night and get paid. I love it. And I've been at it ever since!"

That first year Michael came down with his wife Maggie. He added recently

> "...down in Cornwall, flat broke, all I had was the van, the guitar and the remains of a marriage. So I followed a van that had a Folk Club sticker on – god knows where it was, it was pitch black and raining cats and dogs..." When he finally got there and was allowed in, he says "It was an amazing place, I'd never seen anything like it in me life... stone room, no microphones, no nothing... tatty old fishing nets hung up... packed with people. They'd keep getting up and singing, but the thing that hit me most was this rather large lady got up, and she sang a song – She Moves Through The Fair – and she sang it unaccompanied... and I'd never seen anybody do that before, I was astonished... I mean, how brave is that? And that was the first time I saw Brenda. Also, part of the package, of course, was Fish... and then there was a dumpy Scotsman standing on a stool playing the Maori Fertility Dance which got faster at the end – that was Alex Atterson."

Michael & Maggie had been living in his van down at Cot Valley, but he says the weather was so bad, Brenda took pity on them and offered them a room...

> "I mean, it was astonishing hospitality... that's a word that I associate most with Brenda, was her relentless hospitality. She used to collect people – after the gigs, we'd go back to Brenda's, and her front room, which was not stadium-sized, would be packed with people drinking coffee or cider or something, and it was just so sociable. I'd been playing gigs for years, but once the gig was over, you were on the street and you were on your own... and these guys were being so nice to us – I mean, I just couldn't get me head round it. And I seemed to be existing on a diet of cornflakes, and thunder and lightning – treacle and clotted cream on bread – which was like, heart attack on a plate! And we'd get up in the morning, get in the car – Brenda would stop off at Harveys and pick up a couple of crayfish, we'd have a couple of bottles of wine, and we'd be off for a picnic down Prah Sands or somewhere... they were so lovely to us... it was great..."

Michael playing guitar at a picnic on Hayle Towans, with Andru, Brenda, me and others

On future occasions we met the beautiful and elfin Andru – she had been a student of Michael's when he taught photography at Bolton, and then went on to Hull College of Art. They too celebrated 50 wonderful years together in 2016 – and she's still beautiful and elfin, damn her. They live in a big old farmhouse on the Northumbrian fells half a mile from Hadrian's Wall, from where Andru runs her designer knitwear business. Michael recalled recently... "it might have been the last summer that we saw Brenda, and maybe she already was suffering from dementia, but she and I were sitting at the end of the garden in the sunshine up at the Stack, and Andru walked past on her way up to that top cabin where we were staying – and Brenda just said –'She used to be pretty, but now she's beautiful' – and that really touched me." (She never had dementia, Michael... she was just telling it like it is...)

I remember a small, black, chunky and totally square young pup called Arthur, who grew with us through the years. The daft and adorable Arthur (the first of several black labs) was known to stroll languidly onto the stage and collapse in a big black heap during Michael's spirited rendition of 'She Came In Like the 6:15'. With the sad demise of Arthur, came Wellie, or Wellington, and then Alfie. When Alf was looking particularly soft and floppy, Michael would explain earnestly that, despite all appearances to the contrary, he was actually a killer. "Sic him, Alf! Kill! ... Kill, Alf!!" Michael would urge him – and Alf would sit gazing at Michael in adoration, dribbling gently, tongue lolling. Or at Michael's prompting "Gie'us a grin, Alf", Alfie's face would widen into a very un-doglike tooth-baring grimace.

On one of our seemingly endless days of picnics, I was in Michael's old van when we were heading for Gwithian, a region of extensive rolling grassy sand dunes with random tracks it was just possible to get a car along, by the beach at Hayle. Michael just took off, the old van rolling and rocking at high speed in a straight line over the dunes, everything in the back, including me, being thrown into chaos, until, suddenly and randomly deciding it was time to stop with just the sky visible through the windscreen, he slammed his foot on the brakes. I emerged, battered and bruised, to find the van perched precariously at the top of a 10-foot sheer drop down a dune. Alex Atterson and his then-wife Glynis were with us on several such trips... as were other regulars such as the Yetties, the Piggies (Pigsty Hill Light Orchestra), Derek Brimstone, Ralph McTell and others, too numerous to mention.

Michael sometimes took me, as a teenager, to school, in that old van. Nowadays, when in his cups, he sometimes drunkenly reminisces about those occasions, saying how he had visions of my regulation navy blue school knickers, but managed to control himself... "She was ready..." he will say wistfully, maudlin. But he was always a gentleman, and my virtue was intact.

Brenda and Michael in The Quiet Woman at St Ives

In those early days, Michael and Brenda very occasionally paired up to do brief 'cabaret' style sets at a couple of local venues: one was The Quiet Woman, a restaurant in St Ives near the Malakoff bus station; the other, the Pednevounder, a restaurant/nightclub on the Lizard – although the arrangement was a very informal one. The tempo for these evenings was usually laid back classics, jazzy and bluesy: 'Girl from Ipanema', 'Autumn Leaves' and 'September Song', 'The Shadow of Your Smile', 'Laura' and 'Misty' I remember, amongst others. As a very transient duo, these were some of Michael and Brenda's finest performances – I wish we'd had the foresight to record them. The Quiet Woman burned to the ground a few years later – an unrelated incident, I believe.

Here are Michael's comments on their musical relationship:

> "But me and Brenda – we'd be sitting in her front room in the afternoon, and I'd pick up me guitar and start playing these old-time ballads – sometimes called torch songs – and I soon found out that Brenda knew most of them, cos she'd been brought up in that era – so we'd get it together, and every now and then we'd do a few songs at a folk club or wherever we were. The first Christmas I was down with Andru, we were broke again – I remember Christmas Day we shared a packet of 5 Woodbines, and all we had left was a halfpenny – and on Boxing Day we played a posh restaurant in St Ives called The Quiet Woman. We did that sort of torch song stuff, and it was an ideal place for it – it was lovely. And we got paid some money, but I grabbed it all, because we were going to do it again the next night, and I said, 'I'll have the first lot, Brenda, you can have the second lot...' – we were so skint!

> "The thing with Brenda – it didn't happen all that often – we never did gigs at folk clubs or festivals or toured together... it was just stuff we liked to do for ourselves... and people gravitated towards it – and I don't think we'd have cared if they didn't... But the difference between me and Brenda – Brenda always wanted to be an entertainer – and that's one thing that I dread. She had Fish to kick off with, and then other guitarists – but I'd run away from that... just not up my street. So – yeh, it was very short-lived, but it was very good... some things aren't meant to last all that long. But I'm glad it happened – it was great."

And Mike Sagar-Fenton remembers the magic of Brenda and Michael performing together:

> "One fringe benefit for Brenda had been the chance visit of a gruff young schoolteacher from Hull called Mike Chapman. Mike didn't sing at all originally but just sat there and played. One tune turned into another, sometimes a medley ten minutes long,

> folk, jazz, Beatles, which would normally have turned an audience off. But Mike was something else, and rows of folkies, mums and dads, farmers and shopkeepers, many of whom had never heard anyone playing extended pieces before, leaned forward and pricked up their ears, listening in silent stillness, before roaring their applause; almost as profound an impact as Brenda's own. When and how they got together I don't know but it was probably the most productive and creative musical partnership she ever had. Mike could put his hand to anything, blues, jazz, bossa nova, the standards Brenda loved, anything, and they became musically inseparable."

Michael has become a national treasure amongst his thousands of fans, and is an international guitarist of high repute, regularly performing in the USA, principally the Southern states, Memphis and Nashville, and elsewhere around the world. I've lost count of his album production, but he was a favourite of John Peel, and is adored and respected, and rightly so, as the 'guitarists' guitar master'...

From his website: 'This self-styled old white blues guy from Yorkshire is one of the most under-rated heroes of our time. With his uniquely English melancholic perspective and emotive guitar style he deserves wider recognition.'

Alex Atterson

Another regular visitor to the club, travelling down from his own club in Norwich, was Scotsman Alex Atterson. What a darling – he could sing a traditional ballad to make you weep, or play a lively ragtime number on the piano to make you dance – his 'Dr Jazz' was irresistible.

Science trained, he had worked for Colman's Mustard, but then took up teaching, and was the instigator and original organiser of the Norwich Folk Festival, held annually in the University of East Anglia. Mike Sagar-Fenton describes him as "...a jazzer at heart who preferred playing piano, but folk was a broad church and he was very popular in the clubs." He was a fine jazz musician, a moving traditional singer, and a hilarious comedian – I always begged for his rendition of 'The Pudden', in broad Scots dialect. He played piano, guitar and accordion with equal ease and was a great all-round entertainer. He was also a great songwriter, particularly when writing the music to another's words. One of his two published LP

Alex Atterson

albums features many poems by Cornish poet Charles Causley which he has set to music, but one of his most successful, for me, is Bilbo's Last Song by Tolkien... I put it on YouTube – do listen. Makes me weep every time.

Alex came down often, initially with wife Glenys, and subsequently with Gill, and their two sons, Tom and Will. We often picnicked together, and he spent Christmas at our house a few times. Another firm friend and a lot of fun, Alex became one of the prime movers in Brenda's musical career, but by the '80s, he realised that the life of a travelling musician was not secure enough for a man with a young family, and he went back to teaching.

And away...

Alex talked Brenda and Fish (which I shall call him from now on, to save any confusion with the plethora of Johns) into taking a booking at his club in Norwich, with some additional gigs in other venues en route. Their first ever booking away from home was with their greatest fans, Bedminster Down Boys Club in Bristol in October 1966, but by 1967 they were already touring extensively around the UK. On their first booking at the UEA folk club, they were the support act for Tom Paxton. One of the earliest bookings was at the Royal Naval Engineering College at Manadon near Plymouth, in a bill they shared with Des Hannigan. The subsequent review in the College Mag described the novelty of the situation, as a "brave – or foolish – experiment"... folk music not being something with which most of the inmates would have been familiar, or indeed with which they would have had much truck. The reviewer's first impressions dismissed Des as "a beatnik", John the Fish as having "a brine-blasted mop of hair with a spiky set of whiskers to match", while Brenda was apparently "...a woman of immense proportions who wore gypsy rings in her ears and a Cornish fisherwoman's smock." However – he was soon enlightened. "Beardy..." says the reviewer, "immediately delighted the audience with his slightly harsh voice and his adroit fingering of the guitar..." while Brenda "...completely captivated the audience with her magnificent soprano voice and some of the most beautiful melodies ever to be sung...". The reviewer declares the "brave experiment" a success, and closes with thanks to the singers for undertaking the journey from "the Land's (Very) End." (I'm not sure I'd describe Brenda's voice as soprano. It was bigger than that...)

Brenda's photo from the Manadon review – on her first tour away with Fish

So Brenda and Fish started touring. Normally, they left Des and Handshake holding the fort. Fish and Carrie both remembered a couple of slightly hair-raising experiences when on their travels with Brenda. "I'd been driving for ages and was tired, and Brenda said 'oh, it's alright – I'll take over'... so I climbed in the back to have a sleep, and Brenda took over the wheel, with Carrie sitting next to her. I almost immediately went to sleep, and then was woken by this scream, shouting and honking of horns...". Carrie: "...she'd stopped for petrol, and she was trying to get back into the traffic, weaving in and out, drivers were honking at her... I think we stopped and changed over again with John driving. Another time, coming back from Plymouth, we'd stopped for a break, and she just reversed out into the traffic – saying, 'oops! I think I've gone wrong!', with marvellous understatement... That was the only time I ever knew her to drive". Driving was not her forte, and from then on she left it to other people.

Brenda made some great and long-term friendships on those early tours, and established links with people and with clubs that she would return to many times. Significant ones included Jacqui and Bridie's club in Liverpool, Mick Peat's club in Derbyshire (he's now a presenter on BBC East Midlands 'Folkwaves' show), the club in Castle Hedingham with Sylvie from Stained Glass, Jasper Carrott and his Boggery Folk Club in Solihull, Ewen Carruthers' Red Bear club in Sherburn-in-Elmet, The Swan at Ascott-under-Wychwood, and many others too numerous to name. Some Festivals became favourites too – as well as the annual trip to Norwich, the frequent visits to Lacock & Chippenham, later Trowbridge Village Pump Festival – so ably managed for years by John Alderslade and the team – made her one of their most popular guests; her name is immortalised with others on a 'memory bench' near the festival entrance (I hope it's still there – the festival was cancelled last year, but now appears to have been reinvented back at the historic Stowbridge Manor Farm, after several years sited in the Vale of the White Horse). She sang at Cambridge Folk Festival at Cherry Hinton a few times too: in 1970, Brenda and Fish compered in the Cambridge Club Tent,[15] and the review of their set in the local paper in 1971 was very flattering:

> "It was a touch of inspiration for Brenda Wootton, a cheerful Cornish girl of enormous girth, to follow Miss Farina (sister to Joan Baez) in the programme yesterday, for here was a singer with a high, clear voice, and a pure conventional sound, adaptable to any style or humour. On a predominantly sun-drenched after-

---

[15] *'Thirty Years of the Cambridge Folk Festival', Dave Laing & Richard Newman*

noon, Miss Wootton, during a cloudy patch, asked the audience to invoke the sun to shine again by saying 'If you were all to lift your heads up and *blow*...' It did the trick and she responded with a perfect rendition of 'Summertime'... Here was an artist with real presence, a wide vocal range, perfect diction both in song and announcing her numbers (an essential so many folk singers neglect), and an unforgettable comic delivery of an oldie... 'A Good Man is Hard to Find'."

However, some local nuns, delivering some school-children to the site to sing, were appalled at the state of the Festival fans, decrying the invasion of 'long-haired hippies'... One said "I didn't think it would be this kind of folk festival. If we'd known I don't think we would have come. I don't want the children to see people lying around listening to music, and think that's all there is to life. I don't like the hippy atmosphere."[16]

As Brenda became more well-known, selling records and signing autographs became a regular feature after each performance. She developed her own unique style, which certainly didn't speed the process up: below her signature, a little cartoon of a roly-poly Brenda figure with a bun on her head, a seagull (for her Bardic name), four kisses and a pair of musical notes. I've even found one in similar vein that John the Fish created – a little scruffy-haired bearded face, on a ticket to their gig at the UEA Folk Club in Norwich.

Memorabilia... Brenda's autograph, a ticket to the UEA Folk Club in Norwich with both autographs, an early Count House membership card, and Brenda's logo

[16] *Cambridge Evening News, August 2nd 1971*

It was shortly after that gig, while they were away on tour in Norfolk in late April 1967, that Ian Todd dropped a bombshell – he was closing the Count House, with just three weeks' notice. A surgical strike, Des called it. Brenda was horrified – she and Fish had come to rely on the Club as a way of life, not just as a relatively small source of income. She instantly resolved to do something about it.

From Norfolk, she made phone calls and wrote letters, looking for a new venue and artists to sing there. On their return from that tour, the Count House closed on May 20th, and without a break, the very next week, Pipers Folk Club opened on Saturday May 27th 1967, in the Village Hall in St Buryan, 6 miles west of Penzance – her diary for that date just says 'Open'. The Count House was dead – long live Pipers!

Sue, Jan Yeates and Brenda at St Buryan Village Hall at the launch of Pipers

Mike Sagar-Fenton recalls Brenda's first moves towards the big time:

> "For John, it was another gig, rather a long way to go in days before motorways or by-passes, but just another show. But Brenda had seen the light, discovered that she could entrance an audience far from her native home who'd never heard of her, and she let her imagination fly. She had never been shy about her own achievements but after Norwich she acquired a habit of spending the first ten minutes of any conversation expounding how well they had gone down here or there, what bit of praise

she'd received, which of the folk club A-list (yes, there really was one) she'd impressed, and on and on and on. It was exciting at first but soon became tiresome, a ritual one had to get through before a normal conversation with her – and she was great to talk to, wonderful company – could begin. It was the beginning of the self-obsession which everyone who consorted with her had to accept, a continuous assertion of her talent, importance and popularity, no doubt based on a chasm of inner self-consciousness and insecurity.

"However, her progress justified almost every hyperbole she applied to herself. She went away any time she could cajole John to travel, and never failed to rouse the audience to whoops and cheers. Her face and figure, along with John's own individual appeal, took them into the larger folk-club world.

"Then Ian Todd quietly announced that the Count House was closing and had been leased to some idiot to run as the A-Go-Go disco [*Chris, who visited it a few times, remembers it as NUA – 'No Urging Action' – equally absurd, bearing a logo with the acronym in puffy psychedelic letters*]. Ian was within his rights of course, but that didn't stop him feeling the fury of the local and up-country folk fraternity who were losing their favourite club. But Ian's heart had never been in folk. It had just been a rather fascinating and quite lucrative by-way in his life.

"Brenda was now head and shoulders into the folk scene and wasn't about to lose her local club so in about ten minutes (as she told it to me) she had hired St Buryan Church Hall and started the Pipers' Folk Club, complete with a cute logo from Peter. It had taken over her life – no more pantos, recitals, Socials... although she did keep her stagehand in with the famous Choughs.

"I came back home with a bit of guitar skill and started playing with Steve Hall as a duo. We rehearsed and wrote songs together and one night made our debut at Buryan. Brenda was pleased and we gradually became a fixture, then, when she moved the club back to the Count House, and later in the Western Hotel."

Mike soon had experiences of his own as an accompanist to Brenda with 'foreign' audiences...

"I once stood in as Brenda's accompanist at a festival on the Isle of Wight. She was highly billed, but faced an audience of hard-core traditional folkies, not to be easily jollied along. We had forty minutes to turn them around and I wondered how she would manage. Brenda was extraordinarily sensitive to her audiences and recognised each one for the different animal it was. This night she started by saying little and sang a few melodic and musically challenging songs. The audience began to perk up. The lady was no joke. Then, gradually, she began to talk to them. She drew them in, bit by bit, until they were in her hands, laughing, joining in, stamping and cheering. The forty minutes had passed and they were hers. Even I, who was standing right beside her, could not quite see how she had done it. It was as close as I've ever come to seeing natural genius at work.

"We had left Cornwall at 4.30 in the morning, and the last thing I remember as I passed out at 2.30 the following morning was Brenda at the centre of a group of adoring musicians, still going strong."

Pipers Folk Club – Brenda & John the Fish

So by June 1967, the fishnet drapes had migrated south to St Buryan to adorn the walls of the new club. Brenda ignored the high stage in the village hall, and set up a low platform stage on one side of the hall, beside an old pot-bellied stove heater. Her brother Peter designed for her an iconic logo of the god Pan as a Piper, faithfully reproduced by husband John in plywood, which stood behind the performers throughout the lifetime of the club – it can be seen in many of the photos.

I am proud to own that I was responsible for the name of 'Pipers'. Hunting around the local map for inspiration, I spotted the names of the two large megalithic standing stones on Boleigh Farm land near St Buryan... the Pipers... supposedly two naughty musicians who played their pipes for the equally naughty Merry Maidens, and all turned to stone for playing and dancing on a Sunday. I have to say, it never stopped us.

The hall was packed for the opening night at Buryan – word had obviously spread. Ralph McTell was the compere on that first evening, and the audience numbered 280. Brenda later recalled: "Mike Chapman sent a message saying he couldn't get down as he was singing in Scotland. But he got in his car after the gig and drove all the way down – arrived about 9'o'clock with his eyeballs out on stalks..."[17]

Ralph McTell, Wizz Jones & Pete Stanley with Brenda & Fish at Pipers at St Buryan

[17] *'Folk in Cornwall', Rupert White*

The first guests, in order, were Cliff Aungier, Derek Brimstone, Ralph McTell, Pete Stanley & Wizz Jones and Noel Murphy... and within a month the club was opening five nights a week.

Pipers fell into the regular routine of opening at least four nights a week in the summer and one in the winter, and another long-standing tradition began – all back to Brenda and John's in Penzance after the club. Willing volunteers filled the kitchen, producing endless supplies of coffee and platefuls of toast, and chat and music continued in the front room till the early hours. It was usually the case that the guest artist was staying at our house – in the summer months, for the week – so it was a busy time. I can't hope to do justice to all of those guests here, but will mention a few who really became part of our family for a time.

In an interview in the Western Morning News Mike Sagar-Fenton commented:

> "Those were days when folk clubs could run for five nights a week in the summer, with a top-class range of visiting artists. None of them had met anyone quite like Brenda before, a figure who was fussing around them like their mum one minute, and singing them off the stage the next..."[18]

In 1968 Pipers first record, Pipers Folk, was produced, by a similar private subscription method to the recordings made by the Count House, and featuring Brenda and Fish – using an early form of Crowdfunding! Supporters paid £1 each to help with the production costs, then as the record sold, at a certain point they received their investment back, with 2/6 profit. Peter created two possible album covers – they were both stunners, one of Zennor and the Men-an-Tol – but the one selected was an abstract design of boats in Newlyn Harbour.

The audience photo taken at St Buryan on the back of the LP cover has many recognisable faces. In the front row, from the left, are Scott Tutthill (who, following every particularly quiet and beautiful song from Brenda, would yell out an appreciative 'Yes!!' before anyone had a chance to breathe), Avril (who with husband Brian ran a boutique in Penzance), Mary Ellery (Peter's wife), and Dominique Denut (who lived in Lamorna Pottery at that time). Seated beside them on the floor at far right are Leslie and Trevor Male (the blacksmith at St Buryan).

---

[18] *Western Morning News, April 27th 2010*

The audience at Pipers at St Buryan

Even on nights when it wasn't packed to the doors, the atmosphere was warm and welcoming. In an interview with Tony Jasper in Folk Review, Brenda said:

> "I don't mind getting up when it's early in the club mid-week, when there's only a few people there. They've come in to listen. I find on a night when there's a poor audience, we don't have a 'performer and audience' situation... we have friends... it's almost like having an evening sitting at home and making music. We're more inclined to look at their faces and identify with them. I do love performing to a very large audience, it's a marvellous feeling – but I'm just as content with a few..."[19]

Ralph McTell

The community that was to spring up under the auspices of Pipers Folk Club was a fairly unique family at that time, and one of its earliest members was a young guitarist fresh from busking on the streets of Paris (not London!) – Ralph McTell. Ralph was booked as one of the resident singers at Pipers for that first summer season in 1967, for the princely sum of £3 per night. Even then, his guitar playing was magical and his warm and charismatic personality won over everyone who heard him.

He often stayed with us, but eventually chose to live down in Cornwall in a caravan at Mitchell, by the Folk Cottage, with his wife Nanna and, by 1968, baby Sam, and I remember so many happy times with them. There is a lovely photo of me bottle-feeding Sam in Brenda's front garden.

[19] *Folk Review, June 1973*

Sue photo-bombing Brenda and Ralph McTell, Norwich Festival 1974; Paul in the background

We had some memorable picnics, one down at Lamorna is photographed. There is a walkway in the harbour just below the car park, and we are all sat there in the sunshine. An elderly Cornish lady is in the background, wearing her best hat, watching Ralph seated on a deckchair playing the guitar. I often wondered what she thought of us all. Andru Chapman remembers one of those picnics:

> "It was one of the summers when everyone seemed to go down to Cornwall… It was hot, and we were all down on the beach one day with Ralph and Nanna and Sammy their son, Michael, and Alex Atterson. Everyone was stripped off and having a great time except Ralph, who hates the sun. He was sitting there fully clothed in 95 degrees, and we finally persuaded him to take his shoes and socks off – and he got sunstroke on his feet!" [20]

[20] *'Folk in Cornwall', Rupert White*

Ralph later appeared with friends 'Whispering' Mick Bennett on rhythm and keyboards, Pete Berryman on guitar, and Henry 'the VIII' Bartlett, as Henry's Jug Band, and they performed regularly at the Folk Cottage, Pipers' sister club at Mitchell further up in Cornwall. Ralph was to take his significant talent further than almost any other regular performer at Pipers, reaching Number 2 in the British charts and becoming known worldwide for 'Streets of London', first released in 1969 on his Spiral Staircase album. Apparently, in 1968, Ralph played his new song to Fish, offering it to him to perform – but Fish wasn't keen, saying it was 'a bit sad'. Ralph, disheartened, left the song alone for a while, eventually offering it to Derek Brimstone – another favourite at Pipers – who reportedly got amazing reactions to it, and encouraged Ralph to perform it himself – which of course, he did, to universal acclaim. There are currently over 200 cover versions, I believe. Sadly, the message of the song is probably more relevant than ever, nearly 50 years later, with the numbers of the homeless in Britain rising so fast. Ralph recently released a new version in December 2017, with Annie Lennox and a choir formed from members of Crisis, a housing charity, as a fundraiser for the cause.

Ralph and Nanna loved Cornwall so much they eventually ended up buying a house at London Apprentice, and now live down here.

Noel Murphy

Another regular guest from the early days, Noel was a crazy Irishman with some beautiful lilting songs, and some rip-roaring ones too. In tune with the hippy ethos of the time, he was prone to wearing a small brass bell in the lace-up flies of his jeans.

He found a young Scottish protégé he called Shaggis, due to his flowing blonde locks, and together with bass-player Ron Chesterman (from The Strawbs) they went under the stage name of Draught Porridge. Shaggis was a diffident and shy lad, but proved to be something of a child genius on the guitar, banjo, or any other instrument he picked up, and he could play just as brilliantly if the instrument were behind his head. His name was actually Davey Johnstone, and for a while was married to a Cornish lass called Di Partridge from Newquay; their cheerful baby appeared on the cover of his only solo album, 'Smiling Face'. He went on to become a world-class guitarist in Elton John's band, where he still plays today, and for a time was the partner of Kiki Dee.

Noel Murphy and Shaggis (Davey Johnstone) at Pipers

Noel has said: "Brenda was a massive influence on Cornish folk. She would open Pipers six nights a week, and she had her favourites, and I was one of them – Mike Chapman was another... Pipers and Folk Cottage had something special going for them..."[21]

One minor incident relating to Noel Murphy: we were all off on a picnic down to Nanjizal – a glorious but somewhat inaccessible beach near Porthcurno. We parked the car in a field at the top, and had to pass a horse in a field to our left on the path down. The huge horse came up to the fence and looked at us enquiringly, and Murph gave him a green apple. As Brenda approached, wearing an apple green dress, the horse trotted over and attempted to take a huge bite out of Brenda's bosom. The skin wasn't broken, but the bruise was spectacular for weeks after.

There was great excitement when 'Pipers Folk' was invited to sing in a film being produced by Westward TV, called 'Mayday! Mayday!'. The film was an entry in the Dublin Festival of Folksong & Folklore in 1967, and starred actor Ralph Bates (the Warleggan character from the first TV series of Poldark) as a sailor, shipwrecked in Napoleonic times, who is washed up on Porthcurno beach in the 1960s, to be discovered by two '60s dolly birds.

A fairly nonsensical story, the film was broadcast on Westward TV on October 5th 1967, and members of Pipers up for the task were required to be at the Minack Theatre, on the cliffs above Porthcurno beach, by dawn for the filming.

---

[21] *'Folk in Cornwall,' Rupert White*

Brenda arranged an 'all-nighter' at Pipers the night before, and Murphy was the guest. At 3 am he was flat on his back on a trestle table in the coffee bar with a top hat on his belly, dead to the world and snoring loudly. However, despite his bad example, the task was achieved, and on August 27th 1967 sufficient 'Pipers Folk' joined Brenda, Fish, Murph, Ralph with baby Sam and Nanna, Jan Yeates and me above the Minack, to film in the light of the rising sun. But typically, there was no rising sun that day, of course, just thick fog. We were singing Lamorna, and the producer kept calling for retakes, hoping the weather would improve – so Murphy kept on making up more verses. Noel said 'I remember peering over the edge of the cliff at first light, and because it was late summer, the water was full of sharks...'. They would have been the impressively big but harmless basking sharks, often seen from the Minack. For many years, Noel has been retired and living quietly in Cornwall, close to his favourite golf club, although he is recently undergoing an enforced sojourn away from home.

Derek Brimstone

'Brimmers' was a hugely popular and regular guest at Pipers. He lived in Hemel Hempstead with his wife Jeannie and a horde of kids, and was a brilliant comedian with a broad Cockney accent, and an excellent musician to boot – sadly he died only a year or so ago. He took to bringing the whole family down to Cornwall for a week's stint in the summer, and again, huge picnics loom large in my memory, and improvised football matches with all his kids. He famously christened the Count House at Botallack, 'Bollock Attack'.

He was the most under-rated musician ever, but some of his stories, delivered in the broadest cockney, were legendary. With unashamed delight, I am going to pass on a few Brimstone specials recounted to me by Mike Silver.

Derek says he was at a festival in Scotland, and there was a band staying in the same hotel, among whose number was a mandolin player. This guy was big: huge, tall and well-muscled – so big, the mandolin looked like a table tennis bat in his hands. Derek was there when he came down to breakfast one morning, and watched him plough through everything on the menu – porridge, cereal, then a fry with eggs, bacon, sausages, the works, until he finally got to his last piece of toast. He asked the waitress if they had any honey... "Oh, yes, of course" she said, and went off to fetch some for him, returning with a small single pre-packed sachet. He held it up in his huge fingers and studied it solemnly. "Ah..." he said, in his strong Scottish accent... "I see the hotel keeps a bee..."

On another occasion Derek was doing an outdoor performance at a seaside resort, due to play in a shelter on the promenade, in front of which rows of folding chairs were laid out ready. But the weather was awful, and it was absolutely bucketing down. There was just one punter sitting out front, holding up his umbrella in the pouring rain. Derek started by explaining that he was booked to do two forty-five minute sets, but as there were so few there, would the guy mind if he just did the one set? The guy said, no, he didn't mind at all, that was fine, so Derek went ahead and did his one set. At the end he apologised to the guy, still sitting there under his umbrella, for the shortness of his performance. "Oh, that's ok," was the reply... "I'm only here because I was hired to put the chairs away afterwards..."

Finally – for those who know Michael Chapman's guitar style – Derek was at a concert where he was booked to follow Michael. Michael did a blistering set, with his usual phenomenal guitar riffs, sounding like a six-man group on his one guitar. For his final number, he tuned up all his strings bar one, one at a time until they snapped, to devastating musical effect, then tuned down the final string until there was no more sound to be heard. The audience went wild with delight. Derek was the next up... "Well... that was lovely wannit?" he commented... "Funny – I was going to start with that one..."

Apocryphal? Probably – but does it really matter? Brenda turned one of Derek's sagas into a poem... for the full story, look at 'The Bun' in Pantomime Stew... and listen to his 'Mrs Fisher' on YouTube for a further flavour of the performer...

Decameron

One group that turned up at Whitsun in 1970 and were to prove enduring friends forever after, was Decameron – "four hairies and guitars in a car with a cello on top". Once described by Brenda in Folk Review as a 'six-man quartet', this lovely bunch of lads hailed from Cheltenham, and included the original duo, Dave Bell and Johnny Coppin, Geoff March and Al Fenn, the next to show up – making the quartet – then the late-comer, bassist Dik Cadbury... and the sixth man, and just as essential as the rest, Geoff's brother Jonathan March, the sound man who worked the knobs.

Decameron outside Brenda's house at Leskinnick Street (note Mike Sagar-Fenton's expression, front left) with Sue & boyfriend Tony Lyons

Brenda describes their first appearance:

> "I couldn't tell one from the other at first, but their collective sound was easy, the Count House was packed, that night's guest, Johnny Silvo, had supped overlong at the local hostelry, and the band played for over half an hour to rapturous applause. So when Ralph told us he could only do two nights of his usual week at the Club, we booked Decameron, and the initial link with Cornwall was formed."

> "It's good to remember their first encounter with 'The Murf'... they had just finished their week at Pipers and Murphy had arrived early for his, so for a whole day we were a big family. It was to be the final week of the celebrated 'Draught Porridge', a somewhat emotional time for our Noel, and we skated around him gingerly. But what a day we had, 14 of us all told, beer and pasties up the Radjel Inn at Pendeen for lunch with our dear old pal Willie Warren, football and swimming all afternoon, and we ended the day in The Meadery at Trewellard singing everything we could lay our tongues to..."[22]

Both Al Fenn and Dik Cadbury later went on to work with Brenda as guitarists. Decameron became justly popular and produced several excellent albums, and for a short while wrote and produced pantomimes annually in their native Cheltenham. They had a few

[22] *Interview in Folk Review*

'Farewell' concerts, and memorably all showed up for Brenda and John's Ruby wedding celebrations at the Count House in 1986. Their alter egos, the more than manic Magnificent Mercury Brothers, were hugely popular. Dik and Johnny still pursue their own successful musical careers and perform regularly.

Decameron with Jonathan March, Steve Hall, Denise Dawson, Brenda, Willie Warren and me outside The Radjel at Pendeen

Mike Silver

A supreme singer-songwriter and guitarist, with a fabulous voice that can still make me weep and smile all at once...

Mike was first brought down to Cornwall by the remarkable guitarist Gerry Lockran in 1967. They had met while working in Jersey a while before and become firm friends, and as Gerry was booked to do some gigs in Cornwall, he invited Mike along.

One of those gigs was at Pipers at St Buryan, and so Brenda and Mike met for the first time. He came down again the following year, and did some gigs on his own, and was offered a 'season' at the Railway Inn in Penzance, then run by Henry the Jug – three nights a week on his own, and one night with jazz musician Goudie Charles. He was sometimes billed under his real name, Mike Boreham – but, perhaps wisely, stuck with Silver.

Mike's beautiful songs, rich voice and fine guitar playing soon made him a favourite at Pipers, and we booked him regularly. By 1975, Mike had started gigging around Europe, and was living on a house-boat in Amsterdam. He heard on the grapevine that Brenda and guitarist Robert Bartlett were breaking up, and called her to offer her his services for 6 months. It was agreed, and the day after my wedding, Brenda and John left to meet up with Mike in Amsterdam and begin rehearsals.

Mike Silver and Brenda performing in Germany

Mike is married and has lived in north Cornwall for some years and is still performing and touring regularly.

Mike recently told me a horrific story, which neither I nor my Father ever heard from Brenda. He was on tour with Brenda in Germany and France in November 1975, their first tour together. They had left the car in Stuttgart and caught the train down to Paris for some TV work, and Brenda was ill, running a temperature. Her French agent at the time, Gwenn, was very unsympathetic, and only concerned that Brenda should meet her commitments. Back at the hotel in the afternoon, Mike insisted Brenda have some rest, and she went to bed, exhausted. He looked in on her a few hours later, and she was practically delirious, and didn't recognise him. He called Gwenn in, who flatly refused to call a doctor, saying Brenda was just tired, and let out a string of French invective, which Mike didn't understand, but he certainly picked up her meaning. Mike yelled back and demanded a doctor, and in the end Gwenn capitulated.

She spoke to the doctor when he arrived in a stream of rapid French with the same scornful, dismissive attitude – but fortunately the doctor spoke English, and having taken one look at Brenda, ignored Gwenn and addressed his remarks to Mike. After examining Brenda, he gave her a massive injection of penicillin, and told Mike that Brenda had a very serious viral infection, and if she hadn't been treated, she could well have been dead within 4 hours. He said she would have to have complete rest, no work, no stress, no travelling, for at least a week, with further antibiotic injections every day... and then he turned back to Gwenn, and in another stream of rapid French which again Mike didn't follow, but *fully* understood the mood of, he played absolute merry hell with the agent, and left her, for once, speechless. Mike was vindicated, and never spoke one word to Gwenn again.

Brenda, of course, once she had recovered enough to understand what had happened, completely ignored the Doctor's general advice, and the next day at 6.45am they were on the train back to Stuttgart, and she did a gig in a different town every day for the next 5 days, then driving 400 miles back to their base in Braunschweig ('Don't knaw and wain't be told...')... She did, however, note his specific advice, and in each town they visited, Mike took her to the nearest hospital for an injection of antibiotics... Her diary just reads: "realised I was ill, called doctor, gave me penicillin injection, and told me caput in 4 days if not...".

I don't think she even realised Mike had saved her life. Thanks for that, Mike.

Folky Friends

There were numerous other good and long-standing friendships formed at Pipers and I can't do a resume of every one here, but some others with happy memories attached include:

Martin Carthy – another firm friend of Brenda's, Martin, apart from being a superb guitarist and performer, and a folk legend, was a barrel of laughs. There's a great photo of him fooling around with Brenda up at the Stack – her home on the hills in west Cornwall. An early mentor of Mic McCreadie.

Diz Disley – what a character. Canadian born, he played with top jazz violinist Stephane Grappelli, and with the Hot Club de France. We once visited him in his flat in London, and discovered him living on carrot juice, which he swore by. His vehicle of choice was a hearse, which he eventually sold to the Pigsty Hill Light Orchestra. Known for: "It may be rubbish, but by gad, it's British rubbish!"

Allan Taylor – a particular favourite of Brenda's, his 'Old Joe' was a memorable and moving song. We got to know him and his family well. Brenda definitely looks three sheets to the wind with Allan in this photo...

Pete Berryman – a phenomenal musician who later became one of Brenda's occasional guitarists. Pete's musical CV reads like a folk musician's star hit list.

Allan Taylor, with a very laid-back Brenda

Pete Berryman being accosted by Brenda, Tish Lewington behind, at Norwich Festival, 1974

Wizz Jones – phenomenal performer, mentor of Ralph McTell, Pete Berryman and so many others. First appeared at Pipers in St Buryan with Pete Stanley.

The Yetties – the four large (apart from Bonny) and large-hearted lads from Dorset spent their week at Pipers one summer stripping the surface of Brenda's front room wall down to the granite. Hard work, removing years of paper and plaster. They were also present at a few of our large and memorable picnics down on Hayle Towans.

John Alderslade & Will Whitmarsh are still great friends of mine after, what, 40 or more years? Hailing from Wiltshire, they had a terrific fun act with puppets and suchlike, aimed at kids, as well as the more serious folky stuff, and both were involved in the organisation of the Lacock & Chippenham and the Trowbridge Folk Festivals since forever. John and wife Mo and Will and wife Joy are mates for always.

Pigsty Hill Light Orchestra – a goodtime 'scrumpy & western' band from Somerset, one of whose number famously did an amazing take-off of Brenda, wearing a pink corduroy dress of hers, on stage at St John's Hall in Penzance – interrupting Brenda & Fish in the process. He took his life in his hands, but fortunately she saw the funny side. The group bought Diz Disley's hearse, and wrote a song for it, including the memorable words: 'When driving on the motorway, the sign you love to see, is a petrol pump and a knife and fork, a cup of tea, and a P'.

Pigsty Hill Light Orchestra with Brenda and Fish

Tony Capstick – a lovable rogue, who was also a presenter on BBC Radio Sheffield for 30 years, and, I've just discovered, played a policeman on Last of the Summer Wine for many years, as well as being single-handedly responsible for getting the dialect word 'wazzock' accepted in the OED! Sadly developed an alcohol problem, and died in 2003.

Gerry Lockran – a great musician, with the most manoeuvrable mouth. I adored him. With **Cliff Aungier**, another much-loved Pipers' regular, he founded the Half Moon Club in Putney which is still going today. He died tragically young of a stroke at age 45, having earlier lost the use of one hand, curtailing his performing career.

Donovan – a guest at the early Pipers, at the time when he was starting to get attention with his 'hippy' friends on the beaches of St Ives.

Jasper Carrot – a hilarious comic and a gifted performer, who went on to achieve great things on TV and was awarded an OBE; he also managed Decameron in the early days with his agency Fingamajig.

The Humblebums: Billy Connolly & Gerry Rafferty – yes, THE Billy Connolly... a fabulously funny guy and a great entertainer.

Jon Betmead – what a great guy, and a great friend. We've recently reconnected on Facebook, I'm happy to say.

Brenda, I'm sure, would be appalled at the brevity of this list; she could have written a book about every one of them... however, a more complete account can be found in the Appendix.

Back to Botallack...

By early 1969 Ian Todd's follow-up venture at the Count House – a disco – had failed, and once again the venue became available. Brenda took it on, and Pipers moved back to 'Bollock Attack'.

My husband Chris Ellery-Hill, at that time a teenager living in nearby Carnyorth, attended a few of those disco sessions. He recalls it ran a few nights a week, and the walls were painted a bright orange inside (which accounts for the later pink bleeding through the white-wash). It was named NUA – 'No Urging Action', (weird or what?) and had a logo with NUA picked out in fat psychedelic-style letters in a circle. There was a bar serving a choice of coffee or coke, and he thinks the music being played was probably Northern Soul. Chris says he went along as there was precious little else to do in Pendeen at that time... sometimes he went with a friend, and once he remembers two couples on holiday turning up. It was that good...

Given that Pipers at St Buryan was regularly pulling in around 50-100 fans a night, Ian Todd may have regretted his decision to close the folk club.

So, the orange paint of the disco was once more restored to (pinkish) white, the fishnet and the Piper migrated north, and Pipers Folk Club re-opened at Botallack on March 29th 1969, with guest artists Keith Chetwin (*not* Chegwin!) and John Sleep (from Folk Cottage), and with residents Brenda, Fish and Steve Hall. Steve (latterly organiser of Golowan Festival in Penzance), along with Mike Sagar-Fenton (also a later Golowan organiser), had both been in the Penzance Young Playgoers, and both became long-term residents at Pipers.

Opening night of Pipers back at the Count House, with Fish and Mike Sagar-Fenton

Both Mike and Steve also wrote a few memorable songs for Brenda. Mike's wistful 'I'm Counting Stars' appeared on Pipers first album, 'Pipers Folk', his 'Abel George' on 'Boy Jan – Cornishman' and 'The Lifeboat' is on 'Gwavas Lake'. He wrote others which were never recorded ('The Mackerel', 'Johnny Roscoff' and 'Migrants'), and also wrote beautiful music to Kipling's 'Harp Song of the Dane Women'. Steve's 'To the Sea' appears on 'Pasties & Cream' – the first album to feature Brenda and Fish produced by Job Morris of Sentinel Records, which came out in 1971.

This began what was really Piper's heyday – audiences were regularly over 100 per night, with fans travelling from all over Cornwall to drive down the little country lanes out onto the cliffs for the experience. All-nighters became an occasional feature in the summer. The audience paid for the evening show, and at midnight were turfed out into the night and had to pay for the early morning session before re-entering. All came equipped with sleeping bags or blankets, and the performers got used to trying to keep everyone awake with rousing chorus songs, striding up and down the rows of the somnolent stalwarts, struggling to make it through to the dawn. The thing that Brenda particularly remarked on in later years was how innocent it all was – certainly in those early days – no alcohol, no drugs, no trouble, no rabble-rousers... just a bunch of people enjoying some great songs.

By the early '70s, Pipers was proving a bit of a movable feast. The club moved into the Western Hotel in Clarence Street in Penzance in 1971, as it was obviously more accessible than the old mine building on the cliffs – perhaps an indication that the initial impetus of the Folk Revival was slowing down. The Western was where Mic McCreadie made his debut appearance, and stuck with it to the bitter end, and many other new friends were made here – the lovely Roger Brooks and countless more.

Alex Atterson, Creeping Jane & Fish at the Western Hotel

There was parking in a yard behind the Hotel, but the owner, Bill, was an unhelpful and unfriendly chap, and none too popular with the Folkies. When the local Council decided to change the road markings in Penzance, turning Clarence Street into a one-way street, he created merry hell. He was pictured on the front page of the Cornishman, in a 'High Noon' like stance standing in the middle of the empty road in Clarence Street beside the hotel, with the headline "The Loneliest Man in Town". It caused great hilarity in the club.

With the move to Penzance, Brenda had started to run occasional big concerts in St John's Hall or in The Garden (formerly the 'Wints', or the Winter Gardens) on the Promenade. It meant she could bring down some bigger names, and offer a larger fee to some of our most popular guests. Regulars who were booked there for 'specials' included Ralph McTell, Michael Chapman, Decameron and Martin Carthy – and a real treat, the native American Buffy Sainte Marie who was tiny, but thrilling to watch – all appeared in spectacular concerts. On one memorable occasion at a Piper's concert in St John's Hall which featured the Pigsty Hill Light Orchestra, Brenda and Fish were singing on stage, when their set was interrupted with the news that a folk superstar had turned up expectedly, and was now waiting to appear. Brenda was horrified at this appalling rudeness, and responded with icy calm. Even the audience held their breath... then Dave Creech from Pigsty Hill Light Orchestra came out wearing a pink corduroy dress of Brenda's and a wig, with a 'John the Fish' guitarist, and sang one of Brenda's songs falsetto, causing general hysterics all round. She forgave him, and hooted with laughter.

Mike Sagar-Fenton again:

> "I went back to London, and saw Brenda and Fish in the Half-Moon at Putney. It was full of Cornish of course. Brenda pretended to be pissed off: "We thought we could get away with all our old stuff!" She came to my horrible bed-sit in Marylebone and sang 'Forbidden Fruit' to me which she'd just learned. When I ran a folk club in Greenwich they did a gig for me.
>
> "On another occasion, early one summer's evening as the Count House (which Brenda was running by then) was about to open, eight or ten volunteers were setting out chairs and benches, distributing ashtrays, sorting out food and drinks and generally making a hullabaloo.

"Brenda had agreed to sing a song at my wedding and she had chosen the lovely Irish air 'My Lagan Love'. There were only two verses, so she sang them to me, very quietly, in a corner. As she sang, I noticed the movements of the helpers becoming slower and slower, and their noise decreasing. Eventually, none of them could bear to mar the sound, and she finished the song, still quietly, against a background of motionless, enchanted helpers, standing in various parts of the room in a perfect and spontaneous silence. As she finished, we all drew in a deep breath; and life went on.

"When she actually sang the song at the ceremony in St Peter's church, so sweetly and beautifully, you could hear the congregation aching to applaud afterwards.

"Then I came home for good. The Western Hotel was hard work. Steve and I were residents, at least three nights a week in the summer, often while Brenda was away, but the soirees afterwards at Coombe Dingle were as lovely as ever, the kitchen generously serving out tea and prime baking to as many as came. We took it for granted then but I think now of the work and the cost, and of John's forbearance. I only once heard him complain about the 'sodding musicians'.

"Decameron had started at the Count House doing a floor spot. They were so hip – their first number was "I wasn't born to follow" by the Byrds which I knew as I was then running a record shop, but had never been heard in a folk club. After their third number I was rushing up the aisle to Brenda saying "Book them!" and she laughed back at me "I just have!" They became firm friends of Liz and me, Dave Bell in particular, and were a much-anticipated fixture at the Western. A rival favourite was Noel Murphy. I remember Steve and I once doing the residents' spot before his first set – at the end of every song the audience sat up, smiling in anticipation, only to slump again as we started another song. Uncomfortable for us but we could see their point – he really was that good."

Once Brenda had turned professional in 1974, Father and I continued to run the club for another 3 years, with Brenda and Robert turning up when they could to do a spot. Mike Silver says that once Brenda had left the club, it was never the same – she was the centrepiece around which it all revolved, and her absence left a large Brenda-sized gap.

On November 8th 1975 Pipers changed venue yet again, opening in an upstairs room at the back of the London Inn on Causewayhead.

There was one very regular member of Piper's audience who, over a period of many years and completely unsolicited, brought his own tape recorders, both cassette and reel-to-reel, and recorded everything that happened in the club. **Dennis Clixby** was a lovely congenial fellow who lived at The Belyars in St Ives, and he was also involved with Trencrom Revellers Theatre Club.

After Dennis died a few years ago, there was concern that his collection of tapes should be preserved for posterity. Initially it was held by John the Fish until someone could be found to sort and archive it properly. After a few false starts, long-term Pipers' resident Mic McCreadie stepped up to the plate, and he has since spent countless hours listening to, tidying up and copying the archive onto more durable and accessible CDs, and subsequently, Richard Prest has achieved even more success with the old tapes. The collection is remarkable, and Mic and Richard's work on it has been a labour of love – they have managed to pull out and combine the performances of several individuals, including Brenda, Ralph McTell and others. The painstaking work continues, and there may still be more gems to be found. Details can be found on Mic's blog here: http://www.micmccreadie.com/archivist/.

Eventually, after nearly 10 years of running Pipers, we decided to pass it on to others. My other commitments were making too many calls on my attention, Brenda of course was away most of the time, and Mr Wooty couldn't run it unaided. So on 15 Jan 1977, we officially handed over to Niall & Cathy Timmins. Niall was an accomplished performer himself, and lived with Cathy in Nancledra. They managed to keep the club going for another few years, while it moved from the London Inn to the Old Meadhouse at Gulval, briefly to the Trencrom Revellers hut at Nancledra, to the Old Quay House at Hayle, and finally back to where it all started, almost 20 years before, to the Turks Head in Chapel Street in Penzance, being run by that most faithful of all folk fans, Dennis Clixby.

As to the Count House, as John the Fish says, "It became that famous that the National Trust now own it..." – and sadly it's now been fully 'Poldarked'. One of the first performers at the folk club there, Michael Chapman, has been going back every June for many years to do a couple of nights – a real trip down memory lane for the old regulars – but even that came to an end in June 2016, with Michael's final appearance at the Count House – almost fifty years on from that first rainy night in 1966.

By the time she was to move away from small clubs to the big-time, Brenda had already had some interesting encounters, having appeared with the likes of Terry Wogan, Robin Ellis (the first TV Poldark), Angela Rippon, BBC broadcaster Kenneth Kendall, and opera singer Ben Luxon. These were the first of many famous names she was to mix with over the course of a long and successful career.

Ben Luxon, Brenda and broadcaster Kenneth Kendall

The Folk Cottage at Mitchell

Folk music first came to the attention of John Sleep on visits to the Count House in the early days, and he became keen to start something similar in his own neck of the woods near Newquay. He joined forces with a like-minded friend, John Hayday, and they took on a barn on a farm near Mitchell, owned by another friend called Willoughby Braxton. A lot of work was needed on the old barn, but around the time Pipers was becoming established in St Buryan, the Folk Cottage in Mitchell was also starting up. The two Johns became the residents, and with regular performers of the calibre of Ralph McTell, Wizz Jones, Pete Berryman and others, Folk Cottage was destined for success. Instead of the perky Piper, Folk Cottage had a stylish and stylised nude in silhouette at the back of the stage.

Pipers and Folk Cottage worked closely together. Both clubs were way out in the countryside, and they were soon able to establish a circuit. Bringing artists down from 'up-country' was expensive, and the two clubs were far enough apart that they were not likely to 'poach' audiences, so artists could get at least two bookings in Cornwall, which made getting top performers so far down the country a little more achievable. So the 'seasons' at Pipers and Folk Cottage were often a close reflection of each other. During the 1970s, Pipers and Folk Cottage became two of the most popular folk venues in the country, and just about all the top acts from the folk scene wanted a piece of the action.

Other clubs soon started up – after all, the 1960s were the start of the 'folk revival' as it became known – and thrived throughout the '70s: the Mermaid Folk Club at the Gurnards Head with Chrissie Quayle, Tell Mann's Tell-a-Tale Club in Penzance, Room at the Top at Redruth, Bodmin Traditional Folk Club with Lar Cann and Vic Legg, which started in May 1968, and even one on the Isles of Scilly, with organiser Roz Hicks – and those last two are still going! Around the same time, Martin Val Baker was also bringing down a remarkable list of world-class performers to St Ives and elsewhere, so Cornwall was really buzzing. (For a detailed account of the entire folk music scene in Cornwall in that period, read Rupert White's excellent 'Folk in Cornwall'.)

Ella Knight

One person who became inextricably linked with the Truro Folk Club and the folk scene in general throughout Cornwall, and was certainly a vital member of our 'folk family', was Ella Knight. For as long as I knew her, until very recently, Ella lived in a caravan in a farmer's field on the outskirts of Truro, usually with a dog or two, and surrounded by a lovely garden (much lovelier than the caravan, it has to be said) housing some quite rare camellias.

Like Pipers, the Folk Cottage went through a number of incarnations. Ella & Fish's wife Carrie took over running the club from John Battensby, and moved the club to Rose; it then moved to Goonhavern, and later to the Green Parrot at Perranporth, finishing up at the Swan in Truro.

Ella was well known to all folkies in Cornwall and across the country, and at Folk Festivals near and far. She almost never, it seemed, wore shoes, despite working as a horticulturalist at Killiow Estate and elsewhere, and outside in all weathers. She was a self-taught expert on camellias. Initially her little Jack Russell terrier, Ben, was at least as well-known as Ella herself – Ben was infamous on the folk scene as 'Supertool', from his habit of gamely trying to mount dogs much, much larger than himself, at Festivals; John Alderslade's beautiful, if slightly vacant, Afghan hound, Karl, was one target I recall.

From the left: Will & Joy Whitmarsh, unknown & John from Stained Glass, Brenda, Andy & Ella, Me (looking sulky) and John, John & Mo Alderslade and Karl the Afghan, at Tredinnick Stack

Brenda and Ella formed a formidable team at Festivals and Clubs. They appointed themselves Honorary President and Chairwoman of the Bum Appreciation Society, and were prone to firmly grasping the nether regions of some of their prime targets, sometimes even with one in each hand – Martin Carthy, Michael Chapman, Al Fenn, Dik Cadbury, Pete Berryman – all have suffered at their hands, although it didn't seem to leave them with any permanent damage – I can't speak for the psychological effect. Certainly today they would be done for sexual harassment in the workplace ('That would be a fine thing, if you could get it', Mic McCreadie dryly commented). I'm only jealous, as I was only allowed to be secretary, and didn't have Brenda and Ella's savoir faire about these things. Joy Whitmarsh was also a member, and, probably fortunately, minutes were never recorded.

Ella was somewhat accident prone, unfortunately. She suffered permanent damage to one eye when she was hit by a baton at a clog dancing performance, and had to give up driving her beloved Morris Minor, a vehicle of some character she used to take to all the Folk Festivals. She lost one little dog when a crane accidentally dropped something heavy on her van, and she suffered a huge loss when her caravan burned to the ground. A fund-raising venture launched at Brenda's Memorial concert was able to help buy her a 'new' second-hand caravan home in the same field north of Truro, where she lived until a couple of years ago, when she became too ill and was moved into a care home in Mabe Burnthouse. Sadly she died in March 2017, but we did manage to get her along to the last session in the Count House.

Michael Chapman, John the Fish and Ella Knight, at the last night at the Count House

Richard Gendall

One incredibly influential person Brenda was introduced to in 1972 was Cornish Bard, Richard Gendall. Richard was born in the Turks & Caicos Islands in 1924 and started learning the Cornish language at the age of 4; he spent his youth in Lanndreth and St Winnow. Richard joined the Royal Navy in WWII, and after the war went on to teach French, and then Cornish, at Helston School, taking students to exam level in the language.

Brenda with Richard Gendall at Lorient Festival

Brenda had been invited to sing in Cornish at the Pan-Celtic Festival in Killarney, and not knowing any songs in the language, was introduced to Richard, who could maybe write one for her.

He did as asked (addressing his first letter to 'Barbara'!), but she had only three weeks to learn the song, and not having spoken Kernewek before, her interpretation was somewhat lacking, and she did not win that year. However, it was the first appearance of Cornwall at that Festival, and gratifying in that it was the first time that the Cornish language had been represented abroad in song. She has said that singing in Kernewek and listening to its lovely sound excited her, and that experience of the power of the Celtic languages, and the importance of the heritage, convinced her that she would sing at least one song in Cornish at every concert she performed from then on – a pledge she kept throughout her career, also ensuring that Cornish was heard on every album.

Richard was a fascinating character, an extremely knowledgeable academic, a linguist, somewhat of a melancholic, and a gifted song-writer. In later life he lived in North Cornwall with his wife Jan, but when he and Brenda first met, he was teaching in Helston School and living alone in a barn in a wood in Wall, Gwinear. The wood was one he had created himself on his own land. He had travelled extensively, and wherever he went he collected tree seeds, bringing them back to Cornwall to create his own exotic wilderness. In amongst the trees on his land, he excavated large lined pools to encourage wildlife, and created what he called 'The Sanctuary'. He was made a Bard of the Cornish Gorsedh in 1949, and characteristically, his Bardic name was Gelvinak, Cornish for Curlew.

Often, in his numerous letters to Brenda, he described at length the joy it gave him to sit and watch the many wild visitors to his Sanctuary, or to spend time on his boat 'Alargh' in Hayle estuary with his sons, studying the birdlife... adding at one point: 'Meanwhile, you sing, and sing, and sing – as voraciously as a mole tunnelling for worms....'

She sometimes acted as a muse for Richard's songs – he called her 'Breage', who was the nursemaid to King Germoe – and he once described Brenda as 'the midwife' to his melodies. She remembered one occasion when she was in Germany and heard nightingales singing for the first time. She was so thrilled that she joined in, and the birds answered her – interesting, given the circumstances of her first adult public appearance. She wrote to tell Richard of the experience, and a few days later he presented her with a beautiful song about the nightingale and the Cornish thrush.

Brenda was fascinated by the Cornish language, and for the next year she worked with Richard to bring out an album of songs and prose in Kernewek, titled Crowdy Crawn. Richard also played guitar, and as he wrote more songs, she learned them to sing, picking up some of the language as she went, although she never became fluent. Of their joint Sentinel album, he later said "No thoughts of mine have been more heartfelt than the verses we put on Crowdy Crawn".

Clive Betts, writing about the resurgence of interest in the language in the Western Mail in 1974, said "Seventy years ago, even the Cornish had forgotten they once had their own language, but now the tongue is heard in folk clubs throughout the county, publicised by a very large, and very able, folk singer, Brenda Wootton. Her activities, which include a long-playing record, have given the language a boost and a status it has never had since the Saxons defeated the last Cornish king, Hywel, in 936 BC."[23]

Their professional relationship, and their close friendship, was to last many years. Their extensive correspondence was often intense and personal, as they frequently used each other as confidantes, both apparently lacking that special someone to whom they could unburden their innermost thoughts and worries – of which both had plenty.

Richard's attitude to their working partnership is illuminating...

> "At the risk of sounding a trifle mad – which could be true – I'd like to reiterate and also extend what I already in the past have said about these songs... I am as it were a woman who has given birth to them, motley and inconsistent bunch of bastards though they may be, and if their fathers have been several... the midwife without whom they would certainly all have been stillborn, has been, and is, yourself, Brenda... it is meant as a compliment, with almost inexpressible thanks, that you were responsible for their safe birth.
>
> "...These songs of mine only came to be written as a result of Donald Rawe and others putting me in touch with you... I am still surprised that you find my songs worth working on... I try never to push my songs with you, preferring to leave it and see whether you take to them or not, but I would like you to know, that however little I *say* normally, your use of these songs is a tremendous joy to me. I would say it makes me feel proud, only

[23] *Western Mail, September 23rd 1974*

> that is not the right word – it's more a matter of being amazed to see these songs 'work'"[24], he says in August 1975.

Although music was his first love, (he had memories of composing 'sad songs' in the family garden at the age of 6), he initially had little opportunity to exploit it when sent away to school, until a music teacher took pity on him and gave him the "'luxury" of piano lessons, and ultimately, daily lessons in the "delicious mysteries of harmony". From then, he says it was a "gap of something like 30 years frustration, Brenda, until you began to sing me... you, and a few others, have given me my first and probably last chance to shout to the world". Richard was no performer – he had no wish to stand on a stage in front of an audience – but he needed his works performed, and Brenda fulfilled that need for him. He said that he was a "supplier, in that I tend to rise to the occasion, but only when the occasion arises – there's something in me that responds when somebody says we need this or that, that stirs me into thought and action where otherwise I'd be sitting around dreaming or watching the birds. Thus it is that if you order a song you usually get it..."

With Richard's support, Brenda became involved in many projects relating to Cornwall and its history, especially with schools, and if she was visiting an area, would often phone Richard and ask for a song about a particular Cornish character, or an historical event associated with it. Usually, within a few days, the requested song would arrive by post: the words, hand-written, with notes, the 'dots', or chords, notes for a musician to read from, and a simple version of the song on tape as sung and played by Richard, as Brenda never learned to read music – that was the normal package. Often she would visit him in his barn to rehearse the new songs.

Richard's Wikipedia entry states he 'founded Teere ha Tavaz, an organisation which seeks to promote the Cornish language in its Modern Cornish or Curnoack Nowedga variety.' It was slightly more complicated than that – as Matthi ab Dewi notes in his Cornish News blog, 'Dick Gendall used to support Unified Cornish at the outset, and published a book 'Cornish alive'. He started using and researching Late Cornish after becoming unhappy with Unified.' [25]

---

[24] *All of Richard's unattributed quotes are from his private letters to Brenda*

[25] *http://news.bitesizecornish.co.uk/mernans-richard-gendall-death-of-richard-gendall/*

In practice, this meant that all the songs he'd given Brenda early on in their relationship had to be re-written by Richard and re-learned by Brenda before he was happy for her to go on singing them! Many academic battles have been fought over the 'acceptable' versions of Cornish over the years, which Richard was often embroiled in, but as a non-speaker, it is not for me to stir them up again...

Ultimately, he was to write over 450 songs for her – about a third in Cornish, most in English, and a few in French, Spanish and even German – as well as major projects such as operettas or musical dramas, some at her request, some unsolicited, and some of which she never ever performed. I still have them all – they are now all detailed on a spreadsheet, and will hopefully be available soon, via Brenda's website or the Cornish Music Archive.

In an interview in the Melody Maker in 1978,[26] Brenda commented: "He can be an aggravating bugger, but the gift of knowing Richard makes me so positive. The thing is he doesn't see his own talent, and of course he's a very shy man..."

Here is what Richard had to say about his relationship with Brenda and the songs he wrote for her, in an interview with Cornwall Live in 2010:[27]

> "Music, along with languages and history, were his chosen subjects at Leeds University, where Richard taught himself composition and harmony after immersing himself in Scottish and Irish traditional songs.
>
> "But it wasn't until he met Brenda Wootton in the Irish town of Killarney that his song-writing career really took off. Cornwall's 'first woman of song' was performing there and she and Richard immediately saw the potential for a productive working partnership. In all, Richard wrote some 90 [*sic*] songs for Brenda, which she sang live and recorded for a string of albums.
>
> "'Brenda was a very good performer and very good at putting it across and I was able to provide the language "handle" to her Cornish repertoire,' he says.
>
> "In 1973 they released Crowdy Crawn, the first recording of songs in the Cornish language. But while Brenda enjoyed the limelight,

---

[26] *Melody Maker, December 30th 1978*
[27] *Cornwall Live interview, 2010*

Richard eschewed self-promotion, and this may explain why his contribution to Cornish music is sometimes overlooked.

> 'I was extremely aware that we in Cornwall were missing a body of songs in Cornish about Cornwall and I wanted to help redress that,' he says. 'So I would tell Brenda not to bother saying they were my songs but to just get on and sing them.'
>
> 'In many ways Brenda changed the course of my life.
>
> 'I had always been writing songs but she was the catalyst for that period. If it hadn't been for Brenda I wouldn't have written nearly so much.
>
> 'With Brenda it was a supply and demand situation — she would come to me all the time, asking if I had a song about a particular subject. And if I didn't have one, I'd write one.'

"Richard Gendall was a man of many parts: a Cornish language champion, author, poet, teacher, folklorist, dialectician, song-writer and composer. His contribution to Cornwall's cultural integrity is immense and perhaps without the efforts of him and others during those early days, Cornwall's distinct culture and language may have been subsumed still further into a homogenous uniformity."

In 1982, Richard met and married Jan – he had often expressed in his correspondence with Brenda, his loneliness, and his desire to find a wife. Unfortunately, while his marriage satisfied one need, it seemed to eventually estrange him from his music and his musical friends, and gradually the supply of songs dried up. However, this coincided, for better or worse, with Brenda's own poor health limiting her ability to perform, and she still had an enormous cache of unperformed material of Richard's should she have wanted something new.

I was much saddened to lose all contact with Richard after Brenda died, despite making several efforts to speak to him. He and Jan bought an ancient house in Menheniot, which became an ongoing project, and Richard became a Professor at Exeter University with his work on the Cornish language – his wife Jan steadfastly guarding his privacy.

In an article in the Observer in 2005, he was described as then being a 'linguistically vigorous 81'. He sadly died in November 2017, aged 93, and I have dedicated this book to his memory.

Mic McCreadie

Mic McCreadie has been an almost constant presence on the Cornish folk scene since the '70s. He first visited the Folk Club at Rose in 1970, and was made a resident the following year. It was there that he first became aware of Brenda and John the Fish, and in 1972 Fish invited him down to Pipers, which was then at the Western Hotel in Penzance.

Mic McCreadie with Brenda at the Penventon Hotel, Redruth, at his first wedding

He was made a resident there soon after, and with his usual impeccable taste, says he was...

> "...just gobsmacked, that I could be considered good enough to be someone who was booked and paid every single week to sing in Brenda Wootton's folk club – and it did me no end of good, because I got so much joy out of all that, all down the years. But then I lost my licence driving – Bert Biscoe was in the back and tried to get out in the main street in Helston, when we'd all had a few... I tried to stop him, but the police officer wasn't impressed. I used to come down on the train then and stay overnight in Leskinnick Street, before and after the club, then I'd get the train back after breakfast the next morning – and she made us so welcome, ever so nice. Loads of people would come back after the club, friends, fans, not just the per-

formers. Some of us would go to the Chinese takeaway round the corner, and bring back our food, and she'd warm up plates for us, and then we'd all sit in her front room: Ralph McTell, Derek Brimstone, Alex Atterson, Tony Capstick, Jon Betmead, Martin Carthy – everybody, all of them, drinking coffee, and eating toast... lovely nights, lovely – I've so many memories...

"Your Dad and I, trying to put Tony Capstick to bed – Tony and I were sitting on the floor, 'cos there were no seats left... and Ella was there with her dog, the little Jack Russell, Ben. Tony says to me 'Will you look at the size of the dick on that dog? Look at the size of that dog, and look at the dick. It's disproportionate.' I'm saying, 'yeh, right, Tony... sorry, but'... 'Brenda! Look at the size of the dick on that dog!' – and he then proceeded to invite everyone in the room, in a loud voice, to compare the size of the dog and its dick. Ella's there, getting really peed off... 'Shut up, Tony...', and in the end Brenda, trying to diffuse the situation, hands Tony a bottle of whisky, nearly three quarters full. 'Here Tony, have a drink – forget about the dog...' and we're all there listening to the Eagles (first time I'd heard them, that night at Brenda's), and Tony starts necking it, wraps himself round this bottle of whisky, forgets the dog and everything else, and ends up semi-comatose.

Your dad said we'd have to get him to bed, couldn't just leave him there – so he and I hung Tony between us and staggered up the circular staircase to the first bedroom, and got him onto the bed against the wall. I decided to try and get him into the bed, get at least some of his clothes off... should have left him there, should have known better. Your dad took his jumper off, and I got Tony's shoes off, and he's unconscious, and I undid his zipper and pulled down his jeans – and it was the first time ever I'd seen a pair of unisex knickers on a man... y'know, instead of boxers or underpants, it was a one-piece, women's red knickers, and I'm there staring in amazement when there's a thump and a blue blinding light, and a voice says 'You're not shagging me, ya Scotch poof...'.

"There was another great honour accorded to me – when Brenda asked me to be her guitarist... August of '75, it would be, or thereabouts – around the time I got married. I couldn't do it, as it happened, but I was amazed that she asked me... Brenda actually wrote a letter to my wife, Yvonne, and said I'm not trying to steal your husband off you, I just want to borrow him for a couple of months...

"But going back to those nights at Brenda's, I learnt a lot of music there, because Martin Carthy and others would teach you stuff. He taught me versions of several songs, like 'The Wind That Shakes the Barley', and said he'd write the lyrics down for me and send it to me, but by then I'd gone back temporarily to Scotland, so he posted me the lyrics up there... y'know, that was the level of friendliness that went on then... It was a great big family."

Brenda did often have to have 'serious words' with some of the performers, those who occasionally took it too far with the drinking or other pursuits... and 'having words with Brenda' they soon learnt, was certainly something best avoided – both Noel Murphy and Tony Capstick were miscreants hauled off to the naughty step at different times. As Brenda's still young daughter, most of such drunken sauciness passed me by. I think Brenda would have played merry hell with anyone who tried anything untoward with her daughter – sadly.

And Mic was also one of those with whom Brenda had felt it necessary to 'have words'. It was his habit, when not performing, to stand in the bar or the entrance to the Western, and chat with his mates. At one point he was 'summoned' to Brenda's office, where Brenda pointed out to him clearly the error of his ways. As club resident, he represented the club, she said, and it was his job to stay in the club room, not to spend his spare time chatting to his mates and drinking, even if it was just in the next room... he should show willing and be prepared to sit in the club room throughout, and enjoy the performances of others, or be ready to step in if needed. All for the princely sum of £4 a night – the most he ever got paid.

As he explains, resident singers were paid according to the number of people who'd paid the entrance fee, and what was left over after the guest's fees and other expenses was split between them – so if you were the only resident who turned up that night, you did ok. "Mind you, we were never in it for the money," he says... "and I was doing a few other clubs each week: Truro, Camelford, Padstow." At a concert staged in Piran Round by Folk Cottage organisers, the Johns Sleep and Battensby, Mic was the warm-up act for Steeleye Span. He remembers John Battensby telling him he'd get £2.50 per song – so he hastily re-arranged his normal 4-song set into 5 short songs – only to be told by John Sleep later that there was a ceiling of £10 for the night.

Mic survived the experience, and his musical career developed through several line-ups – initially as Creeping Jane, with Sue Bushnell and John Visick, through numerous other musical reincarnations to the present day. Nowadays he performs regularly with skilled bass-player John Martyn, and another old Piper's favourite, the extremely talented guitarist Adrian O'Reilly, as 'Handpicked'. He also runs his own small recording studio and has produced several CDs of memorial concerts he's arranged, such as those of Larry Law and Clive Palmer, and of the very successful Folk Cottage reunions he's organised over the last couple of years. He has also been good enough to help me out with my last two CDs of Brenda's recordings.

He recalled one occasion when he was providing a support act for Brenda and Rob Bartlett at Treswithian Village Hall. Mic said he'd done a fabulous set, and received a rapturous reception from the audience; he thought he'd be a hard act to follow, and was filled with the warm glow of a job well done. Brenda and Robert came on, and did a couple of introductory numbers, which were well received. Then she sang such a sweet, sensitive song, so gently and softly, you could have heard a pin drop... she got to the end and Mic straightaway let out a loud 'Yeeeeesss!!' roar of appreciation. Brenda shot Mic her trademark, withering, scathing look that would have turned milk sour, and carried on singing; she hadn't finished the song. That stuck a pin in his party balloon, for sure.

Brenda's influences – other song-writers and songs...

As explained elsewhere, Brenda's musical influences were many and various – from the hymns and chapel music of her youth, through the old piano standards of the '30s and '40s played by her mother Lena, and the early blues, soul, rock and pop influences of the '50s – it was always an eclectic mix. One of her favourite forms of music was the musical – she adored the old movies on TV with Fred Astaire and Ginger Rogers, Gene Kelly, Bing Crosby, and Howard Keel (Lena's favourite), and knew all the songs off by heart – I grew up listening to them. Coming across her sheet music for 'Laura' (from the 1944 film noir of the same name) the other day reduced me to nostalgic tears... I still miss her singing these beautiful old songs around the house.

This is a completely random and by no means comprehensive list of performers and composers Brenda admired – influences, if you like:

Nina Simone, Mahalia Jackson, Tony Bennett, Peggy Lee, Ella Fitzgerald, Sophie Tucker, Bessie Smith, Nellie Lutcher, Artie Shaw, Edith Piaf, Jacques Brel, Ewen Carruthers, Billie Holiday, Aretha Franklin, Sarah Vaughan, Dinah Washington, the Fisk Jubilee Singers, Mel Torme, Judy Collins, Odetta, Harry Nilson, James Taylor, John Sebastian, J J Cale, Ry Cooder, Antonio Carlos Jobim, Dorsey Brothers Orchestra

She also enjoyed listening to classical music occasionally – these would certainly have been amongst her favourite pieces: Vaughan Williams: Fantasia on a Theme by Thomas Tallis; Sibelius: Swan of Tuonela, Finlandia; Rachmaninov: Piano Concerto No 2; Grieg: Morning Mood & Death of Ase; Debussy: L'Apres Midi D'Un Faun; Holst: Planets Suite

Apart from Richard – although by far the lion's share of her source material came from him – there were a few songwriters whose work she particularly favoured. These were among them...

When she started working with Madron Players in the early 1960s, Brenda met a lovely lady called **Molly Bartlett**, who was then a member of Madron WI. In 1961, Brenda produced Molly's play 'The Smugglers of Sennen' with Madron Players – the play in which Brenda first performed Lamorna for an audience. When we knew Molly, she lived at Red Lodge at Tremethick Cross near Penzance. She was a playwright and a published author, and often won prizes at the Cornish Gorsedh for her Cornish Dialect poems and stories, and in 1970 Molly was made a Bard – Bardic name: 'Scryfer Ranyeth', Dialect Writer. (The Cornish Gorsedh is a charitable organisation based on the Welsh Eisteddfod, and 'exists to maintain the national Celtic spirit of Cornwall'. The ceremony is held annually in a different part of Cornwall each time, and apart from the main business of appointing new Bards, also awards prizes and trophies for the best Cornish language and dialect pieces.)

At Brenda's request, Richard set some of Molly's lyrics to music, and Brenda recorded her 'Mount Misery' on the 'Crowdy Crawn' LP with Richard accompanying. Molly was also an excellent cook, who took her fine baking to Penzance Farmers Market every week; her Australian Fruit Cake was moist and memorable, and Brenda often ordered one from her for special occasions, as all would sell out at the Market.

Brenda probably met **Ewen Carruthers** when guesting at his folk club at The Red Bear in Sherburn-in-Elmet in North Yorkshire in the early '70s. Ewen was a Northumberland-born singer-songwriter, and Brenda sometimes stayed with him and his family when she was touring in the area, and he gave her many songs to sing. They kept in touch over the years, and Ewen said in a letter "It's good to know you're still singing some of my songs...". She was to record four of them on her albums – 'Love's Own Sweet Refrain', 'In Love Again', 'What's in a Name?' and 'Paris'... all beautiful and lyrical songs, and much loved by Brenda and her audiences.

Dave Semmens at Tredinnick Stack

Dave Semmens is a Cornish lad, currently working as a lawyer in London. I remember him as a gentle long-haired guitarist who used to come to the club, and who often visited Brenda up at her hideaway on the moors at Tredinnick Stack. He recalls:

"I would collect her from the (Tremaen) shop in Penzance. Somehow she would squeeze into my 2 seater MG Midget and we would trundle up to the Stack to practice some songs. As a contrast to all her Cornish material she would love to sing American classics as well as others, including one or two of mine. I can remember her singing my 'Unbelievable', 'A Day Away', 'Missing You' and of course, 'Vanity' – and I remember teaching her 'Memphis in June' and 'Over the Rainbow', amongst others. 'Here There and Everywhere' I particularly enjoyed performing with her.

"For a while I was a regular weekly resident at Pipers in Penzance and we would always do a couple of songs. However, she was always very modest and careful not to upstage whoever was the guest. At some stage I remember we hawked ourselves around one or two promoters/A & R people in London. Can't remember if we were trying to sell her or both of us or my songs! Nothing came of it. Shortly after that she asked me to be her permanent accompanist. Gave it a bit of thought but said no, so I could finish university. Then along came Rob!"

Brenda and Dave did make some recordings together at Sentinel Music; I've now found seven of Dave's song lyrics, and I am hopeful we may find recordings of some of these among the recently-acquired Sentinel Music tapes...

From the moody and dramatic French singer-songwriter **Jacques Brel**, she learned 'Song for Old Lovers', and 'Ne Me Quitte Pas'. She also sang several of **Mike Silver**'s songs, including 'Soon I'll Be Home', 'Saturday Night in the Country', and 'Come On In', which was used as the familiar opening number to her 'Sunday Best' programme on Radio Cornwall throughout the show's reign. She performed the works of a huge variety of modern songwriters, such as 'Send in the Clowns' from Steven Sondheim, Bob Dylan's 'Forever Young', and 'Forbidden Fruit' by Oscar Brown. **Mike Sagar-Fenton**'s songs have also been mentioned.

Of her more traditional Cornish songs, Lamorna has proved probably the most popular and enduring – and also possibly the most contentious in terms of its origin. She has said she learnt it from the Matthews brothers at St Levan, but it is believed now that it originated from a Manchester song called Pomona – there is an Albert Square and a Pomona in Manchester, but *not* in Lamorna. Mike O'Connor has commented: "I have a growing confidence the song was written by the author Charles Lee, who lived in Cornwall from 1900 to 1907 and resided for much of that time in Lamorna. He had a great reputation for writing very clever parodies and light-hearted songs, some for reviews, pantomimes and the like. Brenda told me that in the 1950s an old man told her 'I wrote that' after a performance of Lamorna in Newlyn – he was apparently revisiting 'old haunts'. At the time Brenda did not believe the claim, but in later life she suspected it might have been true. I think the visitor might have been Charles Lee making a farewell visit to Cornwall, knowing his days were numbered." If so, it is unlikely to have been sung by Brenda at that time, as she didn't sing Lamorna in public until 1961, and Charles Lee died in 1956 – but she could have been in the audience. And Charles Lee could certainly have adapted the popular Manchester song... (Penzance's Town Crier, Philip Rowley – aka Piglet – insists she 'stole' it from him. Not so, Piglet – her knowledge of it predates her knowledge of you! And songs are anybody's...)

She sang, with relish, old traditional Cornish favourites such as 'The White Rose, 'The Old Grey Duck', 'Little Eyes', 'Sweet Nightingale', and 'Camborne Hill', and of course, 'Trelawney'. 'Tryphena Trenary', a lovely bright song, was written by former editor of the Cornishman newspaper, **Herbert Thomas**, as was the eponymous 'Pasties and Cream', used as the title of one of her early albums. Traditional songs in the Cornish language are few and far between, but one she particularly loved and recorded was 'Delyo Syvy' ('Leaves of Strawberries'). Hopeful songwriters frequently sent her material, which she rarely used, the exception being 'Cornwall' by **Tom Kolinsky**, which she adapted, with his permission, and recorded for her final album, 'Seagull'. Taking on any new song, especially from an unknown and untried author, involved hours of work rehearsing, and she was always conscious of her commitment and the time element.

I should maybe make one comment on Brenda's rehearsing when she was at home. She sometimes used a little Casio piano for picking out a tune, or working out a harmony – but if I was around, she occasionally asked me to help. Unlikely as it sounds, as I most definitely did *not* inherit that voice of hers, I was, however, capable of holding a tune and hitting the right notes, and sometimes she just needed someone to sing the straight melody to enable her to explore the harmonies, above and below the tune. Father was hopeless... as soon as she began harmonising, he'd follow her...

Crowdy Crawn – Brenda & Robert Bartlett

Brenda and Robert probably first met in Norwich, sometime in the early 1970s. Robert was a one-time member of contemporary folk group Totem (as was Dik Cadbury), a former rock guitarist, and most recently an editor of Beat Instrumental, a national music monthly. He was and is a versatile musician and a charismatic performer, and it probably didn't take them long to realise that they made an excellent musical partnership. Michael Chapman found them an early gig at the Greenhead Hotel in Haltwhistle when they were en route to bookings in Scotland, which he says went down great – and as the sleeve of their first record notes, they had almost 'No Song To Sing' (one of Michael's own songs).

Brenda and Robert Bartlett as Crowdy Crawn

When Brenda called me into Tremaen Craft Market in the winter of 1973 and asked me if I was willing to take over her role as Shop Manager, it was as a result of Robert's encouraging her to join him and turn professional as a duo. They had done some gigs together, but while Brenda was still involved with the shop, she could not devote her attention to a professional career. My agreement freed her to follow her star... (She did later tell a number of journalists in interviews that I had approached her and 'persuaded' her to turn professional... but the impetus did *not* come from me.)

They decided on the name of Crowdy Crawn – the title of Brenda and Richard's album the previous year, from the Cornish 'Croder Croghan', a small leather sieve hung by the fire in old Cornish homes, which held little treasures or precious things. Their mentor and songwriter supreme was Richard Gendall, so Cornish songs featured heavily, although they were even then singing an eclectic mix of traditional folk, pop, blues and jazz numbers as well. Robert and Brenda spent many a happy hour in Richard's white-washed barn in Gwinear, playing around with music and learning new songs. Along the way, new friendships were formed with Robert's friend Steve Shearsby, and his brother Nick.

Robert & Richard in Richard's barn at Wall, Gwinear

From the start, it was a love affair. When they officially began as a professional partnership in the spring of 1974, she was like a giddy schoolgirl with the excitement of it all. Their first professional tour was in Brittany – and when she wakes in the hotel room in St Pol de Leon and gazes out of the window at the lacelike bell-tower of the church at the start of that tour, her world is fresh and new; (the song, 'An Tour Dantelezet', on their Starry Gazey Pie LP, is Breton for 'lacelike bell-tower', a common feature of the district in northern Brittany). They had several tours booked in the UK and Europe over the next few months, including a concert in Paris and a booking at the Pan Celtic Festival in Ireland in May, together with a return visit for Brenda to the Kertalg Festival, with other French gigs booked by French agent Gwenn Le Goarnig.

The line-up for this festival was amazing: Dick Gaughan, The Dransfields, The Boys of the Lough, Martin Carthy and The Watersons. When all the dust had settled, Brenda and Robert discovered that Gwenn had recorded their set, and had brought out 2 albums – one featured Brenda with the rest of the line-up from Kertalg Festival in 1973, and there was one track with Brenda and Robert on Festival Pop Kertalg 1974. Amazingly, Gwenn claimed full copyright, to the best of my knowledge without even consulting the artists concerned – certainly, Brenda and Robert were told nothing of her plans. She also brought out an album titled 'Pamplemousse', which Brenda and Robert *had* agreed to record for her, but once again, claimed full copyright. Legal battles followed, but again, to the best of my knowledge, Crowdy Crawn never received a penny from those records.

So – nasty taste at the start of their professional career there – but Brenda and Rob went on to make their own first official album, 'No Song To Sing', for Sentinel Records and the following year, 'Starry Gazey Pie'. Apart from the pirated Kertalg albums mentioned above, 'Tin in the Stream' was another great album they made, this time produced by German company Stockfisch. One look at the cover photo gives a hint at the closeness of their relationship at that time. They went on to perform at Cambridge Folk Festival, Trowbridge Folk Festival and others further afield in Scotland, and toured in Brittany, Belgium, France and Germany.

Cousin Malc

Her cousin Malcolm Rowe was one of Brenda's greatest fans, and followed her career avidly, frequently accompanying her to concerts and on trips abroad. When Brenda and Robert had been together about six months, she got word one day that Malc had had a serious accident. In February 1975 he had been cycling back from a Valentine's fancy dress party late at night, and somewhere near St Just a car came round a bend in the narrow road too fast, and both Malc and the bike went through the front windscreen and out at the back. Worse – the driver somehow managed to drive off and leave him lying in the road, with serious head injuries.

Brenda was beside herself with worry, and she and Robert cancelled current bookings and returned from their UK tour immediately to be by his side. Malcolm's severe injuries resulted in significant brain damage, and it was over a year before he could even begin to learn to speak again. His first, and for some time, only, word, was 'curses'.

Malc's damaged brain believed he was talking normally, so trying to hold a conversation with him was very difficult: "Hi Malc – how are you feeling today?" would be met with "Curses... curses curses, curses?" but when he realised you couldn't understand him he would start to get very distressed. The factor that was most effective in bringing about a breakthrough in his speech was listening to cassettes of Brenda's music. She had taken up several of her music tapes to see if they helped, and their familiarity would reassure him. Amazingly, he began singing along with all the correct words to the songs he loved, even if he then resorted again to 'curses' for his speech. It was a classic demonstration of how the brain responds differently to music than to speech. In his memory, the lyrics were stored in a different part of the brain to the words he used for speech, but eventually, thanks in part to his love of Brenda's music, much of his spoken language did come back to him, albeit in a stumbling, incomplete fashion.

Brenda and cousin Malc on the boat to Spain

He spent a long period at Stoke Mandeville hospital, in the department that dealt with soldiers brain-damaged from gunshot wounds, and eventually was returned to St Lawrence's Hospital at Bodmin. This establishment was known as a mental health institution, and visiting him there was so distressing – for the visitor at least. He was put in a large ward filled with geriatric and Alzheimers patients and the 'elderly confused', and the place stank of overcooked food and stale pee, and worse. The one ray of light in all this was that part of the damage to his brain had left him with an ongoing state of 'diminished responsibility', and he was generally quite happy and unconcerned by his surroundings.

The driver who had caused all of this heartache was identified, but as a compensation claim was deemed to be likely to take too long, the family decided to settle out of court. After two or three years recovering, Malc came back to his little cottage near St Buryan, and even attempted to return to his old job, working at Peter Ley's garage in St Levan. But his condition of 'diminished responsibility' really made this situation untenable – he couldn't look after himself properly at all, and his cottage soon just filled up with rubbish and dirty plates. Peter Ley realised he was unfit to work when he dropped a car down from the jacks too fast and burst the tyres, and set fire to a car he was supposed to be respraying, for my cousin Diane's dad, Ken Rumsey. He spent his days from then on walking to his favourite pubs at Treen and Lamorna, and helped out polishing the brasswork.

For some years when I lived out of Cornwall, I lost touch with Malc, and had difficulty tracking him down when I went looking for him. He had been placed in the live-in care of a retired nurse in Penzance, was then moved to a Care Home in Alexandra Road, and finally has ended up in a very good nursing home in Newlyn – where he is still living, relatively happily. We visit him when we can, but his speech has deteriorated again somewhat, and he now has to be moved in a wheelchair. In his 70s now, he still remembers and mourns Brenda, and what little conversation he attempts is likely to be about her, but he remains cheerful.

Norwich Festival

Norwich Festival 1974 – Brenda & Decameron (Al, Johnny, Geoff & Dave) with Cousin Malc outside his tent

Ah... Norwich. Happy memories. We first visited the festival in the early 1970s, set on the campus of the University of East Anglia, and returned every August. It was more like a huge family reunion, as we knew all of the performers from their visits to Pipers, and Brenda and Fish were also booked to perform at the Festival. Everyone camped – the grounds by the river would be littered with the tent homes of all the musicians, so there was no need to do anything other than roll out of your sleeping bag in the (late) mornings to be amongst music and music-makers. Martin Carthy, Michael Chapman, Decameron, Ralph McTell, Derek Brimstone – all the usual suspects – gathered to have fun for a long weekend.

Norwich Festival football match; visible are Brenda in goal, Pete Berryman, Michael Chapman, Robert Bartlett, Henry the Jug and others

In 1974, a remarkable football match took place, with Carthy, Chapman and many of the other performers – and, for the one and only time ever, Brenda in goal. Below is a great shot of Michael Chapman, Rick Kemp, Martin Carthy and Norma Waterson sitting around chatting, while Brenda stands behind...

Michael Chapman, Martin Carthy, Norma Waterson, Rick Kemp and Brenda at Norwich

It was at Norwich Festival in August 1975 that the cracks first appeared in Crowdy Crawn's protective shell. It was always on the cards – their personalities were both too volatile, their egos too fragile, their emotional entanglement too intense. Raging arguments could be heard by anyone who cared to listen, emanating from Brenda's tent. Sour expressions and pointed comments developed into outright nastiness on both sides, embarrassing for witnesses and not conducive to a happy festival. To add to the excitement, Robert and my cousin Diane, who was visiting the festival for the first time, had met and fallen in love. Brenda's diary over the next few months records her concerns about the future of Crowdy Crawn, and about Robert's reticence to cooperate or to make plans. Eventually, Father received a tearful phone call from Brenda, touring with Robert in Scotland, saying that she'd cancelled further bookings on the tour and was flying home. One of her dresses had been ripped up and she had a split lip. We were aghast and outraged in equal measure, and determined to get on the next plane up to Scotland to 'rescue' her, but she was adamant she had it under control. When they returned, and I had a chance to see Robert again in our house, I presented him with a long letter I'd written to him, and demanded he read it in front of me, there and then. They parted amicably enough, with Robert having to sign a legal document, which amongst other things, confirmed Brenda's ownership of the Martin guitar – Robert kept the many other musical instruments they'd acquired.

Brenda as songwriter: One interesting upshot of Brenda and Robert's relationship only really became clear to me very recently... perhaps as a result of their partnership, in the 1970s, Brenda apparently wrote several songs. Sorting through the huge boxes of lyrics, I found evidence of Brenda as songwriter – there are a handful of poems, obviously intended to have melodies, signed by Brenda, from this period – the music may well still turn up. She had often written comical ditties for pantomimes – 'My Donkey Can Sing Like a Nightingale', 'Something About a Pasty', and 'Thunder & Lightning'... then we had the beautiful 'Everybody Knows', recorded on the Maxi Single... and she also wrote the lyrics for the lament for the Cornish fishing industry, 'Fish to Find', recorded on the 'Gwavas Lake' album. Now we also have 'Monday Morning Spring', 'Station Prayer', 'Brenda's Lullaby', 'Woman Here', and 'Go For Broke'. To top that – I've discovered that a wonderful song I heard her sing many times, 'Now and Then', is not the work of some unknown songsmith from the 40s, but with lyrics by Brenda, and a sweet melody by local jazzman Phil King. Rest assured I will be following this up...

Incidentally – it seems obvious to me that these verses were mostly love songs to Robert. Some people may find the notion of Brenda as a sensual being a bit difficult to cope with, but she was always a passionate character, and still at that time an attractive woman, and being large does not preclude feelings of wanting to love and be loved (and please – for god's sake, no tasteless jokes or shrieking headlines). I think it very likely indeed that she had one or more physical relationships while on the road. In a way, it would have been surprising if she didn't – the 'permissive society' was in full swing, and for a lonely, homesick, woman, being 'out on the road and on her own', to paraphrase a Mike Silver song, might well have led her to occasionally seek comfort and reassurance where she could find it. Certainly, from her poems and the photos it is obvious to see she adored Robert, at least initially, and from his writings to her, it seems the feeling was mutual – for a while. I'm not condoning this – but I'm not condemning it either. It is what it is. And she never stopped loving Father... although what he knew or thought about it is not recorded. It is worth mentioning he was not always as pure as the driven snow himself. I'll say no more...

Most of my family, from my wedding photos – clockwise from front left: cousin Adam Ellery, Auntie Ellen Morris, cousin Gillian Argent, Peter, Brenda, me, cousin Malc, Auntie Kate Hey, cousin Jonathan Ellery, and Great Great Aunt Bessie Osborne

But the timing of the break-up was significant, for me. Robert was to be our best man at my wedding to John Luscombe that September, and my cousin Diane was one of my best friends, would have been a bridesmaid, and had made my wedding dress. Sadly, due to the split with Brenda, neither Robert nor Diane attended the wedding, and nor did her parents. Robert and Diane eventually married and emigrated to Australia with Barnaby (her son from her first marriage, now renamed Ben), and the couple were to have three more sons, and were soon joined by her parents Marjorie and Ken. It still upsets me that I lost my best friend for years as a result of Robert and Brenda's split.

Years later in the 1980s, Brenda travelled to Australia to sing in the Cornish Kernewek Lowender Festival near Adelaide. Amazingly, Robert, Diane and all four of their sons turned up at the concert, and there was a delighted and genuine reunion. Subsequently, Diane wrote me a long letter, and I sat up all night and cried... but we established a new relationship from that. So as soon as I was able to afford it, after selling the house at Tredinnick in 1995, inherited following the deaths of Brenda and John the previous year, my first big spend was on a trip to Australia for me and the boys.

Unfortunately, by then the relationship between Robert and Diane had also broken down, and she was a single mum struggling to look after her four sons and working full-time in the care of the elderly. Nevertheless, it was an amazing and emotional seven weeks – and I couldn't have been more delighted when Diane was able to pay me a return visit back to Cornwall in April 2017 – her first in well over 30 years. She returned the following year, but the cost is prohibitive, and we don't know when or if we will meet again. Beware the life of the Cornish exile, living 10,000 miles from home...

Robert is now back in the UK and living in Derbyshire, and has no contact with his sons. He sometimes performs in a group called Rule of Thumb, I believe, though word from him is rare.

Brenda Wootton – Cornwall's Ambassador for Song

So began Brenda's solo career, with her name heading the bill, plus a succession of musicians... usually, but not always, guitarists. She was 47, a large, middle-aged, Cornish housewife, about to start an international singing career. She was just as scared as she had been when starting as a duo with Robert – probably more so. Now she was the one bearing the responsibility virtually alone of finding sufficient, and sufficiently well-paid, employment to keep both herself and an accompanist in business.

Her first steps, immediately after my wedding day, involved a trip to Amsterdam with husband John to meet and begin rehearsals with Mike Silver. From the Netherlands, Brenda's career over the next few years fanned out across Europe, and she performed as far afield as Canada and Australia. The intensity of the tours, sometimes lasting months, and the sheer number of gigs, make a detailed time-line unrealistic (there is a rough timeline in the Appendices), so instead I will take a look at her work in the individual countries.

In those early days, it took her a while to establish her own understanding of her role and its significance, and to come to terms with her new lifestyle... "As far as being a professional artist is concerned, I'm very grateful that something I'm really interested in and love is being asked of me. I didn't think it could be commercial, because how can it – what I'm doing? But I suppose it's because they like the personality, they recognise the fact that I'm a deeply-rooted person, heritage-wise, and they want to know about it," she said in an interview with Karl Dallas in 1979. "I don't really think I've learned my trade too much yet. But I know who I am at last – I found that out about 18 months ago... I'm a Cornish woman, middle-aged – and I've stopped being ashamed if I can't get the housework done. I've stopped worrying about all that sort of thing, which did bother me, because I was brought up very traditionally in Cornwall."[28] Eighteen months earlier, she had been made a Cornish Bard, and had become a grandmother for the first time.

Brenda eventually developed very clear views on her role as a singer. She definitely came to see herself, as she was so often described, as an Ambassador for Cornwall. Wherever she went, she promoted Cornwall, and Cornish traditions, Cornish history, Cornish culture

[28] *From Folk News no 22, Interview with Karl Dallas, 1979*

and the Cornish people, tirelessly – but it was not the *only* thing she was. Her pledge to sing at least one song in Cornish at every concert had resulted in a wealth of new material from Richard Gendall, and she used it to the full. This didn't stop her also singing at least one blues or jazz number on the programme – anything and everything from a negro spiritual to a hymn to a ballsy burlesque number was fair game. But her priorities were clear, and French audiences responded with delight to her ringing cry to open any large French concert: "Je ... suis ... Cornouaillaise!", especially when delivered by this overlarge middle-aged granny in her vibrant flowing robes, with arms flung wide, and rings sparkling on every finger...

These aspects of Brenda, almost without her instigation, became part of the 'branding of Brenda', her image that was instantly recognisable to her legion of foreign fans. She had long enjoyed wearing silver rings, and over time her collection grew until every finger and both thumbs glittered in the spotlights. She had also long ago given up wearing knee-length skirts, and for comfort, lived in long flowing dresses that were all handmade – a skill and an interest which sprang from her days designing costumes for the drama stage. She was even known to take her sewing machine on tours, to buy colourful fabric and exotic braids in foreign towns and to run up a dramatic gown for that night's performance in her hotel room – she never once used a pattern.

She selected bright, bold designs in easy-care fabrics, which could be quickly washed and dried and stuffed in a suitcase, and still come out looking good enough for the stage. Colourful silk scarves, too, were part of her persona, and beaded necklaces that she often made herself out of upcycled charity shop finds. As her appeal in and love for Brittany grew, she commissioned a special silver brooch in the form of a large Breton triskele, a swirling three-legged Celtic symbol, with three purple amethysts at the heart, and she wore it at every concert – as an Aquarius, amethyst was her birthstone. She also took great pains designing her own logo, a Celtic-styled 'Brenda' enclosed within swirling letter trails with triskele-like curls.

She was very conscious of her image, and deeply resented any attempt to pigeonhole her as simply 'a folk singer', which she found insulting in the extreme. In an interview with Colin Irwin in the Melody Maker in December 1976, Brenda explained: "You're called a folk singer because you work the only scene available to you and that's the folk scene. But I learnt to sing the blues and chapel, and I learnt Bing Crosby songs. I love the English folk scene but I fit just as easily in a chapel choir or a traditional jazz band. The blues in me is bursting to get out somewhere."[29]

And later in the same interview: "She's terrifically proud of Cornwall... but at the same time, she's anxious not to allow Cornwall to become dominant to the point where it becomes a gimmick or a trademark, with choruses of 'ooo-aarhh' greeting her wherever she goes". Despite her love of her land and her pride, Brenda wanted little to do with the politicisation of Cornwall and the too-ardent nationalism of some Cornish... she felt such movements sometimes got 'a bit heavy', and were potentially divisive, leading to a 'them and us' situation, and has said that during her years spent touring in Europe, her strongest feelings of nationalism were often as a European – she would have had no truck with Brexit! "I'm not just a Cornishwoman – my work is on the Continent, and I'm a European, a member of the Common Market... anyway, I'm a singer, and my voice is my passport", she has said... (whatever the colour of the document!). One of her press releases reveals: "She believes she sings to communicate... with ALL ages, creeds and countries."

The question has been asked – why did Brenda become such a success abroad, and not in her own country? It's a difficult one – certainly, she had loyal Cornish fans who followed her avidly on her weekly Radio Cornwall programme, Sunday Best – but she never pushed her own material, and rarely bragged on the show about her remarkable achievements, conscious that it would have sounded like just that – showing off. The internet was not 'a thing' in those days, so unless you followed music journals closely, you might easily have missed news of the superstardom that she was experiencing elsewhere. Her singing, her personality and her programme were unique – and the French, in particular, adored eccentrics... they fell for her onstage seduction techniques in a way British audiences never quite did. Although she was much admired and lauded in Britain, she was more often described, and too easily dismissed, as a 'folk singer', her humble origins in the folk scene too well known here to admit her to the higher echelons of musical star. And she certainly did not fit the image of the conventional female folkie.

From 1975 for about 15 years, Brenda toured extensively around Europe, and visited Australia and Canada too, with a succession of

---

[29] *Melody Maker, Interview with Colin Irwin, December 1976*

guitarists and other musicians, choirs and bands. This often resulted in long months away from home, and bouts of extreme homesickness. In an interview in 1979, she confessed: "When I got married all I wanted to do was be a good housewife, a good cook, and a good mother to my children. My family have helped so much, and always supported me with my singing. But I do get terribly homesick sometimes. Sunday dinner times are the worst..."[30] And her homesickness on those long tours was a tangible thing that was sometimes almost an illness, especially if she felt she was not getting the support she needed from her guitarist. Combined with her perpetual exhaustion from the stress and pressure and the long drives between gigs, her efforts to appear pleasant and delightful to her hosts and to put on a totally professional performance, and the endless late nights, it did sometimes contribute to a real illness. Her mood vacillated from doom and depression if there were money worries, if the music wasn't going well, or if there were fears for the future with guitarist problems, to one of euphoria after every successful gig – which they mostly were – so she was often capable of going from hell to heaven and back in one day.

But she regarded herself very much as a professional musician, and would tolerate nothing less in those she worked with, which as her guitarists will testify, sometimes made her a difficult taskmaster. She was a member of Equity and the Musicians Union, and insisted her musicians should also comply, and did everything she could to present a totally efficient and professional face to the world – 'the show must go on' was definitely her mantra. Every time she finished a gig, at home or abroad, the very next day, if she had some spare hours, she was straight into her 'housework': hand-washing and drying her clothes in her hotel or bedroom sink, cleaning the flat where they were staying, rehearsing the songs for the next gig, cooking for all and sundry, phoning or writing to organisers, agents, family and friends, arranging new bookings, sending cards home, or doing her accounts, song lists for copyright and other paperwork, to ensure she brought every scrap of paper back for the resourceful Jacquie Harding in Heamoor, who kept her books reliably up to date.

Newspaper reviews from those days are many and almost invariably fulsome and glowing in their praise. From the Western Morning News in 1980: "In speech, her Newlyn-bred voice is as rich and

---

[30] *Focus on Folk, Keith Clark, Western Daily Express 1979*

mellifluous as clotted cream. In song, her voice at full strength could crack granite, or just as easily slip into 'Summertime' with a tenderness that moves to tears"[31]; "...combines the husky tones of Cleo Laine and the sweet lyrical voice of Mary O'Hara ...an exceptional singer, whose familiar, almost cosy, approach to her audience is intermixed with an absolute professionalism in her singing"...[32]

For some reason I can't quite fathom, from the early 1980s, the invitations to Germany, Belgium, Holland and other European countries seem to have mostly dried up – she was still going great guns in Australia, the marvellous successes in Canada were still to come, and France, as always, was her bread and butter... But the huge protracted tours of Germany and elsewhere were no more – just the odd gig, here and there. Her bookings in these countries were mostly under the stewardship of her agents Hansi Dobratz and Leon Lamal, but I have found no evidence as to why this rich vein of bookings ended; a few years later, it could have been down to her health, but not at this period...

Her Accompanists...

In the early days at the Count House, Brenda would happily accept accompaniment from whoever was available and could work out the chords... usually, it was **John the Fish**, but in the late 1960s she sometimes performed with **Mike Sagar-Fenton**, **Dave Semmens**, or **Michael Chapman**, principally on jazz and blues standards, and also sang with Cornish Bard and songwriter **Richard Gendall** from time to time, recording the Crowdy Crawn LP with him.

Decameron's **Dik Cadbury** played for Brenda occasionally, notably in Brittany. He remembers it thusly:

> "I got a call towards the end of 1972 from Brenda saying that Fish's father was very ill in hospital and that he might have to bail out of a tour they were in the middle of so would I consider standing in as guitarist for the remaining dates? I did a number of folk club gigs with her at the end of that year, then Brenda asked whether I would do the Killarney Festival and one in Harlech with Alan Stivell – I know Malc drove us in Killarney because I have some lovely slides of us driving round the Ring

---

[31] *Western Morning News, 27th August 1980*

[32] *Probably Welwyn Hatfield Times, 1980*

Of Kerry with gorse in bloom – one of Brenda sitting in the open tailgate of the car learning her lines. In Harlech, I have a clear memory of sitting on the roof of the castle with Stivell's guitarist Dan ar Braz trying to work out the chords to Paul Simon's 'America' – happy days.

"Brenda and I played Kertalg Festival in 1973, shortly before I joined Decameron. We took the car from Plymouth to Roscoff with Malc (Brenda's cousin) at the wheel and Robin Dransfield as a passenger. It was the third Celtic festival I played with Brenda after Killarney and Harlech. We initially learned the songs of Richard Gendall in Robert's basement flat in Hampstead (if I recall correctly). My Breton friend Mique Lefevre asked me if I fancied playing a Celtic festival in Brittany – I said I didn't play Celtic music but that I was working with a singer from Cornwall (Brenda) who sang songs in the Cornish language and perhaps that would be of interest. He spoke to Gwenn Le Goarneg who put us on the bill. Robert and Brenda joined forces after that.

"There was a day in 1972 when Al Schmidt, Brenda and I drove off into the Cornish countryside, round the coast, (with a hamper and some vino, natch!) and ended up shouting at the tops of our voices: "Who are the beautiful people? We are!!" I wrote the song 'Beautiful People' as a snapshot of that day out."

Brenda in the back of Dik's car, with Pipers stickers

Dik was in a group called Totem, with John Bidwell, Al Schmidt and Robert Bartlett. It was the appearance of **Robert Bartlett** on the scene that persuaded Brenda to leave her role as Manageress of Tremaen Craft Market, and make singing her career. They worked together from January 1974 for nearly two years, and she was then joined by **Mike Silver**, who could only offer her a few months – but turning professional as a singer had upped the stakes, and as she had determined to only use musicians that could meet her exacting standards, finding a reliable and committed replacement guitarist was an almost constant headache for Brenda.

Brenda sitting in Dik's car in Killarney, learning her words

By December 1975, she had high hopes of **John Dunkerley**, but he cried off at the last minute – apparently he'd received a better offer elsewhere. **Andy Dickson** was next, and she did actually start working with him for a few weeks, although being convinced from early on that he wouldn't be up to scratch. She had offers from **Jake Walton** and others that after long chats came to nothing; **Dave Semmens** declined her request, to finish his University course; she asked the newly-wed **Mic McCreadie**, who wasn't in a position to help. **John Alderslade** was the next to step up, and although a competent guitarist, he too was not able to offer the commitment Brenda needed.

Time was running out, as she needed to be working, and Brenda, near to desperation, placed ads in the Melody Maker, and interviewed a couple more potential guitarists, finally selecting **John**

Molyneux, a versatile musician who played several instruments. Anxiously she waited to see what the downside would be. They got on reasonably well, and he was certainly a more than competent musician who learned fast. However, it transpired he didn't really gel with Brenda's choice of material.

For Brenda, each new guitarist meant going back to Stage 1 – preparing tapes and chords for them, often having them to stay for weeks at a time, with hours and hours of rehearsal work before she could get together enough material for even one night's concert. It would never be a matter of a simple interview. The rehearsals would be continuous, filling every spare hour for the first few weeks, until both she and the guitarist gained sufficient confidence to be able to relax into the programme. Eventually, **Al Fenn** from Decameron stepped in... and she worked with Al for about 8 months.

Brenda and Al Fenn performing at Pipers at Gulval Meadhouse

In the Spring of 1978, **Dave Penhale** responded to an ad of Brenda's in the Melody Maker. He came down for an interview to Leskinnick Street, and met Al Fenn there, who was on site both to help Dave with learning some of the songs, and because he and Brenda were due to leave shortly for another European tour. Uniquely, Dave's appointment as Brenda's guitarist was a salaried position. He recalls she went to some pains to make sure his stamp was paid, and that all the paperwork was correct. He soon realised, having left teaching, he was going into another 'profession'...

> "...and that's the key word, really... professional. Every interview she did, she reinforced that she was a professional. And it was that reinforcement that emphasised discipline, and preparation

> – that in order to present a show, entertain and tell a story, to an audience of 10, or an audience of 10,000, you just had to be right on the button – every time – and I had to *learn* that. I really had to learn that. You see them now, coming into the business, up there doing their bit, and ooh, the edges are a bit rough... but you see a great professional at work, and you can relax. And Bren had that...".

Which isn't to say that Brenda could not fool around on stage... Dave, like Al and the others, had a lot to put up with when she went into one of her 'comedy' routines. For 'Raise the Portcullis', she created a plastic bucket 'knight's helmet' to wear on stage, and played a kazoo, and a guitarist's pride could well have been dented with having to don a toy policeman's helmet and a fake moustache, as Al Fenn did, for 'The Policemen's Ball' (another ex-panto 'hit')...

Brenda in knight's helmet, with Dave Penhale

Audiences willingly, it seemed, were happy to make fools of themselves doing the 'actions' to 'Something About a Pasty', flapping their arms to fly home when '...heading for the river, Tamar', or pulling the chain to 'Turn On the Steam' – "whoo whoo"! Sometimes the musician had to lead the audience in one direction while Brenda went off on harmonies of her own, or be prepared to be the butt of a Brenda joke. Most took it in good part – let's face it, they had little choice. What they *must* be able to do was to know exactly what the next song – always a big contrast – was going to be, and be ready to play it correctly, and at the right speed and pitch.

Dave also had to learn a new discipline in moving over to the adored Martin guitar – a Treble 0-18 – "I had to live with it, it was never out of my sight, in my room every night – thinking back, I spent more time with that guitar than I did with my wife..." he said. It had been bought in Germany on Brenda and Robert's first tour, but was stolen in Paris a couple of years later when left briefly unattended at a concert.

Learning new songs with Brenda, he says they would try them out to see "if they could walk and talk"... if they had a future. As well as the UK, Dave toured Brittany, Belgium, Denmark and Germany with Brenda, and they recorded four albums together. During a festival in the Isle of Man, where they spent some time with The Chieftains, he and Brenda went off for a picnic one day, and spent ages in a field working out the arrangements for 'The Mermaid' to record on the 'Boy Jan' album – which in the end weren't used, as she decided on a church organ accompaniment instead as more suitable.

He also accompanied her on her first trip to Australia in 1979. He recalls, at the end of an arduous 36-hour journey, coming into Adelaide airport, and looking down to see flocks of children on the runway... who they then discovered were there to welcome Brenda, all bearing armfuls of flowers. Apparently, the Irish community of Newcastle in New South Wales were most tickled when Brenda started talking about fairies... "you believe in fairies?" she was asked incredulously. "Well, course I do – don't you?" she replied. One of their 'gigs' was to record 'Humphry Davy' for the children on the School of the Air, and teach them all about his inventions and discoveries.

Dave remembered Brenda's superlative record-keeping. "She kept meticulous notebooks, where she would record everything that she performed, including any encores, and then if she returned to that venue, she would look back and check to make sure she could present a balanced programme the next time, with sufficient new material mixed in with the old favourites...". This data was also needed for her regular accounts to the Performing Rights Society, who required notification of every public performance of a song for copyright purposes. I think at the last count I have at least 30 of those notebooks, plus the petty cash books, the payment books for musicians' fees, the financial breakdown books for each gig, the records sales books, the address books for every contact...

In 1978 Dave accompanied Brenda in the 'War & Pieces' Show in Buckland Abbey for the Serenade 78 Festival. He left Brenda to work on his own projects in August 1980.

Unfortunately, after Dave, it was never again possible for her to be in a position to employ someone full-time on a regular basis, and over the next few years Brenda was sometimes compelled to use a number of different guitarists, dependent on who was likely to be available for a forthcoming tour.

By the early 1980s, she had added a few more to her 'stable' (apologies for my inefficient memories of some of these worthy folk – for a more complete list, look in the appendix):

- Alex Atterson, long-term mate and catalyst for Brenda and John starting to tour, played piano and guitar for Brenda when circumstances allowed
- Pete Berryman joined Brenda for some tours, principally to Brittany and the Lorient Festival
- Andy Dickson, whose sister ran a folk club in Worthing
- Steve Gordon – a tall chap, and a very competent guitarist
- Steve Hall – one-time resident at Pipers Folk Club, sometimes played for Brenda in the early days; now leads the Boilerhouse Singers
- David King, a classical guitarist, who can be seen accompanying her singing 'Lyonesse' on a BBC SW Spotlight programme[33], also recorded guitar backings for her on the Gwavas Lake album, and on Lyonesse
- John Knight, the recording engineer who worked on several of her albums, had become a great friend, and played backing guitar for her on a few recordings
- Mike Morgan, who I remember had black hair and beard, and I believe toured with her in France
- Mike Sagar-Fenton – a lifelong friend who had written several songs for Brenda, helped out on several occasions
- David Snell, who played the harp for her on a few occasions, including the World Travel Fair attended by Princess Diana
- Ashley Staton, a great jazz pianist, who adapted well to Brenda's material and played on several albums for her.

By 1983, Brenda had found a brilliant guitarist able to do the job reliably and with the skill and patience she needed – **Chris Newman**, and he was to become her longest-serving accompanist. Chris had experience of playing guitar in a wide range of genres, and could cope with most of Brenda's varied material comfortably, as well as

[33] *See Brenda website, video section*

the demands and rigours of working and touring with Brenda. He had his own career – and still does, a very successful one – but was able to take time out, if well planned in advance.

He did live a long way from Cornwall, in Yorkshire, so she usually tried to arrange tours that would make the travelling worth his while. From the history on his website, it is easy to see how they moved in the same circles:

> "Chris met the great swing guitarist and humourist Diz Disley in his late teens and played with him in folk clubs the length and breadth of the UK for a number of years. Diz was responsible for re-launching Stéphane Grappelli onto the world stage after a period of relative obscurity, and through him, Chris had the good fortune to play with Grappelli's band for a while...
>
> "He toured for six months with Clive's Original Band's solo project (COB, with Clive Palmer of the Incredible String Band), before moving to Bristol in 1973.
>
> "He soon involved himself in Bristol's musical life, becoming involved initially in the hugely-popular comedy band Pigsty Hill Light Orchestra and subsequently in a number of other outfits, including White on Black and a couple of his own projects, the wonderfully-named Overdraft and Fallen Arches. He became a regular on regional TV and radio, and presented BBC Radio Bristol's Folk Tempo programme for a period. In the midst of all this, he started working with folk comedian Fred Wedlock. Spotting the commercial potential of Fred's material, he applied his compositional, production and arrangement talents to it, thus launching Fred's career into the mainstream. Chris received a silver disc for producing Fred's 1981 hit The Oldest Swinger in Town – to which he also composed the tune and which reached No 2 in the charts in the UK and No 1 in several other countries. As Fred's Musical Director and bandleader, appearances on such iconic national TV programmes as BBC's Top of the Pops, Pebble Mill, Tiswas and That's Life, followed.
>
> "In the mid-1980s, Chris was bandleader and Musical Director for the French tours of Cornish singer Brenda Wootton – a big star in France though little-known at home. With her, he played on iconic national French TV programmes such as TF1's "Champs Élysées", in iconic venues such as the Paris Olympia and Théâtre de la Ville (where they regularly played sell-out three-night runs)

and at prestigious festivals such as the Printemps de Bourges. At this period, when he was spending almost six months of the year in France, he also got to know and perform with the revered Colette Magny and the even-more-revered and then-exiled Argentinian singer and activist, Mercedes Sosa."

Brenda on stage with Chris Newman

Chris plays on the albums 'My Land', 'B Comme Brenda' and 'Seagull', as well as the Australian single, and on the later CD brought out by John Knight from his Bobino recording: 'All Of Me'.

He sent me this lovely memory of Brenda, from a tour he did with her to France:

"I worked with Brenda off and on from 1980 until 1988. We spent most of that time touring in France, where she became extremely well-known, but I also had the opportunity to visit Australia (twice) and Canada too.

"She had an extremely sound fundamental understanding of her business. On French tours we'd play six concerts every week (Mondays were always days off) and this of course involved a considerable amount of travelling. Without fail, the morning after a show, she'd sit in the back of the car, or at a table in an airport coffee shop, and handwrite a personal letter to the organisers of the previous event thanking them for giving her the opportunity to play in whatever-town-it-was, and for arranging such a well-run event. Occasionally, of course, the event wasn't particularly well organised, but she'd write the letter anyway.

"She taught me a lot about how to deal with sound guys in such a way that they'd do a really good job. Our technical requirements were extremely simple: 2 microphones, one each for her voice and my guitar. Generally speaking it was pretty easy to balance the two channels but from time to time we'd come across some guy who couldn't resist fiddling with the settings as the show continued. This is one of the most irritating things that can happen as it's really easy to lose concentration as one's being distracted by altered volume levels etc.

"I remember one concert where the sound guy was constantly messing around with the settings, and at the end of each song, while the audience applauded, Brenda turned to me with a fixed grin on her face and implied she was going to murder the technician if this persisted. However, at the end of the show, she publicly thanked the organisers, me ('Monsieur l'Orchestre'), and then, to my absolute astonishment, the useless sound guy. 'Un grand merçi à Jean-Claude (or whatever his name was) pour le bon son ce soir.' I was amazed, as the guy had just done the worst job imaginable, so later I asked her why she'd gone out of her way to praise him. She replied, 'Well, you know, we might be back here again next year and have the same crew, and this means that *next* time he'll do a good job.'

"And she was right."

There were often accompanists of other musical persuasions, who stood in as session musicians on albums, or as members of a jazz combo when Brenda was in 'cabaret mode'... a reasonably comprehensive list is in the Appendices.

Her Albums...

In all, there were over 30 audio recordings published by or of Brenda, mostly LPs and a handful of singles, during her professional musical career – and they could all be generally expected to reflect a sample cross-section of her current programme as performed on stage. (Look in the Appendix for a full discography, and Brenda's website address, where you can find photos of front and back covers, samples, and in some cases, lyrics.)

The first album she appeared on, together with John the Fish, Des Hannigan and Mel and Miles, was **'More Singing at the Count House'**, produced by J Ian Todd in 1965. Once Pipers Folk Club had returned to the Count House from St Buryan, there was interest in producing another album, this time with just Brenda and Fish – but no money to fund it. Brenda took up Ian Todd's idea of asking for help from their loyal audience of regulars, and in 1968 a 'shared profit' scheme was announced (an early variation on Crowdfunding!), where individuals could buy 'shares' in the proposed album for £1 each, with a guaranteed return of 2/6 together with their stake money after a certain interval. The scheme was enthusiastically taken up, and a very staid gentleman recording engineer from Stourbridge came down and recorded a live session of the folk club, with several retakes. A few songs were also recorded at a riotous evening in the Newlyn Meadery, with Pipers' fans in attendance – the audience was very patient, and, as '**Pipers Folk**', provided the name of the album they had participated in. In a very short time, sufficient albums had been sold to repay all the investors.

Three years later in 1971 came '**Pasties and Cream**', again featuring Brenda and Fish... by this time the club had made sufficient impact on the local music scene for the album to be produced by Job Morris of Sentinel Records, based in Riverside Studios in Newlyn. Mike Sagar-Fenton recalls that part of the recording was again done in the Newlyn Meadery. The 'audience' included a party from Bedminster Down Boys Club, (huge Pipers fans), and members of Madron Young Farmers – and Job and his equipment were sited in another room. Brenda, not being as familiar with the recording process at this stage, forgot that her microphone was open throughout the proceedings, and Mike, who was sitting close by, could hear her audibly complaining between takes about some aspects of the recording. Suddenly Job's voice came over the loudspeakers: "I'm doing the best I can, Brenda!".

Brenda spent some time setting up the cover photo for this in the kitchen of a Mrs Hitchens in Trewarveneth Street in Newlyn – close to where Brenda herself had lived as a young girl. (Amazingly I recently happened upon Mrs Hitchens granddaughter, who turns out to have taught Davy in primary school – small world, idna?) Brenda accessorised it to look exactly as she remembered, with the nostalgic feel of the kitchens of old Cornish families worldwide. Obviously, it had to have a proper Cornish range, with the china dogs on the mantelpiece above and the pinny (or 'apernt') hanging on the door. The table was properly set with a blue and white gingham tablecloth, the old 'brown betty' teapot and patchwork tea-cosy, my gran's cut glass pedestal sugar bowl, the old-style Cornishman (it had recently changed format to a more modern tabloid with photos on the front, which was, of course, unacceptable – so an earlier version had to be found) propped up ready to read, and the cup of hot sweet tea ready to drink with, of course, the home-made pasty... which apparently was later eaten and enjoyed by Geoff March of Decameron!

Both her earlier albums had used existing material, old folk songs or favourite tunes from Cornwall known to many locally, so this was the first time she had used 'new' material, with 'To the Sea' from guitarist Steve Hall, and two numbers of her own devising: 'Something About a Pasty' and the 'Cornish Alphabet'.

By 1972, Brenda had been introduced to Cornish language expert Richard Gendall, as a result of being invited to represent Cornwall at the Pan Celtic Music Festival in Killarney in Ireland, and her next album, '**Crowdy Crawn'** – another from Sentinel Records – reflected this new interest. In a departure from her previous albums, she and Richard performed, with Richard strumming on the guitar and sometimes accompanying Brenda on a song, or speaking verse. Many of the numbers were actually in the Cornish language, all written by Richard or traditional, and it may have been the first time the Cornish language was heard recorded. The artwork on the cover was again Peter's design, presented as an illuminated manuscript. Irene Morris, Job's wife, explains on the sleeve notes that the album was intended as a 'Cornish sampler', and all the words, those in Cornish with English translations, are printed on the inner sleeve.

Here is what Cornish poet Charles Causley had to say when Brenda sent him a copy of the album:

"Dear Brenda, that was very kind of you to send me a copy of the splendid Crowdy Crawn. What a record! Beautifully performed, and entirely original in concept. Only you and Richard could have made it just what it is. I'm full of admiration.

"One thing that's an extra delight is the echo of the true Cornish accent (as one hears it in ordinary spoken English) that inhabits, with a marvellous authenticity, the speech and the song here in Cornish. One can see the link, the connection: something so simple, yet so profoundly moving.

"I've just done an anthology of magic verse (for children), and wish I had known of Hus Gans Mynfel: it would have fitted in perfectly. The record is so fine, that it's invidious to pick out single items, though: I like them all! Thanks again... Shalom! Yours, Charles Causley"

A year later, and Brenda had turned professional as a singer with guitarist Robert Bartlett as the duo Crowdy Crawn, and her head was full of new and exciting musical possibilities. **'No Sing to Sing'** was a result of this happy collaboration, and was a more exhilarating and challenging collection of tunes than previously. Robert played guitar and concertina and sang, and there was tremendous support from a gaggle of musician friends. To see how Brenda felt about Robert at this stage, just look at her face on the very 'hippified' cover picture.

That same year, Brenda and Robert were invited to Brittany to sing in the festival at Kertalg near Moelan-sur-Mer by Gwenn Le Goarnig. Gwenn encouraged them to record their next album, **'Pamplemousse'**, and it was produced by Barclay in France under the Kertalg name. Pamplemousse is French for Grapefruit, one of the tracks on the album, and Brenda, perhaps ill-advisedly, made herself a voluminous grapefruit yellow dress for the cover. The financial arrangements were precarious to say the least, and the album was also produced under a different cover and without the 'Pamplemousse' name, and as a promo single with the track '**Grapefruit**' backed by 'Mordonnow'. Gwenn also produced an album of all the artists performing at the Festival in 1974, titled '**Kertalg 74 – Pop Celtic et Folk International**', which included one pirated track of Brenda's: 'A Good Man is Hard to Find', again with Barclay under the Kertalg label. The other artists on this album included Dick Gaughan, The Boys of the Lough, Robin & Barry Dransfield, Martin Carthy and The Watersons.

In 1975 **'Starry Gazey Pie'** was produced back home with Sentinel Records again – Brenda and Robert's third album together. The cover features a sepia Francis Frith photo of Vine Cottages in Boase Street in Newlyn, Brenda's childhood home. By this time, Brenda and Robert were touring extensively on the Continent, and spending a lot of time in Germany. Their final album as a duo, **'Tin in the Stream'**, was produced by the German recording company, Stockfisch Records – once again, Brenda is gazing adoringly at Robert on the front cover.

In 1976 Brenda responded to a long-held desire of Irene Morris of Sentinel Records to produce an album with Cornish school-children singing about Cornish heroes, legends and traditions. All the songs are written by Richard Gendall, and the album **'Children Singing'** features the voices of 80 children from three local schools: Ludgvan, Alverton and St Mary's RCP in Penzance. The cover drawing was done by one of the pupils at Alverton School; Al Fenn from Decameron was the guitarist.

Brenda's next album, **'Carillon'** (Bells) was produced by Transatlantic Records in 1979. Most of the songs are again by Richard, but there is a lovely selection from Ewen Carruthers and one from Mike Silver – Dave Penhale is the guitarist. John Bidwell's gentle '**Apple Wine**' from the album was released as a promo single, with 'Silver Net' on the flip side.

Brenda then took up with Burlington Records, run by John Garrad and Nigel Pegrum and based at their Plant Life Studios in Hitchin in Hertfordshire. Nigel Pegrum, who had also produced 'Carillon', had been a member of Steeleye Span for 17 years before becoming a producer. Three Burlington albums were produced in one year in 1980. The first, **'Boy Jan...Cornishman'**, with Dave Penhale as guitarist, was probably the first album where Brenda had had quite so much control over the sleeve and the production – she packed everything in, but you do need a magnifying glass to read the sleeve notes. The wistful title track was written as a love song for my son Jan Luscombe. Brenda used a grid of black and white photographs on the front cover to illustrate the theme of each track... the line drawings were once again done by Peter. I am there as a sweet little girl at bottom left, to illustrate Mike Silver's beautiful 'Loving Eyes', and my son Davy is at bottom right, for Richard's gentle lullaby 'Pensevyk Beghan' (Little Prince), written for Davy at Brenda's request when he was born.

Brenda in full cry, with Dave Penhale on the roof of Théâtre de la Ville in Paris

Burlington's next project was '**La Grande Cornouaillaise**' – The Great Cornishwoman – produced very much for the French market, and again with Dave Penhale. Most of the songs are in French, one in Breton and three in English, all with translations. The dramatic cover photo was taken on the roof of the Théâtre de la Ville in Paris.

The final Burlington album was supposed to be the first of several 'themed' albums, although the others (on mining, famous Cornish characters, etc) never materialised. '**Gwavas Lake**' contained songs exclusively about the sea and fishing, and has the famous Newlyn School painting 'Fish Sale on a Cornish Beach' by Stanhope Forbes on the front cover. It was timed to coincide with the 400th Anniversary of the completion of Sir Francis Drake's famous voyage around the world in 1580. The tracks were all Richard's, apart from Mike Sagar-Fenton's moving 'The Lifeboat', and a powerful poem by Charles Causley, set to music by Alex Atterson – 'The Bristol Christ'. Dave Penhale and Four Lanes Choir accompany.

Brenda then recorded four albums with engineer John Knight at his studio near the Lizard – a multi-track recording studio in a derelict RAF radar bunker on the edge of Goonhilly Downs, where he recorded and engineered local bands and choirs. I'll let his wife Gloria pick up the story:

> "Following on from the Sentinel and Burlington recordings, and as Brenda's career was evolving beyond folk music, her love of jazz and blues meant that she really needed the kind of musicians and studio that could help take her on the next step of her

musical journey – so Brenda contacted John Knight, who had a recording studio at Trelan, down on the Lizard. In the '70s, John played guitar in an uber-cool, jazz-funk band, 'Matrix', and in Cornwall, where everyone knew what everyone else was up to, news travelled along the grapevine that John might be available. He wasn't playing professionally at this time as he was concentrating on recording bands and musicians in his studio, a disused wartime radar bunker. John and Brenda knew each other and John had 'sat in' with Brenda on occasions.

"From 1982, they commenced a musical relationship that lasted almost a decade. Brenda and John's collaboration cemented a platform for an outstanding collection of recordings. They co-produced four albums and a number of singles. Both perfectionists with a shared creativity and vision, each brought their individual skills to the production. Brenda's voice and arrangements added to John's engineering and production dexterity, and their mutual respect and shared musicality culminated in a collection of first-class albums.

"The first album John produced with Brenda was **'Lyonesse'**, in 1982, when she was signed with RCA France. Most of the tracks are beautiful, haunting melodies written by Cornishman, Richard Gendall. However, the running order indicates Brenda's transition from folk into jazz and blues with arrangements of 'Autumn Leaves' and even, 'Honky Tonk Woman'. Her guitarist Dave Penhale recorded with her, with additional session musicians including Dave King on classical acoustic guitar, who also arranged some of the songs. Camborne Town Band feature on a couple of the tracks.

"John has some unforgettable recollections of studio time spent with Brenda. Brenda and her husband John were every inch a team. He took care of her. While she was working in the studio, he would fill in his time sitting in the car, either having a snooze or preparing her Radio Cornwall Show, 'Sunday Best'. This was a very popular request programme and 'Mr. Wootie' worked on the running order ahead of the broadcast. Brenda was a homely lady and they didn't travel without a picnic basket of goodies... buns, pasties and sandwiches filled with boiled egg and sandwich spread, plenty for themselves and any hungry musician that had missed his breakfast."

Sue: 'Lyonesse' was somewhat of a new departure for Brenda. Although the majority of the tracks were once again Richard's, she certainly demonstrated her versatility by including the haunting John Sebastian number 'The Room Nobody Lives In', and in particular, 'House of the Rising Sun' and both a Beatles and a Rolling Stones track. And she sings 'September Song' and 'Autumn Leaves' better than anyone else I've heard... gives me goosebumps every time. The front cover photo was taken on the cliffs at Land's End with a misty Longships lighthouse in the distance; sleeve-notes for both the RCA albums are in French.

Gloria: "However, once working, Brenda took on her professional persona and she knew exactly what she wanted for each track. In the case of 'Silver Net', recorded for their next collaborative effort, '**My Land**' in 1983, that was an ethereal effect with a violin string section. There was no budget for a string section, and little prospect of finding such a thing, and this was back in the dark ages before synthesisers sampled sounds. Violinist Sally Holmes was on the studio session, and John had an idea. He asked Sally to record every note on the violin for a few seconds, and then he wrote an arrangement and copied every note needed, one at a time, onto the multi-track machine, in four parts – and the final result was Brenda's 'string section'. Happy days!

"Again recorded for RCA France, the balance of the material on 'My Land' tipped more towards jazz and blues. Brenda used a number of the best jazz musicians in Cornwall: Ashley Staton, Ray Roberts, Phil King, Mike Higgs, Cass Caswell and Bob Crooks, in addition to her brilliant regular guitarist, Chris Newman; Treviscoe Male Voice Choir also featured. The album included a personal favourite, Richard Gendall's 'Silver Net', alongside good-time swing numbers, 'All of Me', 'Ain't She Sweet' and 'Summertime'. Retrospectively, I can see what a clever move this was on Brenda's part as the content of the album is a 'catch-all' for her international market... plenty of jazz standards, yet still retaining her Cornish roots. This album was distributed in Belgium, France, Germany, Italy, Holland and the UK."

Sue: 'My Land' has a great mix of material from Richard, Mike Silver and Ewen Carruthers, together with traditional blues and swing numbers – but just listen to her version of Gershwin's 'Summertime' – breathtaking. Trevor Nunn described this classic Gershwin song as 'plangent'... which it most certainly is, and I've not heard a finer version than Brenda's. The front cover photograph was taken in Morrab Gardens in Penzance, and you can't miss the beautiful silver and amethyst triskele brooch she always wore. The back cover features my lads, looking angelic in their Cornish tartan kilts with their Damawyn down on Mousehole Pier. 'Dus Tre' and 'Paris' from My Land were released separately as a promo single.

In 1983 John Knight took his recording equipment down to St John's Church in Penzance to record a single for Brenda, produced again for RCA France. '**The Christmas single**' featured Mousehole Male Voice Choir and Camborne Town Band performing the much-loved Cornish carol by Thomas Merritt: 'Hark the Glad Sound' and the beautiful 'Softly, Sweetly, Thro' the Air' – originally written by an American woman in the late 19th century, but which somehow became firmly entrenched in our West Cornwall family. Brenda wanted a traditional Christmas scene on the cover, and took my boys up to the Engine Inn at Nancledra for the photo shoot. They posed in front of a blazing fire wearing suitably Christmassy thick woolly jumpers, and standing beside a Christmas tree – on the hottest July day we'd had for some time. No wonder Jan looks a bit flushed. But how I wish they'd gone on to produce the full Christmas themed album Brenda had always planned. (We have since remedied the situation, and in December 2017, were able to bring out a re-sampled '**Brenda at Christmas** CD'.)

Sentinel Records brought out a compilation album in 1984, titled '**Way Down To Lamorna**'. It featured 16 of the 'most popular' tracks from Brenda's first five Sentinel LPs: 'Pasties & Cream', 'Crowdy Crawn', 'Children Singing', 'Starry Gazey Pie', and 'No Song to Sing'.

In 1981 Brenda had asked Richard Gendall to write a special song for her forthcoming tour of Australia, for the 3rd Kernewek Lowender Festival in Kadina. He wrote 'Moonta, Wallaroo, Kadina', the names of the three towns in the 'Cornish Triangle' west of Adelaide, where the bi-annual festival took place. When she was planning her next Australian tour in 1985, Richard came up with 'Cornish Australian (Just Like Me)' for all the Cornish in exile in Oz, so Brenda decided to produce both together as a '*Cornish Australian*' **single**. This was entirely devised as a personal project by Brenda, funded by her, and recorded by John Knight, who also played guitar synthesiser. Brenda's guitarist Chris Newman also played guitar on the tracks, and she used the Perran Harmony Singers and a group of children from

Ludgvan School (including Davy and Jan!) as backing. The lyrics are on the cover, and she even enclosed an inner sleeve with information about all those involved: the musicians, the singers, Ludgvan School, John Knight's studio, Richard – even Humphry Davy and St Perran!

> Gloria: "In 1985 John recorded **'B Comme Brenda'**, the third album he'd worked on with her, produced for another French label, Disc'AZ. By now, her international reputation was established and Brenda's French agent Olivier Gluzman promoted every album on TV, radio and in live concert tours. The album, an almost whimsical blend of tender ballads, bawdy blues and hymns, included ' Once In A While', 'Oh Holy Lord' and 'Nobody Loves a Fat Girl', and if that's not avoiding being typecast, I don't know what is."

Sue: One of my personal favourites amongst Brenda's albums, 'B Comme Brenda' used a novel concept for the sleeve design. The title loosely translates as ''B' like Brenda', and she gave each track a single French word beginning with 'B' as an explanation: Bénédiction, Brel, Ballade, Beautemps, Bientôt (Soon), Bascule, Belle Grâce, Belmondo, Bistrôt, Burlesque, and Boeuf. Briefly: most are self-explanatory, but 'beautemps' is 'good weather', 'bascule' is a balance, there is a Jacques Brel song, and a tribute to Jean-Paul Belmondo, Belle Grâce is 'fine, thanks', and 'boeuf' in this context is to have a jam, or be a great success. The back cover features Brenda in three similar poses (photos taken by John Knight), to demonstrate that she multi-tracks five times as her own backing group, credited on the sleeve notes as 'The Woottontots'. Camborne Town Band also features on this recording, as well as a group of jazz musicians. 'Once in a While', in English and French, does it for me on this album.

> Gloria: "Brenda's next album '**Tamar**' was remixed in 1986 using previously recorded tracks and was a return to her Cornish roots. An ambassador singing the songs of her beloved country, with her performer's confidence not to conform but to stand in front of an audience and say, 'This is who I am'. Whether singing in the ancient Cornish language, French or traditional songs sung in pubs since Cornishmen first gathered round a pint, the significance of the sea is always lapping at her heart. 'Tamar', 'I Wish I were Crossing Now', 'Waiting for the Tide; all wistful, evocative songs of her homeland. This album for me, sums up Brenda the woman; I can imagine her tired from the journey, alone in a hotel room before going on stage; waiting for the adrenaline

rush to pump her through the next performance. Her bardic name, Gwylan Gwavas (Newlyn Seagull) is encapsulated in the track, 'Gwavas Lake'."

Sue: Her next album was the maxi-single with Brenda's own lyrics on '**Everybody Knows**', backed by 'Walk Across the World', with music by celebrated French songwriter Francis Lai and recorded in Paris. I have described this in full under the section on France. Once again, John Knight took the atmospheric cover photo.

Sometime in the late 1980s Brenda and John the Fish reunited for a charity concert in the Penventon Hotel in Redruth. The cause was one dear to John and Carrie's hearts, the SIDS charity (Sudden Infant Death Syndrome), now renamed The Lullaby Trust. The concert, which featured many of their fans' old favourites, was recorded by Chris Blount's Chough Tapes and produced as an audio cassette called '**So Long**', and sold to make money for the charity.

Brenda was finishing work on her final album, 'Sailing Gulls', in 1989, when she had a stroke, and was unable to complete the final mixing. Once Olivier, her French agent, realised she would not be able to do any promotion tours, any further work on it was dropped, and it was released as it was, very quietly, under the title '**Seagull**' for the Vogue label some months later. Such a pity she wasn't able to do it full justice, as there were some interesting new tracks on there: 'Cornwall', the song contributed by Tom Kolinsky, which she had adapted, and 'The Shadow of Your Smile', which I particularly like.

The French recording company Le Chante du Monde recorded four lullabies with Brenda in the late eighties which were used on both a four-track EP and a full album, with other performers, later. The EP, **'Berceuses Celtes des Isles Britanniques**' (Celtic Lullabies of the British Isles) had Brenda singing a traditional lullaby from four of the Celtic countries in Britain: Cornwall, Wales, the Isle of Man and Scotland. It is a remarkable record due mainly to its extremely lavish sleeve, which was created as a colourful pop-up book cover with seals and a mermaid. Three of the four tracks (excluding the Scottish one) were used on an even more lavish LP album, '**Berceuses du Monde Entier**' (Lullabies of the Entire World). The cover when opened reveals a whimsical full-colour 3D pop-up scene of a girl asleep in bed surrounded by her toys, with a gigantic clockwork bird outside her window. As well as Brenda's contributions, there are Jewish and Russian lullabies, Berceuses Noires (black lullabies), and three from France, sung by Brenda's friend, French chanteuse Colette Magny.

Other recordings surfaced after she died. In 1996 Keltia Music in Brittany (run by Bob Brimley, formerly of Brio Music in Cornwall, who had bought out the Sentinel Music catalogue) released a CD titled '**The Voice of Cornwall**', which was virtually a straight copy of Sentinel's compilation 'Way Down To Lamorna', with a few more of Sentinel's tracks added. It was later released in France as 'La Grande Cornouaillaise' (they'd obviously failed to notice there was already an album of that name), its only real virtue being its CD format – most people can't play vinyl any more. I have recently come across a recording apparently being offered by Amazon in Australia on a 'print on demand' basis, which has just four unlisted tracks. I have no idea what they are, and I can't seem to track it down.

A much more welcome CD released in 2010 was '**All of Me**', John Knight's wonderful recording done in the Bobino Theatre in 1984 – again, the story is told elsewhere in this book, but it is a marvellous memory of a live concert when Brenda was at the height of her musical career.

Finally – I will always be grateful to Mike Gluyas for the gift of his excellent recordings taken of Brenda in Pipers Folk Club at St Buryan in the late 1960s, which I was able to bring out on a CD as '**Brenda at Buryan**', in 2013. For more information, look in 'Brenda's Legacy...'.

There are a few more random recordings around – not least, Dennis Clixby's tapes recorded over many years at Pipers – and I have, as explained, now produced a '**Brenda at Christmas**' album in 2017, taken from some seasonal tracks from earlier records with some new Christmas-related tracks added.

For most of those 30+ recordings listed above, Brenda took a very 'hands-on' approach to both the musical arrangement and the cover design of her albums. She was a perfectionist who was almost always her own arranger, and she planned out the various parts for voice or instrument carefully. She spent much time studying photographs and planning design and layout. Brother Peter designed the artwork for two of the earlier albums, Pipers Folk and Crowdy Crawn, and she used a succession of excellent local photographers for promotion shots: Ander Gunn, Abed Shah, David Hills and many others. If at all possible she determined that the lyrics should be included, sometimes on an inner printed sleeve, or if not, on the back cover –

although these are sometimes almost too small to read. She ensured that everyone who had contributed had a mention on the cover, and that anything in the Cornish (or French) language was translated or explained – and every track always had a small paragraph of explanation. Sadly, none of this detailed preparation she had done for 'Seagull' was used, and all information on the musicians and technical detail is missing.

Each album is a snapshot into the life of a remarkable woman, taken at different times. I am grateful to have them.

Brittany – La Marraine des Celtes

In August 1971, Brenda had her first foreign booking – at the Lorient Festival, with John the Fish. The die was cast, and Brenda's lifelong love affair with Brittany had begun. Two years later, she had another engagement in Brittany at Kertalg, a large old chateau in Morbihan, not far from Lorient. The chateau was owned by the Le Goarnigs, an old Breton family. The daughter, Gwenn, had arranged a folk festival in Moelan-sur-Mer, including some big names in the folk world: Planxty, Robin Dransfield, and Happy Traum, and from Brittany, Celtic legend Allan Stivell and the remarkable Soeurs Goadec, amongst others. Brenda did the festival with Dik Cadbury, and was to meet Breton musicians Allan Stivell, René Werneer and Dan ar Bras, all of whom she later worked with.

Brenda and Dik rehearsing with René Werneer at Kertalg Festival

Brenda and Dik on stage at Kertalg

I love this photo of her wearing an enormous black and white Cornish flag as a cloak on the festival stage – an early indicator of her determination to take Cornwall to the world. The festival was a great success, with 15,000 attending. Brenda wrote of it in Folk Review:

> "Planxty were late arriving, and there was no-one on stage, so an instant group was formed. Two of Stivell's band, Broken Consort, Robin Dransfield, Dik and I belted out 'Martin said to his man', and took all the fear out of our 'official' set later on.... Dik and I were very lucky. The sun was shining, the crowd was all warmed up, and they received the Cornish songs with gusto; but then I stepped aside into the blues with 'Broke Down Gal', thus nearly getting raped by an over-enthusiastic Breton. It was nice... but with all those people watching?"[34]

Brenda singing at Kertalg

Brenda related to the Bretons as her Celtic cousins right from the start, and to Brittany as a sister country to Cornwall – so Brittany was naturally 'family' to her, and obviously she to them, as she became known there as La Marraine des Celtes – The Godmother of the Celts.

---

[34] *Folk Review, September 1973*

On her first arrival on the ferry at Roscoff, she visited a restaurant above the harbour beach and met Mamique – a wonderfully colourful character, who became a loyal fan and a huge friend for years. Mamique's husband had been killed working for the French Resistance during the war, and a grateful French government had presented his widow with Le Blokhaus – an old German blockhouse by the harbour – as a very bizarre compensation gift. Mamique and her daughter Soazig ran the restaurant. Dave Penhale recalls that if customers were believed to be German, Mamique would secretly spit in their dinner before serving it. However, she was always thrilled to see Brenda arrive, making a big fuss of her, and we had many memorable evenings with her there, Brenda usually singing for her too.

Brenda with Praze Male Choir singing in Mamique's restaurant in Roscoff ferryport

Mamique serving lobster bisque in Brenda's house, with her daughters and Richard Gendall

She and her daughter came over to stay with Brenda in Penzance for a holiday in the mid-70s, and she made an amazing Lobster Bisque in Brenda's kitchen. She later sold Le Blokhaus and bought a fancy new eatery on the hill above the ferryport, impossible to miss on the right as you leave the port – I believe her daughter may still run it.

Food is definitely a big issue with Bretons – especially seafood... they do it so well, eating everything edible that comes out of the sea. I really don't know why we are so squeamish on this side of the Channel. There is a small town on the Atlantic coast called Le Guilvinec, a fishing village the Breton equivalent of Newlyn. In Le Guilvinec was a bar called Le Pub, run by an adorable guy called George Gloagen. George (pronounced 'shorsh') was maybe in his 50s when we knew him; tall and rangy with a wry sense of humour, he always wore slippers as he had damaged his feet playing football in his youth – now he was reduced to playing only boules or petanque. We called him, at his request, Georges Le Roi – George the King.

Georges Gloagen – 'Georges Le Roi'

Le Pub had a glass showcase on the wall outside, containing a bowler hat, rolled umbrella and a briefcase – George's little joke, for presenting an 'English Pub'; he had brightly coloured t-shirts made for staff and customers with the same motifs. Le Pub was open at 4am every morning (it only ever closed at all if there was an important football game on TV), and on the counter would be a long row of shot glasses each filled with red wine, all ready for the fishermen as they came off the boats in the dark before the dawn – to take the chill off. George booked Brenda to sing in Le Pub many times, and we would stay upstairs in his flat above the bar – the windows looked over a courtyard containing a huge fig tree. The night would be so packed, the wildly appreciative audience sitting cross-legged on the floor left little room to move.

George was a fantastic cook, and one day he decided to make us a 7-course banquet. We went with him in the morning to the fish market on the docks, where every kind of fish and shellfish was being offered from large wooden barrels… weather-worn men with lined brown faces, and women in shawls, knife in one hand, oyster in the other, offering us a free sample. Each of those seven courses turned out to be fish. From memory, we had spider crab legs, langoustine and fruits de mer ('fruits of the sea') on a bed of ice and seaweed, queens (small seashells, for which you needed a pin), shore crab legs (for which you needed a hammer), raw oysters, la lotte (monkfish), and a huge and bubbling fish stew.

The guitarist accompanying Brenda on that trip was effectively 'on trial' following Mike Silver's departure. The following morning we all set off in her VW camper for the next gig, 250 miles away. We discussed the amazing meal of the night before, and the words 'raw oysters' were mentioned. The guitarist demurred: no no, the oysters were cooked, he insisted. We assured him that they were, in fact, raw… and when he finally accepted that we weren't lying, his face instantly changed colour – sort of an ombre effect, shading to green from the bottom up. We had to stop the van immediately for him to be violently sick by the roadside. He'd shown no ill effects at all up to that point. Shame.

Brenda made friends all over Brittany – everywhere she went, she amassed a network of friends and fans that would happily offer her and her troupe (at the very least, Brenda, guitarist, and a roadie) a bed for the night. The only difficulty with this was that she would feel compelled to sit up till the early hours drinking wine and being sociable, which would leave her drained for the next day.

She made long-term friends with Breton musicians Dan Ar Braz, René Werneer, Pascal Stive and Gweltaz Ar Fur – fine musicians all – and they sometimes performed with her at Breton gigs or sat in on some of the recordings for an album. For many years, until quite recently, Gweltaz ran Brittany's best music shop in Quimper, as well as performing. (I re-encountered Dan ar Braz on a recent return trip to Lorient Festival, where we joined the queue of fans

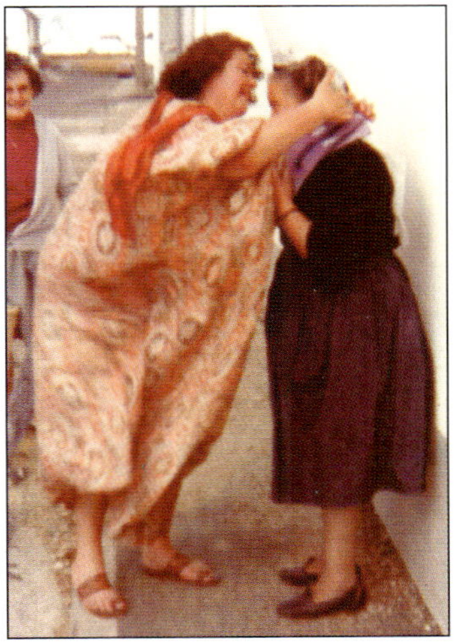

Brenda adjusting the 'coif' of a Breton lady

waiting for him to sign their CDs... unfortunately, when I introduced myself to him, I was so overcome with emotion on seeing him again I must have appeared a total fool. It was probably 30 years since I had last seen him – and always in the company of Brenda, of course.)

Sue and Dan ar Braz at Lorient

But her warmth and generosity won over not just musicians – she made long-term friendships with many 'ordinary' fans she met on her travels. Here is an extract from a letter from a Cornish couple, written to Radio Cornwall in 1989, with whom they had taken a short coach trip to Brittany for a break:

> "Two very lonely people, my wife and I, were sat in a café in Quimper, wondering what to do with ourselves in the few hours before we had to meet our coach. A couple entered the café, John and Brenda Wootton – we started chatting, and from then on, they both took over – and what we anticipated would be a dull few hours, turned out to be a great morning out for both of us.
>
> "Brenda with her knowledge of French helped us out enormously, so instead of us struggling to make ourselves understood, we had a morning to remember. Neither my wife or I will ever forget the taxi ride – we thought we would never get back to our coaches, as we did a complete tour of Quimper, with Brenda explaining to the driver the place where the coaches were parked..."

Wherever Brenda appeared abroad, she said Cornish people would appear 'out of the woodwork'. Meeting Cornish exiles abroad was something that delighted both her and them... they loved to hear again the warm Cornish dialect so far from home, and she reports one saying to her: "Keep on talkin', maid – your voice is like a pound of cream". John Farndon of Falmouth wrote to tell her "I was at Concarneau on October 4th, and found you hanging from every lamp-post!"

Lorient Festival – La Grand-mère du Fête

Brenda was a guest at the first ever Lorient Festival in 1971, together with John the Fish, with Alain Stivell and The Dubliners on the same bill – and she was an immediate and enormous success; so began a long love affair between Brenda and the festival. She returned there in 1973 with Dik Cadbury, in 1974 with Robert Bartlett, and on other occasions with Pete Berryman, Steve Gordon, Chris Newman and others – frequently also with Cornish choirs. Apart from Brenda herself, Cornwall as a Celtic nation was only represented in a small way on their first official year as a delegation, in 1978, with organiser Betty Pitman from Perranporth taking over a group of about a dozen or so. The pioneering Cornish dance group Bucca, with the Davey brothers and Morwenna Jenkin, were part of that vanguard, and Brenda was once again booked for the Festival. She decided that Cornwall's profile at this Inter-Celtic shindig was in no way high enough, so she proposed to the Festival committee that her daughter, one Sue Luscombe (as I then was), should be taken on as the Delegate (Coordinator) for Cornwall. Thanks, Brenda.

No, really... thanks. I loved it, although it was a killer. That first year, 1979, I think I took over a team of about 40 participants from Cornwall, but within a couple of years the numbers had swelled to around 140. The Cornish contingent at that time, in the early 1980s, included choirs, bands, dance groups, musicians, artists and craftsmen and sportsmen. At different times, as well as all the musicians and dancers, we had Cornish tennis players, darts players, gig rowers, chess players, and once an entire Tug of War team from Launceston to take part in the Celtic Games. In 1981 I had organised a Celtic Sports Day in St Ives to select potential sportsmen from Cornwall to take part in Lorient's Celtic Games the following year – the winning team, from South Petherwin near Launceston, were a lovely bunch of lads and did a smashing job, but couldn't compete with the huge

Scottish and Breton caber tossers, and in specialist Celtic sports they'd never before encountered – such as lifting a cart-axle, running with a heavy sack of grain, and the mysteriously named (and potentially dangerous) 'porridge stick'.

Betty Pitman & Bucca at Lorient in 1978

The logistics for such trips were harrowing: I found that in order to prepare adequately for the next year's festival, I had to begin working on the arrangements from the minute I got back from this year's... visiting summer arts and crafts festivals to select and commission items for the following years exhibition in Lorient, and selecting and contacting potential performers before they became too booked up. The paperwork for Customs and Excise alone was a nightmare.

Over time Lorient became so big that it ran (and still runs) for 10 full days, and included thousands of performers. The Breton contingent alone – the largest, of course, by far – was several thousand strong, for as well as their top performers and musicians, every small village in Brittany sent their own pipe band with bombards and binious, and dance groups in full costume. An important part of the festival were the parades, the biggest, on the first Sunday usually, when the pipe bands and dance teams from every country involved paraded throughout the town, ending up in the huge Parc du Moustoir stadium. Especially fascinating were the fiercely proud Breton family groups, often led by the toddlers; the groups included grandmothers, schoolchildren and babies in antique prams, all wearing their uniquely and exquisitely hand-embroidered outfits, the women and girls in their ornate white lace bigouden or coif headdresses, the exquisite designs unique to each town – and the fathers bringing up the rear, raising aloft their town's huge flag, heads held high, striding forward with piercing eyes and backs ramrod straight.

Every year for four years I took over a fantastic collection of selected artwork and craft items from Cornish artists, usually worth up to £50,000 or more in total value, to be used as part of a full exhibition in a huge marquee set up for that purpose in the town centre. Each country had their own gallery space, and could fill it with their nation's best art, for exhibition and for sale – subject to the approval of Exhibition organisers Jean-Yves and Rosenn Dubois. I fell foul of Jean-Yves one year, when I took over two spectacular and huge paintings of Nubian heads – vivid and dramatic, photo-realist, larger-than-life giant portraits of the heads of native tribesmen in costume, by Cornish artist Colin Scott – let's just say I had to fight to get permission to mount them; I was amazed by the organisers' intolerance of the subject matter, something I'd never before experienced.

Each year we were able to take over volunteer 'staff' to man our space. One year the artist Ken Symonds and his wife Jane from Newlyn came with us, another year it was Cornish potter Jason Wason and his family, or Leach potter Nic Harrison and his talented weaver wife, Jackie. The trials and tribulations involved with the customs in both countries for all this artwork were many and various. That first year, 1979, when I was pregnant with Jan, our boat arrived late at night, and the Bretons wouldn't let the goods into the country until the relevant staff to check our cargo had arrived the following morning; I was not about to leave all that valuable artwork unattended, and so myself (pregnant, remember), my family and all the artwork were stranded on the dock overnight. Ensuring a bed on the ferry to Roscoff was always a challenge – so many wanted to travel at the same time. One year I had to share a tiny 2-berth cabin down in the bilges with Brenda's guitarist Pete Berryman and Neil Plummer from Stithians Male Choir – I can't remember who slept on the floor, but it wasn't me.

The entire town of Lorient – about the same size and feel as Plymouth, having been bombed in the war and largely rebuilt – is taken over for the festival. If you're not a fan of bagpipes, stay away

– loudspeakers on every street corner belt out the strident sounds of pipe bands and Celtic music from all the nations all day and most of the night – actually, no – all night and most of the day: early mornings were mercifully peaceful while everyone recovered.

The Celtic nations: Brittany, Scotland, Ireland, Cornwall, Wales, the Isle of Man, and Galicia and Asturias in northern Spain – together with a few other random pockets of Celts worldwide – send delegations to Lorient every year; it is by far the biggest Celtic gathering globally.

Sue with the delegates from the other Celtic countries in Lorient

It was a huge privilege to be the Delegate for Cornwall, but a huge headache also, especially as the time for the festival neared when the sense of growing mild panic would mount to downright frantic fever-pitch. From the start I had had Davy with me as a toddler of course, and once my son Jan was born in January 1980 things became even more fraught.

Being in charge of a group of 140 Cornish people away from their homes for 10 days or more, travelling on coaches and sleeping in school dormitories, together with the assorted performances throughout that time for which I was responsible, was more than a fulltime commitment for me. I was Mother Hen. I carried a 'stage manager's' box everywhere (a hangover from Brenda's amdram days) with anything I felt I might be called on to produce instantly, which could include everything from scissors and sellotape to a French dictionary, local maps and even ladies sanitary accoutrements. And most of it would be needed, at some point...

Brenda singing with Terry Broad's Four-Fifths Jug Band and an octet from Carnon Vale Male Voice choir in the exhibition marquee at Lorient, 1980

The Cornish, generally, lapped up the whole experience. John Robert King, in an article in Cornish Life in 1980, reported "they soon worked out 'Right on, my bird' as 'Droit sur, mon oiseau'... and delighted in the confusion it caused" – especially when spoken with a broad Cornish accent. The Carnon Vale Octet, he says, had two impromptu moments of glory... the first when they got their heads together outside the Palais des Congrès and sang for nobody except themselves and the enthralled passers-by... the second, when an enthusiastic Breton spectator passed down a bottle of wine from his first floor window with approving and respectful nods towards the Cornish flag."[35]

Brenda was booked at Lorient for every one of my four years stint as Cornish delegate, and several times since. We loved it. The atmosphere was exciting, warm and vibrant, and the people – organisers, performers and punters – all adored Brenda. She became known as La Grand-mère du Fête, Grandmother of the Festival, and each year put on one of the biggest concerts of the week – usually beginning with the ringing cry... "Bonsoir Lorient!! Comment ca va?"

That first year in 1979, I was allowed to take the 2-year old Davy backstage during Brenda's evening concert in the Palais de Congres, and he had his own little bedroom with a couch made up for him to sleep in one of the greenrooms... very optimistic; of course the excitement proved too much, and no sleeping took place at all. Before her last number, Brenda called for him to be brought on stage, and he appeared in his pyjamas, grinning shyly as the audience went

[35] *Cornish Life magazine, 7th Feb 1980*

wild with delight at seeing Brenda's adorable grandson. In 1982, with Jan at 2½ and Davy 5, both boys were brought on stage in their Cornish tartan kilts for Brenda's last number and wowed everybody. After the concert, and well after midnight, we were all sitting in a bar next to the concert hall, the boys sipping hot cocoa and playing on the slot machines, while everyone wound down...

Davy on stage with Brenda at Lorient, in his jimjams

The Lorient committee, in those early days, thought it would be a good idea if they held an advance planning meeting with the delegates from all the countries in a different host country each time, all expenses paid. One year I visited Killarney for this meeting, and the following year, Father and I went over on the ferry to Brittany, driving the 2-3 hours down to Lorient for the meeting. The correspondence had given 10am as the time for the committee and delegates to meet the following morning, in a room in the Town Hall, so Father and I duly presented ourselves there at the appointed time. There wasn't a soul in sight. About half an hour later, the delegates from Wales turned up, then gradually over the next hour, more people arrived. Eventually, at around 12 midday, Monsieur Le President, Pierre Guergadic, turned up, and spent 10 minutes unloading all the booze from his car. Once we were all installed in the committee room and everyone was given their choice of drinks (top-notch wine or premium Scotch whisky, mainly), the meeting began. Scotland, the largest non-Breton contingent, was up first to explain their plans for the next Festival; after much discussion, it was then Ireland's turn, then Wales... and then Pierrot ('El Presidente') announced it was time for lunch.

We were all bundled into our cars and headed off to Fort Bloque, some 10 miles or so down the coast. A lengthy table was laid ready in the restaurant to accommodate us all, and the fantastic 'lunch' took us through from about 1.30pm to past 6pm before we got back. All the ladies were given bouquets of flowers and gifts of perfume, the gents were given whisky and cigars, and much fun was had by all. Eventually Father and I got back to our hotel, and the next day drove back up to Roscoff to get the ferry back to Cornwall. At no point did I get an opportunity to discuss my plans for Cornwall at the coming festival, and neither, I believe, did the Isle of Man. The Bretons always have their own set of priorities, but I think such extravagance has moderated now. Needs must...

One of the key events during the week was always the Mayor's Reception. This took place in a huge 'Salon' in the Town Hall, with a large hand-painted mural covering all of one wall. Every Celtic country was supposed to send a delegate to this 'do'. It was expected that they would bring a gift for the Mayor – certainly, the town of Lorient always had gifts it would present to each delegate – and there would be some token entertainment from each delegation too. In my time I remember receiving a large hand-carved slate plaque inscribed with the Lorient coat of arms, and a glass oil lamp, amongst other things. Our gift for the Mayor was usually a Brenda album, or maybe a small Tremaen pottery lampbase, and our offer of entertainment was usually Brenda singing a song, or maybe one of the Cornish dance teams. In 1979, Morley Eathorne, a monumental mason and member of his village choir, multi-tasked – between commitments to sing with Four Lanes Choir, he was demonstrating his skills as a slate carver in the Craft Marquee, and it was one of his creations that was that year's gift from Cornwall to the Mayor, M. Jean Lagarde.

That same year, John Robert King was amongst the party when M. Lagarde demonstrated a singularly unhurried approach to the opening of the Arts & Crafts Exhibition, and commented... "later, at his formal reception, he dazzled the Mayor of Cwmbran in Torfaen in Wales with a similar lack of urgency... 'How does he get through?' asked Jim Davies incredulously... 'I have 4 or 5 meetings most days. I couldn't do it.' He clutched his gift of a miner's safety lamp nervously, almost as if he were in two minds about presenting it to M. Lagarde at all... Brenda took one look at the lamp, and boomed out with inimitable cheerfulness 'You can't give him that, old cock. Cornishman invented that..."[36]

[36] *Cornish Life magazine, 7th February 1980*

There was always much champagne flowing freely at this event, distributed by a team of ladies from the kitchens next door. Brenda took to befriending these ladies, showing them pictures of her grandsons, over which they all cooed. Hence Brenda and I received much more than our fair share of champagne, and after several hours we would toddle out of there in a very merry state, Father already aware we would need collecting by car from the door for this very reason. Brenda's favourite bit was 'snogging the Mayor', who at one time was a very handsome and congenial fellow.

Eventually after four ridiculously busy years (I was still involved with my other local activities, playgroups and suchlike, as well, at this point), I had to give it up, and the role was taken over by ardent Kernowphile Beatrice Kerno, who stayed in post for over 25 years. Unfortunately during that time the Lorient committee reined back on expenditure significantly, and the numbers of the Cornish delegation were never as high again.

In August 1986, at Lorient's request, Brenda was involved in taking over a huge production from Cornwall for the festival – an opera almost, written especially by Richard Gendall in the Cornish language, which had taken many months and mammoth effort on everyone's part to prepare. Richard came along too, as advisor. The story was 'Anne Jeffery Ha Bobel Vean' – (Anne Jeffrey and the Little People), described as 'A Chronicle in Song, Dance and Mime' – an old Cornish story about a young woman who supposedly was able to talk to the 'little people' and ultimately was viewed as a sort of white witch. Anne Jeffery was born in St Teath, near Bodmin, in 1625, and the most remarkable aspect of her story was that she survived incarceration for six months with no food, apparently thriving, having been fed by her friends, the 'little people'.

The main performers were members of Cornish dance group Cam Kernewek and their families, in particular Merv Davey (the recent Grand Bard of the Cornish Gorsedh) and his wife Alison, who played the part of Anne Jeffrey. The chorus was the Denzil Richards Singers, and with a cast of over 20, and a total crew of twice that size, the organisation of the rehearsals and other preparation was a mighty task. Even after the team had arrived in Lorient, Brenda had difficulties with the administration of the spectacle, and wrote to organiser Jean-Pierre Pichard with her concerns... explaining that after 'many grinding months of constant labour' – since arriving she had felt 'unsupported' by the festival. All was eventually ironed out, and the sell-out performances took place in a vast 6000-seater marquee, the 'Kergroise Space', reputedly the biggest such in Europe, and the production received great acclaim. They shared top billing that year with the headliners Alain Stivell and The Pogues.

Terry Pascoe's lovely painting of 'Anne Jeffrey and the Little People'

Unfortunately, although the enthusiasm was certainly there for the show to be performed again back in Cornwall at the Minack Theatre – which would have been stupendous – Richard, most likely taking advice from elsewhere, refused to allow that to happen. A wonderful opportunity missed. Sadly, it was symptomatic of an uncharacteristic change in Richard's temperament later in life, when he seemed to withdraw into academia and became less and less accessible and amenable, and much less involved in his music.

Brenda's concert in that huge Space at its inception in 1984 drew this comment from the Festival organisers: "The mascot of this year's festival was none other than the great Brenda Wootton, the Cornish Seagull, who was well able to spread her wings and adapt to the size of this new venue..." Breton singer Gilles Servat was thrilled to be able perform on stage with Brenda and described her as 'a real character'.[37] The Western Morning News reported Brenda, in her introduction to the song 'Tamar', as saying:

> "...'the River Tamar is the border of Cornwall', in a way that seemed to consign mainland England to irrevocable isolation. When she had finished and the cheering had subsided, the thin sound of the Celtic Harp was heard as Alain Stivell joined Brenda on stage for 'Amazing Grace', a finale that eventually combined the efforts of the symphony orchestra, the pipe band, the Mousehole Male Voice Choir and a Welsh chorale, alongside the voices of the festival's two great stars. This was still being cheered 10 minutes after the TV cameras had been turned off and all the musicians had left the stage..."[38]

A great cartoon of Brenda at Lorient, by talented local cartoonist Clive Wakfer; it appeared in Peninsula Voice

Chris and I were invited back to Lorient Festival as guests in 2015, I think partly because Cornwall and the Isle of Man were the featured countries of the year and I was a former Delegate, but principally in honour of Brenda's place as the Festival's Cornish icon. It was over 20 years since my last visit, and the Festival was bigger than ever – certainly in terms of audience numbers – and just as thrilling. Much had changed, but the buzz and the excitement were the same. We were astonished to be placed in a top hotel in the very centre of the action, and to receive a phenomenal 'goody bag' brimming with loveliness, and it was marvellous to meet up with old friends and to absorb the Festival's heady atmosphere once more. So, yes – thanks Brenda... and thanks for everything, Lorient...

---

[37] *'The Lorient Interceltic Festival', Alain Cabon*

[38] *Western Morning News, August 25th, 1984*

France – La Grande Cornouaillaise

To say to a Breton that Brittany is in France is almost worse than saying to a Cornishman that Cornwall is in England – and that's bad enough. Brenda's success in Brittany had to be fought for and won again in France, but she managed it with her usual flair – to become known as La Grande Cornouaillaise... The Great Cornishwoman.

Brenda's first agent in France was Gwenn Le Goarnig. Although her family home was in the Chateau of Kertalg in Brittany, Gwenn had a flat in Paris, from where she managed a stable of artists. Brenda had sung at Gwenn's Kertalg Festival in 1973 with Dik Cadbury, with Robert in 1974, and again with Dik and others in 1975. Unfortunately, the Festival in 1975, like the others, lost money, and Brenda was among those not paid for her performance, which led to much dissatisfaction all round. Gwenn had arranged for Brenda with various musicians to make an album, but by the time all of the recording was done, matters were getting very fraught, and the whole arrangement fell apart. Brenda realised she needed to look for a new agent in France, and while she was wondering what to do about her 2-year contract with Gwenn, she received a call from her, and says Gwenn apparently 'blew up' and said she was finished with Brenda. Brenda's reaction was, well, thank goodness for that – at least she was now free to look for another agent.

After that slightly dodgy start, Brenda managed to find an excellent French agent: Olivier Gluzman. Olivier managed all Brenda's French bookings for many years, and we got to know him and his family well. They visited with Brenda and John in Cornwall for Christmas in 1984, with their two sweet little girls, and one of Brenda's most frequent roadies, the ever-cheerful Dominique Bourdin.

Brenda and French agent Olivier in Cornwall

A review in Paris Soir of Brenda's concert at Theatre de la Ville, with typical Gallic flamboyance, describes the novelty of her performance for French audiences:

> "It is difficult to compare Brenda with any other singer... with her Cornish origin, she carries on stage a kind of soufflé of sea and air... this large lady with eyes wide with expression, a fringe of little laughs like champagne corks, with rings on every finger, her uncertain French... she is all of the grandmothers in fairy tales, warm and friendly as in children's dreams... She is funny, enthusiastic, open, this lady in her 50s who decided only 6 years ago to sing around the world, and throw her cookery books in the stinging nettles..."[39]

France became Brenda's biggest fan base... she appeared many times on French TV and radio, and played at the biggest venues in practically every French town, especially of course, in Paris. Her concerts at Theatre de la Ville, also called the Sarah Bernhardt Theatre, at the Palais de Glace and at Olympia were sell-outs – huge promotions, with audiences of 1000s. She became a family name in France. When I started taking evening classes here in French, to try and keep up, my French teacher told a friend of hers in Paris who my mother was, and says she 'went berserk'!

Diana Lawer, who became a friend, explained her experience of this phenomenon:

> "I used to go to as many of her concerts as I could, including the Paris ones. The French idolised her; I remember, I think it was at the Paris Olympia, that she was given star billing over Johnny Halliday! I started a little tradition of giving her a posy of yellow roses tied with black and gold ribbons at her curtain calls, and over the years, we became friends.
>
> "I was at the Bobino in Montparnasse, Paris, when she did the concerts with Camborne Town Band, and a lasting memory of this week is that wherever you went on the Metro system there were life-size billboards of Brenda all along the walkways and on the platforms. People here think of her as just a folk singer. They have absolutely no idea of her star status in France, due mainly to her jazz and ballads."

The posters for these affairs were almost larger than life, and smothered all the huge publicity bollards – the iconic 'colonne Morris' – and the subways around central Paris. At this time, in the

---

[39] *Paris Soir, 10 May 1979*

early 1980s, Brenda was likely to get besieged by fans if she walked down any Paris street, and large crowds queued after her concerts to buy her albums and get them signed – Dave Penhale recalls they sold 50 albums after one concert – a record (no pun intended)! Her cousin Barbara was very impressed with the lines of huge posters of Brenda in the Metro, when she came to Paris for Brenda's Bobino concert.

Brenda and Dave Penhale, standing beside a large French 'colonne Morris'

Cousin Barbara, so impressed with the avenue of large posters in the Metro

However – as with the production of her records, Brenda often had to be prepared to invest her own money up front for this type of promotion, and rarely got it all back. Nevertheless, she often commented on the difference between the French and English attitudes to musical events... the French as a nation held such things in high regard, and invested heavily in Culture, Sports and the Arts. In France, even small towns would have a professionally run concert hall or theatre, with full-time staff, lighting and sound engineers – they were very proud of their home-grown talent and welcomed foreign artists of all genres, and the French people responded well – it was very rare to find a concert poorly publicised or attended, and wherever she went she played to packed houses. She felt Britain was very much the poor relation in comparison.

Perhaps because of this Gallic interest in culture, Brenda's time in France put her in the spotlight with some big names. Brenda sang for the French President, Francois Mitterand, and compared notes with him on the joys of being a grandparent. She sang in the Palace of the Popes in Avignon... She sang at a special trip on the Venice Simplon Orient Express, with guitarist Chris Newman... She sang in the notorious Isle de Ré penitentiarie – Saint-Martin-de-Ré at La Rochelle – for 'lifers' of 30 years or more, locked in their cages... She appeared on a French chat show with Paul McCartney and Jacqueline Bisset, on other shows with David Cassidy and David Essex, and performed in Brest with the legendary jazz violinist Stéphane Grappelli.

In one year, 1981-1982, she appeared alongside such well-known international celebrities as Jacques Loussier, Gilbert Becaud and Yves Montand (France), Rita Streicher (Austria), Anna Prucnal (Poland), Mercedes Sosa (Argentina), Maria Carta (Sardinia), Giovana Marini (Italy), Barbara Hendricks (Metropolitan Opera, New York), Luther Allison Blues Band (Chicago), jazz musician Lionel Hampton, racing driver Jacques Lafitte, and ballet dancer Rudolf Nureyev.

She appeared at a mega Fête d'Humanites – an International Festival for Women – and was a little at a loss amongst such a crowd of strongly militant feminists, as she did not see herself in that role. She introduced her set by explaining that yes, she was a mother and a grandmother, a sister, a wife, a lover, a cook, a home-maker, "... mais ce soir", she cried, "je suis une putain!!" – "but tonight, I am a whore!"... and then launched into riotous versions of 'House of the Rising Sun' and 'Honky Tonk Woman' – which subsequently went to number 2 in the French charts. It went down a storm – and appropriately, the set was recorded by the Rolling Stones mobile truck.

The series of concerts in Olympia were special events staged by Olivier and billed as the Three Divas – three top singers from very different cultural backgrounds: Maria Carta from Sardinia, Mercedes Sosa from Argentina, and Brenda of course from Cornwall. The three did their own numbers, and also performed together, and were filmed for French TV (this is still viewable on YouTube). Brenda and Mercedes particularly hit it off. Mercedes, a large woman like Brenda who wore dramatic South American ponchos, had a strikingly powerful voice and sang wild and bewitching tunes from her native country – her 'Gracias a la Vida' ('Thank you for Life') was played at my wedding. I remember there was one other celebrity at the concert I attended – Charlene Tilton, famously cast as Lucy Ewing in 'Dallas', and nicknamed the 'Poison Dwarf' by Terry Wogan – who had scored a hit in Europe with her song 'C'est la vie'. Unfortunately she did not score a hit with Brenda and Mercedes when she threw a little paddy, demanding that Brenda change dressing rooms, as she wanted the one allocated to Brenda. Brenda concurred... politely, of course.

Brenda in curlers, backstage with Mercedes Sosa

Olivier was Brenda's agent in France from 1982 until 1990, and their relationship, although generally very positive and friendly, did go through some 'troubled' patches – increasingly so in the final years. Brenda wrote many long and angry letters to him with complaints about the failure of plans they had discussed and agreed upon, often plans in which she had invested heavily in terms of both time and money, which had gone wrong, or had come to nothing. As was her style, she did not hold back – but usually ended on a conciliatory note, ensuring their continued friendship:

> "The exciting thing about Olivier Gluzman is that he is an optimist, positive (sometimes a little *too* positive!), and his eyes look up – but now and again his head is in the clouds! Which is wonderful – but this practical Cornishwoman Brenda Wootton will always endeavour – *while she dreams* – to keep both her feet firmly on the ground... so if we have a storm, I will catch you by the shirt tails and hang on, till it is calm again..."

Brenda won two prestigious awards in France: in 1981, she was presented with the Loisir des Jeunes Award for her 'Celtic Lullabies' single, in Paris; and in 1987, she received the 'Academie Charles Cros' Award from the French Minister of Culture in Paris on March 17th, for the best 'stranger' album of the year, for her LP 'Tamar'. A remarkable achievement for a fat, middle-aged Cornish housewife and granny...

She made a good friend in one of the Artistic Directors of Theatre de la Ville, the former journalist and TV producer, Jacques Erwan, and the great (in both senses) French singer-songwriter Colette

Magny, and they had plans to work together, which sadly never came to fruition...

The French songwriter Francis Lai (who wrote the music for 'Une Homme et Un Femme' and 'Love Story', amongst other great movies), having heard her voice on her ''B' Comme Brenda' album, asked to write a song especially for her to sing. His song, 'Walk Across the World', was written for a global charity effort of the same name – encouraging people everywhere to fundraise by walking for charity, and raising funds for children's causes worldwide. Brenda performed the song at a massive 'World Travel Market' event in Olympia in London, with accompanist David Snell on harp, which was opened by HRH Princess Diana, whom she met. The song later appeared on a maxi-single together with a rare flip side: a beautiful love song written by Brenda, titled 'Everybody Knows', with the music once again written by Francis Lai. Amazingly the single wowed the Japanese, enthusiastic supporters of the 'Walk Across the World' initiative, and the record smashed through to the top of the pop charts in Japan, staying at Number 1 for some weeks.

So how did Brenda achieve that stellar shift, how did she make that transition from small English folk clubs to the heady heights of international folk fame? Certainly the vast numbers of her Radio Cornwall 'Sunday Best' fans never suspected the extent of her achievements abroad.

Why her? What made Brenda stand out from the numerous other talented wannabee folk stars? Yes, the voice was astonishing – her vocal range and the purity of that voice were remarkable. But for me, in addition to that, it was her homeliness. She struck up a relationship with every member of her audience, and made each of them feel like she was talking just to them – a rare ability; they were part of her family, and she laughed with them and cried with them. She always chatted easily to her audiences, whatever their nationality, speaking no differently than she would speak to an old friend she'd met in the street in Penzance.

Charles Aznavour – whom she met, performing on the same bill in 1986 – has said that for 'les chansons française', the lyrics are more important than the music... sensitive, emotive lyrics matter more than a marvellous tune – whereas for 'les chansons anglaises', "it is the music that matters more... that is the difference". Perhaps Brenda gave them both – with her choice of material, her stage presence, her easy familiarity, and that magical voice. The French language is famously lyrical, and when singing in France, Brenda spoke in French, and usually included at least one song in French in her repertoire.

For the French, she had that colourful Bohemian flair and personality they had always admired – she was their larger-than-life grandma, or a much-loved eccentric mother or sister. She taught herself to become fluent, and chatted amiably about each song before singing it, in a language her audience understood, in a chatty, conversational tone – and they were charmed by her. So she was able to explain what each song was about, especially important if it was in Cornish of course.

As with all her public performances at home and abroad, Brenda's music was liberally seasoned with yarns, with Angus's story-telling skills strongly to the fore. For example: several old Cornish tales she sang about include references to the Devil – and Brenda was fond of explaining how the Devil was afraid to come into Cornwall, as the Cornish were forever getting the better of him – she said he 'ran off screeching like a whitnick (weasel) when one Cornishwoman threatened to put him in a pasty...'. Not sure how that translated into French...

Sometimes she caught them off their guard – she would spend several minutes telling a jokey story about how the Cornish had asked their friends the Danes for help to fight the English, whistling to them and beckoning, and how the Danish had rowed across the Channel in their little boats, comically mimicking their rowing action. They would be laughing with her at this funny image – and then she would start into the painfully beautiful and wistful song 'Tamar', describing how the river ran red with the blood of Cornish and Dane at Callington Down, the lilting tune flowing like the river itself. Few could resist such a pull on their emotions...

She sometimes introduced her French concerts with "Mes chansons sont comme mes amis, chacun avec son personalité, son ambience. Et perdant que je les chants, ma tête peints leur portraits – puis je vous introduis mes amis?" ("My songs are like my friends, each one with its own personality, its own mood. And while I sing the songs, my mind paints their portraits. May I introduce you to my friends?"). She was different, unique, and the French audiences adored her, and lapped up her slightly imperfect French and her warmth. Normally known to be famously cool and chic and disdainful of joining in with chorus songs, it was astonishing to hear a French audience of thousands in a huge hall joyfully trying to get their collective tongues around "Leetle eyes, I loff you, leetle eyes, I loff you..."

For Brenda's cousin Barbara and husband Ron, for close friends Colleen and Bill, and for Donald Jarvis, John Knight, brother Peter and others from home who attended one of her big Parisian concerts, it was a real eye-opener. I stood at the back of the vast auditorium of Olympia, darkened into a huge warm cave and filled with barely visible humanity, all attention focused on one point in the far distance, the small jewel-like figure in the spotlight, rings flashing, arms wide, bright robes swirling. The voice, like a crystal bird, rose to the ceiling and swept back to the listeners below – I was family, but even I could feel the strength of the bond flowing both ways, a tangible exchange of affection, respect and kinship between performer and audience.

Brenda on stage at Bobino Theatre in Paris

On one big tour in 1983, Brenda travelled with Camborne Town Band and guitarist Chris Newman, who formed a jazz combo with Ray Roberts on sax and flute and Dave Freeman on electric bass. They were booked to do a series of concerts at a theatre called Bobino, in one of the back streets of Paris. Bobino had a prestigious and notorious history, as the theatre of the black burlesque performer, Josephine Baker, famous for her erotic dancing and nearly nude costumes in the risqué and racy art deco era of the 1920s. Baker's last performance at Bobino was in 1975 at the age of 68, a concert attended by a stellar audience including Prince Rainier, Princess Grace, Jackie Kennedy, Sophia Loren, Mick Jagger, Diana

Ross and Liza Minelli. Josephine Baker died four days later. The significance of the concerts with Brenda and her team was that they too were the last – the final nights of Josephine Baker's theatre. One of Brenda's songs was called The Last Performance – and it was. Bobino itself closed down after their final show.

The theatre inside was magical, all red plush and gold cherubs, ornate rococo décor and tiers of Victorian seating. Camborne Town Band – a bunch of local Cornish lads after all – were star struck by the whole experience. They appeared on French TV with Brenda singing 'Somewhere Over the Rainbow', but I think one of my most lasting memories was seeing some of the band members standing in awe outside a sex shop opposite the theatre, daring each other to go in.

From the Cornish Guardian:

> "The band had travelled to Paris by coach, crossing via the Roscoff ferry, and within a few hours they found themselves on a national television station for a prime-time Saturday evening broadcast from the Champs Elysee. They accompanied Brenda singing 'Over the Rainbow', while another guest was Charlene Tilton from the hit TV series, Dallas. Marcus Dunstan, who was in the Camborne Town Band at that time, had this to say: "We performed to thousands at an Amnesty International concert alongside rock bands, it was a far cry from life in Cornwall – we were truly amazed at Brenda's popularity."

They often performed until late in the evening, but were rewarded with the sights of Paris including the Eiffel Tower and the Palace of Versailles, and also played on a boat sailing up the River Seine. Brenda ensured they had time to enjoy the best food and drink to keep them in good spirits.[40] Regular meals were booked in advance at huge French restaurants, and mealtimes were chaotic affairs – upwards of 80 people to be fed at a sitting, most not speaking the language, and many of them wondering whether, if they asked nicely, could they please just have ham, egg and chips.

A Cornishman who happened to be on holiday in Paris and had been invited to the theatre by his French hosts, was also in the audience that night. Following an appreciation of Brenda in the Western Morning News, after her death, he wrote to Frank Ruhrmund:

---

[40] *Cornish Guardian 6/11/2013*

> "With regard to the 'French connection', I can vouch for her popularity there [*in Paris*]. We were invited to the theatre one evening by our hosts... and Brenda was performing, accompanied by Raymond Roberts, an old school friend of mine, plus Camborne Town Band! It was an amazing evening – we ended up singing Trelawney. I could not believe that a sophisticated audience such as that found in Montparnasse could be won over in such a short time. Brenda taught them the words, and they sang them with fervour. They loved her fractured French too.
>
> "My friend Raymond spotted us in the audience and came out after the show and invited us backstage. We met Brenda and she immediately invited us and our friends to dinner. We could not accept, but that warm-heartedness seemed to typify Brenda's approach to life. Our friends never forgot that evening and will be very sorry to hear of her death."

Many years later, Brenda's former guitarist and Recording Engineer, John Knight of Coverack, discovered his recording of this prestigious concert... see under 'Brenda's legacy...' at the end for what happened to that tape.

Brenda acquired one very interesting long-term pen pal in France – a remarkable woman called **Nina Katorza-Freeman**.[41] Nina had first seen Brenda on French TV, and wrote to tell her of her links with Brenda's home town, Penzance. She says "I determined to write to you when I saw you chez that charming Jewish boy Drucker [Michel Drucker, a famous French TV host, had interviewed Brenda on his TV programme] – nice intelligent boy, so kind – after you he had Barbra Streisand, most interesting girl... but you, you were born for the stage, my dear, and can act like nobody's business!"

Born in Penzance in 1900, Nina posed for several of the Newlyn School artists as a young girl, and for the artists of Montparnasse in her 20s, where she also became friendly and performed with Josephine Baker and her crowd in the Moulin Rouge and the Folies Bergere. In the Second World War she was imprisoned in a concentration camp near Marseilles for her Resistance activities. She later moved to the south of France, and in 1956 sang at the wedding of Prince Rainier and Grace Kelly. She knew the painter Marc Chagall, lamenting his death in 1985: "I knew him in the 70s – a charming

---

[41] *See under 'About' on Brenda's website*

lovely old man – Fun, & oh! So good looking! He called me Ninouska like all my Russian friends…". Her stories are astonishing, although her large scrawled handwriting is difficult to read, but she wrote long chatty letters to Brenda in the mid-1980s. I have promised myself I will not let her story die, and you can read it on the Brenda website, and coming soon, on the 'CornishStory.com' blog.

Germany – Mama Cornwall

Brenda's original contacts in Germany had come through Alex Atterson. She found a great agent, Hansi Dobratz, and for around 8 years from the mid-1970s proceeded to perform in practically every town in the country, becoming well known as 'Mama Cornwall'. In one year she worked out, when she checked her diary, that she had spent more nights in her hotel bed in Germany than she had in her own.

With Hansi's help Brenda and Robert made a record titled 'Tin in the Stream' with Stockfisch Records in 1974. I travelled with Brenda on one tour in 1980, taking baby Jan with us. I remember sitting in the empty darkness of a big theatre in Berlin one afternoon, while Brenda was waiting for a sound check. She offered to change Jan's nappy while we waited, and he took the opportunity of the fresh air to pee all over her stage dress – dear boy. Neither Jan nor Brenda was fazed by this…

Brenda and Jan in Berlin

One concert which Brenda found particularly moving took place in the courtroom in Nurembourg where the trials of the key players in the Nazi holocaust had taken place some 40 years earlier.

Brenda made many great friends in Germany, including singer Cobi Schrier, and Hildegard Doebner of Witten, in whose club she performed many times, and Ray Austin, an English-born jazz/folk musician and radio presenter living in Freiburg, who also performed at Pipers Folk Club.

Kathleen Bayersdorf in Coburg described Brenda as "...one of those badly needed public relations experts who advertise Cornwall's originality and fascination..."

Belgium and beyond – Lady Cornwall

In Belgium, Brenda's long-term agent was Leon Lamal. Leon and his family lived in Hoeilaart, an area famed for its grapes and with large old greenhouses on all sides – the small town was sometimes called the Glass Village, for this reason. Leon had the most wonderful grape-vines in a number of ancient greenhouses – the luscious grapes were large, black and sweet. He showed us the delicate operation necessary to pick them, laying a box lined in soft material gently beneath each bunch, and using a tiny silver scissors to cut the bunch from the vine without touching and ruining the bloom.

Leon had a flat in Hoeilaart which was used as a base for any visiting performers touring in Belgium, as he had a whole stable of them. Brenda often met up there with Alex Campbell, Decameron, Martin Carthy, Alex Atterson and many others, and sometimes made pasties for them in the flat. If they were there for a while – which was often the case – she set up her sewing machine and made new dresses for the stage. I believe the toilet arrangements there left a lot to be desired though...

Dave Penhale remembers touring with her in Europe... on that occasion, unusually, they visited Denmark and Luxembourg. Brenda discovered that a Cornish woman she knew would be travelling to Denmark, and would be coming to one of her concerts, so she put in a special request for her to bring a load of saffron with her so that Brenda could make saffron cake for Alex Campbell, who was also on the tour. On one tour, they were sharing the flat in Hoeilaart with Davey Graham for a week. He was being looked after by his mum, and doing his own series of gigs around and about. Dave says

Brenda came to an arrangement with Davey that she would cook the supper every day, before they went out to their respective gigs, and in return, Davey would do some one-to-one guitar sessions with Dave – "which is what we did for a week!" says Dave – "and I've never forgotten it..."

I went with Brenda on her first Belgian tour with Robert in 1974, and they did a fantastic gig in Tournai; I was also witness to their amazing performance at a festival in Boechout. As a duo, they certainly did wow audiences. The organisers put us all up in their own house, and we spent a delightful if quite drunken afternoon in their sunny courtyard.

On tour in Holland in November 1975, Brenda and Mike Silver did a gig in a cellar club called La Pochinelle in Amsterdam, at a Literary Luncheon for British ex-PM Edward Heath, to celebrate the launch of his book 'Sailing'. In the photo, Mike looks very unimpressed (understandable, I would have felt the same), but now says he has no memory of it at all. Brenda obviously has no qualms, and is chatting gaily with Ted.

Brenda chatting to Ted Heath, with Mike Silver, in a club in Amsterdam

As well as France, Germany and Belgium, Brenda's principal European haunts, she also toured extensively in Holland, Austria, Switzerland – where she made a point of visiting Sir Humphry Davy's grave in Geneva – and Luxembourg, where she made some firm friends in graphic designers Lex, Anne & Pit Weyer, who for many years sent us huge posters of their graphic New Year cartoons, and once an amazing collage-laden scrapbook featuring Brenda. She was equally popular all over Europe.

Ireland – Herself: The Cornishwoman

Ireland was Brenda's second voyage across the sea as a performer, when in 1972 she was asked by Donald Rawe and the Celtic Congress to take part in the Pan-Celtic Festival in Killarney. She chose the song, and needed help with translation and pronunciation, so it led to her first meeting with writer, composer and linguist Richard Gendall, and became the catalyst for her interest in and absorption with the wider Celtic nations.

On that first occasion, Brenda travelled to Killarney with guitarist Steve Hall, brother Peter and cousin Malcolm Rowe. It was Brenda's first attempt at singing in Kernewek, the language of Cornwall, and she didn't win; but it inspired her to learn as much as she could about the language, and to coax some more songs from Richard, in both Cornish and English – not that he needed much encouragement. They had time for some sight-seeing in Killarney as well, and enjoyed visiting the races.

Brenda with Malc, Peter and John, at the races in Killarney

In 1988 she attended the Pan-Celtic Festival with Merv Davey, and entered the competition with the Richard Gendall song 'Cala Mea'. It was the first chance she'd had to attend for 10 years, as she had been so busy working, performing in the UK and abroad, but from the correspondence with the Kernow Pan-Celtic Committee, there was a definite dispute or 'misunderstanding' about her appearance there. It appears that Cornwall had not sent a contestant the previous year, as there was some difficulty in getting performers to commit to the trip when they couldn't know in advance whether or not they would win through the selection process, and there appeared a strong likelihood that the same situation would prevail in this year... so Irish organiser Con O'Conaill asked Brenda if she would go. As she was free at that time, she readily agreed, saying she would be happy to visit the Festival anyway, as she'd not managed it for so long. However – this obviously broke the rules of the Kernow Pan-Celtic selection process... and Brenda was not happy with being 'told off' for attending and representing Cornwall – better her than no-one, was her feeling.

She became well-loved in Ireland, where they took to calling her 'Herself – The Cornishwoman', and went back a few times, mostly to the Pan-Celtic Festival, and once on a personal holiday with John, visiting the beautiful Dingle Peninsula and the Ring of Kerry.

Australia – Little Cornwall

They may have awarded Brenda different honorary 'titles' in every country she visited, but with typical Aussie pragmatism and restraint, in South Australia, they just claimed: "...we call her Brenda..."

Brenda was invited to take part in the Kernewek Lowender, the Cornish Festival that takes place every two years in South Australia, on three occasions, in 1979, 1981 and 1985. The Festival centres on the towns of Moonta, Wallaroo and Kadina, otherwise known as the Cornish or Copper Triangle, in the Yorke Peninsula west of Adelaide, where some 50% of the residents are believed to be of Cornish descent. The organiser of the first trip was John Nicholls from the Arts Council of South Australia, the body which was part funding her visit, and Brenda made many friends out there amongst the ex-pat Cornish, including Festival organisers Ros Patterson, Diana Hancock and Irene Barnes, Kim Bonython and others.

The Cornish exiles and their families who first came out in the 19th century were principally miners looking for work in the copper mines. They brought with them all of their memories of their Cornish experience of home, and preserved them at all costs, with the result that those Australian families with a Cornish background seem now almost twice as Cornish as the Cornish themselves. They love their gook bonnets and their Cornish costumes and traditions, their Cousin Jacks and Jennys and their Cornish food, celebrating the pasty as a major icon (62,000 were sold over the festival weekend!) – and they loved Brenda. There are other towns in the region associated with the Cornish: I visited Burra Burra, Silverton and Broken Hill on my own trip to South Australia in 1995, and the barren desert landscape littered with the ruins of such obviously Cornish mine stacks is very bizarre, and quite poignant and emotional to view. Brenda, like me, visited Redruth Gaol, and saw Ludgvan Street, and was particularly affected by the small dugouts in the ground where some of the miners lived, in abject poverty – yet still they managed to fashion a fake fireplace and mantelpiece out of the clay walls of their homes, on which they placed the china dogs they had brought with them from home, 10,000 miles away.

The Adelaide Advertiser said of her first visit in May 1979: "Like a galleon in full sail with her Cornish tartan cloak billowing around her, Brenda Wootton swept across Moonta Oval... eddying in her wake was a stream of admirers..."[42] Brenda was envious of the tremendous spirit in Australia's 'Little Cornwall', saying "We'd never be able to have a fair like this... the economy couldn't afford it, and we're too blasé about our customs now. Here, there's still a lovely naiveté and Cousin Jacks are embracing their customs and heritage with a vigour that would shame their Cornish kin." (Hmmm. See my comment at the end.)

On that first visit Brenda was taken to the Headquarters of the School of the Air – Australia's unique Outback School Radio that links children throughout the region with broadcasts of lessons for their schooling. Brenda went on the radio at Silver City, Broken Hill, and spent some time talking and singing with children up to 500 miles away, teaching them the song 'Humphry Davy'. The children were aged from 5-12 years old, and there were 160 on roll at that time, with seven teachers taking their lessons at 20 minute intervals. All the children operate their own transmitter/receivers.

Also on her first visit in 1979, an old school friend saw her on TV and phoned to say "I don't suppose you'll remember me..." – but of course, Brenda did...it was her old pal Sylvia Hosking from Penzance. "I've been looking for you everywhere!" Brenda replied. Sylvia had gone to Australia as a nurse, married, and had four sons... and the couple met up and had a great time talking about the old days.[43] Another school friend, then living in Canberra, Doreen Biggs, also turned up, so there was a grand reunion.

One event booked on that trip was at the tiny hamlet of Penneshaw on Kangaroo Island off the coast of Adelaide. The trip there involved Brenda and her entourage taking a plane flight from Adelaide to Kingscote on Kangaroo Island, then a 40 mile drive to Penneshaw.

---

[42] *The Adelaide Advertiser 25.5.79*

[43] *The Cornishman, June 28th 1979*

Two hours before they were to depart, the skies opened and torrential rain poured down, forcing the closure of both airports. Visibility was down to 15 yards. Despite various alternative plans being discussed and rejected, Brenda was determined – she was all for setting off in a small boat across the 22 miles of ocean, an idea quickly scotched by her tour manager. There was great relief when the clouds finally lifted, and they left on the plane 2 hours late. There followed a hair-raising drive at break-neck speed, with all Brenda's party crammed into one small car, along a lonely and deserted track in a thunderstorm, the 40 miles to Penneshaw – where they arrived with 20 minutes to spare.

Guitarist Chris Newman sent me this memory of his time spent in Australia with Brenda:

"In May 1981 I was delighted to be asked to accompany Brenda on her second visit to Australia to appear at the biennial Kernewek Lowender festival that took place in three small South Australian towns that had strong connections to Cornwall, due to the presence of the mines that had attracted many Cornish immigrants in the nineteenth century.

"It was an exciting journey for me as it was my first time travelling outside Europe. In those days it was a really long trip: London/Abu Dhabi/Singapore/Sydney/Melbourne on British Airways then an internal flight to Adelaide. I can't precisely remember the total duration from Heathrow to Adelaide, but it was well in excess of 36 hours, so by the time we arrived at our final destination we were both pretty zonked.

"As the Boeing 727 taxied in to the terminal in Adelaide I noticed a crowd of people gathered near the arrivals area. Some were carrying placards, and there were also a couple of news vans from radio or TV stations. We were both wondering what this was all about when one of the stewardesses came up and told Brenda that this was in fact a welcoming committee from the festival.

"She was amazing: all the passengers got off the plane while she went into one of the washrooms in order to, as she put it, 'put her face on'. Satisfied that she was presentable, and showing no sign of over 36 hours of constant travelling, she stood by the open front door of the plane, waved and descended the steps into the waiting crowd, all the time being filmed by the local TV channel.

"She certainly was a trouper!"

During that 1981 visit, part of Brenda's schedule was to judge a VIP Pasty-Making Competition, where she got several of the smart-suited dignitaries to have a go, all suitably pinnied-up, and taught them, by example, the basic rules of making a proper Cornish pasty. One of them turned out to be the top-hatted Premier of South Australia, who joined in with great good humour.

Brenda teaching the dignitaries how to make a pasty at Kernewek Lowender

She was fascinated to learn about the Cornish convict, James Ruse, who was one of the first to be deported to Australia in 1788 for some minor misdemeanour. On his arrival in New South Wales he told the authorities that he was a farmer, and as they were desperate to make the new colony self-supporting, he was allocated a small plot of land, and became the first white farmer in Australia. He went on to become a successful citizen, and there is now a James Ruse Agricultural High School in Sydney. Inspired by the story, Brenda asked Richard to write his story in song, which he did, using these lines from his tombstone: "My mother reared me tenderly, with me she took much pain, and when I arrived in this colony, I sowed the first grain."

She also took the story of the Mystery for another song – the Cornish lugger that sailed from Mounts Bay to Australia in 1845 with seven fishermen on board – an event recreated in 2008 in a replica boat commissioned by yachtsman Pete Goss.

For her final appearance at the Festival, she'd once again asked Richard Gendall to write a special song for the event, and recorded that and an earlier one onto a privately-produced single to take with her: 'Cornish Australian (Just Like Me!)' and 'Do You Come From Moonta, Wallaroo, Kadina?'. She had a lot of fun with the cover photo: she is holding a pasty, a can of Fosters and a bottle of Devenish (Devenish, Brenda?!), and wearing a stereotypical Aussie corked hat with a little Koala, and Cornish and Aussie flags on the brim.

Irene Barnes, one of the Festival organisers in 1983, said of her concert: "...the magic of her music so captured the audience you could hear a pin drop. The way Brenda changed from 'red hot mamma' to finish her Saturday concert with a sweet lullaby was something I shall always remember..."

She was given a specially commissioned copper and silver brooch depicting a seagull and a eucalyptus, and planted a eucalypt in Queen's Square, Moonta. She had asked to visit the home of a Cornish family, and was taken to meet a couple in an old cottage – she told them their front room reminded her so much of her own granny's house in Cornwall... but then cut straight to the chase with "Now then, my birds... where's the outside loo?" Irene took a photo of her standing in the doorway of the privy singing 'I wouldn't leave my little wooden hut for you-hoo-hoo...'!

I've mentioned Robert Bartlett and Diane, my cousin, turning up with their passel of boys at a concert in Adelaide – and another ex-pat Cornish woman who showed up was Cherry Hall, whose parents Olga and Barney Hall lived at Trendrennen Farm near Porthcurno, and were friendly with some of Brenda's oldest friends, Jean and Nicky Hards. Cherry had emigrated a while back, and had written to Brenda telling her the story of her family's large wooden kitchen table. Everything in her family's history had happened on this table – kids had done their homework on it, Christmases and birthdays had happened around it, wedding and funeral parties too – babies had been born on it and the dead laid out – so when she emigrated, Cherry paid a huge sum of money to have the table shipped out to Australia. Brenda was very taken with the story, and – courtesy of Richard – was able to sing the song of 'Trendrennen Table' for her in Australia. As a thank you, Cherry presented Brenda with a large chalk portrait of her she had done herself.

Spain

With the Galicians and the Asturians in Northern Spain featuring so prominently with their Celtic cousins at the Lorient Festival, it was perhaps inevitable that Brenda would end up touring in that region. As with all her other trips to foreign parts, it was Richard Gendall who provided her with a fully translated dialogue, enabling her to communicate with her audiences. She toured in Spain on a few occasions, and always went prepared with written introductions to all her songs translated into Spanish by the multi-lingual Richard. He even wrote her a couple of songs in the language...

Here is one, written by Richard, which she sang for them in Spanish:

> "How happy I am to be in Galicia, seventh sister of our Celtic family!
> From all of us living so far away, I bring you greetings – we do not forget you!
> To this green land and its kindly people, a warm embrace – we shall always love you!"

In August 1982, La Coruna, the capital of the region, formed her base, and one of the organisers for Galicia to Lorient Festival, Geranio Torreiro, showed her around – she did TV and radio while there, and a big concert in Santiago. She visited Galicia again in 1984, and in 1986, and flew to Barcelona, where she did a series of five concerts with Chris Newman, and the Catalonian singer-songwriter and activist, Lluís Llach (now a member of the Catalan parliament). The outdoor concerts were held in the Plaça del Rei, a fantastic medieval square in a royal building in Barcelona; the palace was the residence of the Catalan counts from the 13th to the early 15th centuries, and the history of the building can be traced back to the Barcelona of the 11th century – so, an appropriate place to be performing with a Catalonian artiste – thanks to Richard, she even had some words in Catalan for the largely partisan audience.

Canada

Brenda visited Canada in July of both 1984 and 1985. The trip to Canada in July 1984 with Chris Newman was her first foray across the big pond; there were plans for her to tour in the States, but they never came to fruition.

She sang in three of the big Eastern cities, starting with a first for her, a Jazz Festival in Montreal, at which Ray Charles was also booked

– which she says was a huge success. The following day she was recording all day for Canadian TV Station Soleil. After three days when she says it was 'too hot to move', her French agent Olivier joined them, and they went on to Quebec, where the venue was Le Pigeoniere – another 'great success'! Then it was back to Montreal for three nights at the Club Soda, then on to Ottawa, where she finished the tour with five nights in the National Arts Centre.

While she was there, a Cornishman called Albert, living in Ottawa, came to the performance nearly every night. Brenda later wrote to his sister Sylvia Symons:

> "...on my first night I opened with 'Cornwall the Land I Love', and I could hear this audible sobbing somewhere to my left... they were breaking their hearts! It turned out to be two homesick sisters from St Ives..."

Brenda standing beside a huge flagpole announcing her concert in Canada

The press release from the National Arts Centre says she had...

> "...contributed enormously to the renaissance of the ancient Cornish tongue, Kernewek, a close relative of Breton and Welsh – she sings in English, Cornish and French... She identifies strongly with her homeland, saying 'I sing of my country not through duty, but by choice.'
>
> "She is capable of any genre... but no matter what she sings, the listener's pleasure is the same – she has one of those tornado-like voices that encompass a dizzying range of emotions. Her generosity is overwhelming, her warmth and humour the kind that make instant friends of first acquaintances.
>
> "'In Penzance, my home, the old folks come up to me with their problems,' she says. 'I can't take two steps in the street without someone coming up to me... husbands and wives confide in me secrets they've hidden from each other all their lives – I am the vehicle of love!!' she laughs."

Brenda wowed them in Canada as she did everywhere else. The review in Ottawa's The Citizen paper reported:

> "What sets Wootton apart from many performers of recent memory – and can't help but endear her to even the most cynical of audiences – is her tremendous stage presence. It's as if she refuses to admit she's onstage, and would rather think of her performance as a get-together in the living room of a dear friend. She explains her songs – not simply recounting what the ones in Cornish, the ancient language of Kernewek, are about – but describing the atmosphere and the people of the homeland she so obviously loves..."[44]

Chris Newman has happy memories of that tour:

> "In the early spring of 1984 Brenda called to see if I'd be interested in doing some shows in Canada with her in the summer. Interested? I'd been waiting my whole life (or so it seemed) for the chance to cross the Atlantic and visit North America.
>
> "The short tour, in July of that year, included appearances at the Montréal and Québec festivals, shows that had clearly come about as a result of the 'French connection' as by this time, Brenda was doing extremely well in France and becoming very well known. We flew to Montréal and made a few appearances that seemed to go down well. Then we went to Québec City: another world.
>
> "Montréal's situated in the French part of Canada, but in reality is a completely bilingual city. The city of Québec, however, was a very different proposition, being far more French than any city I was, by now, very used to visiting in France itself.
>
> "We arrived at the airport and were waiting by the carousel for the luggage to appear, when I became aware of two uniformed guys, obviously military, who seemed to be taking a keen interest in us. I thought this slightly odd, but wasn't concerned until our luggage arrived on the belt. No sooner had I lifted the cases and guitar onto the floor that these two guys grabbed the bags and put them onto trolleys. It turned out that these two chaps were our drivers.

---

[44] *The Citizen, Ottawa, July 17th 1985*

> "Drivers. Plural.
>
> "The organisers of the festival had assigned Brenda and me two separate Army drivers, with two separate cars! I seem to remember that hers was a bit bigger than mine, but they were both massive vehicles that were put at our disposal for the duration of our visit. We stayed in a very fancy hotel (complete with a revolving restaurant on the top floor) and each day when there was a concert performance, we'd come down to the lobby to be greeted by our assigned drivers who would then whisk us to the venue...in two different cars. After the show the same thing would happen in reverse. It was somewhat bizarre, but a lot of fun.
>
> "You could get used to that sort of treatment..."

She had had very little time for sight-seeing, but did manage to visit a First Nation site. Even then, it was France she returned to, for a concert in Avignon, before flying home the next day.

Sunday Best, Radio Cornwall, and UK media

In early 1983, Brenda was approached by BBC Radio Cornwall to present a regular weekly radio programme of listeners' requests, a notion which really appealed to her. Again – buffing my nails with a blasé air – it was I who come up with the title 'Sunday Best'.

It was to prove a labour of love for both Brenda and John for a number of years, for little reward – unless you count the main reason for her doing it, which was to connect with her Cornish fans and to raise her profile amongst the people of Cornwall, the vast majority of whom had no idea at all of Brenda's fame abroad. It is true she performed professionally far less in the UK than elsewhere – she has said: 'I trot across to Paris like I'm catching the Marazion bus – it's not that I don't want to work in my own country, I'd much prefer to... but I'm just not getting the offers'.

Justin Leigh, for many years a stalwart BBC presenter, remembers the early days of Radio Cornwall when he was a starry-eyed young wannabe...

> "I still have the very first Radio Cornwall magazine with autographs from some of the presenters, including Brenda Wootton. Brenda's Sunday request programme had become a family favourite in our household and we even wrote in to get a request played. I can't tell you how exciting it was to wait with anticipation for our names to be read out. Little did I know at the time that I would later go on to produce Brenda's programme. I was Justin 'twiddling the knobs', as Brenda used to put it."

She built up an enormous weekly following amongst Radio Cornwall listeners, attracting sometimes 600 postcards a week, all with requests for songs to be played. Now just imagine the work involved in reading through those 600 cards – selecting those she could include in the show, and arranging the requests in such a way that made for a well-balanced listening programme, without repeating songs from recent shows, making a few guideline notes for each track played, and ensuring that the records needed were indeed available in Radio Cornwall's archive.

She always played one or two of her own songs – not a lot in a 2-hour programme – but there were some requests that could be guaranteed to come up every week: 'My Way' and 'One Day at a Time' were definitely top favourites, although she would only play them periodically – there is a limit to how much of that sort of thing one can take. An unusual request stood a much better chance of being chosen.

Brenda recording her Sunday Best programme in Radio Cornwall

For Brenda and John, who went through every card, selecting, sorting, choosing and rejecting, it was many hours work every week, over and above the 2-hour broadcast programme. Then there was the drive from Newmill, north of Penzance, up to the studio in Truro, recording the show, and the driving back. If she was likely to be away, she pre-recorded a show. She certainly didn't do it for the money... I think it was about £30 a programme, by the end.

Browsing through a few of those requests which Brenda kept, I came across one from a rather remarkable chap called Sibley George Richards, of Penzance... born in Newlyn in 1911, and then aged 75, he was one of the few remaining (at that time) survivors of the Titanic disaster. He said in his letter "I am the youngest living survivor of the Titanic, being 10 months old at the time; we were saved in Lifeboat number 13 (official records have him in Lifeboat 4)... we were 6 hours in the open Atlantic Ocean, bitter cold, but my wonderful mother held me all the time and did her best to keep me warm until we were picked up at 6.30 am by the Carpathia and taken to New York...". His request was for a hymn reputedly played by the band as the Titanic went down... 'Nearer My God To Thee'...

At Christmas time and for events like Children-in-Need, she usually made special efforts. In early November, she sometimes wrote 'porchery' on demand for a donation to Children In Need, and in 1986, even milked a cow for the cause. A friend remembered her walking with Ian Botham on his first charity marathon from John O'Groats to Lands End in 1985 – on the very last leg, presumably! There were invariably special Radio Cornwall events at Christmas time: in 1981 she starred in the Radio Cornwall organised 'Cornwall Christmas Cracker Show' at the Coliseum at St Austell. On one of her trips to Australia, she even managed to set up an Aussie Sunday Best, pre-recording Cornish listeners' requests to be broadcast for family in Oz, and vice versa... it was very successful.

She won friends at home as easily as she did abroad. One subscriber to this biography, an American singer called Barbara Tresidder Ryan, has commented:

> "My husband and I met Brenda and John in Oct. '91. We all hit it off immediately and they took us on a tour of their favourite places and to find Tresidder Farm (my maiden name is Tresidder), then on to the Rogers' farm, Rosenithon, for a massive Sunday meal. Brenda played our music on her programme and had us open at the Star Inn in Redruth for the Rum and Shrub shanty singers. We are Celtic musicians [from a band called Iona] and I sing in Cornish. This was one of the most magical times of my life and I want to give your book to my husband to rekindle our memories of your magnificent mother."

She always tried to get to the Royal Cornwall Show each year, where Radio Cornwall invariably had a presence. Presenter Duncan Warren remembers it coincided with his wedding anniversary – and every year, she showed up with a bouquet for his wife... he was astonished she always remembered!

In her last year at Radio Cornwall, there were plans for her to do a new series of programmes called 'Brenda's Cornwall'. Here are her notes for an introductory piece she planned to record:

> "What is Brenda's Cornwall? For me it is wherever I meet Cornish people, from the banks of the Tamar to the last rocks of the Western Isles off Scilly... As I cross the Bridge, I'm in my own back garden... downhill all the way... on a boat, in a barrow, in a car or on a bus... Talk to me, tell me, when we meet, in Penzance, Padstow, Pendeen or Par, Hayle to Egloshayle, Skilly Gap to Kelly

> Bray... Tell me when it's your Feast or anniversary, gathering or revel, we'll try and get there, John and I, to your shows, gymkhanas... to meet you, who live in Cornwall, in a Calendar of the Cornish year. We'll have a yarn, perhaps a bit of music, a cup of tea, and a laugh, eh?"

Five weekly programmes were contracted for August 1992. It never happened, of course – though I think it would have been popular. Here is a bit of yarn she wrote for the proposed programme, about the much-loved and mourned Cornish MP, David Penhaligon:

> "Some years ago I had to go to London with our lovely David Penhaligon to judge a fiasco of a Pasty Competition put on by a big superstore. Beforehand I said to him, 'David – do you know *how* to make a pasty?'... 'Never 'ad to', he said... 'got a wife and a mother to do that – but I know how to eat them!' ... so I gave him a few pointers on what to look out for. My dear life – no wonder he was a politician! To listen to him 10 minutes later, you'd have believed he'd made pasties all his life... he picked the competitors up on everything! Some gab!

> "Years ago I wrote a song about a pasty for a pantomime, and we recorded it for the Pasties & Cream LP. About 8 or 9 of us went up to Stithians to record it with their band... we were all stood around a microphone at one end of the room – me with my back to the band, who were all sat up the other end of the room... I'd asked for it to start with a fanfare... we waited... all was silent, and I couldn't see the conductor... Then suddenly – My gar!! There was this great blast of sound! We couldn't sing a note, we all just fell about laughin'!"

Although her final illness had curtailed her activities abroad, she did manage to keep her Sunday Best programme on air for a while longer, finally announcing her retirement on 28th Jan 1992, which prompted a flood of cards from her listeners with get well messages and condolences.

As she became better known in the UK – although she was never as famous here as she was in Europe – it became the norm for her to do a spot on TV and/or radio just about anywhere she was booked to appear. There were a few special programmes, where she was given her own half-hour or hour-long broadcast, and I have managed to preserve poor copies of some of these on a CD – the quality is pretty dire in places, but as television companies generally seem to have been very bad at archiving their programmes at that time most cannot now be found elsewhere.

Back in the early '80s, she did two charming half hour shows for Westward TV – one called 'Cornwall the Land I Love' and the other 'Pasties and Cream'. Both shows had the same format: they featured a number of songs introduced and sung by Brenda, over a pre-recorded backing track, and filmed in some context that related to the song. Where possible, she interviewed someone of interest – such as Edward Waters, custodian of Geevor Tin Mine Museum, about the mining at Pendeen.

Brenda interviewing Edward Waters at Levant Mine for Westward TV

For 'Allan Apple', Brenda was filmed in Newlyn explaining the Allan Apple tradition, and interviewing a few friends about their memories of being given such apples in their youth. Newlyn fisherman Joe Brownfield joined her to talk about the fishing industry, for 'The Rape of the Mackerel Shoals', and for 'The Mermaid of Zennor', she was filmed at Zennor hearing the story from Cyril Orchard (who swore it was true), then singing from a bank of heather on the cliff above the sea. Both Davy and Jan also featured in the filming: for Pasties and Cream, she took a coachload of Cornish men and women to a field somewhere in Cornwall, where they sat on folding chairs amid the cows (odd choice of site!), and joined in with the singing – and there she was filmed chasing the 2-year old Jan around while he grins mischievously, and she sings the lovely tribute song she had asked Richard to write: Boy Jan; Davy also appeared in Allan Apple. I treasure these scraps of film of my two young lads!

There was a programme recorded in Penzance at Ponsandane, then a hotel, one Christmas – Noswyth Lowen, which featured Brenda singing with Cornish baritone Ben Luxon, along with Ros Keltek, Neil and Mervyn Davey and others. Brenda usually recorded a song for BBC Spotlight at Plymouth whenever she had a new record or was about to leave for a major tour or a prestigious event, but almost all of these 5-minute slots have been lost.

There is surprisingly little of Brenda in action to be found online. She had a half hour TV programme recorded in Bristol in 1978 with guitarist Chris Newman, on the Louis Robinson show, called 'Down the Club'; it was filmed in Bedminster Down Boys Club, already devoted fans – three tracks from this are now available on YouTube. Another half-hour show for TSW was rather insensitively titled 'Brenda Wootton, In the Round'. The French TV footage of her appearing with Mercedes Sosa and Maria Carta in Paris for the Three Divas tour in 1983 is very good.

She did significant interviews over the years for many newspapers, magazines and journals, including She Magazine with Leonard Pearcey (see appendix) and Annabel magazine, and for the folk scene: Folk Review, Melody Maker and Folk Roots.

In 1987 she was involved in organising a major musical event at Towednack. The small village and abbey of Landavennec in north-west Brittany is named for the same saint as Towednack near St Ives – St Winwaloe – and to celebrate the 1500th anniversary of the founding of the Benedictine Abbey at Landévennec, a special event was planned with the Abbot and four Breton monks visiting Towednack. Once again, Brenda requested some special songs for the event from Richard Gendall, who wrote a cycle of songs dramatizing the life of St Winwaloe.

The song cycle was sung by Brenda, accompanied by Praze Male Voice Choir, and with the attendance of a large gathering of Clerics, French and Cornish, including the Bishops of Plymouth and Truro – choirs from eight local churches also took part, and the event was attended by over 1000 people. Amazingly, the South West Film & Television Archive do hold some footage of this event.

They also, I believe, hold footage of the 'War & Pieces Show', though I haven't yet seen it... In 1978 a friend called John Dane asked Brenda to take part in a production he was putting on for the 'Serenade 78' Arts Festival in Plymouth – the 'War & Pieces Show'.

Brenda and Richard with Abbé Jean De La Croix of Landévennec at the Winwaloe celebrations at Towednack, 1987

It was staged in Buckland Abbey near Yelverton, the home of Francis Drake, I believe to celebrate the 400th anniversary of the voyage of the Golden Hind around the world. The production had a cast of actors and dancers, all lavishly dressed as clowns, doing readings, monologues, songs, dances etc on the general theme of war and peace. Ian Stirling, a presenter on Westward TV, and a great mate of Brenda's, though more usually seen with one hand up the TV puppet Gus Honeybun, was also in the cast. Brenda and Dave had fabulous clown and harlequin-styled costumes, themed, like the rest of the cast, in red, purple, orange and yellow, and with professional clown make-up. Brenda sang Richard's Cornish lullaby 'Pensevyk Byghan' and Ewen Carruther's 'In Love Again', as well as, in a departure from her usual programme – 'The White Cliffs of Dover', 'Johnny I Hardly Knew You', 'When You're Smiling', 'When Morning Breaks', and 'Send in the Clowns', with chilling effect.

Dave Penhale recalls one 'single song' slot they pre-recorded in Plymouth for Westward TV... they were on their way back home to Penzance, and the recording had been done only a couple of hours before the programme was due to be broadcast. Driving down through Cornwall after doing their spot, Brenda realised they wouldn't be back in time to see their performance on air. She had the notion of stopping somewhere en route to see if they could watch the show on someone else's TV – no programme playback option in those days! So somewhere near Trago Mills, she asked Dave to pull in at a complete stranger's residence, and knocked on the door, asking politely if they would mind if Brenda and Dave came in to watch Westward on their TV, as they would be performing in a few minutes. The surprised elderly couple apparently agreed readily.

Brenda with Ian Stirling as clowns in the War & Pieces Show, 1978

Gwylan Gwavas – Seagull of Newlyn, Bard of the Gorsedh Kernow

One title which Brenda apparently felt a little uneasy about was 'Cornwall's First Lady of Song' – in a letter to one reporter she protested: "...but I do not claim that!", offering the name of Dame Fanny Moody, the 'Cornish Nightingale', as a more likely contender. She may not have claimed it – but that is how many referred to her.

Brenda in her new bardic robes at her first Gorsedh, with Ben Luxon, 1977

Probably one of the proudest days in Brenda's life was on a Saturday in September 1977, when at Nine Maidens, St Columb Major, she was made a Bard of the Gorsedh Kernow, for her services to music and the language in Cornwall. That year, in her blue Bardic robes, she walked with Cornish singer Ben Luxon, already a Bard, and took quite seriously her pledge of allegiance to King Arthur. She chose the Bardic name 'Gwylan Gwavas', Kernewek for 'Seagull of Newlyn'... Gwylan is Seagull, and Gwavas is an old name for that part of Newlyn from where Brenda's family hailed, and can also mean 'the winter place'. Brenda once explained it as "It means Newlyn or winter seagull, and it's right because I'm always flying across the water with my mouth wide open!"...[45] Some will have heard, and been startled by, Brenda's sudden and amazingly realistic imitation of a seagull in full cry – occasionally she was known to throw her head back and give a long and loud, full-throated 'gooooooolla gulla gulla gullagullagulla!!', followed by the characteristically perky 'parp parp parp parp...'! But the 'Gwylan' of her Bardic name was intended more as a reference to her singing like a bird, seagulls being Newlyn's most common, although not necessarily most tuneful, bird... the ever-present noisy flocks around Cornish harbours are more often seen as 'flying rats' than songbirds, particularly in view of their indiscriminate theft of anything edible from 'gullible' hands! Although I confess to looking

[45] *Western Morning News, 27th August 1980*

on them a lot more kindly in recent years, now that Brenda may be among them... and they were here first... (Richard once wrote a song about an incident from her childhood – she had rescued an injured gull and a kindly bus driver took pity on her when she had no money for the bus fare to Mousehole Bird Hospital to get it fixed.)

The area of sea outside Newlyn harbour has long been known as Gwavas Lake, possibly a folk memory from the time when it was indeed a lake, before the sea level rose. It is known that at some time in the distant past, St Michael's Mount was four miles inland, and its Cornish name, 'Carrek Los yn Cos', means 'Hoar rock in the wood'. The submerged forest that is sometimes visible in Mounts Bay at low Spring tides offers proof, and contributes to the stories of the lost land of Lyonesse... the title of an album and a song of Brenda's.

She attended the Gorsedh whenever she could, and saw it as part of her Bardic role to be an Ambassador for Cornwall wherever her career should take her.

1977 was a great year for Brenda, as a few weeks after the Gorsedh in October, her first grandchild was born. With typical Brenda restraint, she encouraged me to name him after Penzance's most famous son, Sir Humphry Davy... although I did like the name Davy, and had no reservations. Every opportunity she had, she pushed Cornwall, the Cornish people, or the Cornish language to the fore. Even though she didn't speak Cornish, if anything needed naming, she phoned Richard for suggestions in Kernewek... so the playgroup I ran in Canon's Town became Bagas Gwary, for example. Pets were given Cornish names, cars, boats, babies...

Many and various were the bookings, festivals and concerts she was called to... and whenever the situation demanded it, especially if there was a snippet of Cornish history or a legend to be explained, or a Cornish character or a place to talk about, she would ask Richard for a special song for the occasion. So, she had songs relating to Humphry Davy, Richard Trevithick, China Clay, tin mining or miners, fishing or fishermen, pirates, Padstow May Day and accordionist

A proud Brenda in bardic robes with Davy and Jan

Charlie Bate, Helston Flora Day, and the Well of St Keyne, the River Tamar, Luxulyan or the Scilly Isles, the Mermaid of Zennor or the King of Prussia Cove... or simply about her love for Cornwall.

It is true that wherever she went she took Cornwall with her. When she began touring in Europe, she kept a lump of Cornish granite beneath the seat in her car, to 'ground' her. When news was broadcast about the dangers of Radon gas in homes built of Cornish granite, she didn't mind in the least... she cheerfully decided she was addicted to it.

I have a vivid memory of Brenda and the boys, whom she had persuaded into their Cornish Tartan kilts for the occasion, standing alone on the empty streets of Camborne, waving her Cornish flag proudly and singing Trelawney with tears in her eyes, to welcome home the coach carrying the Cornish rugby team who had on that occasion *failed* to win the cup at Twickenham.

It soon became clear, especially once Sunday Best was established, that the Cornish had indeed taken Brenda to their hearts, and claimed her as their own. One rather comical instance of this became evident in the late 1980s, when she was approached for permission to use her name by a local entrepreneur: he had produced a line of cuddly, colourful and furry pasties to sell, called the Oggy Family. Most of the 'family' had humorous names... Soggy was the surfer dude, Joggy was the exercise freak – but the (pink!) mother of the outfit he called Brenda.

Brenda was constantly approached by charities asking for her to perform at their events, or to donate a record or a scarf for a raffle. She did have certain charities she favoured – she had great respect for the Cheshire Home at Long Rock who had helped some old friends and relatives, and later in her career she sang to open the Green Fair in Penzance for several years. It would have been impossible for her to accept every one of these charitable calls on her time, although she did what she could. She often donated her time to work with local Cornish bands and choirs, maybe introducing their concerts and singing a couple of numbers with them...

For some years in the mid-1980s, she undertook to do a series of workshops with a number of primary schools in Cornwall, under the auspices of the then County Music Adviser, Derek Kitt. She put enormous effort into these workshops, researching local legends and characters that were relevant to each school she visited, and asking Richard Gendall for new songs for each new topic. She created visual aids, drawing pictures herself, with notes, in felt tips on large pieces of card, and wrote out humorous or interesting stories to tell them, dramatizing parts where necessary. She got the children to act out some stories with her, or to do relevant illustrations or make craft items. One headmaster, in his 'thank you' letter to Brenda, recounted comments he later overheard from two, normally truculent, boy pupils: "She 'ad a beautiful voice", said one, and the other responded "She was heck of a good".

What did she get paid for all this effort? Precious little... but she loved to work with the kids, and it was part of her mission, to teach Cornish children about their culture.

She accepted the role of President of Radio Beacon, the voluntarily-run Hospital Radio for St Lawrence's Hospital at Bodmin – it was where her Cousin Malc had stayed for a long while after his dreadful accident. And she had a couple of 'social clubs' that she particularly befriended: Bedminster Down Boys Club in Bristol had first come down to west Cornwall on holiday in the mid-1960s, a coachload of inner-city lads and their leaders, including a marvellous chap called Steve Long, one of the key organisers. They were so thrilled with Brenda and Fish singing at the Count House that they came back every night during their week's holiday, and returned with a fresh group of eager lads year after year.

> "Brenda and Fish would join the older members and helpers (old enough to drink) for lunch during the holiday, and it wasn't long before the duo would be performing their first concert outside their beloved Cornwall – at Bedminster Down Boys Club on 13th October 1966. When the Count House closed, Brenda opened Pipers Folk Club at St Buryan, and BDBC went with them. In 1970, Brenda and Fish were Guests of Honour at the Club's Open Night, the ultimate tribute for the Club's love for the First Lady of Cornwall."[46]

The boys clubbed together and presented Brenda with a copper kettle, in honour of one of their favourite songs of hers, and Brenda and Fish went up to Bristol to sing at the club a few times – once appearing with football legend Jimmy Hill – so she became very friendly with Steve and his family.

---

[46] *"Girls Not Allowed – A History of the BDBC", Andy Lewis*

Brenda and Fish with Jimmy Hill and Bedminster Down Boys Club in Bristol

The Ashtorre Rock Community Centre at the Waterside, almost under the bridge at Saltash, was another favourite. She was filmed cutting the ribbon for the opening of the new centre there in March 1991, when most of her other appearances had already stopped. They adored Brenda, and she went back there many times, even writing one of her Cornish Alphabets for them.

It wasn't all about performing though. Whenever friends or visitors came to call, they would be taken on a guided tour of her favourite places – Sennen Cove maybe, Cot Valley at St Just, Lamorna, Mousehole – Brenda still carrying out the role of Ambassador. But always, if the season was right, they would end up at Newlyn for a Jelberts' ice cream. Best in the world, we all agreed... they're still using the same secret family recipe as when Brenda was a girl, in their shop beside the bridge at Newlyn. I often used to see Stevie or his descendants wheeling the big ice cream cartons up the road to the shop in a converted baby's pram, even in the 1990s... And, as has been mentioned many times – any excuse for a picnic.

One of Cornish culture's most prestigious events was the huge concert with Massed Cornish Choirs in the Royal Albert Hall in 1988. For once, she could attend and just be a member of the audience, and she took all the family with her... Auntie Kate and Cousin Barbara and their families, who lived in London, joined her there, and she took enough flags for them all to wave.

Like a 'busman's holiday', if she had a free evening at home, Brenda would often search out a nice bit of singing. If there was one musical activity which she occasionally became involved in purely for fun, it was jazz. She established a long-term musical relationship with the

Phil King Trio, and individual jazz musicians such as Ray Roberts on clarinet, trombone or sax, Ralph Freeman, Viv Rodd, Ashley Staton or Phil King on piano and Goudie Charles on bass – all performed with her often in various musical line-ups.

Brenda and family at the Royal Albert Hall, and yes, she brought enough flags for everyone

Brenda singing jazz at the Old Quay House, Hayle

She would often try and get along to the Smugglers at St Erth Praze, or to The Old Quay House at Hayle, where like as not she would end up doing an impromptu jazz performance with the band. As she had always wanted, she took her own jazz combo with her to France when she did the Bobino tour, and scored a huge hit in Paris: Chris Newman, on guitar, Ray Roberts on sax and flute, and Dave Freeman on bass; they can be heard on the 'All of Me' CD. Pianist Ashley Staton, if he wasn't working away as an entertainer on cruise ships, often sat in on her album recordings, and she also did some jazz numbers with guitarist John Knight of Coverack, with the Jubilee Jazz Band, and that great outfit from Plymouth, Rod Mason's Jazz Band.

Brenda's versatility as a singer was widely acknowledged, but her ability to sing jazz was less widely known – she was a great 'scat' singer, and could join in and take off at ease with free-style harmonies and improvised trad jazz licks. I hope one day to be able to bring out a CD of Brenda singing jazz and blues numbers – I have several unpublished recordings which I'm sure would be well received by her fans. And as she said to Colin Irwin in an interview in the Melody Maker: "The blues in me is bursting to get out somewhere..."[47]

But any opportunity for a good sing, was her main drive when back home. She'd have loved the regular 'Shouts' that have sprung up around Cornwall in recent years... she attended whenever she could the one that has been happening every Friday in the pub at Cadgwith for years, and enjoyed joining in with the crowd. Local characters Buller Arthur and Hartley Trip (Tripconey) would 'strike sound', and amid shouts of "Give 'er cloth!" and "Like a' organ!!", would make the rafters ring. Cadgwith's gig is now called the Buller in his memory, and the village holds an annual Buller Day.

Lowender Peran Festival

In 1978, the first annual Lowender Peran Festival took place in the Ponsmere Hotel in Perranporth. Brenda appeared pretty much from the beginning, and was a huge supporter. She attended the festival whenever she could, sometimes booking a room in the hotel for the duration, and often performed – doing a proper concert, joining in a singsong, or simply telling yarns (a couple of which I have on film). Here is what the current Festival website has to say about those early days:

> "The Pan Celtic Festival, [*which of course Brenda had attended in 1972 and in later years*] then held in Killarney, was particularly supportive of the Cornish and encouraged performers to attend and take part in the competitions. Con O'Connaill, the executive director of the festival, made frequent visits to Cornwall to drum up support and found an ardent enthusiast in Betty Pitman of Perranporth who lead a party of Cornish to the festival throughout the 70s.
>
> "Encouraged by the successful entry of Kemysk in the Celtic Singing competitions in 1978 Betty was determined that Cornwall should have its own Celtic festival and by October of that year it did.

---

[47] *Melody Maker, December 1976*

There was a weeklong festival of what Betty deemed as Celtic activities which included a variety of water sports, tug of war teams and wrestling as well as music and dance. A short while after the first festival Betty booked up the dates and venues for the next year and called a meeting of interested parties, committed them to running the event and then promptly resigned!

"The festival was named In recognition of [St] Peran and Lowender Peran was born.

"**Cornish Dance** Folk dancing and dance displays were, and are, a key feature of the Celtic festivals as they provide the opportunity for pageant and colour as well as the expression of identity through costume and tradition. Cam Kernewek formed late in 1979 and were quickly followed by Ros Keltek in early 1980 so that Cornish dance displays and troyls were a feature of the 1980 festival and have remained a core part of the festival since that time.

Brenda on stage at Lowender Peran Festival, with guitarist Chris Newman

"**Cornish Music** Whilst main stage concerts are enjoyed by all and our own bands are regularly joined by well-known performers from the Celtic Diaspora, the opportunity to participate has been a key feature of Lowender Peran from the outset. From the informal sessions that spring up throughout the festival to the opportunity for a spot on the acoustic stage or the Droll Adro storytellers tale swop this continues to be a part of the culture of Lowender Peran.

"**Celebrating a wider Cornish heritag***e* The cover of the 20th anniversary programme for Lowender Peran depicted a fish wife in work wear costume and marked a move in emphasis towards the celebration of a wider Cornish heritage. This shift in emphasis eventually lead to the launch of the 'An Daras Cornish Folk Arts

Project' in 2003 and the regular inclusion of events involving dialect, verbal arts, costume and Cornish history and folklore as well as an extended range of crafts in the 'Celtic Market'."

In 2013 the Festival committee asked me to present a talk on Brenda as part of their programme. They had arranged a 'Brenda Wootton' evening, in recognition of her support for both the festival and Cornish culture and the language. The festival also invited four young Cornish performers to select a song of Brenda's from one of her recorded albums, and perform it in their own style during the evening. Camborne Town Band was also invited, and reprised their version of Over the Rainbow that they had performed with Brenda at the Bobino Theatre in Paris and on French TV in 1983, 30 years earlier. It was a very moving evening, and I was heartened to see the enthusiasm and skill with which the young performers tackled Brenda's songs, and the love and appreciation from the audience.

One of those performers, Richard Trethewey, an extremely talented and committed Cornish musician with a great love for Cornwall, was again asked to prepare several tracks with Camborne Town Band for Lowender Peran in 2017, by then located at Newquay. An earlier presentation was planned that afternoon, as part of the Cornish Music Symposium, with Richard providing an illustrated talk on the Cornish language songs recorded by Brenda which are available for performers to learn. He had most of the information from my recently created Brenda website, but wanted to come down and have a chat with me about Richard Gendall and the Cornish songs – and his bribe, for my time, was his own hand-made pasties, using his gran's recipe. That lad makes an *ansum* pasty!! He can come back *any*time. He did a marvellous presentation, singing a couple of the songs as well with Stephen Hunt accompanying, and the concert with Camborne Town Band was fantastic. And I was awestruck to meet his Granny – a pasty maker supreme.

With all of this attention from the next generation of performers in Cornwall, I was left so thrilled to feel that Brenda's legacy is indeed not only intact, but stronger than ever.

St Ives September Festival

Martin Val Baker began the institution that is St Ives September Festival many years ago, and it is still bringing down innovative and prestigious performers annually, as well as the best of local acts. Here is his take on a concert featuring Brenda in 1979...

"The wide diversity of acts and cultures made for some strange bedfellows, and for one night we decided to try and mix them together on one stage, something which seemed a very good idea at the time. Topping the bill we had the Cornish folk diva Brenda Wootton with a couple of I.M.S. chamber musicians, some other folkies, Bob Devereux and two poets from the north. The northern poets had only just arrived in town, not expecting to have to perform that night, and consequently had had a few drinks on the way down.

"The large audience consisted mostly of elderly St Ives folk who had come to see Brenda, who was very popular at that time, and I rather suspect that their familiarity with the work of alternative poets from the north was fairly minimal. Anyway the poets started the evening off and after about fifteen minutes the St Ives lady who was selling raffle tickets for us came out to me on the door and said 'Martin, there doesn't seem to be much applause in there – oh, hang on... they're beginning to clap...'.

"And so they were... slowly – very slowly, they clapped. The poets had misjudged the situation – or rather we had given them the wrong audience. As I poked my head into the hall they were going on about dog mess in St Ives – not quite right for the local audience at all. It was the first and only time I have heard a slow handclap, but the northern poets, rather bewildered, still did not take the hint that their time had come. Bob, who was also acting as compere, had to move on to the stage and carefully manoeuvre them off it. The rest of the evening went down relatively well and at last the audience were able to see their favourite in full song. Another lesson learned, don't mix chalk and cheese. The following year we put Brenda on with the Four Lanes Choir – a much more comfortable situation for her..."

He added: "I will always remember Brenda and John doing a fantastic rendition of 'Tishomingo Blues' at The Half Moon, Putney, in the Seventies ..."

Did she get there?

Did Brenda achieve what she set out to do? She did not choose the epithets that she was awarded by the different countries in which she appeared. She made no claims to be Cornwall's Queen of Song, or the Grandmother of the Celts. She rejected the title of 'Cornwall's First Lady of Song', and said that belonged to Fanny Moody, as she had 'earned it'. She often described herself as simply 'a Cornish granny who dearly loves to sing'. But she certainly made her name, whichever one it was, wherever she went – and to my mind, she did achieve something wonderful...

Initially, she wanted to fight through the inevitable prejudices associated with being a middle-aged, fat, Cornish housewife – to prove to the naysayers that she was different, she was special, she had a demonstrable and singular talent that others would pay to see. She made it OK for an older woman to suddenly grasp her talent and thrust herself onto the world stage. Age was not a barrier – her size was not a barrier... together with that astonishing voice, they became almost an asset, highlighting how far removed she was from the legion of pretty young women with a nice-enough voice and a song to sing. Every glowing press review marvelled how someone such as her could come from nowhere, a middle-aged granny from a rural backwater, and become such a shining star for all the Celts. She recounted a revealing anecdote...

> "I did a concert just before Christmas and a lady came up to me after and said 'I saw you on the telly last year, and I told my husband I thought you were crackers, going off round the world like that at your age. I only came along to your concert because I was curious to see what you were like for real. And I've been suffering from depression lately, and you came on and you gave me the 'andsomest night I've ever had. I'm 52, and I've not been coping well – but you've done me the world of good. I'm going to go out and do more things from now on. I thank you for what you've done for me..."[48]

She boosted the confidence of women around the world, made them feel that – if Brenda could do it, follow her dreams, and win through, maybe they could too. She was quoted in an interview for the West Briton Argus in 1980:

---

[48] *'Cornish Life', Vol 6 No 2*

"Middle age does not daunt her. In fact she loves to drive home to her audiences the fact that everything doesn't grind to a halt between 40 and 50... 'Too many people look on their middle years as a time of takings things easy and giving up, and their talents can all too easily go to waste.' Age, concludes Brenda, has nothing to do with capability and ambition..."[49].

So her goal, when she started singing on stage, was almost certainly personal success, the ambition to achieve recognition for her own talents – and to demonstrate that a fat, middle-aged Cornish woman could be a force to be reckoned with. Over the years I think that morphed into a serious mission – a bold endeavour to bring Cornwall and its culture to a much wider world, to use her own Cornishness as a vehicle with an irresistible message, that I think as time went on became less and less about her, and more and more about Cornwall. One French fan certainly got the message, writing to say "Dear Mrs Wootton – Thank you for giving us Cornwall..."

Although it wasn't there when she began her journey, the desire to tell the world about Cornwall soon became a driving force. As he had wanted, she got Richard Gendall's music out to a huge global audience, and won thousands of converts. A Metropolitan Police Officer wrote to the Cornishman after one of her concerts: "As long as this jolly lady travels the country, and I believe soon, the world, Cornishmen like myself will be reunited through song with the homeland they so deeply love..."

At every single concert she performed, on every TV or radio programme, in every newspaper interview, and with every record she sold, her audiences around the world would hear some of the Cornish language and the dialect, they would hear her telling stories – yarns – about her childhood, about her country and its culture, about its people. This was one role she totally embraced – Ambassador for Cornwall. And in that too, she definitely succeeded, handsomely. She nailed it.

After she died, Neil Kennedy, Secretary of the Cornish Language Council, said in a letter to the Western Morning News... "Cornwall, and more specifically, the Cornish language, has lost a great ambassador..." Pretty good for someone who never really learned to speak it properly.

---

[49] *West Briton Argus, July 28th 1980*

So – yes – I think she got there. She achieved both goals – recognition for her country and its culture, and an appreciation of its language – *and* she won an army of fans around the world for her superlative singing voice and her larger-than-life personality. I think she *did* earn that accolade – Cornwall's First Lady of Song. (Shame Fanny Moody got in there first with 'Cornwall's Nightingale', really.)

Brenda was justifiably proud of her victorias

Paying the piper...

Brenda's meteoric success as a performer came at a price. It was always a fine balancing act, between what she felt she needed to do, and what she was physically capable of. She effectively built herself a gilded cage, and, desirable as global recognition and success obviously were, she inevitably had to continuously push herself higher and harder, often at the expense of her personal relationships, her health and her home life. Once fame hit, she was not free to choose to take time out at whim, or to decide not to do a tour because she wanted to spend time with her grandsons.

It was almost an addiction – if a new prospect was offered, some new opportunity to perform before an untried audience, with a celebrity, or for a prestigious event – she would move heaven and earth to make it happen.

But where she had once been so excited and thrilled to visit new places, to have new experiences, to learn new material, eventually the excitement faded and it became, at times, a chore. When she had bragged to John that *she* was now the breadwinner in the house, that *she* owned the car, maybe she hadn't fully thought through the implications – that *she* was now the one responsible for paying for it all – which meant she *must* keep working, no matter what; it was a treadmill she couldn't step off. Learning new material meant unpaid hours, sometimes weeks, of rehearsals to bring the current guitarist up to scratch... Visiting new places meant unpaid hours of travel to get to unknown venues and deal with people with whom she was unfamiliar. In Paris, the golden city she had loved, she had experienced a number of troubling thefts – her valuable Martin guitar, sums of money – a couple of times her vehicle was damaged in break-ins, and it all shook her confidence.

With Robert, the exciting new career had been a joint venture, a duo – but ever after – she was on her own. She was a solo performer with an accompanist. She was not only responsible for keeping her own family going, but also for ensuring the guitarist got paid, that the other business-related bills were paid, that her agents in different countries were on the ball and new tours and publicity were being booked, that her Radio Cornwall programme requests were prepared and pre-recorded, that records were planned, to the tiniest detail, that her programme remained balanced with enough new material – that she always appeared *professional*. Inevitably there were times on long tours abroad when she was aching with tiredness, when depression and exhaustion completely overcame her – but often the only people to know that at the time would have been the people she was travelling with – her guitarists. They would have to suffer her resulting mood swings and impatience – we left at home only knew what she chose to tell us.

Raymond Delf performed with a dance group and travelled with Brenda to Lorient, and remembers a charity concert in the late '70s...

> "Cam Kernewek was the support group for a charity gig that 'Our Brenda' was holding in Camborne. We had been in Lorient with her, and she had also completed a rather long tour of Brittany prior to this charity event. This tour had taken an awful lot out of her, she was both in pain, and physically exhausted, but her performance that night was flawless, and Brenda was her usual exuberant personality. That is until she turned her back to the audience, and let the pain and exhaustion show both in between her performances, and on completion, it was then that we all realised exactly what was meant by the words 'True Professional'. Amazing, wonderful, Lady, with a superb voice, who will never be forgotten by any who knew her.."

As a woman, as a very large woman, as an older woman with health issues, as a woman travelling and working in foreign countries, often trying to cope with languages she didn't know... she had a lot of obstacles and prejudices to overcome, and the extra weight she carried was as much emotional as it was physical. The pressure became worse when there were grandsons to leave behind... She shouldered these burdens alone, for the most part. She rarely complained, or revealed how much the stresses and strains affected her – certainly to anyone outside immediate family; after all, she had made her own choices. In a rare confessional letter home from Paris in 1977 she admits "I woke up here yesterday morning crawling with fright and thought the car had been stolen – Paris does things like this to you – as you well know! But no, it was ok..." However, she later discovers a large sum of money is missing from her handbag, decimating the profits from the tour: "It's no use breaking my heart – I feel angry, frustrated – I'm *not* a careless person... but I get scared... all the other things in my bag are precious too... my god, how I hate Paris! Sorry, so mixed up – oh how I miss you all – shall be glad to be too busy to think..."

Brenda was not a deeply religious person – she was not a regular attender at any church, although I think she did have some religious convictions. Obviously she had been brought up as 'chapel', and was comfortable enough in that environment. If she was buoyed up by any kind of faith, it was more likely to be her faith in her Cornish roots and in her own abilities. But this could, and did, frequently take a beating. It was not something she ever really discussed with me, but I know she was, nevertheless, deeply spiritual. She certainly found a spiritual lift from certain places... old churches, or wild and beautiful countryside, in the presence of certain people or listening to some particular music. She would happily attend any religious ceremony or service if there was a specific reason, but I sensed she enjoyed the experience as much for the shared joy of the music and the singing as anything.

This lovely story I came across recently in the Guardian perhaps best illustrates Brenda's belief system:

> 'At a meeting of west Cornwall's pagans, a Cornish speaker told me a story to illustrate the complex web of belief and identity. When he was a boy, his grandfather had taken him to the top of Carn Brea, one of the hills believed to have been significant in prehistory. The old man grabbed his hand and thrust it into the soil. "Feel that, boy," he said, "that's the beating heart of Cornwall. But don't you go telling Grandma – she thinks I'm a good Methodist."'[50]

Dik Cadbury, during the time he spent with Brenda rehearsing material, was responsible for introducing her to Quakerism – it is a belief system strongly associated with all the Cadbury family, including Dik's mother Marion, who became a good friend to Brenda. Dik took Brenda to the beautiful Quaker Meeting House at Come-To-Good, which she later visited with Robert Bartlett – who was a friend of Dik's, of course, from their time in the group Totem. Although she never became a regular attender, Brenda seemed to get comfort from such visits, and appreciated the tranquillity. Her friend Gerald Priestland was also a Quaker, and I know they shared similar beliefs.

As to her career, she obviously felt that the cost to her health and her peace-of-mind was justified. Yet although it was clear to all that

---

[50] *Philip Marsden, "Cornish identity: why Cornwall has always been a separate place", Guardian newspaper, 26/4/2014*

she obviously did achieve her main goals, that was never enough – there was always more she wanted to achieve, and couldn't… she never wanted it to stop, she fought to keep going, when all around her knew it was fruitless. That was Brenda… always strothin'…

Damawyn

Amazing to think that, with everything else that was going on in her professional life, Brenda had time for any personal life away from the pressure and the crowds. But meanwhile, back at the ranch...

Grandchildren

On September 10th 1975, I married Arthur John Luscombe in Penzance Registry Office, and that evening we had a reception at the Trewellard Meadery. It was a memorable event – John and I had met at the folk club, and many of our friends from the folk scene were there, and from the various drama groups. There was entertainment throughout the evening: from the Choughs, from Brenda's great friend Geoff Hudd from Padstow, from John & Sue Visick, from Fish, Donald Jarvis and Vera Round, Mike Sagar-Fenton, Steve Hall, Mic McCreadie and all the usual suspects. Richard Gendall wrote and performed a special song for our wedding, and of course Brenda sang. It was a lovely day, marred only by the fact that there were some important people missing: Robert, who should have been our Best Man, my best friend and cousin, Diane, who had made my wedding dress, and her parents, Marjorie and Ken – my Great-Aunt and Uncle. Whatever had happened between Brenda and Robert, it was my wedding day, and I felt they should all have been there. That still saddens me now.

The very next morning Brenda was off on her trip to Amsterdam to work with her new guitarist, Mike Silver.

John and I had moved into our first house, in Jamaica Terrace in Heamoor, earlier in 1975, and the following year we managed to get a mortgage on a lovely property in Canon's Town, midway between Penzance and Hayle. A long string of a village with no real centre, it was difficult to find any sort of community to become a part of – one little village shop, a church with a strict Methodist Church steward who guarded it with a vengeance, and a pub, was all that was on offer. Husband John was working as a fitter & turner at Holmans in Camborne, where he was to stay for many years, then moving to Bassets of Hayle and finally back to Compair at Pool, always working in light engineering roles.

After Brenda had turned professional in 1974, as well as taking on her role of Shop Manager at Tremaen Craft Market, at some point I seem to have also taken on the role of her PA in the UK. I felt singularly ill-equipped for the task, but did the best I could, handling the correspondence, record production and UK bookings. It's difficult to sell your mother... I certainly always felt a little awkward trying to convince potential venues of how wonderful she was, even though I knew her voice was astonishing – it felt like boasting.

Managing Tremaens and working for Brenda certainly kept me busy for a while, but by the summer of 1977 when my first baby was due, I gave up the shop to concentrate on being a mum.

By the due date, I was staggering around like a ship in full sail, but there were no signs of imminent birth. Brenda was booked to appear at Landithy Hall at Madron that night, where BBC Radio 2 was staging their popular Barn Dance programme, hosted by Terry Wogan. I was in no fit state to be barn dancing or dosey-doe-ing up and down the hall, although it was suggested as a remedy for my condition. Brenda had to sing a couple of songs on stage, accompanied by Mike Sagar-Fenton. Of course she announced to the world that her first grandchild was due that night, much to the delight of Terry Wogan and the audience in the hall, although probably of little interest to the millions listening around the UK. But Davy, laid back as he later proved to be, didn't appear for another 10 days.

When Davy was born (at 9lb 10oz!), I took one look at the little cross and crumpled face and burst into tears, saying "It's another bloody Ellery!" They were tears of joy – the newborn face reminded me so much of Angus, who often talked of the "the divine right of the bloody Ellerys"... their conviction that they could and should do whatever they felt was right at whatever cost, with a strong tendency to bloody-mindedness.

Brenda was ecstatic with her new grandson, and with her new role as grandmother.

But the new arrival cost her dear in terms of her emotional state, and her ability to cope with her job. This is from a letter she wrote home from Paris, a fortnight after Davy was born:

Brenda with baby Davy – an all-embracing love

"Paris depresses me, and I was sad before I arrived, and these grey hotel rooms only make it all worse. When I'm really busy it'll be easier. In an hour we go to the theatre and an interview on the radio etc – feel numb, as though it's really nothing to do with me.

"When you and John first announced a baby coming, I felt happy at the idea – but didn't realise the impact he would have on me. Not the usual 'look at his little fingernails' etc – that's all there of course, but this immense awe of his existence. You two are the mother and father but he's there (25% anyway) because of me – a living miracle – the shape of his head, the set of his eyes – already a little personality who will grow up in his own manner in spite of us. He is unique, as we all are – one day he'll have to worry and care over you, when you're old, and I'll be long gone... it's the continuity of it all... past and future are already in him – he's been to Belgium even now! [*I'd been with Brenda on her recent tour, heavily pregnant*]. Our everyday surface was predictable and calm, and then he dropped in and caused such a splash, and his circle is widening, and we are caught up in it...

"And what a lot of love he has created in two weeks... Alice's eyes were a joy to behold – last year she was painful and prickly in her loss – the loss is still there, but softened by the fact that Davy Arthur Ellery Luscombe exists... [*my mother-in-law, a year after her husband Arthur died*]"

She was desperately missing her hands-on experience of the new love of her life, baby Davy – but also was particularly depressed that day, as she'd discovered some money had been stolen from her purse – inexplicably, as she kept her bag close beside her at all times. It effectively meant she had little profit from the trip, and Christmas was coming...

She was on her way back from Brittany when Davy was due to be christened, and told her Breton hosts, and the audiences, and the men working on the ferry boat (whom she also sang for on the crossing) of her good news. When she arrived at our house, there was barely room in the car – she was loaded up with their gifts of bottles of wine, bags of langoustine and lobster, Breton cakes and sweets, huge bouquets of flowers – all given for Davy's christening party. His full name is Davy Arthur Ellery Luscombe – Davy for Penzance's most famous son, Sir Humphry, Arthur for his Grandad in Camborne and for King Arthur, to whom Brenda had pledged allegiance when she was made a Bard, and Ellery for Angus, because I couldn't leave him out, and it was the first name I'd thought of when Davy was born...

She consulted Richard for an appropriate granny name for herself in Cornish, and was delighted with his suggestion: Damawyn. Dama is Dame, and wyn is fair or beautiful... so 'Fair Dame', and it is only applicable to the oldest matriarch in any family, given as a mark of respect. There can be only one! And she was it – neither of the boys had any problem with calling her 'Damwyn' from the moment they could speak... and today, for my sins, I am the Damawyn for my six grandchildren.

I carried on with my homemaking – against all sensible advice, re-decorating and wallpapering every room in our house at once, and sorting out our 150' long but very narrow garden. In January 1980, Jan Gwavas Luscombe was born – at 10lb 3oz (thanks to his 6' 2" dad, who apparently had been a 12lb-er, *and* delivered at home with no midwife!). His size caused some comment, including one from my midwife, who said, memorably, if not reassuringly "Well, I shouldn't worry Mrs Luscombe... if you want any more you won't have any trouble... you could drive a train through there." Bless. After that experience, I resolved then and there that two was quite enough, thank you. Jan was so-named as the Cornish version of John, as both his father and his grandfather were Johns (let alone John the Fish!) – and a generic name for a Cornishman is Boy Jan or

Janner – and he was born in January! And Gwavas was the second part of Brenda's Bardic name: Gwylan Gwavas, or Seagull of Newlyn, her home town – but Gwavas can also mean the winter place, and Jan was born in winter.

Jan-Jan Luscombe (Brenda's pet name for him) proved an 'interesting' baby. He had a very creative side. 'One morning, to my absolute horror, I discovered that not only could Jan get out of his cot unaided, but that he was capable of getting down the stairs too... neither of which we had realised. I found him beneath the table in the kitchen, sitting happily in a home-made 'soup' of black Gestetner ink, the contents of a tube of my face make-up, and a packet of Swoop wild bird food, and completely covered, from head to toe. I had to use a towel to pick him up and carry him at arms' length to the bathroom, where I hosed him down in the bath. On another occasion he made a similar 'soup' on the tray on his high chair with chocolate cake and vinegar. "They bring their love..." Brenda was fond of saying, at such moments...

Brenda told a French journalist about her grandsons: "'I live for them. One day they'll carry on my life...'... Waiting to hand down her life to those she loves, Brenda makes her Cornish heritage bear fruit..." he added.

Sue – Canon's Town Playgroup – Bagas Gwary

Once Davy was over 2 years old I started looking for a playgroup for him – but the nearest one was in Crowlas, a bus journey distant, and as I had no car then, it was a bit of a struggle to get to with the baby as well. Brenda suggested (she was prone to this sort of thing) – why didn't I look into starting a playgroup in Canon's Town, in the church hall? After all, she said, "... you did use to be a teacher...".

I did, of course, and soon learned that having been a teacher had little if anything to do with running a good playgroup. So I signed up for Playgroup leader training, and when Jan was 6 months old in 1980 he and his big brother attended the first Canon's Town Playgroup in the church hall, much to the complete disgust of the Chapel steward, Mr W, who obviously felt playgroups were the work of the devil. Despite Mr W's determined efforts to put a lid on us, the playgroup was a great success, drawing in children from St Erth and Hayle as well, and I took on a wonderful helper, Marlene James, who stayed with me throughout, and is still a great friend. Brenda did everything she could to help out with the constant fundraising, and while she was at it, suggested that what this village really needed was a Women's Institute.

Sue – Canon's Town WI

So – of course, I started up a WI – and with the by then well-known local celebrity Brenda as a member, attending whenever she wasn't away on tour, sufficient numbers of interested ladies did join up to make it viable, and for a few years it was a very successful group, becoming involved in many of the CFWI County events. We submitted an entry for the Royal Cornwall Show one year when the topic was Famous Cornish People... and of course we had one of our very own, so the display featured Brenda against a map of Europe with little strings depicting her trips around the world.

Brenda and me at the Royal Cornwall Show with Canon's Town WI display

I don't think we won, but it excited a lot of interest. We made a beautiful patchwork quilt, and an embroidered banner, and even put on Village Fairs and a couple of Village Horticultural Shows in conjunction with the Playgroup. Thankfully, the days of nudie WI calendars had not yet arrived, so the world was spared that.

One novel project Brenda did initiate in the WI was Twinning between WIs in different parts of Cornwall, with a view to supporting each other and discovering something of each other's areas. Her suggestion was reported in the CFWI County Newsletter, and I believe others took up the notion. We twinned with Carharrack WI, and had a couple of happy evenings when coach-loads of ladies migrated to each other's premises. When it was our turn to host, we held a Zodiac party (any WI worth its salt never missed a chance for a good 'Theme')... and Brenda spent hours drawing by hand large, surprisingly good, dotted pictures for each Zodiac sign, which were placed one on each table, and photocopied and hung above too – so all those with the same Zodiac sign sat on the same table... a brilliant notion for an ice-breaker at a party. We played Zodiac-themed games and sang songs, and made some new friends. Brenda's drawings were beautifully executed, and I still have them.

I can't leave this topic without including a letter Brenda wrote in 1987 to the 'troublesome' Chapel Steward in Canon's Town, Mr W... here is Brenda at her most acerbic:

> "Dear Mr W... Have just returned from hospital to hear from Susan of the accident to the chapel lawnmower, which, you believe, was caused by our WI on their Show Day? To our knowledge the horseshoes were not used outside on that occasion... but they are our property, and we had left them in the hall. With the number of children that visit the premises it is most probable that the horseshoes were taken out by a child at the show or during a playgroup session... so in that case, yes, we *are* responsible, for which I personally wish to pay, since I wasn't able to help that day, having to attend 3 other charity events.
>
> "It would be a shame if the garden around such a nice little building could not be kept tidy, there's enough vandalism and neglect around already. Talking of vandalism, we were most distressed within the WI to find our prize-winning entry to the Royal Cornwall Show (which we were saving to display in August) had been, it appears, deliberately smashed and thrown in a back shed. We were not aware it was in anyone's way – can you help us? I believe our Secretary will be writing to the Chapel Committee on the matter... we certainly do not want any further happenings of this nature, do we?

"Trust that the enclosed will be sufficient to allay the damage to the lawnmower. As a family, we all try never to hurt or inconvenience anyone else and to do as good a job as we are able... as a Christian should, is that not right?

"Hoping that you and Mrs W are in good health, Yours sincerely..."

Establishing the WI, and the Playgroup, did mean that at last Canon's Town began to feel like a community. I then – not having enough to do, obviously – got involved in local politics and stood successfully for Ludgvan Parish Council, which led to me becoming a Ludgvan School Governor, and later to representing Ludgvan as a LibDem on the County Council.

John, me and the boys, a publicity shot for the County Council elections...

Brenda having set me up with these activities, of course she was often away singing in exotic places. But for me, the reality was that as my children were growing up, I had become involved in so many community affairs that I was seeing less and less of my own sons, and was in danger of going under. Not all Brenda's fault, of course – like her, I'd made my own choices – but at one stage by the mid-1980s, this is what I was spending my time doing:

Working as Brenda's UK secretary, running Canon's Town Playgroup and its Committee, serving on Penwith Playgroups Branch Committee (plus many associated training courses and events), Cornwall Playgroups County Committee, National Playgroups Exeter Conference Newsletter Editor, Cornwall Playbus Committee, Canon's Town WI Committee, CFWI County Committee, Ludgvan Parish Councillor, Cornwall County Councillor for Ludgvan, Ludgvan School Governor, and HUMPTY Group

> Committee (a small action group working to improve facilities for toddlers and parents locally, with this mouthful of a tortuous acronym: Helping Under-fives and their Mothers [and fathers] by Providing for and Thinking of the Young)...

A completely absurd timetable of course, and totally unsustainable in the long term.

So then I decided to set up a voluntarily-run, full-time, family centre in Penzance. They say, if you want a job done properly, ask a busy person.

Sue – Penwith Family Playspace

Penwith Family Playspace opened in an old warehouse off Bread Street in Penzance in 1986, and managed to stay open 365 full days a year for 6 years, run by a management committee and a team of volunteer parents. We provided a drop-in café, a crèche, a playgroup, parenting workshops, a toy loan scheme, toilets and baby-changing facilities in the town centre, and various other related activities. It was really a mammoth enterprise, and gave much-needed help and support, and increasingly, self-confidence, to a lot of families who would likely otherwise have suffered in silence. For one heady period of about a year I was actually paid a grant-aided £15 per week to run it, but more often the effort was indeed all voluntary. The costs were never entirely met by the customers – it was inevitably a case of huge and continuous fund-raising efforts and numerous grant applications to a wide range of potential funders every year. Frustratingly, many grant-aiding bodies were happy enough to provide capital for 'start-up' projects, but getting revenue funding to keep us going was always a nightmare. It was really a question of finding some new service we could offer, stretching ourselves even thinner, in order to attract enough grant income to keep open. Infuriatingly, one of our main users was Social Services, who often sent us schoolgirl mums and inexperienced young parents for support and help, but who never considered us worth funding.

In 1987 we in Playspace were collectively appalled to hear that our midwife-led, low-tech Bolitho Maternity Home in Penzance was scheduled for closure. It was where both my sons had been born, for heaven's sake, and the next nearest unit was at Treliske, over 40 miles away from some local mothers. We decided immediate action was called for, and with fierce determination we planned an assault.

At 6am on the day the Home was due to close, we were waiting just out of sight up the road from Bolitho, with an attendant media circus who were signally failing to keep the low profile we'd requested, with floodlights and large furry sound booms akimbo. We stormed the front door to be met by two bewildered nurses, pushed straight past them and ran into the kitchen – a sympathetic midwife had given us a plan of the layout earlier – where three of us chained and padlocked ourselves to the radiator. The kitchen had been chosen as it had a separate back door and porch at the front of the building, plus cooking and washing facilities of course.

On that first day Radio Cornwall reporter Steven Strong insisted on joining us in the barricaded kitchen, and began sending out bulletins every half-hour... but by midday he was running out of news, so declared that "the ladies currently padlocked to the radiators in Bolitho Maternity Home are now applying their lipstick..." – we protested strongly at this total fabrication, of course. Very vocal and supportive crowds gathered outside, fish and chips were passed in for lunch, and we passed out cups of tea to the policemen who'd been detailed to stand guard. It really was a very jolly atmosphere. There was intense media interest for a week, which slackened off as time went on, and to my horror I found I had become the media mouthpiece – taking a deep breath and conducting interviews with visions of my speech teacher Doris Wernhard floating before me. A rota of around 100 supporters kept the kitchen occupied, with 'squatters rights', of course, even through Christmas; and even the electric and water companies kept their services going for us. A number of local musicians and bands were drawn in to hold fund-raising concerts outside the kitchen, even a choir on one occasion, and we held parties for the children there. We cooked meals – it was a kitchen, after all – kept spare sleeping bags and pillows in the pantry, an Elsan in the back entrance porch, and children regularly stayed over with their parents.

Our dogged persistence eventually attracted the attention of a film crew from Scarlett TV, and we had a half-hour programme made about our sit-in. We even hired a coach, with the assistance of the local Labour Party and Unison members, and with a team of supporters took our case up to Westminster, taking tea in the Members Tea Room with Harriet Harman (in whom I have since lost all faith I have to say). Ultimately after 4 months (and rest assured, we were only chained to the radiator for the first few hours), we had to concede defeat, and dragged out our sleeping bags and saucepans to leave the former Bolitho Maternity Home to its fate. At least we had seriously incommoded the ruthless powers-that-be and held up their plans for 4 months. Millions were then spent turning the building into a home for the elderly confused – good job I didn't book myself a bed, as within not too many more years, that too bit the dust, and millions more were spent turning it into NHS offices. What a crying shame.

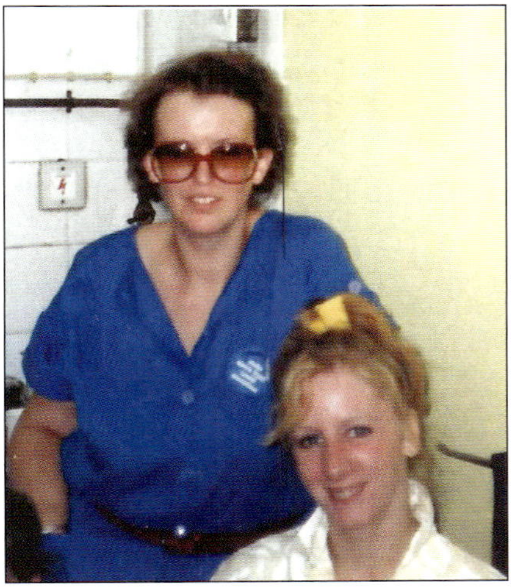

In the kitchen at Bolitho, with cousin Sarah Morris (who sadly died too young.)

My activities at this time impinged little on Brenda's career abroad, which by the mid-80s had turned stratospheric. And of course, most of this feverish activity on my part was non-Brenda related – and I felt sure I was constantly letting her down as regards my supposed secretarial tasks on her behalf. She often talked of my efforts in Playspace as "picking up waifs and strays" (once describing it to an old school friend in Australia as "a welfare centre for losers"!), but did once tell me she was proud of what I was achieving, and I think saw our occupation of Bolitho Maternity Home as typical of the actions of her slightly mad daughter.

One surprising thing I came away with after reading her private diaries recently was the realisation that every time she mentioned my name, it was in a positive context: "Spoke to Sue on phone today... lovely", or "John and Sue came up to meet us at the gig... glory, glory, to see them". Nowhere did I see any criticism of my work on her behalf (and she was certainly not shy of criticism if she felt it was called for), and I don't recall her nagging me much either. Perhaps I wasn't the constant disappointment to her that I felt I was...

Here are her comments to Olivier in February 1988: "Susan and Davy were with many 1000s of people at the Houses of Parliament yesterday, and we saw them on TV going to 10 Downing Street. They presented a big petition for Margaret Thatcher, but did not meet her... It was very exciting for Davy to actually see our

Government at work... They are trying to save two of our local hospitals from closing. Susan speaks well in public, she is becoming a true heroine for the people [*sheesh*] – BUT, John and I had to look after Jan, for which we deserve a medal – no! He is lovely!"

Sue – Paradise Park

By the end of the 80s, I had managed to shed the bulk of my commitments to random committees, although I was still running the playgroup in Canon's Town and Playspace, and was still a School Governor. In 1990, in need of actual funds instead of just kudos, I applied for and got a job at Paradise Park in Hayle, working in the shop and café and on the entrance gate. The owner, Mike Reynolds, asked me one day how it was that I sold more Guide Books on the entrance gate than anyone else. All I knew was that I'd done what was asked, and offered the book to everyone paying for entrance. On the strength of this amazing feat, he offered me a job running his leaflet distribution company, Warleggan. The job needed me to operate a computer database, and having never touched a computer, I undertook to learn – which resulted in my making a friend for life in computer wizard Dot Moore (later Campbell), a large Irish grandmother then living in Penzance. I had to appoint a team of 13 distributors throughout Cornwall and coordinate the distribution of 1000s of leaflets for around 6 tourist attractions to guest houses, hotels, cafes, shops – everywhere, really ... challenging work, but I enjoyed the job. By 1993 Dot and I (my input being by far the lesser!) had perfected the database to such an extent that Mike Reynolds decided he didn't need an administrator any more, just a secretary to input the data. I returned from a week's holiday in Wales to find a letter from my boss on the doormat telling me my services were no longer required – the only time in my life I've ever been sacked. I was grateful to then get a job working with computers at Soft Warehouse in Penzance for Steve Simmons, where I stayed for several years, improving my computer skills and technical knowledge somewhat.

Steve then inspired and inveigled me into joining the LibDems and standing, successfully, for the County Council. The amount of effort and energy, time and travelling, and sheer frustration of serving as a County Councillor, coupled with the costs, which were never quite met by allowances and expenses, meant I only stayed in position for a couple of years... though I did enjoy serving on the Newlyn Orion committee with Peter, and on the Archaeological Unit, especially when site trips were involved. So much for my brief sojourn into politics....

Sometime in the early 90s, out of the blue, we heard from Robert Bartlett. He and Diane had been living in Australia for many years, with their three sons, Thomas, Fraser and Daniel, and Diane's son from her first marriage, Barnaby – who had re-christened himself Ben. Robert had been working as a lecturer in journalism at Adelaide University, and was looking for a way to get back to Cornwall. Brenda told him of a position coming up at Camborne College, and Robert was short-listed for an interview – failing that, he had also arranged an interview for a job with the Cornishman newspaper, and was coming to stay with Brenda soon, hoping to be able to relocate his family back home in Cornwall. I knew that Brenda and Robert had had an amicable reunion on her visits to Australia, and for some reason I still don't understand, I was absolutely beside myself with excitement to be seeing him again. On the day he was due to arrive, by rented car, at Brenda and John's home at Tredinnick, I couldn't sit still and wait in the house and took myself off down the lane so that I could watch the approach road for his arrival.

He didn't get either of the positions he'd applied for, but he did leave a lasting impact on my family – as ever. He turned up at Paradise Park one day while I was working there, and we sat in the café and chatted in my lunch break. My relationship with husband John had not been good of late... maybe we were just tired of each other, but the communication between us was poor, no matter how hard I tried. Inevitably, when Robert asked, "Yes – but how are *you*?" it all came tumbling out, and Robert's incisive reaction was clear. "Go!" he said firmly, "Take no prisoners". His words had massive impact, and for the next few days I agonised, spending time with friends, some of it in a drunken stupor, discussing what I should do – time away from John, of course, who by now had realised something was up. It wasn't all Robert's fault – I was on an emotional roller-coaster, and buzzing with possibilities; a fortune cookie would have had a similar impact I'm sure. Finally on the Monday morning I told John I was leaving, with the boys, and I would get a flat in Penzance. The next few hours were without a doubt the most terrifying of my life. John had a total nervous breakdown, and underwent a frightening personality change I could never have anticipated. It took several visits to and from our local priest, and many weeks of sick leave from work, before he was able to resume some kind of normal life. Robert was long gone and completely forgotten by then, and in fact John and I stayed together, trying to comfort each other and re-discover whatever we had lost, for another 3-4 years before we finally separated in 1995.

Brenda didn't understand what was going on at all. I tried and failed to explain it to her, but it was Father who appreciated the full impact of what John and I had experienced and gave me the most comfort. But by this time, Brenda was ill, and had been for some time, and was reluctantly forced to accept that her international career was now behind her.

Grandchildren 2

Somehow the boys survived all this manic activity of mine and emerged as relatively stable, if sporadically stoned, teenagers. They both went on to Ludgvan School, where they made some good friends, some of whom have stayed with them ever since. They also both started as Cubs with the St Erth Scout Group, which I like to think taught them a lot. In due course, they went into Humphry Davy School in Penzance, which they also survived intact and hopefully a whole bunch wiser.

As brothers with a 2¼ year age gap, they fought and argued regularly, although there were signs (increasingly, since they grew up), that they actually love each other to bits. Aggravating everyone around them seemed to be their chief pleasure in their youth, although they've not entirely grown out of that. But for their dad John, whenever we were out together in the car as a family, it could sometimes become too much to bear. When they were squabbling loudly in the back, he frequently threatened that at the next sign of a ruckus, he would throw both of them out of the car, whoever was at fault, and they would have to walk home – and was actually moved to make good his threat on one occasion. (It was not too far from home, and they did survive.)

For Brenda, generally, they could do no wrong – she adored them both, but one of her main concerns was that they should absorb everything she could teach them about their Cornish heritage. She took them with her to musical, cultural and social events across Cornwall whenever she could, if possible, wearing their Cornish tartan kilts.

At Christmas time, she made sure they were involved in the carol singing and took them to see the lights at Mousehole and Newlyn. She told them about the Cornish legends, read them stories, told them about her childhood and the things she remembered.

Davy and Jan in kilts for Brenda and John's Ruby Wedding celebrations

Davy seemed to drink this in a little more than Jan at the time, and along the way he developed a genuine pleasure in helping older people. He regularly took himself off to visit one little old lady who lived just up the road at the Stack, who was always thrilled to see him and gave him tea and cakes. Both boys seemed to enjoy wearing their kilts, and looked entirely at home in them. When Davy was a lanky 13-14 year old, he left the house at Canon's Town one day for a 'walk' up to Trencrom Hill, wearing his kilt, a leather bomber jacket, an enormous scarf, a hat and a huge pair of inline roller skates. He always did have an 'interesting' dress sense, and loved to pose, such that I often took to calling him 'Burlington Boy'.

Jan was a lively baby and a rambunctious toddler. Whenever he saw Brenda, his first reaction was to charge across the room at her yelling 'Damwyn!', and if she had made the mistake of bending forward to kiss him, she would inevitably end up with a bruised nose or forehead – she was lucky she didn't lose any teeth. Davy was a little more reserved. His favourite thing was always trees – interestingly, as it became his career as an adult. I hadn't realised this until I created a lifetime's photo album for his 21st birthday – on almost every page there was at least one photo of Davy up a tree.

One year Brenda took Davy on a holiday to Brittany with Hendas (John) and herself, which he loved. But by far our biggest and most memorable family holiday happened in 1988, when all four of us went to Canada for a few weeks, a long-held dream of John's. We arrived in Vancouver, and hired a brand new RV (a 'recreational vehicle', which we christened Harvey, of course), and took off inland and up through the Rockies. I have never seen such awesome scenery – we had to stop Harvey every few yards it seemed, to take more shots and stare open-mouthed at the wonder of it all. We travelled up to Banff, across to Calgary, down through Alberta to Head-Smashed-in-Buffalo-Jump (as amazing as it sounds), down into the States and through Montana, Utah and Washington and back up to Vancouver. Fabulous – it made a lasting impression on John, who has always yearned to go back, and actually managed it this year.

After John and I had split up, with the money from the sale of Tredinnick Stack, once the mortgage and other debts had been cleared, Davy, Jan and I went to Australia for 7 weeks. We were to stay with Diane – the first time I had seen her since before I married. For me it was the most incredible emotionally-charged experience.

I remember Diane and me in a slow-motion, soft-focus dream, wrapped in each other's arms, dancing together around the airport when we arrived. For the boys, it was a magical experience to meet up with some real cousins about their own age – Ben, Tom, Fraser and Daniel – and they got on famously.

Of course by this time, that generally involved smoking out together in a friendly fuzz, but hey... We went off on our own up to the awe-inspiring Uluru (Ayers Rock) in the Red Centre, travelling by coach, and returned through the desert on the Ghan – one of those 'World's Most Amazing Railway Journeys' that I really wouldn't have missed...

After returning to Cornwall, I was finally able to gather all mine and my parents' belongings into my own 'new' property at St Just – a wonderful 200-year-old granite ashlar house near the town centre. Bought from phenomenal local artist Kurt Jackson and his family, the house had been built as the town's first police station in the early 1800s and had bags of character.

Davy and Jan came and went at different intervals, and went through the usual teenage angst. After a few years trying to sort myself out and find my feet, I finally settled on a self-employed route of buying and selling antiques and collectables online – principally on Ebay, and latterly, on sales outlet Etsy. I specialise in finding art deco and art nouveau delights, ceramics and glassware mostly, and also in the retro mid-century household items I remembered fondly from my childhood. I pride myself that I've become quite knowledgeable in certain fields; it was never going to make me rich, but it has helped the cashflow considerably over the years.

Anyway – back to Brenda...

Tredinnick Stack

An escape... that was something Brenda had long relished. By the early 1970s Brenda's house in Leskinnick Street was regularly packed with people – guests, invited and otherwise, to the folk club, or just friends dropping in, down in Cornwall on their holidays and making the inevitable assumption that Brenda and John had as much free time as them. Much as she enjoyed the company, it often left Brenda feeling drained. She dreamt of finding a bolt-hole, somewhere she could dash off to and hide for a while.

One day, working in the shop, she got a call from her solicitor and friend, Bryan Harvey, telling her about a property that had come up for sale near Newmill. An old wooden chalet up on the moors, in its own grounds of about ¾ of an acre; it was wildly overgrown, but available at a very good price of £1500. He said he found it very peaceful up there, and had taken to driving up there on quiet afternoons to sit and smoke his pipe. There were wonderful views from the top plat, overlooking Mounts Bay.

The chalet had been sited on Marazion beach, but had been moved during the war due to the threat of invasion, and re-sited in a disused mine quarry belonging to Tredinnick Mine, one of the Ding Dong group of tin mines. Brenda and John went up to take a look. They had to fight their way through waist high mint, brambles and ferns to reach the front door; the chalet was actually on the middle of three levels – the bottom level being so deep in wild mint and weeds that it wasn't visible. At the back of the topmost level was the Tredinnick Stack itself, an iconic and chimneyless broken granite tower visible for miles around. And across the lane, a few feet from the front gate, an entrance to a second plot, so overgrown that it was difficult to discern what was there. It was possible to make out the battered remains of an old railway carriage, which apparently had been lived in briefly years before. Much later Brenda drew up plans to create a small performing space there, and christened it the Platt, but unfortunately it never happened.

The chalet itself was in reasonable order. The windows in the front room ran in a broad sweep along the entire front and one side of the house, with views across the valley to the hill in the distance, topped by the ancient granite stones of Mulfra Quoit. There was a little kitchen with a counter opening into the front room, a small bedroom and a toilet. There was even a garage and a shed, ideal for John's ham radio gear.

Brenda fell in love. Back at the shop, with no more ado, she impetuously wrote out a cheque for £1500 and addressed it to the owner, with a covering letter, putting the envelope in the out-tray for the girls to post later. Then she contacted the owner by phone (as she would have said, an 'ass-about-face' way of doing things really), to be told that she was too late – a buyer had already been agreed for the chalet. Heartbroken, she tried to put the idea out of her head.

But she had forgotten that the letter with the cheque was still in the out-tray, and later that day it was posted by one of the shop girls. It transpired that the deal with the original buyer fell through, and when the owner received her letter and cheque, he was so impressed with her trust and openness, that a day or two after thinking she'd lost it, Brenda heard that she was after all the proud owner of Tredinnick Stack. She turned up at Brian Harvey's office the next day to sort out the paperwork, and she knew she was in trouble – imitating throwing her hat into the room first with a contrite face. He was incensed. "What on earth did you think you were doing??" he demanded… "How did you know that guy actually owned the place at all?!"

She loved it there, spending every spare minute sorting it out, and sleeping there when she could. John cleared the ground, and over the next few years, they built a garden with colourful shrubs, and a pond with goldfish, and in the centre, a little oak tree Brenda had smuggled back from Daoulas in Brittany in her suitcase, for Davy's birth – now fully grown, and in a stranger's garden, sadly. At one side was the Piper – a sculpture made by John Battensby from the Folk Cottage and presented to Brenda when she left the Club (looking much the worse for wear now, but still in my back garden). Eventually she invested in two large garden chalets, and placed one on the top garden and one in the bottom. Lined and insulated, they made spare rooms acceptably warm enough, even in winter, to form a painting chalet and an office respectively, and they were used for spare bedrooms when necessary. Inside the house, they installed a shower. It was a nest that was solely their own, the beauty being of course, that unless someone was specifically invited, no-one would be able to just 'drop in' unexpectedly. She had her bolt-hole…

Brenda and the Piper, at Tredinnick Stack

Within a few years, Brenda decided she wanted to live at the Stack permanently, and they agreed to sell Leskinnick Street. The money from the sale enabled her to make major renovations to the Stack, to make it more habitable on a full-time basis. She drew up the designs for exactly what she wanted, and the builders took away the entire front of the chalet, leaving just the wooden-built kitchen and bedroom areas at the back, which were to be clad in granite chippings. But in order to build on solid ground, they had to dig down through 9 feet of mine rubble to reach bedrock. The chalet had just been sitting on top of the mine rubble when it was first placed there – and the back part still was. The front, however, when it was newly built, was sitting on 9 feet of solid concrete. Unfortunately the open-plan layout soon proved impracticable, so John built a partition wall, dividing off a small bedroom area for their own room, which also had a pair of glass patio doors opening onto a small terrace, and a separate small bunk bedroom so that the boys could stay overnight. The moving date was set for June 8th 1987.

She had by then acquired her beautiful cream point Siamese/Devon Rex cross cat, Tikkydew – Cornish for butterfly, because of her butterfly ears – from Peter and Mary. She soon started to see signs of another cat, a huge and scruffy tabby, who would dart out of the cat-flap when she came home and disappear. Eventually she tempted him to stay, and discovered him to be a stray, in need of some serious TLC. He soon responded to her ministrations, and became the daftest, most gorgeous and most loving friend, stretched out on top of her when she was in bed and purring like a steam engine. She named him Bucca – the wild spirit of the moors.

Both of these lovely cats outlived Brenda and John – but after we'd moved up to the Stack in 1995, after Father's death, I returned from a trip to the Lorient Festival to be told a horrific story. While I was away, a lad that was staying in the bottom chalet was woken at 8am one morning by a huge ruckus in the garden. When he opened his door, the bottom garden was filled with the hounds of the Western Hunt, leaping in and out of the fishpond, trampling all over the plants in the garden, and forming a general squabbling mass in the middle. It was some minutes before he realised that underneath that squabbling mass was Tikkydew. The huntsmen were sitting on their horses, looking down into the bottom garden and calling ineffectually for the dogs to come away. Apparently they had been out early exercising the pack around the country lanes, and had surprised Tikkydew across the lane, who had raced for the supposed safety of her own garden. But she was not safe there, or anywhere, from the terror of the dogs. Is it any wonder I despise hunting and all those who hunt and kill animals for fun? Bucca, dear of him, had had a kinder end, sliding gently off his favourite perch, the warm car bonnet, with a fatal heart attack a few months earlier.

The approach to Newmill was usually to drive up Bone Valley from Heamoor, a long and pretty country lane, and part way along was an old single story barn on the left, on its own, with no sign of activity and boarded up windows. After Brenda and John had been travelling this road for a while, Brenda noticed one day that the old boards in one of the windows had been crudely painted in black with the message: "I HAVE STARTED SHOEING HORSES". After a few more months of passing by this slightly puzzling message, and with still no signs of activity at the site, she suddenly noticed one day that the boards had been replaced with brand new boards, and a few yards up the road, the original painted board was thrown in the hedge. "Stop the car" she told Father – "I'm having that". John was aghast – "Whatever for? It's a load of junk" he protested... but she insisted it was Folk Art. It turned out that the farmer who owned the barn had once shoed horses, but had stopped – his sons painted the message when they started up the business again. 'Shoeing Horses' was hanging on her wall at the Stack for many years, and is now proudly hanging on mine. I have been offered serious money for it (not least by Michael Chapman), but it is bequeathed to Davy.

Various minor incidents happened up at the Stack. One stormy night two huge white goats escaped from somewhere nearby, and woke Brenda and John banging on their French windows in the early hours. Opening the curtains to see these two huge white figures pressed against the glass, standing taller than either of them on their hind legs and starkly outlined against the dark rainy night, was completely terrifying – but she did write a funny poem about the experience.[51] Another time they were snowed in – one of the hazards of living on the moors way out in the country – and it was three days before we could get a car up to them with supplies.

The local Trythall primary school at Newmill is a small one – and as a result, frequently under threat of closure – but they are very active and enthusiastic. One hot summer's day they arranged a charity event with the children walking around the road loop of Newmill, Tredinnick, and Carfury, a matter of some miles, to raise funds for the school. Brenda wrote out a big sign, and pinned it on her front gate, which was on the route being walked: 'Stop here for lemonade and buns!', and put a table out on the patio laden with jugs of cool lemonade and plates of food for the walkers; she sat there all day serving them.

The little Trythall chapel at Newmill, next to the school, was neglected for some years and had become very overgrown with weedy shrubs. In the mid-1980s some young people from a local youth group took it on as a project, cleared all the ground around and smartened and painted it up. Brenda had been really impressed with the work they'd done, and had talked about it on her Sunday Best Radio Cornwall programme. The story was picked up by Harry Secombe, and was used in an edition of 'Highway', his 'god slot' TV programme on Sunday evenings. Harry and his TV crew came down

---

[51] *See Pantomime Stew: 'The Night We Got the Goat'*

for the reopening and interviewed Brenda and the volunteer workers – and children from local schools joined in with Brenda singing a couple of songs. The Chapel was used for a service once a month for a while, eventually falling once again back into disuse.

Brenda enjoyed the Stack's beautiful scenery and secluded location for many years, and welcomed many of her folk friends and family there for tea or a meal. She was filmed and photographed making pasties in the kitchen there, an image that was used in Cornwall tourist guides, on tea-towels and on postcards. Her pasty recipe was Lena's... she was asked for it so often, that eventually she wrote it out and photocopied it as a little leaflet that she sold at the folk club. Her long and rambling narrative explains much of the basic logic behind the making of a good Cornish pasty.

Brenda making pasties at the Stack

The BBC broadcaster Gerald Priestland and his wife Sylvia lived just over the hill from Tredinnick Stack, and they became firm friends, such that, following his death in 1991, Brenda was asked to sing and say a few words at his Memorial Service. She chose the beautiful song of Richard Gendall's, 'The Hills of Penwith', a song he loved himself, and had played on one of his programmes on Radio 4. She then recounted this story of her first meeting with Gerald:

> "The very first time I met Gerald Priestland was – to say the least – a bit unusual. It was November time, and we were up at our little wooden holiday house at Tredinnick, which we were planning to make into a more substantial home... so we were pulling it apart prior to its being rebuilt.

"Outside in the dark we had a roaring bonfire – old bits of shelves, lino, etc, were all going up in smoke. Then, there in the little doorway, appeared this somewhat large-framed gentleman... Gerald Priestland, come a-calling. We were covered in cobwebs and black dust, but we offered him tea, and we all three sat on what there was, dirt and all, and proceeded to discuss Cornish archaeology, and the world – which he soon put to rights. Putting things to rights seems to have been one of Gerald's talents. He's still doing it – a friend sent me his article on depression, and I refer to it often. Thank you Gerald... it's been good to know you."

Brenda's social life in Cornwall, when she could manage any, revolved around a few really close friends... apart from Donald Jarvis and Vee, there were Colleen and Bill at St Keverne, and in Padstow lived Geoff and Veronica Hudd. They had met Brenda at one of the folk clubs in north Cornwall, and were very close pals of hers for many, many years. Geoff Hudd was a Lloyds Bank manager – a tall handsome man, well-spoken and with a heart of gold. His wife Veronica was born in Germany, and was a fascinating lady. She had a fantastic talent for anything to do with fabrics: she made and sold her own colourful tie-dyed silk scarves and spun her own wool, and one small bedroom in their house was completely filled with a massive weaving loom, on which she created woven scarves, bags and rugs; Father used one of her woven tapestry shoulder bags for many years. For some time she was President of the Cornwall Guild of Weavers, Spinners & Dyers.

Every year we used to drive up to Padstow for the May Day 'Obby 'Oss celebrations, and always managed to find a parking space outside their house, from where we would walk down the hill to the centre... and the thrill in the blood from hearing the beat of the drums rising up towards us never palled. Their house was always busy with friends coming and going on May Day, and there was always food there for anyone who dropped in. One year we stayed in their little holiday apartment, virtually opposite the stable behind the Golden Lion pub – the home of the Red 'Oss. It was so exciting to have that bird's eye view of the first emergence of the 'Oss from the window of the flat, with the crowds swarming below us, and the dozens of accordions playing in the band.

Some years after Brenda had died, Geoff and Veronica came down to see me in St Just, where I was then living with just my son Jan... they picked up that I was struggling to make ends meet, though I tried to hide it, and making dreamcatchers for sale was one hare-brained money-raising scheme I was attempting (talk about an ageing hippy...). Not only did Geoff send me money as a loan to tide me over until some payment I was expecting came through, but one morning I received a small parcel from Veronica. It contained a most wonderful selection of silk threads and braids, and a complete rainbow of hand-dyed hand-spun wools, to be used as accessories for my dreamcatchers... it was such a thoughtful and thrilling present to receive, and I was really touched. They had lost their son Anthony at a tragically young age, but their daughter-in-law was very close, and they were able to enjoy being grandparents to his two children. I was saddened to hear of Geoff's death a few years ago, and in January 2015 we attended Veronica's funeral... so sad.

Bill and Colleen Rogers, Brenda, John, Vera Round and Donald Jarvis, enjoying a wet and blustery May Day at Padstow

Another friend who had started as a fan of Brenda's was Sally at Port Navas... she and her brother Robin became great pals. Sally was a nurse in Truro, and Robin was training as a Priest in Bristol. We spent some happy times with them, at Port Navas Regatta and at the Carnival there. Brenda also made a good friend in Marion Cadbury, Dik's mother, and often stayed with her when she was touring. Marion sent her a hand-written quote from the Venerable Bede, which Brenda had pinned up in her kitchen for many years:

> "Music is the most worthy, courteous, pleasant, joyous and lovely of all knowledge; it makes a man gentlemanly in his demeanour, for it acts upon his feelings... Music encourages us to bear the heavyest afflictions, administers consolation in every difficulty, refreshes the broken spirit, removes head-ache and sorrow, expells foul spirits, and cures crossness and melancholy."

An old friend from Brenda's amdram days was Peggy Burkin, who with husband Tim had moved to somewhere north of Bristol. Brenda used Peggy's house as a base many times when she was on tour in the Midlands, and the two often sat up talking through the night. Brenda greatly valued the friendship, and used Peggy as a trusted confidante.

One of Brenda's greatest mates, and fans, was Cousin Malc. The son of her Uncle Tom Rowe, Malc is a few years older than me, and apparently used to wheel me out in my pram for walks on the Prom when I was a baby. When Brenda began singing and started running the club, Malc enjoyed coming along, and soon became a regular. He often came with us to Folk Festivals and Concerts, accompanied Brenda on her first trip to the Pan-Celtic Festival in Killarney, and went to Spain with Brenda and John on holiday, staying with her ex-pat pal, artist Rowland Fade.

Malc has always been a part of my life, and was one of the few who bridged the gap between 'family' and 'folk'. One person Brenda always felt she never saw enough of, once she started touring, was her brother Peter. He did come to see her sing in one of the big concerts in Paris once, and was astonished at her popularity.

Brenda's year always included the Festivals and celebrations she remembered from her childhood... and if she was not away working, she attended every one she could. Helston Flora was a very important one... she had asked Richard for a song especially for Flora Day, and he wrote the beautiful Eighth of May... she interviewed couples at Flora Day for one of her half-hour TV programmes, and the song was played. When Camborne started up the Trevithick Festival, she supported them whole-heartedly, publicising it on her Radio Cornwall programme, and turning up to enjoy the fun. She attended Cornish Wrassling events too, a sport she entirely approved of. For a while we tried to get the boys involved, and they attended some training sessions in Penzance, and took part in a Wrassling event in Lostwithiel – with little success, but it was the taking part that mattered – gwary whek yu gwary tek!! (good play is fair play – the motto of Cornish wrestlers).

Holidays and happy days

Every year we tried to have one good family holiday all together, usually with Brenda and John, and my John, me and the boys – and I have so many happy memories of these special times. The first I recall was way back when I was at college in 1970: Brenda and John hired a little cabin cruiser on the Norfolk Broads and I and my then boyfriend, Tony Lyons, went with them.

We had a couple of wonderful holidays on the Isles of Scilly, travelling by the sometimes stomach-churning route of the Scillonian ferry, as the helicopter ride adds just too much to the almost prohibitive cost. We stayed in rented self-catering cottages, once with my sister-in-law Florence Luscombe as an extra guest.

Brenda and John paddling at Old Town on the Scillies

If you've never been, the Scillies are a joy to visit – they are Cornwall's South Sea islands, with palm trees and beautiful golden arcs of unspoilt sandy beaches, and for Brenda, worn out to the point of exhaustion from her demanding career, it was sheer heaven. I had a good friend living on St Mary's, the main island, at that time – Gail – we'd met when she turned up to support our efforts in Bolitho Maternity Home. She and her then husband Gord had a boat, and on one glorious day they took us over to the tiny island of Nornour. Seals came up and investigated the boat, and Father in particular was thrilled at the opportunity to explore such an inaccessible known prehistoric archaeological site, especially when he discovered half of a quern, a grinding stone, buried beneath a low sandbank (and left it there of course, taking only photos).

One summer, at my request, we went up to Shropshire, to explore the territory around my dad's birthplace of Badger in Salop, completely unknown territory for me. We stayed in a lovely converted barn, close to a lake near Tenbury Wells. We had with us on that occasion, Tikkydew – Brenda's beautiful and still very young blonde cat, a Siamese crossed with a Devon Rex. We took her everywhere on a lead, which she soon got used to – but took the lead off when she was indoors, a mistake we discovered when she fell out of the kitchen window, three storeys up, and landed in the woodpile below, emerging, thankfully, unhurt, if shocked. We explored thoroughly, and discovered Father's birthplace, a beautiful half-timbered gatehouse at Stableford, and the ancient 17th century thatched cottage where his father's family had lived, in the picturesque village of Badger.

We had a fabulous holiday closer to home, at Polruan across the river from Fowey in North Cornwall, one year – up to a point. We were staying in a beautiful house amongst trees above the river, and Polruan was not an area we knew, so there was plenty to explore, but just to sit and watch the activity of the boats coming and going below us was a pleasure. Brenda's best mates, Colleen and her husband Bill from St Keverne, came up and joined us there one happy day, pic-nicking in the sunshine on the grass. But there was one very unpleasant incident to come while we were there: Father suddenly started yelling in agony, and once we'd called an ambulance, it was discovered he had a burst appendix with possible peritonitis, and he was taken to Derriford Hospital in Plymouth for several days, which sort of put a damper on the whole holiday – especially for him.

Another year we were much further from home in Appleby-in-Westmoreland, on the edge of the Lake District. This again would have been a wonderful holiday, were it not for the fact that Brenda's diabetes was starting to affect her badly... by then she was wearing a rigid right-angled brace on one foot, as the foot wasn't lifting properly when she walked, and she was finding it very uncomfortable. And the pain she was suffering in her legs and feet completely dis-tracted her from enjoying trips out, even to visit Michael Chapman, whose house was within striking distance. She got most relief during the week from engaging with a 2000 piece jigsaw puzzle.

We did manage some 'half-holidays' away in Brittany with Brenda and John too – where Brenda still had some bookings to fulfil, but with plenty of days where we could laze on beautiful Breton beaches, or enjoy some fabulous Breton food in a restaurant in the evenings.

Brenda and John had some marvellous holidays away together. They spent a couple of weeks exploring the beauties of the Dingle Peninsula in southern Ireland, and on another occasion, travelled down to Almuñécar in southern Spain, together with Cousin Malc, to stay with her good friend, artist Rowland Fade. At his request, they had to pay for their keep with supplies of Marmite and English chocolate bars, unobtainable locally. Ro lived in a community of ex-pat Brits in Almunecar, and was a successful abstract artist – I still have a few of his large dramatic canvases. He took Brenda and John to some very hippyish parties, where she seemed to be having a very jolly time! Rowland sadly died in 2017, before I was able to get in touch with him for a comment – but if you're in the area, there is an exhibition room dedicated to him in Almuñécar's Casa de la Cultura.

But for Brenda, a holiday might just mean one day snatched from her absurdly busy schedule, to drive off into the country and spend some quality time with her grandchildren or her friends. We spent a lovely day with Auntie Vee (aka amdram pal Vera Round) exploring Cornwall's china clay area, amongst the moonscapes of the grey-white mine tips. We settled on a broad grassy verge way out in the country for our picnic lunch, and the boys (then aged about 5 and 2) played happily in the grass. Too happily, it turned out; Jan, true to his nature, had found a rotten old rubber lorry tyre buried in the hedge, and after sitting in it, lying on it and generally immersing himself totally in the whole rotten rubber experience, appeared again black as the ace of spades, dummy intact.

One of her favourite things to do when she was back home, even for a day or two, was to walk up the main street in town, Market Jew Street – not to shop, that was incidental – but just to see what was happening, who was around, what shops had changed hands, meet a few friendly faces and have a bit of a yarn. She'd pop into Mr James Music Shop to see how the LPs were selling, or into Bosher Thomas's for some sweets maybe. Asked if she enjoyed coming home after long trips abroad, Brenda said:

> "Oh, I do so love the peace, and I thank god everywhere and everyone is just the same. Not so long ago I'd just finished a tour

and we all went over to Sennen Feast. We arrived just in time for the Bazaar and when I walked into that church hall where I'd put on all those pantos over 20 years before, it was just as though I'd never left. There was the raffle, the cakes, and all those old friends, Mrs Maitland, Laura and Marjorie, and it was "Ello my bird, what you doin' out 'ere then?', and me showing Davy off like mad. It was a perfect day."[52]

Willie Warren, landlord of the Radjel pub at Pendeen

When we could we visited the landlord of the Radjel Inn at Pendeen, Willie Warren – a wonderful man, who apparently bore the distinction of having been, at different times in his life, both Britain's youngest and longest continually serving pub landlord.

Large and jovial, he always welcomed Brenda and her entourage (there was always an entourage) warmly. Clara Strick was his housekeeper who made a stack of pasties every day to sell in the bar, and her husband Tom had his own seat in the pub which was named in his honour. We usually turned up there with a bunch of hippy-styled long-haired musicians (and their girlfriends) in tow, which fazed Willie not a jot. The photo on the back of Brenda's Carillon album was shot in Willie's snug.

Some of her happiest days were spent in the caravan she acquired. It wasn't Father's favourite thing – any time, especially a short break of a day or two, spent in the caravan, involved him in a very early start and major effort getting it all set up and ready to go, and then setting it up again with their awning and gas bottles and other paraphernalia at their destination. This was often in one of Bill's fields, a relatively short trip to their farm at Rosenithon near St Keverne...

Brenda had met Colleen and Bill on the boat going over to Brittany for a tour one year. Bill was a farmer with a beautiful herd of Guernseys, and they lived close to their family in an old farmhouse near St Keverne.

---

[52] *'Cornish Voice', Vol 6 No 2*

They loved travelling, often touring to far-away places such as Canada, and Colleen was proud to have swum in the Arctic Circle. They drove an old camper van covered in stickers from all the places they had visited, and adorned with a pair of huge cow horns on the front. They met Brenda and John on the ferry travelling to Brittany one year, got chatting, and became firm friends, such that we visited them many times during the year and always at Christmas. They had a clutch of grandchildren who were a range of ages suitable for my lads to play with, and they had a lot of fun together.

Colleen was incapable of providing a frugal meal... she hadn't spent a lifetime as a farmer's wife for nothing. Her feasts at Christmas filled several tables, and Christmas dinner might involve maybe 15-20 vegetables or more, with at least 3 types of meat and the same of stuffings, and of sauces; as for puddings, cakes and sweets... well, words fail me. Not only was the food available in huge quantity and variety, it was also quality. Colleen was a fantastic cook. Her children and grandchildren were always there too, and we played games, the proper games I love, with loads of prizes for everyone, and special crackers and party hats, and – well, everything. Too much really... but Coll loved it as much as anyone, and it gave her enormous joy to offer. Coll and Bill came to Paris to see Brenda in Olympia as her guests, and were wowed by the experience. Brenda loved to take the mickey out of Bill and his cows, and wrote 'porchery' for his birthday about his love affair with them. Colleen and Bill were devastated when they had to give up production of gold top milk, and the herd of cows had ultimately to be sold off.

Sadly, once Brenda and John died, and then Bill, Coll was left living alone with her memories, and told me she couldn't wait to join them. Her meals were provided by her daughter Sally, who had taken over the running of the farm, but eventually after having a stroke, Coll was moved into a care home. We visited when we could, and every time I went in she would look at me fondly in the half-light, her eyes would fill with tears, and she would comment on how much I reminded her of Brenda... she adored Brenda, and often told me that Brenda visited her in the night, to comfort her... Eventually, poor love, she could barely speak, but her eyes were eloquent. She finally got her wish, and died in June 2016.

For Brenda, to escape for a day or two over to their farm, and to sit peacefully outside her caravan in a field, looking out over the sea, was as good a tonic as any a doctor could offer.

Christmas

Christmas was for me, and for Brenda, always one of the most special times of year. Every time we visited anyone at Christmas (and we visited *many*, with gifts), we always stood outside the door, knocked first, then started to sing carols... at least two, and even if the door were opened, we would not be interrupted until we'd finished. Usually, those we were visiting joined in with us on the doorstep.

The carols were and are the most special part of that special time. From the time of Brenda's childhood and before, when the people of Newlyn gathered to sing with the Choir on Newlyn Bridge, remembering all those who had never come home from the war, carol-singing has an emotional tug on many around here. Whenever we were in the car together at Christmas time, we would be singing through all the beautiful Cornish carols we knew. We prided ourselves on knowing 12 different versions of 'While Sheps', including the wonderful 'Lingham' tune, a lovely bouncy version with 'Sweet Chiming Christmas Bells', and we even sang it to the tune of 'Amazing Grace'. 'Lo, He Comes an Infant Stranger' is a beauty my Gran used to sing, as is 'Softly, Sweetly', and 'Cradled in a Manger Meanly'. The Cornish tunes to 'O Little Town of Bethlehem', 'Hark the Glad' and 'Hark the Herald Angels' were always popular, and of course, the much-loved 'Lo the Eastern'.

It was drummed into me that carols must not be sung before Paul Feast (around October 10th, and Davy's birthday – although Mike Sagar-Fenton says he was always told Advent was the start date), and must be sung no more after January 6th, Twelfth Night. But in reality, we usually stopped singing them after Christmas Day... it just never seemed appropriate after that, which may be why Brenda never got around to recording her much-requested Christmas album.

In the lead up to Christmas, the first event worthy of note was the switching on of the lights at Mousehole and Newlyn. Newlyn lights were in operation when I was a young girl, and Mousehole Xmas lights first appeared in 1963, but the spectacle of the villages lit by scores of illuminated wooden structures, and thousands of coloured light bulbs, will always bring me, and countless others, joy. Every year we would look for any new creations – but most were carefully saved and brought out year after year: the whale in Newlyn that spouts blue water, the church on the pier at Mousehole and the Loch Ness Monster floating in the harbour, the little robin high up on a rooftop, the castle turrets on top of the iceworks, even the strings of bulbs encased in colourful plastic buckets that link the whole show.

I am so grateful to those dedicated volunteers who over the years have put so much time and effort into creating such a wonderful spectacle. Nowadays, I'm delighted to see many other towns and villages putting on a great show – Penzance, Hayle, Gulval, and even little Angarrack – which is one of the most spectacular!

I have happy memories of going to see Newlyn lights with my Gran. The switch-on ceremony used to take place inside the old fish market, looking out over the harbour, with a huge Christmas tree in the middle, and burning coal braziers at intervals along the edge. I marvelled at how everyone there seemed to just know all the right harmonies and the endless alleluias to those lovely old tunes. A few times, Brenda was asked to turn on the Christmas lights – a very special honour.

Tom Bawcock's Eve on December 23rd was almost more thrilling than Christmas Day itself. The story is well-known, and probably apocryphal: one year the village of Mousehole was starving, and Tom Bawcock went out in his boat (with or without his cat) and caught seven different types of fish – Fairmaids (pilchards), Scad (horse mackerel), Ling, Hake, Shark, Murgy (dogfish) and Lances (sand eels) – and saved the village. It doesn't sound a very appetising mix, but the fish were supposedly put in a pie with the heads sticking out of the pastry top, gazing at the stars – hence 'Starry Gazey Pie' – various (simpler) versions of which are served up in the local hostelries today.

Tom Bawcock's Eve in the Engine Inn at Nancledra, with cousin Rog Morris and Gay Sagar-Fenton

Brenda was convinced Tom Bawcock's Eve was really just an excuse by the locals for an extra night's drinking at Christmas, but we loved it anyway. The village of Mousehole itself being potentially over-run with drunken revellers on the day, as a family we had long ago looked for an alternative place to sing, and for many years we went up to the Engine Inn at Nancledra, then run by Les Rowe, and sang till we could sing no more. It seemed to be our family who led the proceedings, but the place was always packed, and the beauty of it was that everyone there wanted to sing. Cousin Rog (Roger Morris) took up supplies of carol sheets with words to the most popular tunes, and around the table at the end of the room would be Brenda, Peter, Angus, Rog, Del Johnson (very involved with Penlee Lifeboat), Keith Hall (of the Shell Shop by the Harbour, and brother to Steve Hall who leads the proceedings at the Dock today), Cousin Malc (Malcolm Rowe), solicitor Brian Harvey – and his daughters, who knew all the 'High Church' descants and sang like angels – and Father and me of course (who didn't).

As the evening progressed, other songs, not quite so Christmassy, would creep into the schedule. Cousin Rog's risqué party piece was 'There once was a Vicar of a Country Church', Cousin Malc would invariably pitch in with 'My Brother Sylveste', and Angus would soon be grinning broadly and singing 'Lily the Pink, fell down the sink, caught the scarlet fever, no-one could save her...'. Peter, in his cups, would offer 'Over the Jasper Sea' with great emotion. 'Where be that blackbird to', 'Someone's in the kitchen with Dinah', and other such Cornish favourites, would follow, but the evening always ended with a sweetly sung carol that brought a tear to many an eye.

Sadly, after Les had moved into Penzance to take on the Dock Inn by the harbour, the singing at Nancledra died, and for a few years there were attempts to rekindle it in the Yacht Inn opposite the Jubilee Pool. To my mind it was never successful there – too many people only interested in drinking and talking loudly. It has now become a major event at the Dock, which is a small pub, and the crush of people wanting to be part of the singing on that night makes it quite a challenge. It has been adopted by Steve Hall's singing group, the Boilerhouse Singers, who now run the evening, and don't always appreciate 'rogue elements' striking up. But all credit to them for their thorough research into the local carol tunes – they are preserving some wonderful old songs, and keeping the excitement alive.

In later years, as she had got to know and work with so many of the Cornish choirs, Brenda took to going up to Four Lanes every Christmas morning, where the Four Lanes Male Voice Choir still sing carols outside the Victoria Inn at midday.

New Year's Eve had its own little ritual... I'm sure, common to many. Whether or not we were out celebrating, a small offering had to be left on the front doorstep before midnight, to ensure the wellbeing of everyone in the house in the coming year. A slice of bread (for sufficient food in the coming year), a piece of coal (for warmth), a pinch of salt (for good health), and a small silver coin – an old six-pence, say – for wealth, would be placed in a small heap on the step. At anytime after midnight, a tall dark stranger should, in theory, first foot it over the doorstep and bring the offerings in with him. We rarely managed that – sometimes we would send any male who happened to be there and was willing, outside, just before midnight, to do the job – and sometimes wood substituted for coal. Generally seemed to work, though... we're still here...

Brenda with Four Lanes Choir outside the Victoria Inn on Christmas Day – appropriately singing 'Hark! What music...'

Ruby Wedding at the Count House

Brenda and John married in 1948, and in anticipation of their Ruby Wedding on July 3rd 1988, I began preparations some 3 years earlier. I started collecting names and addresses, trying to re-establish contact with long-lost friends and relations. As the time approached, I booked the Count House for the event, which by then was operating as a high class restaurant run by some Americans, Charlotte and John, who agreed to put on a buffet.

I wanted to make sure I gave all the guests at least a year's notice, as I knew some would arrange their holidays around the date to make the long trip to Cornwall more affordable. I went to some pains to stress that the event was a complete secret, and they must not drop any hints to Brenda or John. I hired a marquee with chandeliers to put on the lawn in front of the building, PAs for both inside the Count House and in the marquee, and a red limo, complete with red flowers and ribbons. I designed and sent out over 400 hand-written invitations, and drew up lists of attendees... warning them all that any gifts or flowers should be sent straight to the Count House, not to the Stack.

On the day, someone nearly let the cat out of the bag by sending a card to the Stack with the message 'see you later at the Count House'... but fortunately Brenda and John thought it would be just a meal. They were astonished when a luxury red limo adorned in red roses drew up outside the house, and Brenda later said, as they drove up to the doors of the Count House, that she thought "oh, looks like someone's having a 'do' here today, look – marquee and all!". Then she spotted some faces she knew – her cousin John Mitch and his wife from South Africa, and Al Fenn, and gradually the penny dropped. The marquee was for them...

It was, I believe, one of the happiest days of my life, up to that point. Everything worked. So many of Brenda and John's friends and relations arrived that she was astonished, and we had entertainment throughout the day. In the Marquee, Decameron did one of their wonderful 'reunion' gigs, John Alderslade thrilled the kids with his daft puppet show and silly songs, and there were some lovely spots from Chucklefoot, Jake Walton, Bert Biscoe, Mike Sagar-Fenton ... "seemed like small 'underds, as we d'say!", commented Brenda later. The boys were dressed in their smart Cornish tartan kilts with red shirts and black ties, and looked fabulous, and there were trestle tables piled high with presents and flowers.

Decameron, aka the Magnificent Mercury Brothers, singing with Brenda at her Ruby Wedding

Sylv (Stained Glass), Johnny Coppin, Mr Wooty, Ralph McTell, Trevor Winter, Terry Broad, Chucklefoot, and John Knight, on stage in the Count House at the Ruby Wedding

"How great to see past guitarist Al Fenn with Jenny down from Cheltenham..." she wrote after the event, in a long thank you letter she sent out to all comers. "Next thing it was Geoff and Frankie March and Jonathon and Nancy March, and Dik and Barbara Cadbury, all with various offspring... all we needed was Dave Bell and Johnny Coppin to have the full line-up of the old Decameron, disbanded over 10 years ago... and suddenly, there they all were! And they'd rehearsed to play *just for us*... can you imagine how we felt!! It was all quite unbelievable, and there walking through the tent door is Ralph McTell and Nanna and their two youngest 'ansum-looking boys..."

Around 150 people turned up – the sun shone, and the folkies, the friends and the family mingled happily, in the marquee, on the grass, and in the newly built conservatory on the front of the building. Everyone loved the food, and in the evening, the music continued inside the Count House, with the stage now at the opposite end from the old folk club days, but no one seemed to mind. Ralph apparently was unaccountably nervous before his performance there in the evening. Brenda and Sylv from Stained Glass did a delightful version of 'My Old Man Said Follow the Van', and we finished up with 'Lamorna' and 'Goodnight Irene'... Brenda commented "...which the old walls of the Count House must surely have remembered... and as I looked down its length, the beautiful paintings, wall hangings and flowers disappeared, and all I could see was the pink bleeding through the whitewash and the old fishnets holding up the ever-increasing amount of plaster falling from above... to left and right, in front and behind, old friends were singing, and Mr Wooty and I were in amongst them! And I looked behind me, and there, guitars thrashing, nose to nose, were Ralph McTell and Terry Broad... we'll not forget that in a hurry..." Magic.

Brenda's husband... John, Mr Wooty, Hendas

To leave 'Brenda's husband, John' – as he was known and introduced to strangers – to almost the end of this narrative, is not to diminish his importance in Brenda's story. John's presence in the background of Brenda's career is a vital – no, *the* vital, element that enabled her to achieve what she did.

From the beginning, John was always Brenda's support. She was ever the leader, the one who took the initiative, as is obvious even in the comments of her friend Marjorie from their days working in the Post Office. There were times when he got precious little thanks for it, but it is obvious from her diaries that his presence, even back in Cornwall when she was far away on arduous lengthy tours, was enough to allow her to just touch base when she needed to, to get that reassurance that he had her corner, he was on her team. It is impossible to imagine that Brenda would have gone on the road had Mr Wooty not been there to back her up.

Mr Wooty

'Mr Wooty' – that's down to me. As a young teenager, I could not bring myself to call my father 'Dad' or 'Daddy'... just *too* demeaning. I reached a happy compromise with the diminutive 'Mr Wooty' – a name that stuck so firmly that just about anyone in the folk world that had any dealings with Cornwall at that time will instantly relate to it. They still talk about Mr Wooty with genuine affection today...

From working for Marshall at Rediffusion, by 1978 John had branched out on his own as 'J E Wootton, Electronics and Electrical', although still doing some freelance work for Marshall – which apparently caused some headaches, as Marshall expected him to be available at his beck and call (he wasn't the only one...). John never made a huge success at it, although his business ticked over, but when Brenda was feeling particularly stressed or vindictive, she never hesitated to remind him that *she* was the breadwinner in the house, or that the car was *her* car, as she had paid for it (she did pass her driving test, but almost never drove, so it was a moot point). It used to make me feel really angry and hurt on his behalf. If he hadn't been doing all the running around for her whenever she wished, he would probably have had more success at his own business. But such unpleasantness never lasted long, and her comments in her diaries and letters home confirm how much she adored him and relied upon him.

She wrote to John from Belgium in 1980 – following weeks of touring, struggling with hard negotiations on record deals that a manager should have dealt with, looking for a new guitarist, living in a foreign country, and not getting the support she so desperately needed:

> "It's been a 'hold on' week – not daring to look too far to left or right, and in no mood to write or phone... I want to thank you for so many things...first of all for all the time you gave to me at home, fixing the p.a. for the concert, and for suggesting the lovely evening when we went out to dinner...I'll be honest, I'm just as frightened as I was, but reassured by your attitude, and by Susan... Kiss our baby for me will you? Am trying hard to restore my sense of proportion... Really looking forward to coming home but mustn't think too much about it – it's a long way off yet, 2½ weeks to go... Love you very much, God bless, Brenda"

Eventually as she became more successful, John did give up his own career to travel with her, for which I know she was grateful. When Brenda's career eventually tailed off, John managed to get a summer job for one season as a doorman on the night club at St Ives Holiday Village in Lelant – not really his thing, but it helped I guess.

Mr Wooty as doorman, St Ives Holiday Village

Mr Wooty was a teddy bear of a man – adorable, nicely rounded, usually cheerful, patient (and he needed to be) and resourceful. He did have a life of his own outside the sphere of Brenda's influence. He had his own bolt-holes, which didn't always make her the happiest of bunnies, but she knew it was the price she had to pay to have his full attention when she needed it. He was a radio ham of long standing. From being a Radio Technician during the war, he never lost his love of all things geekish, anything with knobs and dials, especially anything with valves. He was always a Man with a Shed. In fact, when they moved up to the Stack, he was a Man with Several Sheds. The large garage beside the house was John's prime territory, and was never used for its original purpose from the moment they moved there. Shelving covered every wall, and every shelf was full – with boxes, bits of radio sets, tins full of old valves, partly-finished projects, stacks of radio ham manuals and magazines – there was just space for a workbench. But even this was not enough: at the side of the garage was a shed, at the back was a lean-to shack, and at the back of the house, a fourth 'workshop' – all similarly filled to the gunnels. But he was certainly a great asset when speakers and microphones were needed for the folk club, or at any public event.

He fiddled with things in his sheds for hours, inevitably taking himself out there whenever Brenda became too demanding or life too unpleasant. This was fine while he was alive to enjoy it, but for me, after his death, it was a bit of a nightmare. I was so relieved when his pal Cyril Young offered to come down from Kent and sort through it all for me, pricing up items he felt might be saleable. I did keep two categories of the 'stuff' though, illogically – purely because they fascinated me aesthetically – a few small round gauges or volt meters, and the old glass valves. There were hundreds of these, from tiny to huge, and I had no way of knowing whether they were still functional, but the delicacy and intricacy of the glass structures attracted me. (Given that my father was an electrician for all of my life, it is a bit tragic that as his daughter I am a complete dunce about electrics – the best I can do is wire a plug – and I only learnt that from wiring up Tremaen lampbases in the shop...)

His ham radio call sign was G3DCJ, which since his death has been taken over by his cousin, long-term friend and fellow radio ham, Cyril. He 'worked' stations all over the world, once connecting with the Sultan of Brunei, and in 1991 even managed to pick up the first

British astronaut in space, Helen Sharman. He proudly played the recording of it to Brenda's cousin Barbara and husband Ron when they were down on holiday, and was slightly pink with embarrassment to be interviewed by Radio Cornwall about it. (One of Sharman's tasks while she was on the MIR Space Station was taking part in an amateur radio transmission with children from a British school.)

He loved creating things, evident from the early days at Sennen when he had built his own wind generator in the garden at Treeve Moor. In 1966 while he was working at Skewjack, he received letters of commendation and was awarded a whole £5 for devising a modification to the transmitter which improved the monitoring of aircraft flying overhead, a feat which resulted in a promotion. I remember his excitement at creating a Bat Detector at one time, which picked up the signals of bats flying around at dusk, and a stone grinding wheel, for cutting and polishing slabs of the most interesting beachstones he found. He made me a little 'tumbler', and encouraged me, in my early teens, in my efforts at tumbling and polishing beach stones. My lifelong interest in rocks and geology, which I took at 'O' level, is down to him. As computers started to become more accessible to the general public, he bought up bits and pieces of junk at Radio Ham events, and tinkered with parts from an old Dragon and an early Amstrad computer, being completely thrilled when he managed to get one to do 'ping pong' on the screen. He would have loved the internet, I'm sure... Brenda never once touched a computer, to my knowledge.

Amongst his other interests was, principally, anything to do with archaeology or ancient peoples. For a while in the 1960s he worked in his spare time as a volunteer on digs with the Cornwall Archaeological Society and the West Cornwall Field Club. At one site – if memory serves, the track below Carn Euny – he found a beautiful Neolithic greenstone axe, which I still have.

In 1959 he worked on the dig at Goldherring near Sancreed, a Romano-British hut settlement just off the Penzance/Land's End road, with Mr A Guthrie. It was rumoured that his interest had more to do with the young girl student volunteers who worked there, bent over scraping the soil in the hot summer sun in short hot-pants, but I'm sure that's unfair. Brenda and her paints came with him on one occasion, and I am sitting now beneath her painting of one of the gateways on the site.

Brenda's painting of the dig at Goldherring, 1958

On the back she has written: "John's happiest find – the actual 'post hole' that would have held the pole that swivelled to open the settlement gates. It was a summer of much rain showers. From this height one can see them moving across Mounts Bay, and rain on St Michael's Mount – Faugan in the foreground of the bay – you can see Faugan from many places, east and west. 'Digs' look very bald – it's all grown over again now."

He even found some things to excavate at the Stack. He discovered that the left hand side of the bottom garden incorporated the remains of the walls of an old two-roomed miner's cottage, with a huge fireplace and beside it a 'furzey corner', used to store dry bracken for the fire. He even found the rusting remains of some of the miner's tools. Just outside the hedge at the bottom corner of the garden was a marvellous ancient bottle dump, which we both enjoyed exploring. From somewhere he had found a large quern stone, which he placed on the patio outside the bedroom.

He was fascinated by the ancient cultures of Egypt, Mesopotamia, and Cambodia, by the Chinese Terracotta Army and Easter Island, by the Inca, the Maya and the Aztecs, the Stone and Bronze Ages, and the fabulous Burgess Shale beds of fossils... anything relating to our human ancestors and the history of our planet. The new era of space exploration, with its attention to wavelengths and strange new worlds, fell naturally within his focus. Brenda and John's library of books on such subjects, and particularly on Ancient Cornwall and the Cornish, was extensive – and in the possession of Chris and me, has grown still further.

I remember, growing up, browsing through his collection of magazines and books on his other interests: the paranormal, and any unusual natural phenomena. He was an accomplished dowser, using forked hazel twigs to locate water and objects beneath the ground, or on maps; he even made his own with empty biro tubes and bent copper wire, or sometimes used crystal pendulums. He used to get Fate magazine regularly in the 1950s and 60s, and later sometimes the Fortean Times. 'Fate' usually had lurid articles on reincarnation, spontaneous human combustion, Bigfoot, alien abductions and similar racy stuff. Great fun.

He was a widely read and keenly intelligent man, and so interesting to talk to on any subject within his ken – but he also had a great sense of humour, and his natural state was smiley. He could have passed as the double of comedian Charlie Drake, and loved the Carry On movies and Benny Hill. (Brenda tolerated the Carry Ons as she thought Sid James was hot.)

Me and Mr Wooty, back in the days when I had a waist

He enjoyed the friendships made at the Folk Club, and the social side of touring with Brenda abroad. However he couldn't always take the pace, and was seen to slide headfirst into his dinner fast asleep at a restaurant in France one night. He didn't enjoy the limelight, and went pink with embarrassment one night on a French tour with Brenda. It was his birthday, and Brenda and colleagues had planned a celebratory meal at a night-club/restaurant. They arranged in advance that he should be the main focus of the stripper's attentions, so he ended up in the spotlight enveloped in ostrich feathers and diaphanous scarves and in the arms of a barely clad young lady – tickled pink, you might say. Cruel maybe, but I think he actually quite enjoyed it.

A friend of mine recalled a lovely memory: "Oh I LOVED him! Do you remember the very windy day at some fete when we came upon him on his knees trying to battle the wind and set up, I think it was a loudspeaker or something, and you asked him what he was doing and he said 'I'm praying to the god of flatulence'?"

Mr Wooty's other given name, Hendas, is Cornish for Grandfather, and was Richard's suggestion, when Brenda asked for appropriate Cornish grandparent names on Davy's birth. Both boys, and Brenda and me, called him Hendas, happily. He sometimes gruffly complained that he didn't want to be a granddad, as it would suggest he was growing old, and had a sticker on his bedroom door which read "I'm not an OAP, I'm a recycled teenager" – but he was in fact a doting and patient grandfather to the boys. Here's a fine example of porchery I wrote for his birthday in April 1994 (shortly after Brenda had died):

> There once was a young man called Hendas
> Whose talents were really tremendas,
> He was loved by his grandsons,
> Who, like him, were ansums,
> And his daughter, whose beauty was endlas..."

Brenda – The Last Performance

Without wanting to make an awful pun, Brenda's weight was always the elephant in the room when she appeared anywhere. It was the most obvious thing about her, the thing that no-one dared mention, and the thing that was most quickly forgotten when she started to sing. She always said she didn't care about it, and didn't object if interviewers wanted to ask her how she coped with her weight when touring. 'She is as large as Edith Piaf, The Sparrow, is petite...' said one commentator in Annabel magazine in 1984 – '"But at least they get a lot for their money," she chuckled. "I don't see why, because I'm fat, I should try to hide"'.

That said – if ever I heard anyone recounting some unfunny cruel 'joke' about Brenda's weight, usually when they thought she was out of earshot, and often from those who'd never even heard her sing – it hurt me. And I know it hurt her too, although she would usually pretend she hadn't heard. She was not some freak, to be made fun of. She was a large, extremely talented and charismatic woman whose stomach muscles had collapsed while giving birth to me. I don't pretend she was perfect – lord knows she had her faults, as we all do – but gluttony was not one of them. I've made no attempt to gloss over her sizeable ego, her petulance, her impatience with those around her who failed to meet her exacting standards. No – she never hid herself away – because her weight was not a matter of shame. I feel strongly that her choice of career, literally putting her weight in the spotlight for all to see, drawing attention to it with huge colourful robes and glittering jewellery – was actually an act of defiance. If 'they' were going to stare at her anyway, and make comments, let them stare and comment in awe and appreciation of her exceptional talents. It was a great move – when watching her perform, her size quickly became the least interesting thing about her.

I found a couple of lovely little verses she'd written for the Choughs' revues, sung to the tune from 'That was a cute little rhyme, sing us another one do...':

> Now my name you all know is Brenda
> I sing songs both noisy and tender
> When I make a bow, it's a bow with a wow
> (*And we all have to help to unbend her...*)

So you know that I'm Cornish and proud
You can see by myself I'm a crowd,
I'm not very small... but I can't half bawl!
Of Cornwall I'll sing long and loud!

Laugh at yourself first, so that when they laugh, they laugh with you, not at you...

Mind you, there were journalists who blew it – totally, and woe betide them if they caught the full blast of Brenda's outrage. One such did an interview for the Western Morning News in 1988, insensitively titled 'Our Brenda wishes she wasn't so fat'. In her article she talked of 'heady words' and 'shocking revelations', saying Brenda was 'paranoid' about her weight, and (the clincher) incorrectly used some Devon dialect, 'b'aint', as ersatz Cornish. Brenda was utterly incensed. She fired off a letter to the interviewer (with copies to her Editor, and to Brenda's solicitor)... "I'm wondering exactly what axe you had to grind in that bitchy, nasty, disrespectful and certainly hurtful article... just how good *is* that shorthand of yours that you managed to convey so many distorted pieces of information about me in such a relatively short work?" There was more, much more – it ran into two pages of closely typed fury. I hope her editor took note and fired her on the spot. It really was an appalling piece of trashy journalism.

The fact that she was a professional singer probably did much for Brenda's health; the voice control needed gave her a powerful set of lungs that stood her in good stead in her later years. But the truth is that her large size did affect her, inevitably. Carrying around that extra weight left a toll on her health, and frequently left her breathless and exhausted, although she would do anything rather than let it show.

In 1975, she was approached by doctors at Guy's Hospital in London (*not* the other way around, please note) who proposed a diet for her, one which would take into account her life on the road. It was an experimental research project for them, and a serious challenge for Brenda – the invitation came via a friend associated with the project. She did her best to keep it up, and did lose a couple of stone – and I've never seen her looking so ill. Eventually the doctors at Guy's Hospital ran out of funding for their project and were forced to end it, and by then Brenda had decided she was better off as she was, and went back to her normal lifestyle... which wasn't the hedonistic lifestyle of a big eater. She enjoyed her food, but I would say she ate normally, never huge portions, although not always appropriate choices. She loved a home-made pasty of course (but rarely finished a whole one), and saffron cake and her thunder and lightning. In the '70s she had occasionally made huge buttercream-filled sponges, but her favourite foods were usually savoury – Cornish under-roast say, or mackerel, or langoustines from Brittany... although she never passed up a chance for a Stevie Jelbert's ice cream with cream (neither do I).

By the late 1980s, Brenda was starting to suffer from the effects of mature-onset diabetes. She found walking increasingly difficult, constantly had to check her blood sugar and was permanently exhausted. As early as 1986 she was already losing the interest of Olivier, her French agent, whose attention was diverted towards other, newer – fitter – artists. It was a constant worry for her. By 1988, he obviously felt her failing health was a potential problem, and was curbing his activities on her behalf. She wrote him an angry letter, complaining about his lack of attention: "Olivier... when I telephoned you (after making about 45 expensive phone calls to save your name in Bourges!) you said 'Oh, thank you Brenda! I am sorry, I have not worked so hard for you, I promise I will do much better work for you in future! *I promise!*' Well, Olivier – *NOW IS THE FUTURE*! It is the time for a proper campaign to restore to me the work and the money that I have lost... my situation is becoming desperate..."

In 1989, while she was recording her final album 'Sailing Gulls' in John Knight's studio on the Lizard, she had a stroke. Within the week, she was back in the studio, determined, against all advice, in particular her doctors, to finish the job. Of course, she couldn't do it, and had to admit defeat. She raged against this curb on her activities, and fired off letters to Olivier assuring him she would be better soon, and able to carry out the album promotion tour he had lined up for her later that year. She had been requesting wheelchairs at airports and railway stations for some time, and thought it could all be achieved. In reality, it could not.

'Sailing Gulls' was eventually released quietly some months later, under the title 'Seagull', with a cover which probably took less than five minutes to design, with no supporting information and no promotion whatsoever. She had already arranged all the details for the cover and sent it to Olivier, but he didn't bother with it. Brenda was disgusted, but as she could do nothing about it herself, she was powerless to help matters. Years later, I had to beg Olivier for any spare copies he had. The difficulty was, as she had never finished doing the balancing tracks and laying down the final edits, the record sounds a little raw, and is not her best work. Copies are as rare as hen's teeth, but we are working on re-sampling some of the tracks and re-releasing them – two have recently appeared on the Brenda at Christmas CD.

In 1991, she was still offering herself to work with schools, to Derek Kitt, the County Music Adviser; still agreeing to charity engagements – warning the organisers that she had 'not been well', but swearing them to secrecy about her condition. Her fans in a way made it more difficult for her to make a clean break – always begging for just one more gig, just one more song, and she hated to refuse. And she was steaming ahead making plans for me to accompany her to a concert in Grenoble, and for John to go with her to more dates in Cherbourg and Caen – all of which of course never happened. She wrote me a desperate and determined letter, attempting to make these gigs a fait accompli, insisting I go ahead and make the arrangements – which I really couldn't, in all honesty.

In 1992 she jumped at the chance to go back to Brittany one last time, with John, accompanying the Buriana Singers and others from St Buryan, who were going on an exchange trip with their twin town, Calan. They stayed with host families, and Brenda did sing a couple of songs for the Bretons, much to their delight.

The weight did inevitably contribute to the diabetes, and it was that that was ultimately Brenda's downfall. For a couple of years, it seemed, she went progressively downhill. Her anguish was heart-breaking. She wrote me a letter, begging me to find her some work, *any* work... "so could you, for once, look on me as one of your lost souls in the Family Centre?" she pleaded. She was crying as she wrote it, but even though it hurt me to ignore those pleas, I knew I couldn't help her... whenever she appeared in public, usually to do a charity event at that time, I found listening to her trying to retain some of that old Brenda magic just more than I could bear. Although she always maintained her pride and her dignity, and held her head high, attempting the old companionable chat from the stage, she was losing the Brenda voice of silk and honey.

She was still giving interviews to the Cornishman in 1992, under the hopelessly optimistic title 'Seagull looking forward to full cry'...

saying she had "great expectations for the future... I've had to give up a lot because of my ill health, but I'm glad to say my puff is coming back!" Sadly she was deluding herself. A letter has surfaced from February 1992 that she wrote to the editor of one local paper, who had reported on her retirement from Radio Cornwall...

> "Dear Sir, My name is Brenda Wootton, and I'm very well, thank you. It's come as a great surprise to me to read in your paper recently that an illness was the cause of my retirement from Radio Cornwall. No such thing! Pile of stuff and nonsense!"

She went on to list all the glories that were to come in her career in the coming year. She really was in denial.

Her failing health had already lost her the chance to sing at the bicentenary celebrations of the French Revolution, in company with the great US soprano Jessye Norman. There were other things promised: a TV spectacular, a series of concerts with the French National Jazz Orchestra, and gigs with other famous artists; there were more albums in the planning stages, and prestigious tours further afield, to the States. Olivier couldn't take the risk and they were all cancelled – rightly, as it turned out. Without Brenda's knowledge, I even wrote to Olivier begging him not to listen to her. Her doctor had told me that if she attempted any of this, it would probably kill her.

The song, The Last Performance, was written by Ewen Carruthers about a theatre that was closing – she recorded it on the album 'B Comme Brenda'. What was Brenda's actual Last Performance? I think it may have been for the opening of the Green Fair in St John's Hall, at Easter, the year before she died. I know I couldn't stay in the hall and listen...

Finally she was forced to acknowledge that her singing career was over. In an attempt to salvage something of her self-esteem, Brenda again took up her paint-brushes. When her other activities in drama and music took precedence, she had had no more time for painting. It wasn't until her voice failed her and she grew too ill to perform, that she turned back to her old pastime. But this time, it wasn't solely for enjoyment – she hoped to be able to sell them, tapping into her fame perhaps to still earn a crust. However, by then, painting 'en plein air' wasn't an option, as she wasn't well enough to sit outside for hours. She asked me to drive her around the Land's End district to certain spots she would designate, and then pointed out to me the views she wanted to capture, to paint, for me to take photos. I took hundreds, and actually it proved to be a lovely time for me with her, driving her around in the sunshine to all her favourite haunts. We always chose sunny days, to get the best out of the statuesque cedar trees and the warm granite barn walls she loved to paint.

She set herself up in her little painting chalet in the top garden, and took up her old hobby again, but even this talent was failing her. I never had the courage to tell her, but the spontaneity and liveliness of her earlier paintings I felt was sometimes lacking in these works, although they were technically proficient. Attempts to interest gallery owners or possible buyers met with little response. Peter agreed to mount a display of the paintings in the entrance to Tremaens, but she only sold a handful. After her funeral, I gave many of these later paintings away to close friends and colleagues as mementos.

Brenda's paintings in the entrance to Tremaens

Eventually there came a time when she seemed to be spending more time in hospital than out of it: at St Michael's in Hayle, and then Poltair in Heamoor. I don't want to dwell on Brenda's condition at this time – it was awful for her – demeaning, demoralising and totally depressing. Denied her musical career and with seemingly no control over her activities, she suffered from severe depression, which in turn contributed to her worsening health.

One day Father and I were told that there was no alternative: Brenda must go into a care home. The thought of that awful reality horrified me, but I spent that day on the phone talking to and visiting health professionals and care homes, trying to look at viable and acceptable options, and to make some sort of sensible and realistic plan for the potentially crippling costs. By that evening I'd had enough. I refused to countenance the thought of Brenda living in a care home. I turned up at a friend's house in Hayle in floods of tears, and we sat in the car for hours talking around it. Then I drove to another friend in Newlyn, and dragged her into the Red Lion, where I downed a whole slew of rum-and-cokes, one after the other. She had to phone John to come and collect me, as I was a drunken sobbing mess.

The next morning at 8am I was woken by a call from Hendas. She had just died...

My first emotion was one of total relief. Then guilt, for feeling relief – then the two melded into a hopeless grief...

We drove straight in town to Poltair, and I went into the room with her, on my own... and through the tears I felt a lightness, a sweep of wings... and I felt this bird had flown, and was free at last.

Let us try, like a bird, for a moment to take
Sweet rest on a bough that is ready to break
She feels the bough tremble, yet sweetly she sings...
What is it to her – she has wings... she has wings...

This lovely poem was sent to Brenda by Marion Cadbury, mother of Dik Cadbury. Brenda had it pinned up on her wall at the Stack.

Life goes on…

I still feel Brenda knew what was coming, and, like me, was not prepared to endure it. I'll be forever grateful to her for managing to leave at that particular moment…

Everyone we knew was devastated. The funeral was arranged at Paul Church, and was packed – loudspeakers were placed outside to broadcast the service to the crowds. Davy bravely read a funny poem of Brenda's called Mrs Stone, and I read Downlong, a poem of old Newlyn. 'Waiting for the Tide' and 'The Eternal Year', two beautiful songs of Richards, were played, and Mike Sagar-Fenton read a tribute from Richard Gendall. After the funeral, special friends and family came up to the Stack, and we laughed and cried and remembered.

The response in the media after Brenda's death, both here and especially abroad, was quite overwhelming. It was obvious she was a much-loved lady. Hundreds of fans sent in cards and tributes to Radio Cornwall, and direct to the Stack.

Eventually Father and I began the impossible task of sorting out paperwork and 'stuff'… acres of stuff. Amongst it was Brenda's collection of Richard's songs – all 400 or more of them. I phoned Richard to ask what should be done with the material. I had thought perhaps we could discuss a series of Brenda Wootton/Richard Gendall Song Books – at the very least, I wanted to make sure the collection was properly looked after. He seemed non-committal, until I suggested giving the material to the Cornish Music Guild for safe keeping. Richard refused to allow that to happen – he didn't really care what happened to it all, he said, as long as it was understood it must *not* be given to them. That organisation is no longer in existence, and it is likely that the problem was disagreements over the structure of the language, together with strong influence from another – but the result was that the paperwork has stayed with me ever since, very poorly stored. I have at last made some inroads in properly filing and cataloguing the music, and have made arrangements to deposit all of that material in the new Kresen Kernow archive in Redruth when it opens. I am still hopeful of managing to get music books published… there is such a wealth of wonderful songs there, most now unsung.

Much later, I took down from the wall her earlier paintings, those she had done when we lived at Sennen in the 1950s. I was astonished to find that in 1987 she had written a small paragraph on the back of each one, an explanation of her memory of that day. I was so thrilled... I have now recorded each of those memories and kept them safe – it makes those paintings even more special, to me.

We were contacted, Father and I, a couple of months after Brenda's death, by a lady called Ann Bellingham, who had been commissioned to write a biography of Brenda for the Patten Press in Newmill. After discussion, we agreed, and Ann came up every Monday for months, doing some valuable work cataloguing and sorting the paperwork. Unfortunately, after Father died, and Ann lost her driving licence, it all fizzled out. Some years later Mike Sagar-Fenton took all the boxes of memorabilia away, and also did some very useful sorting of the massive store of memories... but his other commitments and the sheer size of the task, proved impossible bedfellows, and hence this is the third attempt at recording Brenda's life and work for posterity... and I am grateful to both Ann and Mike for saving me a lot of the hard graft!

After Brenda died, it was not long before I realised Father had a 'friend'... I do wish he hadn't felt he had to keep her a secret, as I certainly didn't begrudge him some romance. But he was not well himself. He suffered from angina, and also had diabetes, though not as critically as Brenda. He did manage to spend a few days away in Devon with his 'friend' (which I only know as I found some photos the following year), and I'm glad he did.

It was decided with several of her friends that we should hold a Memorial Concert for Brenda, and it happened in June of that same year, in St John's Hall in Penzance. It was a magical evening... so many lovely old pals turned up, and the evening was recorded by Three S Films, to be produced later on video as 'Brenda's Friends'.[53] Allan Taylor sang 'Old Joe', Mike Silver's fabulous voice was heard singing 'Saturday Night' and some of the other songs they'd performed together, and there were lovely sets from Ralph McTell, Decameron, John Alderslade, John the Fish and many others. Michael Chapman even squeezed himself into the white suit she'd loved to see him wear, and played 'The Coming of the Roads', in his own inimitable style; try name-spotting in the photo below. With the money raised from sales of the video, we were later able to offer a small fund from the briefly formed 'Brenda Trust', to help Pete

[53] *Available on www.brendawootton.org*

Berryman and others to travel to Ireland to represent Cornwall at the next Pan-Celtic Festival.

The line-up of friends performing at Brenda's Memorial Concert in St John's Hall

Brenda had long planned to produce a book of her 'porchery', and for years had been saving poems she had written, for birthdays, or with special memories of people or events, to that purpose. She even had a smart new notebook, on which she had written, 'The Book'... but got no further. The previous year, with her encouragement, I had decided to take on the task, and set about compiling The Book on the computer. Sadly, it was not finished before she died, but I pressed on with it, and with a hefty donation from Father towards the printing costs, 'Pantomime Stew' went straight from my computer to a printer, and by November we published 1000 copies. (I feel slightly abashed now, as I note that it has become common to describe Brenda as a Cornish singer 'and poet' – a description that never appeared when she was alive. I do hope she wouldn't disapprove!)

Here's one of Brenda's epic poems that didn't make it into Pantomime Stew, as I received it some years later, after the book was published. She wrote it for old school-friend Beryl Richards, who sometimes cycled around the district, and had made it up to Tredinnick Stack to see Brenda.

> I never could stay on a bike, it gave me little joy,
> My brother Peter got one, because he was a boy.
> I remember at the Youth Club, I borrowed one one day,
> We went up to Mount Misery. It was Easter holiday...
> We sped down that long hill to Trerieffe (*'Treeve'*), I felt in quite fine fettle,

Then landed in the garlic flowers and every stinging nettle.
The others they were long since gone, I sat there quite alone –
A lady and a gentleman took me into their home.
They gave me something hot to drink, and tended every bruise,
A memory I've no wish to keep, but one I'd wish to lose.
I've never owned a bicycle, but after we were wed,
We had a heavy tandem, and around the country sped...
Poor John, he handled things up front, I gaily pushed behind,
We had some lovely outings, but one night comes to mind...
T'was in the Shropshire countryside, I, singing to the moon,
The chain of course came slipping off – which put *me* out of tune!
We pushed the thing for hours and hours, I cursed that bloomin' bike,
So nowadays we have a car, or else we'd have to hike.
So I commend your energy, and when you come in view,
I wish for you the best of health – it's a darned site cheaper too!
Those wheels will never tempt me now, no matter what you say,
But hope that you will still ride up, to see us, Ding Dong way!

I held a small launch party for Pantomime Stew in the Acorn in Penzance, on a Monday in late November. Father was absolutely and genuinely thrilled with the book. But that Friday he was rushed into hospital with a suspected angina attack, and was in for 10 days before they were able to diagnose it more correctly as a heart attack. His doctor in the hospital was Peter's son, Doctor Adam Ellery. Father was feeling very fragile, and wasn't too keen on Adam's no-nonsense approach, and said he had the bedside manner of a Cornish rugby player – which of course he had been in his youth, and had played for Cornwall at Twickenham.

Father asked to speak to me in hospital, and, very abashed, asked me to get in touch with his lady friend, Stella, and explain to her what had happened (this was *not* the same lady he'd taken to Devon that summer, the old rogue!). When I did, she begged to be allowed to visit him in hospital, and I offered to collect her from her home in Portreath. She wanted to come down every day, and it proved quite a task. At last after about 10 days, the hospital said Father could go home, but only on condition that someone was there to stay with him, and although I was willing and happy to do this, Stella begged and pleaded to come and live with him while he recovered.

So with Father's and my approval, she did. It felt very strange, giving my Father permission to have his girlfriend come and stay. We called in daily, but a week later, on December 16th, we got a phone call at 2am from Stella, panicking and crying. We called an ambulance and raced straight up there, but it was too late. There was no sense of relief this time. I was angry and devastated... it seemed so cruelly unfair.

Stella was inconsolable. It was just coming up to Christmas. Good friends – what would we do without them? Within a couple of days, Michael and Andru Chapman had come down to stay over the Christmas period, and so had Ella Knight. And I had to invite Stella as well, poor soul. Stella's little blind dog Henry came to grief from the unwelcome attentions of Tikkydew, who pounced on him and somehow managed to get her claw stuck in his bottom, poor chap. And having asked Father while he was in hospital what he thought Stella would like for Christmas, I went ahead and bought her an expensive woollen shawl. She selected some personal things of Fathers to take away with her too – including a jumper he wore, which still smelled of him, to put under her pillow, dear of her. So the Stack was full of people, and despite the sadness and the loss, somehow we got through the funeral, and Christmas...

An aside...

While Michael and Andru were still down with us after John's funeral, I started one day to clear out cupboards at the Stack. Andru was keen to help, but was astonished to discover a wardrobe in the back room, lined with shelves and bulging at the seams with old tins, jars, bottles and packets of food. She describes it as 'siege mentality' – almost certainly a hang-over from the era of wartime rationing and austerity in which Brenda had grown up, and her early years struggling to make ends meet in Sennen. Michael Chapman has talked about his experience of Brenda and John's hospitality and generosity when he first came down – and she did seem to have a very real need to keep every cupboard fully stocked with food and supplies, to know that she wasn't going to be caught out if someone turned up unexpectedly, or if some disaster befell them. Freezers were always filled to bursting, and dried milk powder, spare coffee, bottles of sauces or juice, and tins of everything, were always on hand. Michael remembers when Brenda and Robert had first turned up at their house in Greenhead... apart from the guitar and a couple of holdalls, he says the car was just *full* of food. Andru wondered whether Brenda thought they weren't going to feed them, but it was just Brenda being cautious – 'just in case'...

Andru: "I think, probably having come through quite hard times during the War, she just never wanted that kind of feeling again that there wasn't enough – not just for her family, but of course for all us waifs and strays that washed up at her place... but it was that amazing hospitality from both Brenda and John... although John was in the background more, but he really didn't seem to mind us trekking through his house and eating all his food..."

Anyway – on this occasion, we decided it all had to go, as it was all so *old* – and we carried basket-loads down to the rubbish bins. Some of the tins obviously dated back years – possibly pre-dating Scott's Antarctic expedition – including one small pink tin of Shark's Fin Soup which had been in the cupboard for ever. Presumably, no-one ever fancied eating it – unsurprisingly. That, and an ancient jar with *very* pickled onions barely visible through the congealed sediment, exploded violently when we chucked them away, and blew the lid clean off the wheely bin. Dangerous work.

As to Pantomime Stew, I couldn't bring myself to market it. I was so thrilled that Father had seen it, and had loved it, and somehow that was enough for me. To tout the book around bookshops and try to flog it was not something I was prepared to do at that time. I gave a lot away to friends, and it was many years before I finally got around to offering it for sale online and to local shops.

When the dust settled...

Brenda at rest...

So Brenda was finally able to rest – she had 'set her ass to anchor', as she was fond of saying – no more strothin'. Brenda and John are buried in Paul Cemetery above Newlyn, where most of her ancestors also lie. One great worry to me after the death of both Brenda and John was that I had no spare money for a gravestone. I fretted about it for some time, and had worked out exactly what I wanted. When he was clearing out the bottom garden at the Stack, Father had found a huge chunk of granite, right where he wanted to put the goldfish pond. He had a phenomenal struggle to lever and wrest the massive boulder out of the ground, and when he'd finally managed it, he erected it on the top garden. As it happened, the stone was just the right size and shape for a gravestone, but sadly I never had the necessary funds to do anything about it.

The Stack is now someone else's property, but that boulder is not the only significant stone left there. When Angus died, Brenda arranged for Lena's gravestone from Paul Cemetery to be moved up to the Stack and installed in the wall in the bottom garden, to allow for a new gravestone with both Angus's and Lena's names to be placed on their grave at Paul.

Gathering at Brenda & John's graveside at Paul

Finally, Davy came forward with a suggestion. He offered to carve a wooden gravestone from a lovely chunk of Cornish elm – increasingly rare since the onslaught of Dutch Elm disease. He did a wonderful job, and I am so proud of him. He carved out the letters and numbers, and painted them in black, signing it on the back, 'Love, Davy'. He found a large chunk of granite to support the wood, and we placed some lovely Cot Valley egg-shaped boulders in front (collected before it became illegal to do so!).

We had a special ceremony at Paul, with some close friends, Geoff and Veronica Hudd, Malc and Ella, and Fish. Michael Chapman and Mike Sagar-Fenton each played a song. Wood is not an ideal replacement for stone, as it does weather and needs some maintenance from time to time, but the elm is placed there with love, and that is enough for me. So look for a wooden headboard, down near the bottom corner of the main cemetery on the left close to the trees.

Life without Brenda...

Once Father had died, in January 1995 husband John and I decided to move up to the Stack to live. The cats Tikkydew and Bucca still needed looking after, and we took our cat Pussy up there with us. We'd agreed to rent out the house at Canon's Town, and two young local couples moved in.

We struggled to make it all work up at the Stack, but it was not easy. The house felt awkward. It was not designed to be a full-time home for four people, the bedrooms were small, and Jan ended up using Brenda's office shed as a bedroom, which didn't do much for the archived and sorted material Anne Bellingham had left there.

John and I were struggling too, and by the summer we agreed to go our separate ways. No-one else was involved, so in theory there should have been no recriminations, but it was not an easy time. As an only child I had inherited the Stack and all its contents, and much as the site and the view were wonderful, the house itself was impractical and uncomfortable, as well as necessitating a ten minute car journey to the nearest shop and 'civilisation'. By that time, both Tikkydew and Bucca were no more, so I decided to sell up and move. John chose to follow a long-held dream, and went off to India to see the Dalai Lama. I gave over the property at Canon's Town to him entirely – after all, he had worked hard all his life to pay for it, and I had the Stack to sell. For a few years he did amazing work for VSO in Rwanda and Eritrea, teaching light engineering to the locals who were trying to rebuild their country after the horrific genocide and wars there. He is now retired and living in Camborne, not far from both Davy and Jan and his grandchildren (to whom he is a loving and caring granddad), and is now a qualified Spiritual Healer.

Unfortunately, I now discovered that Brenda's rebuilding plans for the Stack had not been that clever... as the 'new' front of the house rested on 9' of solid concrete, and the wooden chalet at the back was still standing directly on mine rubble, the back of the house was falling away from the front, leaving a noticeable gap that really needed some serious money spending on it – money which I did not have. So I was compelled to reduce the asking price for the Stack. Thankfully the sale did still enable me to buy my lovely 200 year old granite house in St Just, where I still live with Chris. It also left me (almost) enough to take that long-awaited holiday to visit my cousin Diane in Australia with the boys... (we ran out of money in Alice Springs, which I understand is traditional for visiting Poms).

So John and I divorced, and needing to change my name, I chose the surname Ellery, in memory of Angus. I was Susan Wootton at school, and decided I'd moved on since then. I also awarded myself another given name: Eles – from a beautiful song of Richards, sung by Brenda; it means 'she angel', and maybe it was an effort to draw one to me... although as anticipated, I continue to be known to all as Sue, which is fine.

By 2004, life had got a bit unfocused. I'd had various lodgers living in my attic bedsit, which hadn't always been a success, both boys came and went at various times, and I'd just lost the little job I'd had as a sales assistant in a local Cornish gift shop. Fed up with living virtually on my own, and too embarrassed to let on to the boys, I secretly signed up to a dating website, and by some random miracle I still find astonishing today, managed to meet up with my soul-mate Chris Hill. He was born in Mousehole and grew up in Pendeen, had attended Bangor University, settled down, and been trapped in North Wales by work and marriage for 30 years. His mother had also been a Cornish Bard, and had known Brenda. He had gone to the Boys' Grammar School and I the Girls', and as they shared a canteen, we would have passed each other daily in the dinner queues (but then, he was three years younger than me, so I probably would not have deigned to notice him). He had two grown-up daughters, I had two sons, and we both had blonde granddaughters the same age. His marriage had been over for some years, as had mine, and we chatted online for hours every day, for months. When I finally owned up to my boys, they were worried that he was probably an axe murderer – which I confronted him with, but he insisted he'd never harmed an axe in his life. Finally I could bear it no longer and went up to Wales to view this prospective match...

And so, gradually, we fell in love. His granddaughter, Katheryn, lived with him, and both his daughters lived close by – one of whom was disabled and required his regular support – and this, as well as his work commitments, meant there was no chance of him moving back home with me to his beloved Cornwall any time soon. So I rented out my house and moved up to North Wales for 8 years to be with him, where I was able to continue running my online antique retailing business from his home – until in 2013 he was able to retire, sell his house, and move back to Cornwall with me. We managed to find a house in Penzance for his daughter Nicki and her son Matthew, and Chris, Katheryn and I moved back into my house in St Just – breathing a sigh of relief all round. Chris's elder daughter, Lorraine, married last year and lives in Chester, and in October 2016, Chris and I were married in Penzance, giving me another 'best day ever', and a double-barrelled surname (no way was I losing that 'Ellery'!).

In the years since Brenda died, her family has grown considerably. Jan, with partner Lydia Reynolds, produced Brenda's first great-grandchild, Tegen Stella Reynolds, in 2000; in 2014 he married Tara, and between them they have created three more: Aaron Arthur John (2009), Lily Jane Ann (2014) and Lena Florence (2016). He works as a bus and coach driver, Tara as a care assistant, and they live in Camborne. Davy is a qualified green oak timber carpenter and tree surgeon, and runs his own business, Belerion Oak Framing, from the home he shares with his Polish partner, Ania – a qualified therapeutic masseuse – in Illogan. They have two children, Olivia Elowen (2013) and Ruben Angus Joseph (2015). So both Brenda's grandsons done good, and I couldn't be happier with their choice of partners. All are well and healthy – and I'm delighted they are all living within an achievable distance from their Damawyn! I may be an only child, but I think I've done my bit to perpetuate a good dollop of Cornishness...

Brenda's legacy...

Brenda may have died, but I'm pleased to say she has not been taking it lying down. The interest in and love for her is almost as strong as ever, and if anything there seems to have been a resurgence of interest in recent years.

When I was completing the 'Pantomime Stew' book in 1994, and looking for someone to write an appreciation for the back cover, I approached Charles Causley, sending him a draft copy of the poems to read. His response still touches me:

> "'Pantomime Stew' is the perfect title for this splendid collection of lyrics, comic verses, ballads and stories by the late, great Brenda Wootton. As a performing artist of world renown she was truly a star in the firmament of 20th century troubadors and story-tellers...
>
> The whole book is irresistible: a marvellous self-portrait, warts and all, by a marvellous Cornishwoman who travelled the world but never forgot her origins.
>
> And at its heart is a remembrance of that never-to-be-forgotten singing voice of pure silver..."

In 2003, the Western Morning News conducted a survey over several weeks to create a list of the '100 Greatest Cornish People'. Unsurprisingly, Richard Trevithick topped the list, followed by Sir Humphry Davy, but the first woman to be mentioned, at number 11, was Brenda Wootton, described as a "Folk singer with an incredible vocal range who toured the world with her ballads and Cornish songs, like 'Pasties and Cream' and 'Lamorna'." Not a well-constructed description, and she would *not* have appreciated the 'folk singer' label, but I'm sure being classed as the 'greatest' Cornish woman would have counted for a lot, especially given that the next woman on the list, Ann Trevenen Jenkin, then the Grand Bard of the Gorsedh, was at number 33.

In 2010, the recording engineer and guitarist friend of Brenda's, John Knight, who had also recorded her more recent albums in his studio near the Lizard, found an old tape in his loft he had forgotten existed. He had been at the Bobino in 1983 when Brenda and her entourage had played at the closing night of the theatre, and at Brenda's request, had recorded the concert for her own personal use. Frequently, old re-discovered recording tape proves to be a colossal disappointment, as the fabric of the tape rots and becomes unusable, but this was some French tape that John had bought abroad, and it was still in good order. Good enough that after a real labour of love working on the tracks for untold hours in his studio, he was able to produce a remarkable CD, called 'All of Me' – a unique recording of a live concert with Brenda at a prestigious French venue.

A few years ago, when we were in Cornwall for a Christmas holiday from our home in exile in Wales, I took Chris up to Four Lanes to hear the carol singing by Four Lanes Males Voice Choir on Christmas morning, as Brenda and I had often done. I noticed a chap filming and recording the choir, and when we went in the pub for a drink with the choir afterwards he was there. He overheard me chatting to the choir, and asked if I was Brenda's daughter, and then told me he had some recordings of Brenda he'd taken years before when Pipers was at St Buryan. His name was Mike Gluyas, and he very kindly offered me the recordings, and together with Mic McCreadie, helped me to prepare a CD, 'Brenda at Buryan'. It was the earliest ever recording of her singing, and the only album to feature Brenda singing at St Buryan.

As I still had all of Brenda's remaining stock of albums, and now had the 'Pantomime Stew' book of her poetry, the 'Brenda's Friends' video, and the 'Brenda at Buryan' CD to sell, I realised I should try and be practical and managed to design a small sales website... all the above (together with 'Gallimaufry', a book I produced containing the largest ever collection of collective nouns!), are now available at www.brendawootton.org. I have also recently set up a Facebook page in Brenda's name for fans and interested parties, and it has been regularly active ever since, gathering nearly 400 'Likes' so far.

In the last few years, we have also had the Tribute Concert for Brenda launched by Lowender Peran, and more recently a talk on her Cornish language songs by Richard Trethewey in a Cornish Symposium there... Richard and the marvellous Bec Applebee, as the duo Didjan, are also performing some of her material, and her songs are increasingly being heard performed by other young people in the region, and further afield: the Welsh singer, Gwenno, is a huge fan, and tells me her 3 year old son loves Brenda and has learnt the Cornish words to two of her songs, which he loves to sing!

In June 2017, I was very pleasantly surprised to hear from Radio Cornwall that Brenda had been awarded a prestigious 'Blue Plaque'. All local BBC Radio stations had been tasked to invite their listeners to submit names of people from their regions that they felt most deserving – and out of all the possible names of Cornish worthies – Brenda's was the most requested. We were invited to Radio Cornwall, together with John the Fish and Grand Bard Mervyn Davey, for the unveiling of the plaque... my son Davy and his family joined us, and as luck would have it, Brenda's cousin Barbara and her daughter Lynette were down on holiday. Barbara was overawed by the BBC surroundings, and delighted to be invited in to watch the interviews being recorded. Unfortunately 'unveiling' was somewhat of a euphemism, as a permanent site for the plaque has yet to be earmarked – nevertheless, I am conscious of the great honour accorded to Brenda by her legion of fans in Cornwall, who still want to make her their top choice over 20 years after her death; it is certainly confirmation of the great affection in which she was held.

I am hopeful that we will be able to continue bringing out new or improved material on Brenda for some time into the future. There are quite a few unpublished recordings that have come to light in the last year or two, and we are discussing 2 or 3 more new CDs. The master tapes of Sentinel Records have been purchased for Cornwall, and there may well be material there that can be used. Likewise, the archive of recordings by Ted Gundry is being digitised, which I suspect may include interviews or recordings of Brenda. There are also meetings planned to discuss – at last – song books of Brenda's material, by Richard Gendall and others.

I will end with comments from four people, spanning the generations, whose lives and viewpoints have been positively impacted by Brenda:

1. Mike Sagar-Fenton knew Brenda in several different roles, almost throughout his life:

> "I visited Brenda at the Stack a few times after her illness. I was sorry to see her ill, but almost glad to see her off the road. Her voice had lost some quality, much of its purity, and her sensitivity for audiences had turned towards entitlement and expectation of praise. I had always hoped she would make a third career of broadcasting, story-telling, writing, all her other great talents which a singer's career had forced her to abandon. She learned my song "Johnny Roscoff" though she never performed it, but we had some easy times together to reminisce.
>
> I'm glad to have known Brenda for a whole raft or reasons.

Some of them are negative. I had a good close-up of the corrosive elements of fame, always being recognised, always being 'on', and then needing it, depending on that stream of praise as she did. Too many times Steve (Hall) or I were reluctantly drummed into action if she felt like impressing someone, entertaining a pub or a restaurant, even after a gig when we just wanted to have a drink and relax. She had to be the centre of attention and could throw a truly massive sulk if she wasn't. She had a mean side, in proportion with the rest. But it cured me of ever wanting to be famous, known wherever I went, never anonymous, no peace. I learned a lot from being with her.

She could also be unexpectedly sensitive. I remember going through some lyrics of a song I was writing. The theme was that there's no such place as 'away' – you can't really (environmentally) throw anything away, you can't wish things away, you can never really run away, all a little depressing. She looked at me and said "But you know you can also never give anything away. Whatever you give away comes back to you, in some other form." She was right. I never finished the song.

I had so much fun with Brenda I'd never have had otherwise. She was intoxicating to be around, her sunny sense of celebration of life, draining each experience to the last drop. All her appetites were huge but so was her enjoyment of them, full-hearted, one hundred per cent, eating, drinking, flirting, touching the heavens with her voice and laughing as few people know how to laugh, right down to her toes. She was a gas."

2. Hilary Coleman, who has become a leading light recording songs and singing and playing in Cornwall, as well as a prime mover in promoting the Cornish language, remembered the inspiration she gained from her first encounter with Brenda:

"In 1983 at the age of 21, I was living in Oxford. Surprisingly there was a small enclave of Cornish musicians there and this was where I learnt my first song in Cornish: 'Kemer Ow Ro', which was one of Brenda's songs. So I was glad to hear she was coming to sing in Oxford. We all went to see her and I remember her singing 'Silver Net' about keeping the young in Cornwall and I felt she was singing to me – go home and look after your country! She awoke a strong feeling of identity in me and that was the beginning of a yearning for home, until I returned several years later."

3. I first met Theo Rodriguez online, after he had placed a succession of orders for Brenda's albums from his home in Denver, Colorado – he has since become a great friend and has even visited Cornwall, coming over for my wedding in 2016. Now just 24, he is already a world-class musician on the harpsichord and other keyboard instruments – playing in a very different genre to anything performed by Brenda. However, he has become totally smitten, and might now be considered her number one fan; as a result, he is an ardent Kernowphile, and is now learning the language. Theo was born around the same time that Brenda died, and but for a happy chance, would never have been exposed to her music. He wrote me a love letter about his feelings for Brenda:

> "It is a cold winter's evening as I sit here and ponder the exquisite voice of Brenda Wootton. Despite the freezing temperatures and the snow piled against my door, hearing Brenda singing always makes me feel warm and cosy. Her pure voice always manages to reach into the depths of my heart, and I often have tears in my eyes as I listen. I shan't refer to her as the late Brenda Wootton because this is not how I see her. For me, she will always be such a deep and intrinsic part of my life, and as a result, she is very much alive and always will be.
>
> "I will never forget the first time I came across Brenda... I chanced upon a YouTube video of her singing with Argentine singer and activist, Mercedes Sosa – and watching it, I was immediately in love. There stood this lovely lady: a long silky maroon dress, blue eyeshadow, delicately curled fair hair, and a ring on every finger. She sang about the land she loved, and as she reiterated this phrase over and over, I felt an overwhelming sense of comfort and love resonating from her. Her performance moved me to look more deeply at Cornwall and its land, people, heritage, and traditions.
>
> "I have always been proud of my English ancestry but was excited to learn about the Cornish culture, which is now at the centre of my life, thanks to Brenda. Not a month goes by where I don't make pasties from her recipe; not a day goes by that I don't listen to her recordings.... I can honestly say that I am a more complete person after knowing Brenda's music and life. If I could have a few moments to speak to Brenda now, I would say, I love you and thank you. All my love Gwylan Gwavas... always."

4. Gloria and John Knight, who spent so many hours working with Brenda in the studio and playing guitar for her on stage, had this to add:

> "Brenda Wootton is an intrinsic element in the musical heritage of Cornwall. It's an enduring tribute to her, that more than twenty years since she passed away, there remain loyal devotees with affectionate memories of her unique voice and charismatic personality.
>
> "Brenda's recorded work was no different from her live performances; a force of nature, switching vocally from a gentle summer breeze to the roar of a gale as she segued effortlessly from number to number. She had the rare ability to make every song she sang her own as she captivated her audience, taking them on a musical ride to Cornwall with humour, passion and honesty while performing the music she loved."

She certainly maintained that 'gallant bravado of style' her composition teacher at school had complained of...

Brenda's living legacy... Jan with wife Tara (pregnant with baby Lena, inset) with Lily, Aaron & the beautiful Tegen; Davy & Ania with their children, Olivia & Ruben – at my wedding to Chris Ellery-Hill, 29/10/2016

Endnote

I am reminded of the comment Brenda made on her first visit to Australia in 1979:

'...She was envious of the tremendous spirit in Australia's 'Little Cornwall', saying "We'd never be able to have a fair like this... the economy couldn't afford it, and we're too blasé about our customs now. Here, there's still a lovely naiveté and Cousin Jacks are embracing their customs and heritage with a vigour that would shame their Cornish kin." '

I think now, nearly 40 years on, Brenda would be heartened with the renewed energy for the Cornish vision. It is well over 20 years since Brenda was here in person to watch Cornwall, its traditions, its businesses, its technology and its culture thrive, and it is thrilling to realise just how much has happened in that relatively short time... she would be amazed...

- The all-embracing efforts of the Cornish Culture Association, led by Simon Reed and others, are preserving all of the old Cornish traditions – Montol, Allantide, guise dancing, and more – and gaining many new adherents
- The Tin Coast is now a World Heritage Site, and Will Coleman's truly awesome Man Engine is wowing everyone and bringing home the true story of Cornish mining
- The broad appeal of comedian Ed Rowe, or Kernow King, with his Cornish humour and dialect, and the popularity of Harry Glasson's music, show the Cornish spirit and soul are blossoming
- Golden Tree and other local theatre groups are focusing on Cornish stories and history and bringing them to a wider public
- Hilary Coleman and Sally Burley's authoritative research and publications on Cornish musical traditions have provided invaluable source material, and encouraged regular monthly 'Shout' sessions which are well-attended in several venues
- The atmosphere, inventiveness and excitement of the old town carnivals has been reborn, bigger and better, in the festivals of Golowan in Penzance, Lafrowda in St Just, Trevithick at Camborne, and elsewhere
- There is sterling work being done in saving and safely archiving the old recordings of Dennis Clixby, Ted Gundry, Chris Blount and Sentinel Music, to be stored in the new...

- ...Kresen Kernow archive in Redruth, currently being built and due to open in 2019
- Cornwall now has its own University campus at Falmouth and Truro, under the aegis of Exeter University
- Home-produced Cornish foods and other products are proliferating, and Food Fairs are burgeoning with Cornish beers, ales and ciders, fish, cheeses and chocolates – and gin! More and more restaurants in Cornwall are offering 'fine dining' fare produced by award-winning chefs
- New art and craft galleries are springing up everywhere, with West Cornwall in particular becoming once again an artistic hub
- There is exciting news for Goonhilly Earth Station with a Deep Space Communication base planned by the European Space Agency, offering the possibility of more local jobs and a promising future for the site
- Revolutionary new technology is working to provide geothermal heating to Penzance's iconic Jubilee Pool
- The Cornish pasty, its status now legally protected, is taking its place beside other more commonly known 'fast food' shops and stalls around the country (not that the proper pasty was ever 'fast food') – and Cornish Clotted Cream too now also has protected status
- The Cornish are now officially recognised for the first time as a National Minority group with the same status as the other Celtic countries in the UK...
- ... and the language, Kernewek, is now protected under the European Charter for Minority Languages.
- Brenda would be particularly thrilled to see that Cornwall's own emblem, the Cornish Chough, after being absent for so many years, has returned, seemingly of its own volition, and is thriving... a potent symbol, if one were needed, of Cornwall's renewed vigour...

And the institutions Brenda knew and loved are still going strong – and in many cases, stronger:

- **Lowender Peran Festival** has survived the demise of the Ponsmere Hotel at Perranporth and moved on to new heights at Newquay – and, as with the **Gorsedh Kernow**, is thriving, and both institutions focus strongly on encouraging more academic research into the Cornish language and traditions

- **St Ives September Festival** is still booking great acts after 30 years or more, and music and literary festivals thrive
- **Tom Bawcock's Eve** is still always packed solid – and, importantly, **Jelbert's ice cream** still draws connoisseurs throughout the season

The resurgence of interest in the Cornish language, culture and traditions is stronger at home and in the Diaspora than it has ever been, and I'm sure Brenda would now be gratified – particularly as she was most likely partly responsible for that herself.

Let's hope – with this renewed interest in all things Cornish – that ultimately Brenda's 'Silver Net' will no longer be necessary, and that large numbers of Cornwall's young people will no longer need to leave their land to find work, as her parents had to.

Brenda took her love of Cornwall to the world – others had the erudition, others worked just as hard to promote Cornwall and the Cornish – but it was the Seagull of Newlyn who got her message loudest, clearest and furthest. Other individuals and groups have since taken up the black and white flag, the Baner Kernow, and are running with it joyfully. New generations are discovering the true value of their heritage. But maybe it was Brenda who made the Cornish themselves feel they were special.

As, indeed, we are.

Appendices

1 Brenda on singing – 'She' Interview, December 1980
2 List of photographs
3 Brenda's accompanists
4 Timeline
5 Brenda's audio recordings
6 Drama Productions 1957-65
7 Performers at Count House & Pipers – residents, itinerants and guests
8 Acknowledgements
9 Bibliography
10 List of Subscribers
11 Index

Brenda on Singing

Extracts from an interview with Brenda conducted by Leonard Pearcey for She Magazine and published in December 1980, in Brenda's own words.

"Nowadays I find that when anyone is singing anything I automatically go straight into harmonies. The nicest thing is when you're with somebody who's already singing, perhaps the melody or perhaps the tenor line, and you find another harmony that fits both of them. It's lovely just searching out harmonies. I should say it's very close to the fact that you've sung in chapel choirs. I remember we were always a bit disgusted when most *church* people just sang unison, or else they did the choirboy high descants which don't seem very natural. It's this getting underneath the melody and just lifting it up. I know it must irritate sometimes, but I don't know I'm doing it to them, when somebody starts to sing and I'm pitching in behind. And then somebody says, do you know such-and-such a song, and I say, yes, been singing it for years, but then I don't know the melody at all because I've always just sung the harmony.

Never had any lessons, but what better training, because there was a pride in singing – I suppose the lessons I had were in the chapel choir. I can remember Irving Thomas saying, "If you can't hear the voice either side of you, you're singing too loud!", because you had to use your voice by using your ears to listen to the others and to the organ. And he used to say "If you can sing soft and you can sing clearly, then you won't have any trouble singing loud, you'll be able to reach the end of anywhere, if you can control your voice singing soft." And that is true – there's nothing better than real soft singing with it all just melding in...

And now I can whisper in a large hall and still be heard at the back, but that is the result of training, because I've been involved in amateur dramatics for many years, and became very keen on it. In the courses that the County used to run, in those days when they had a bit of money, that was where I realised, by listening to a professional they brought down from RADA, just what we can do with our voice. I found that training excellent, because although I was already able to do it, I knew *why* after that, and I very much appreciated understanding it.

I suppose because I had no ambition to be a professional singer, I really never thought of taking training – though I do believe that training for all things is good – but shall I say that singing was so natural to me, it never occurred to me that I should do any training. Like with the jazz band thing: you see, I was 14 or 15 years old in Penzance at the time when our town was bursting with American troops about to cross the Channel and invade France. So of course every corner was filled with those places where they had to buy their goods, and there'd always be a jazz band playing, and many of them visited our houses and were great friends of my mother and father, and mine as well. So this 14-year old kid would be at the side and they'd get me up to sing 'All of Me'; well, I was probably doing it all wrong, but at the same time I gained an enormous love of the 1930s, 1940s music, standards that I loved to sing. Again, I've never studied singing it, or done it professionally, but people say, when I sing that sort of music, I do it well.

One of these days, I'm going to get around to getting a combo [she did], if that's the right word – it sounds very smooth! What I mean is that I'd love to work with say, a bass player, a piano, perhaps a cello, singing standards and jazz that way. I did some work with David Snell, the jazz harpist, and that was a joy. But you do need special arrangements for that sort of thing if you're going to make an album, because you're taking risks with what the world wants to hear. But I love that music.

But how do you decide what song you're going to love? A song arrives in your life by so many different ways, and then there's the various associations: people you were with at the time, the occasion you need to use it, or just the atmosphere of the world at that time. If you were feeling particularly on top of the world in that song, then every time you use it, it brings back that rush of love or affection – or sadness. And you hear this one again and up comes a lump in the throat, and you think, oh yes, I remember – I remember it well. Now *there's* a title for a song!

And again, you see, having been involved in village pantomimes, well, pantomimes are greedy things for songs, and you're digging out all sorts of old music hall songs and new musicals and songs from films... I think there was some excellent music written for films in the 30s and 40s. I don't seem to follow pop very much, I find that it palls on me quickly; I listen to something and think, that's very clever lyrics, or that's an interesting melody, but it never gets beyond that, it never gets inside and hits me in the guts.

I think this is where I'm very lucky with the man who writes my material [Richard Gendall]: he's got the ability to hit me in the guts with what he's doing. I have to get that across to the audience, and that's where the acting bit comes in again, particularly if I sing in other languages, when my personal feelings for the song have to convey the meaning to the audience, even though they may not understand that language, so in order to communicate I have to act the song. It only takes a split second to put the hat on for a song: in Mordonnow, for instance, which means 'sea waves' – it is a rolling song, it has enormous crashing sounds, and then becomes very little and quiet; when you sing a song like that, you've got to give out as much as you know about the sea.

So my hands will be going – I'm always throwing my hands about actually, I've hit guitarists and walls on stage, hurt me fingers an' all when I'm working – but afterwards, people said, well, I could feel the sea, I could hear the sea in that song, and that's because it feels like I'm in the sea. It's a song to the sea waves, saying how much I am frightened of the sea, how cruel it is, how it rises and falls, curls and breaks and hisses, and yet at the end of the song I say, "Oh sea, why is it given to me to love you so?"

But they have to understand, it's a responsibility I have. I'm the only person in the world at the moment who sings professionally in the Cornish language. In audiences there's often somebody with a tape recorder, and there are now some young girls in Germany and in Holland who are singing some of my songs in Kernewek, the old Cornish language, and I want them to be able to do it right. I go back to my teacher Richard Gendall regularly, not just for the songs he writes for me, but to check my pronunciation of some of the songs I've been singing for some time. I do it as properly as I can.

I don't know when I'll ever give up. I always said that I'd give up if it wasn't exciting any more. I've never yet had a concert I didn't get some excitement out of. I'll never forget one week in which I had a real example of the swing from one end to the other. One Tuesday morning I was about to catch the boat back from the Scilly Isles, where I'd been singing, when they asked me if I'd go along to the local playgroup. There were seventeen 3-year olds, and I'd never really done anything with very young children. But I remembered a song me mum had taught me all about a scarf, so I borrowed some and had them all dancing up and down with scarves – I got a terrific kick out of those three-year olds.

At the end of that week I was in Paris doing the Fête des Humanités with an audience of 80,000, and I was very thrilled. But when I look back on it, I got no more kick out of that than I got out of those 17 little children. And the balance between the two, well I suppose that's the kind of buzz that keeps you going.

In the end I just want to be known as a singer, and for the quality of my voice."

List of Photographs

The photographs are of widely varying ages and quality, of necessity, so apologies for any that appear 'fuzzy' – we aren't trying to enter a photo competition, but to offer happy memories. Most are from family archives, but there are many that are of unknown origin. Apologies also to any photographer or copyright owner who is unacknowledged, we did try; please get in touch if you want that information recorded.

Brenda's Accompanists

Dates are often vague and details incomplete; includes musicians, bands and choirs… in random order. (Ashley Staton & Ray Roberts also played in Phil King's Trio)

Name	Instruments	Approx dates	Albums/Some known special events
John the Fish	Guitar	1965-1972, and periodically since	More Singing at the Count House LP 1965 Pipers Folk LP 1968 Pasties & Cream LP 1971 Way Down to Lamorna LP 1984 So Long, Cassette 1987 Voice of Cornwall CD
Richard Gendall	Guitar	1972-73, 1976	Crowdy Crawn LP 1973 Children Singing LP 1976 Boy Jan, Cornishman LP 1980 Gwavas Lake LP 1980 Way Down to Lamorna LP 1984 Voice of Cornwall CD
Alex Atterson	Guitar, keyboards, accordion	1968-73, periodically	No Song To Sing LP 1974
Michael Chapman	Guitar	1966, and periodically	Individual Cabaret/Jazz/Blues
Robert Bartlett	Guitar, as 1st professional duo	1973-75	No Song To Sing LP 1974 Pamplemousse LP 1975 Festival Pop Kertalg LP 1974 Starry Gazey Pie LP 1975 Tin in the Stream LP 1975 Way Down to Lamorna LP 1984 Voice of Cornwall CD
Mike Silver	Guitar	Sep 1975 – for 6 months	France, Germany
Andy Dickson	Guitar	Feb-April 1975	
John Molyneux	Guitar, etc	April 1975-	
Mike Sagar-Fenton	Guitar	Periodically	Pipers Folk LP Pasties & Cream LP 1971 Crowdy Crawn LP
Steve Hall	Guitar	Periodically, early years	Pasties & Cream LP 1971 Killarney
Pete Berryman	Guitar	Periodically	Lorient Festival
Dik Cadbury	Guitar	1972-73	Pan-Celtic Festival 1973 Lorient Festival 1973
Al Fenn	Guitar	1976 and periodically	Children Singing LP 1976

John Alderslade	Guitar	April 1975	
Phil King Trio	Keyboards, guitar, drums	Periodically	My Land LP 1983 Cornish Australian Single 1985 B Comme Brenda LP 1985 Tamar LP 1986 Bourge Concert 1988
Steve Gordon	Guitar	Periodically	Lorient Festival 1979 1-26 Feb Tour 1984 – Truro Twinning Association Valence June 1988
Dave Penhale	Guitar	April 1978 – 1980	Carillon LP 1979 Boy Jan, Cornishman LP 1980 La Grande Cornouaillaise LP 1980 Gwavas Lake LP 1980 Lyonesse LP 1982 Tamar LP 1986
Chris Newman	Guitar	Periodically, over a number of years from the early 1980s	My Land LP 1983 Bobino Theatre, Paris 1984 Canada 1984 & 1985 Cornish Australian Single 1985 'B' Comme Brenda LP 1985 All of Me CD 2010
Brian A Wright	Guitar, Lute		
Mike Morgan	Guitar	1978	Did at least one tour in Germany & in France
David Snell	Harp	27.11.1985	World Travel Market, Olympia
John Knight	Guitar	Periodically, and on several albums	Lyonesse LP 1982 My Land LP 1983 'B' Comme Brenda LP 1985 Cornish Australian Single 1985
David King	Guitar	Periodically	Lyonesse LP 1982 Berceuses Celtes EP 1981 Berceuses du Monde Entier 1983
Ashley Staton	Piano	Periodically	'B' Comme Brenda LP 1985
Ray Roberts	Clarinet, Flute, Sax	Periodically, and on several albums	My Land LP 1983 Bobino Theatre, Paris 1984 'B' Comme Brenda LP 1985 Cornish Australian Single 1985 Tamar LP 1986 All of Me CD 2010
Dave Freeman	Bass	Periodically	Bobino Theatre, Paris 1984 Bourge Festival 1988 All of Me CD 2010
Viv Rodd	Piano	Periodically	Valence June 1988

Francis Lai	Piano		Everybody Knows Maxi Single 1987
Rene Werneer	Violin	Periodically	Pamplemousse LP 1975
Four Lanes MVC	Male Voices	Periodically	Lorient Festival 1979 St Ives September Festival 1980 Gwavas Lake LP 1980 Tamar LP 1986
Mousehole MVC	Male Voices	Periodically	Hark the Glad Sound Single 1983 Lorient Festival 1984
Treviscoe MVC	Male Voices	Periodically	My Land LP 1983
Denzil Richards Singers	Choir		Anne Jeffrey & the Little People, Lorient Festival 1986
Perran Harmony Singers	Mixed voices		Cornish Australian Single 1985
Praze MVC	Male Voices		Winwaloe Event, Towednack 1987 Seagull LP 1989
Camborne Town Band	Silver Band	Periodically, and on several albums	Hark the Glad Sound Single 1983 Bobino Theatre, Paris 1984 'B' Comme Brenda LP 1985 Tamar LP 1986 All of Me CD 2010
St Stythians Silver Band	Silver Band		Pasties & Cream LP 1971
Carnon Vale Octet	Male Voices		Lorient Festival 1980

Session musicians: Gill Butler, Roger Butler, Sally Campbell, Cas Caswell, Bob Crooks, David Etheridge, Jean-Luc Hallereau, Mike Higgs, Sally Holmes, Marion James, Danny Johns, Ken Johns, Mike Lease, Don Lockwood, Nick Jones, Simon Mayor, Jon Press, Alec Shaw, John Sleep, Phil Somers, Paul Timmins, Gerard Trevignon, Paul Triggs, Barry Tuckett. (Apologies to any we've missed...)

Timeline

This is necessarily incomplete – it also does not include time spent doing recordings, rehearsals, interviews, preparation for Sunday Best, or media recording abroad etc. Gleaned from diaries, booking contracts, song lists, correspondence, BBC and other archives. Media is noted where I have the information, but it's likely Brenda would have been appearing on local media on almost every tour.

Year	Key Events	Personal	Music	Media
1925	John born in Badger, Salop, 3rd April	X		
1927	Lena & Angus move up to London to work – they marry there on 3rd September	X		
1928	Brenda Wootton born in Willesden 10th February;	X		
	Lena and Angus move back to Cornwall in August	X		
1932	Brother Peter born in Vine Cottage, Newlyn	X		
1935	John the Fish born		X	
1938	B sings in 'Concert for China', Penzance, age 10	X		
1939	B started at Penzance Girls County School, September	X		
1941	John starts work at Corkes Radio, Service Dept, Wolverhampton, April	X		
1943	B and friend Jean save man from drowning, Perranporth	X		
	B's first dramatic performance, playing Matryona in Tolstoy's 'Michael' with Pz Youth Centre	X		
	John leaves Corkes to serve in RAF in November	X		
1944	B left school	X		
	B started work in Penzance Manual Telephone Exchange	X		
1946	B came 3rd in Ladies 150 yds Open in Newlyn Harbour Sports & Swimming Gala	X		
1947	B first sang solo at choir practice on 24 February	X		
	Mentions 'painting plaques' for daddy	X		
	Meets John Wootton at RAF/Post Office dinner dance	X		
1948	B got engaged to John Wootton on her 20th birthday	X		
	John rejoins Corkes Radio, until October	X		
	Brenda and John married 3rd July	X		
	They move to Wolverhampton to live	X		
1949	B moves back to Cornwall, lives with Angus and Lena; John joins her in June	X		
	Susan born 1st November in Daniel Place, Penzance	X		

	John started work at Skewjack, Sennen	X		
1950	Moved to Atlantic Breezes, Lands End, Sennen, October	X		
1951	Moved to Beachfield, Sennen Cove, 13th November	X		
1954	Moved to Treeve Moor, Sennen, January	X		
	Susan started at Sennen School , September	X		
1955	Brenda's first adult singing performance, for Lands End WI, aged 27		X	
1956	Moved to 18 Atlantic Crescent, Sennen, January	X		
	Susan took piano lessons	X		
	Brenda & others started Sennen Drama Group, November	X		
1959	Moved to 4 Leskinnick Street, Penzance, September	X		
	Susan started St Marys School at Redinnick in Penzance, September	X		
1960	B & J start bed and breakfast business	X		
	Susan took ballet lessons	X		
1961	Susan started at Penzance Girls' Grammar School	X		
1962	John wins fibreglass boat & outboard motor at Culdrose Air Day	X		
1963	Susan started elocution lessons	X		
1964	Lena died April 9th	X		
	First visit to Count House Folk Music Club		X	
1965	Brenda & Fish start touring		X	
	Peter starts Tremaen Pottery at Marazion, with B as Director	X		
1966	Michael Chapman's first visit to Count House		X	
1967	Count House Folk Music Club closed		X	
	Pipers' Folk Club opened at St Buryan, May		X	
	Tremaen moved premises to Newlyn Slip	X		
	'Mayday Mayday' film + Pipers' Folk at Minack Theatre, broadcast October 5th Westward TV in Dublin Film comp.			X
1968	Susan left Grammar School, started Teacher Training course at Philippa Fawcett College of Education in Streatham	X		
1969	John resigned from ROC, March	X		
	John left Skewjack	X		

1970	John resigned from RAF, January	X		
	Started work for Marshall at Rediffusion	X		
1971	Folk on Friday, BBC Radio2 with John the Fish 12 Feb			X
	Susan left college, started teaching in Smallwood Junior School in Tooting	X		
	Pipers' Folk Club relocated to Western Hotel		X	
1972	Folk on Sunday, BBC Radio2 with John the Fish & Tom Paxton 23 January			X
	Lacock Folk Festival + John the Fish, May		X	
	B introduced to Richard Gendall		X	
	Pan-Celtic Festival in Killarney with Steve Hall – Brenda sang first song in Cornish language outside Cornwall		X	
	Crowdy Crawn LP + RG		X	
1973	Killarney Festival with Dik Cadbury		X	
	Harlech Festival with Dik Cadbury		X	
	Kertalg Festival with Dik Cadbury; concert recorded		X	
	Susan returned to Cornwall, working as a Supply Teacher	X		
1974	Crowdy Crawn established as duo with Robert Bartlett		X	
	Susan became Shop Manager at Tremaen Craft Market	X		
	Norwich Folk Festival		X	
	1st professional tour of Brittany + Robert Bartlett		X	
1975	German TV Baden Baden Feb 1st -3rd			X
	TV Glasgow Diary 24 March			X
	BBC TV Glasgow Mar 29th			X
	Angus died April 16th	X		
	German TV Wurzburg May 2nd & 23rd			X
	Norwich Folk Festival		X	
	Brenda and Robert, Crowdy Crawn, split up, September		X	
	Sue married Arthur John Luscombe, September	X		
	Mike Silver starts a 6 month stint as Brenda's guitarist; tours in France and Germany		X	
	HTV Bristol Nov 19th - 21st, 24th-25th Dec 1st-2nd – Sweet Somerset			X
	Sang for Edward Heath Literary Luncheon 13th Feb in Amsterdam		X	
	Folkweave BBC Radio 2 + Crowdy Crawn 11th March			X

1976	Folkweave BBC Radio 2 + Crowdy Crawn 3rd June			X
	BBC TV Cardiff Feb 23rd and Oct 5th			X
	BBC TV Wandsworth Oct 19th			X
	BBC TV Devon October 22nd			X
1977	Folkweave BBC Radio 2 + Tony Capstick with Al Fenn 28th April			X
	Folkweave BBC Radio 2 with Al Fenn 7th July			X
	Concert with Al Fenn in Irvine in Scotland, August		X	
	Wally Whyton BBC Radio 2 with Al Fenn 27th August			X
	Gorsedh – Brenda made a Bard, 'Gwylan Gwavas' 3rd September		X	
	Westward TV Sep 14th 15th			X
	Barn Dance BBC Radio 2 + Terry Wogan, Madron, September			X
	Grandson Davy born 10.10.77	X		
	Barn Dance BBC Radio 2 with Mike Sagar-Fenton 28th October			X
	The Rippon Report with Angela Rippon BBC1 South West			X
	Barn Dance BBC Radio 2 with Mike Sagar-Fenton 30th December			X
1978	Bristol TV – Brenda with Chris Newman and Louis Robinson at Bedminster Down Boys Club half hour show 'Down the Club'			X
	Singing with Dave Penhale in London October		X	
	UK Schools, Humphry Davy, 7 December		X	
1979	Germany 15-24 January		X	
	Belgium 2-18 February		X	
	Germany 1-18 March		X	
	France 19-21 March		X	
	UK 26-31 March		X	
	'War & Pieces' Show, Serenade 78, Plymouth 6-12 April		X	
	UK 13-18 + 24-28 April		X	
	Westward TV 2 May			X
	Theatre de la Ville, Paris, 6-13 May		X	
	Australia Kernewek Lowender 14 May-5 June		X	
	London 9 June		X	

	Pete Murray Show 11 June			X
	Brighton, Radio June 27th			X
	UK, 20 June-7 July		X	
	Isle of Man Tynwald 8-14 July		X	
	UK, 17-21 July, 26, 28, 29, July		X	
	Lorient Festival, 1-12 August		X	
	UK, 16-21, 29 August		X	
	Belgium 31 August-4 September		X	
	UK, 21-23 September, 4,5,9 October		X	
	Germany 12 October-3 November		X	
	1st Lowender Peran Festival at Perranporth		X	
	'Hobsons Choice' Studio recording November 18th			X
	UK, 3-6, 11,27,31 January, 1,3		X	
	Westward TV 12 January + John Bartlett			X
	Grandson Jan born 20.1.80	X		
	BBC Theatre Folk 1980 24 January			X
	BBC Bristol 4 February			X
	UK 15,16,19-24 February		X	
	UK 1-6 March		X	
	France 8-9 March		X	
	UK 10-14 March		X	
	Germany 15 March-10 April		X	
	Belgium 11 April-3 May		X	
	France, Belgium, Denmark 10-26 May		X	
	UK 27-29 May, 1 June		X	
	France 2-16 June, 2-3 July		X	
	Denmark, Germany – 11-17 July		X	
	UK 19-27 July		X	
	Luxembourg, Germany, Switzerland, Belgium, Holland 28 July-3 August		X	
1980	Woman's Hour BBC Radio4 8th August (pre-recorded)			X
	Lorient Festival 4-11 August		X	
	UK – 14,17,19, 22-29 August		X	
	Belgium Festival 6 September		X	

	UK 7,11,13,27 September		X	
	Swiss Radio 29 September			X
	Singing with Four Lanes Choir for 'Drake 400' Festival in Plymouth		X	
	UK 3,4 October		X	
	BBC Bristol TV: An Gof, 6-7 October & Plymouth TV 8 October			X
	Belgium, Germany 30 October-22 November		X	
	UK 23,29 November-2 December		X	
	France 3-15 December		X	
	UK 16-20,22,23 December		X	
	BBC Nationwide 17-18 December			X
	Saturday Night Theatre 'Last Invasion of London' BBC Radio4			X
1981	UK 29 January, 28 February		X	
	UK Schools 19-20 February, Pelynt, Polperro, St Pauls, Nancledra		X	
	France 2-28 March - Palais des Glaces, solo concerts, Paris		X	
	Capital Radio UK 31 March			X
	BBC Plymouth 3-5 April			X
	UK 6,7 April		X	
	Germany, Luxembourg, Austria 8 April- 2 May		X	
	Australia 7-20 May; Kernewek Lowender, South Australia		X	
	UK Lacock Festival 25 May		X	
	UK 28 May, 8 July		X	
	Germany 9-11 June		X	
	UK Norwich Festival 26-28 June		X	
	France, Belgium 15-20 July		X	
	BBC Radio2 Folk on 2 with David Penhale 20th July			X
	France, Lorient Festival + Newlyn MVC 5-18 August		X	
	Netherlands 21-23 August		X	
	UK 28-30 August		X	
	BBC Bristol 1,2 September			X
	Gorsedh Kernow 5 September		X	
	UK 7,16,19 September		X	

	Germany 2-14 October		X	
	UK 18 October		X	
	Belgium 30 October-15 November		X	
	'Cornwall the Land I Love' TV prog BBC 13 November			X
	France 11-18 December			X
	Loisir des Jeunes Award for 'Celtic Lullabies' single, Paris, December		X	
	Cornish Christmas Cracker Show at Cornwall Coliseum, St Austell for Radio Cornwall 26 December-2 January		X	X
1982	France 5,6 January		X	
	BBC Radio4 8 January			X
	BBC Radio4 Down To The Sea Again + Richard Baker 17 January			X
	BBC Radio4 Midweek 20 January			X
	UK Schools 1-3 February		X	
	France 4-21 February		X	
	UK 27 February Concert for Penlee, Ben Luxon + Holman Climax Choir		X	
	France 4-7 March, (Martin guitar stolen)		X	
	Radio Plymouth Sound 20 March			X
	UK 27 March		X	
	France 6-14 April – Bourges Festival, Three Divas Concert, Paris		X	
	Celtic Congress Penzance 16 April		X	
	UK 20 April		X	
	France 21-24 April		X	
	UK 8,11,14,19-23 May		X	
	France 24-30 May		X	
	UK St Germans School 10 June		X	
	France 15-20 June		X	
	UK 22,24-27 June		X	
	UK 6,16-17 July		X	
	France, 20-30 July; Palais de Papes, Avignon		X	
	France, Lorient Festival 9-17 August		X	
	Spain, La Coruna, Galicia, 20-27 August		X	
	UK 3,4 September, Gorsedh Kernow		X	

	France 11-14 September Fete d'Humanite		X	
	UK Schools, Cape Cornwall 4 September, Mullion 24 September		X	
	Richard Gendall married 2 October	X		
	UK 3 October		X	
	France 8-10 October		X	
	UK School 20 October		X	
	France 21-31 October		X	
	France, Paris, New Theatre 6 November		X	
	France 6,7 10-12 December - Brest + Stefan Grappelli		X	
	BBC Radio Cornwall, Sunday Best – first show 23 January			X
	France + Colette Magny 8 February		X	
	'Pasties & Cream' TV prog BBC 11 February			X
	'Cornwall the Land I Love' TV prog BBC 18 February (rpt)			X
	BBC Radio Devon			X
	France 21 February-11 March		X	
	UK 12,13 March		X	
	UK Schools, St Keverne, 16 March		X	
	France & Belgium 14-30 April; Three Divas Paris, 16,18 April		X	
	France 3-10 May		X	
1983	UK 14 May 8-9 June		X	
	France 19 June		X	
	UK Schools Newlyn 25 June		X	
	UK, 3 July, + Trowbridge Festival		X	
	France 21-30 July, Avignon + Treviscoe MVC		X	
	France 6-7 August		X	
	UK 11 August, 12 October		X	
	UK Lowender Peran 16 October		X	
	BBC Roscoff Ferry 11,12 November			X
	UK 18 November		X	
	UK 8, 28 December		X	
	UK 27 January		X	
	France 1-24 February		X	

	UK 27-29 February		X	
	France 1-24 March		X	
	UK Schools 1-6 April		X	
	UK 7, 13, April		X	
	France 16-19 April		X	
	Switzerland, France 10,11 May		X	
	France 10-26 May, Bobino Theatre 14-19 May		X	
	UK Cornwall 4,7,13,16,23 June		X	
	Topped French charts		X	
1984	Canada tour: Montreal, Quebec, Ottawa 2-21 July		X	
	UK 22,26,28 July		X	
	France Lorient 5-12 August		X	
	Spain 14-17 August		X	
	France 18,19 August		X	
	Gorsedh Kernow 1 September		X	
	France Fete d'Humanite 6-10 September		X	
	France 9 September; 12-28 October		X	
	UK 7 November		X	
	France 24,30 November-9 December		X	
	UK Radio Cornwall Coliseum, St Austell Show 16 December		X	X
	UK 8 January		X	
	France 24 January-11 February		X	
	Solicitor suing for cancelled concert at Nantes (1984)		X	
	UK Schools at Goonhilly, 21-25 February		X	
	Celtavision 26 February			X
	French TV: 27 February, 3 March			X
	BBC 7 March			X
	France 8-25 March		X	
	UK 29 March, 6 April		X	
	France 16 April-2 May		X	
1985	UK 9 May		X	
	France 10 May		X	
	Australia 11-21 May		X	

	France 20-26 June		X	
	Canada 2-20 July		X	
	France 21-24		X	
	France Lorient 2-18, 24 August		X	
	Gorsedh Kernow 7 September		X	
	UK 27 September, 5,11 October		X	
	Switzerland, France 5-23 November		X	
	World Travel Market, Olympia, London, opened by Princess of Wales 27 November + David Snell on harp		X	
	France 6-16 December		X	
1986	French tour 24 January–15 February		X	
	UK 18, 27, 29 March		X	
	France 28 April–18 May, Olympia Paris, 9 May		X	
	France 7-9 June		X	
	France 19-22 June, Orient Express + Chris Newman		X	
	BBC Radio4 Jesus Came to Ding Dong + Gerald Priestland 6 July			X
	Spain, Barcelona 14-20 July, + Louis Llach		X	
	France, Lorient Festival 'Anne Jeffery', 10-17 August		X	
	UK 28 September		X	
	France 7-12 October		X	
	France 6-14		X	
	French gigs 6-12th December		X	
1987	Fly Stuttgart for French TV 1-3 February			X
	Reunion Concert + John the Fish, Penventon Hotel, in aid of Cot Death 24 February		X	
	France 25-27 February		X	
	France 13-22 March		X	
	'Academie Charles Cros' Award in France for the best 'stranger' album of the year; Received for album 'Tamar', from the French Minister of Culture in Paris, March 17th		X	
	'Everybody Knows' Maxi single, lyrics by Brenda, music by Francis Lai		X	
	France 12-16 April		X	
	UK 18,24 April, 11 May		X	

	France 8-19 May		X	
	UK 20 May, 17 June		X	
	UK Schools, 13,17 June Nancledra, Bishop School Newquay		X	
	UK 16,19 July		X	
	France inc Lorient 14-18 August		X	
	UK 29-31 August, 15 September		X	
	St Winwaloe Celebration, Towednack 19 September		X	
	Moved from Leskinnick Street to Tredinnick Stack, October		X	
	France 16-21 October		X	
	France 19-30 November		X	
	UK 12 December		X	
	BBC Cornwall Christmas Best 3 December			X
	4 Leskinnick Street sold in January	X		
	France 28-30 January		X	
	BBC Spotlight 9 February			X
	UK 16 March		X	
	BBC Woman's Hour 18 March			X
	UK 10,24 March		X	
	France – Bourges 9 April + Praze MVC		X	
	Ireland, Killarney 8-13 May		X	
1988	UK 22 June		X	
	France 23-26 June Valence + Lluis Llach+ Charles Aznavour		X	
	Ruby Wedding at Count House, 3rd July	X		
	France 16-17 July		X	
	France 5-6 August		X	
	France 24 September		X	
1989	France 28-31 January + Ashley Staton		X	
	Brenda suffered stroke while recording 'Seagull' March 4th	X		
1990	Concert in Bordeaux, December		X	
1991	Sunday Best Radio Cornwall, final show in January			X
	Opened Ashtorre Rock Community Centre, Waterside, Saltash 5th March		X	
1992	Opened Green Fair, Penzance, April		X	

	Brenda in and out of St Michaels Hospital, Hayle	X		
1993	Brenda in and out of St Michaels Hospital and Poltair, Heamoor	X		
1994	Brenda died – 11th March, Poltair Hospital; funeral 18th March, at Paul Church	X		
	Brenda Wootton Memorial Concert – June		X	
	'Pantomime Stew' released, 21st November	X		
	John died – 16th December	X		
	Sue and family moved into Tredinnick Stack, rented out Canon's Town, December	X		
1995	Tremaen Craft Market closed, March	X		
	Sue & John separated, June	X		
	Sue sold Tredinnick Stack, bought house in St Just, took trip to Australia, September	X		
1996	Brother Peter Ellery died, December	X		
2000	1st great-granddaughter Tegen Stella Reynolds born, July	X		
2003	Western Morning News: Brenda voted top woman in poll of '100 Greatest Cornish People', at #11		X	
2005	Sue moved to North Wales to live with Chris Hill, rented out house in St Just	X		
2009	1st great-grandson Aaron Arthur John born, November	X		
2013	2nd great-granddaughter Olivia Elowen born, June	X		
	Sue & Chris sell up in Wales and move back to St Just	X		
	Lowender Peran, Brenda Wootton Tribute Concert		X	
	Release of 'Brenda at Buryan' CD		X	
2014	3rd great-granddaughter Lily Jane Ann born, April	X		
	Jan & Tara married, September	X		
2015	2nd great-grandson Ruben Angus Joseph born, September	X		
2016	Colleen Rogers died	X		
	Sue and Chris Hill married in Penzance, October	X		
	4th great-granddaughter Lena Florence born, November	X		
	Ella Knight died	X		
	Blue Plaque awarded by Radio Cornwall listeners, June		X	
	Lowender Peran – Symposium: Brenda Wootton's Cornish Language Songs, by Richard Trethewey		X	

2017	Lowender Peran – Concert with Richard Trethewey & Camborne Town Band featuring Brenda's songs		X	
	Release of 'Brenda at Christmas' CD		X	
	Richard Gendall died, November	X		
	Sentinel Records Master Tapes purchased by a Consortium, for Cornwall Archives, Kresen Kernow, November		X	
2018	Sue received 2 awards for short story & poem, Creative Writing in English, from Esedhvos Kernow at Gorsedh Kernow, August	X		

Brenda's Audio Recordings

<table>
<tr><td rowspan="4"><u>Folk Music at the Count House EP</u>

Included for posterity, although Brenda did not appear on it. The very first of the 'folk revival' recordings from West Cornwall, it featured the first resident singers at J Ian Todd's new Count House Folk Music Club at Botallack, Pendeen, Cornwall.</td><td>Folk Music at the Count House EP 45rpm</td><td>The Count House</td></tr>
<tr><td colspan="2">John the Fish & Tell Mann, Mel & Miles - 31st Oct 1964</td></tr>
<tr><td>Side 1</td><td>Side 2</td></tr>
<tr><td>1. The Farriers (Mel & Miles)
2. Down in the Mine (John & Tell)</td><td>3. Fly Away (John & Tell)
4. Henry (Mel & Miles)
5. Nightingale (Mel & Miles)</td></tr>
<tr><td rowspan="3"><u>1. More Singing at the Count House LP</u>

More Singing at the Count House, the first full-length album, was an exciting new venture for all concerned, and has now become a very collectable rarity... Recorded at the Count House on November 11th 1965, it featured John the Fish (no Tell Mann, this time - Tell had started his own own 'Tell-a-Tale' folk club in Penzance by then), Mel and Miles again, and Scottish newcomer Des Hannigan, and of course, Brenda Wootton. The record was privately produced with the Count House tin mine logo.</td><td>More Singing at the Count House – LP 33rpm</td><td>The Count House</td></tr>
<tr><td colspan="2">John the Fish (A); Mel & Miles (B); Des Hannigan (C); Brenda Wootton (D) - 11th Nov 1965</td></tr>
<tr><td>1. Green Eyes (A)
2. Johnny I Hardly Knew Ye (C)
3. Fan Me Soldier Man -(B)
4. Lamorna (D)
5. Nobody Knows You (A)
6. Careless Love (D)
7. Haul 'Em Away (B)
8. 100 Years Ago (B)
9. Wild Mountain Thyme (A+D)</td><td>10. There Ain't No More Cane (A)
11. The Flowers Of Spring (C)
12. High Germany (B)
13. Two Brothers (D)
14. I Wish I Was A Rock (A)
15. Mrs McGrath (C)
16. Derby Ram (B)
17. Harp Song of the Dane Women (D)
18. Old Time Religion (All)</td></tr>
<tr><td rowspan="3"><u>2. Pipers' Folk LP</u>

Privately produced, and the first album recorded after Brenda took over running the folk club. The recording engineer, Charles Horrell, from the Video Recording Company in Worcestershire, recorded mostly in the club, although 4 tracks were recorded in the Newlyn Meadery. The sleeve art was one of 2 created by Brenda's brother Peter Ellery, as was the Piper logo - used ever after at the club.</td><td>Pipers' Folk LP
LP 33rpm</td><td>Video Recording Company
VRC 1A</td></tr>
<tr><td colspan="2">Brenda Wootton & John the Fish - 1968</td></tr>
<tr><td>1. Far Side Of The Hill
2. Bradey Bradey
3. Stars
4. Come All Ye Fair & Tender Maidens
5. A Good Man Is Hard To Find
6. When Morning Breaks
7. Chickens
8. I'm Troubled</td><td>9. Stagalee
10. Coming Of The Roads
11. Hold On To Me, Babe
12. Cockleshells
13. Round And Round
14. Winter Winds Of Sorrow
15. The First Time Ever
16. Tom Bawcocks Eve</td></tr>
<tr><td rowspan="3"><u>3. Pasties & Cream LP</u>

The first of Brenda's Sentinel Records albums... Brenda was very particular about the photo on the front... the kitchen belonged to Mrs Hitchens of Trewarveneth Street in Newlyn, who</td><td>Pasties & Cream LP
LP 33rpm</td><td>Sentinel Records SENS1006</td></tr>
<tr><td colspan="2">Brenda Wootton and John the Fish - 1971</td></tr>
<tr><td>1. Pasties & Cream
2. Stern Old Bachelor</td><td>8. Something About A Pasty</td></tr>
</table>

<table>
<tr><td>had the necessary Cornish range. Other musicians who contributed included Stythians Silver Band, Mike Sagar, Steve Hall and John Sleep.</td><td>3. Lamorna
4. To The Sea
5. The Old Grey Duck
6. Betsy Watson
7. Little Eyes (or Lize)</td><td>9. The Oggy Man
10. Old Time Religion
11. Farewell She
12. Bedbugs
13. Camborne Hill
14. Cornish Alphabet</td></tr>
<tr><td rowspan="3"><u>4. Crowdy Crawn LP</u>

An album exploring the Cornish language, with Brenda's mentor, Cornish language expert Richard Gendall, who went on to write over 400 songs for Brenda, many in Kernewek – later Cornoack. Crowdy Crawn is taken from the Cornish 'croder croghan', a skin sieve that was hung by the fire and held small treasures or keepsakes. Confusingly, it was later adopted by Brenda and guitarist Robert Bartlett as their stage name.</td><td>Crowdy Crawn LP
LP 33rpm</td><td>Sentinel Records SENS 1016</td></tr>
<tr><td colspan="2">Brenda Wootton & Richard Gendall - 1973</td></tr>
<tr><td>1. Morvah Fair
2. Kemer Ow Ro
3. Hus Gans
4. Mynfel
5. Well of St. Keyne
6. Tekter
7. Pyu A Wor
8. Merrymaidens
9. Bre Cambron
10. Ow Heryades</td><td>11. An Hos Los Coth
12. An Jowal Carol
13. An Mysyow
14. Newlyn
15. Mount Misery
16. An Scath
17. Tryphena Trenerry
18. Pyth Whrama
19. Lul Ha Lay
20. Farwel</td></tr>
<tr><td rowspan="3"><u>5. Festival Pop Celtic - Kertalg '73 LP</u>

A pirated album, essentially - produced from a Folk Festival held at the Chateau Kertalg in Brittany, for which Brenda and Dik were not consulted and never paid. Other artists featured included Robin & Barry Dransfield, Planxty, Happy Traum, René Werneer from Brittany, and many others. First held in 1972, for 3 years only.</td><td>Festival Pop Celtic '73
LP 33rpm</td><td>Kertalg, France
Barclay 920.452/3</td></tr>
<tr><td colspan="2">Brenda Wootton & Dik Cadbury, Robin & Barry Dransfield, Planxty, Happy Traum, Les Soeurs Goadec & others - July 1973</td></tr>
<tr><td>1. Les Soeurs Goadec - In Plinn
2. Brenda Wootton - Mordonnow
3. Planxty - Si Bheag Si Mhor
4. Robin Dransfield - Scarborough Fair
5. René Werneer - Planxty Irvine & Ash Plant (Reels)
6. Happy Traum - When I Paint my Masterpiece
7. Diaouled Ar Menez - In Fisel
8. Brenda Wootton - A Wennol Wyn
9. Dremmwel - Walk of the Rain
10. Munroe - An Bothan a Baaig Fionnaguala
11. Ar Skloferien - Gavotte of Honor</td><td>12. Brenda Wootton - Jan Knuckey
13. Planxty - Jig
14. Glenmor - Klemm Breizh Izel
15. Soeurs Goadec-Gavotten Ar Menez
16. René Werneer - Reel
17. Robin Dransfield - Adam + Beasts
18. Planxty - Raggle Taggle Gypsy
19. Les Soeurs Goadec - Pach Pi
20. Robin Dransfield-When It's Night-Time in Italy It's Wednesday Here
21. Katell, Drinking a Violin</td></tr>
<tr><td rowspan="3"><u>6. No Song To Sing LP</u>

Brenda's first album as a professional singer was produced in 1974, with guitarist Robert Bartlett. Performing as a duo, they took their stage name</td><td>No Song To Sing LP
LP 33rpm</td><td>Sentinel Records SENS 1021</td></tr>
<tr><td colspan="2">Brenda Wootton & Robert Bartlett - 1974</td></tr>
<tr><td>1. Jan Knuckey
2. Soldier and the Maiden</td><td>8. No Song to Sing
9. Old Joe</td></tr>
</table>

<table>
<tr><td>from Brenda's previous album with Richard Gendall, Crowdy Crawn, and began with a tour of France. The lyrics are printed on the inner sleeve.</td><td>3. Deugh Deugh
4. Djinn Djinn
5. Johnny Groat
6. Mordonnow
7. Black Mountain Blues</td><td>10. Ant and the Grasshopper
11. Good to be Free
12. Port Quin
13. Forever Young</td></tr>
<tr><td rowspan="3"><u>7. Pamplemousse LP</u>

Pamplemousse is French for grapefruit. Produced in Brittany under the aegis of Gwenn Le Goarnig, Brenda's first French agent, Gwenn also released this with a different, bold, red and white cover, possibly for the French market</td><td>Pamplemousse LP
LP 33rpm</td><td>Barclay – France
920.475</td></tr>
<tr><td colspan="2">Brenda Wootton & Robert Bartlett - 1974</td></tr>
<tr><td>1. Mordonnow
2. Maria
3. Dus Tre
4. Grapefruit
5. Sweet Nightingale
6. Jan Knuckey</td><td>7. Danny's Song
8. Delyo Syvy
9. Close Your Eyes
10. A Wennol Wyn
11. Missing You
12. Peaceful Easy Feeling</td></tr>
<tr><td rowspan="3"><u>8. Kertalg '74 LP</u>

The final festival at the Chateau Kertalg in Moelan sur Mer in Brittany, with a phenomenal line-up - but once again, a pirated album. Brenda has just the one song on here: 'A Good Man is Hard to Find'. The cover art was done by Katell Le Goarnig, sister to Gwenn, the organiser - the central figure in front of the bonfire is supposed to represent Brenda, I believe.</td><td>Kertalg 74
LP 33rpm</td><td>Kertalg, France
Barclay 90 011</td></tr>
<tr><td colspan="2">Brenda Wootton & Robert Bartlett, Dick Gaughan, Leon Rosselson, Martin Carthy, Robin & Barry Dransfield, The Boys of the Lough, The Watersons – July 1974</td></tr>
<tr><td colspan="2">1. Dick Gaughan: Seven Yellow Gipsies (3.46)
2. Leon Rosselson: The Fox Chase (4.43)
3. Malicorne: Rossignolet des bois et ronde (4.06)
4. Martin Carthy: Skewbald (3.30)
5. Boys of the Lough: The Streamstown Jig/Johnny MacIljohn's
6. Reel/Sonny's Mazurka (2.08)
7. Brenda Wootton: A Good Man Is Hard To Find (2.37)
8. The Royal Irish Rangers: Tha Mi Sgith (2.49)
9. Robin & Barry Dransfield: The Ballad of Dickie Lubber (4.17)
10. Alistair Anderson & Colin Ross: Marche (3.03)
11. The Watersons: The White Cockade (3.51)
12. La Bamboche: Mazurka, no summer at the Henri Caillaut (3.12)
13. Robin & Barry Dransfield: Hornpipe and Reels (3.28)</td></tr>
<tr><td rowspan="3"><u>9. Tin in the Stream LP</u>

Recorded by Stockfisch Records in Germany, this album reflects Brenda and Robert's increasing popularity on the continent - major European tours took place several times a year, around France, Germany, Belgium and The Netherlands.</td><td>Tin in the Stream LP
LP 33rpm</td><td>Stockfisch Records, Germany SF7001</td></tr>
<tr><td colspan="2">Brenda Wootton & Robert Bartlett - 1974</td></tr>
<tr><td>1. Doro
2. Betsy Watson
3. Careless Love
4. Tryphena Trenary
5. The Sweet Nightingale</td><td>6. The Cock of the North
7. Pasties & Cream
8. Lagan Love
9. Lamorna
10. Summertime
11. Wild Mountain Thyme</td></tr>
<tr><td rowspan="2"><u>10. Starry Gazey Pie LP</u>

Most of the songs on this album by Sentinel Records are Cornish</td><td>Starry Gazey Pie LP
LP 33rpm</td><td>Sentinel Records SENS 1031</td></tr>
<tr><td colspan="2">Brenda Wootton & Robert Bartlett - 1975</td></tr>
</table>

traditional, and a few by Richard Gendall - but all are about Cornwall. The cover picture is an old sepia photograph of Vine Cottages in Trewarveneth Street in Newlyn, where Brenda lived as a little girl...	1. The Story Of My 1. Country 2. Maggie May 3. St Gennys Foxhunt 4. Delyo Syvy 5. The Trees They Are So High 6. Tom Bawcocks Eve	7. King Of Prussia 8. Clegh 9. The Ringers Of Egloshayle 10. The Stratton Carol 11. An Tour Dantelezet 12. Tamar 13. Farewell Shanty
<u>11. Children Singing LP</u> Brenda recorded the album with groups of children from three different schools: Alverton, Ludgvan and St Mary's in Penzance.	**Children Singing LP** LP 33rpm	Sentinel Records SENS 1036
	Brenda Wootton & Alastair Fenn - 1976	
	1. Opie, Davy, Foote, Trevithick & Bone 2. Onen, Deu, Try 3. John Opie 4. Bring Thy Boat 5. 1497 6. Evening Prayer 7. John Dory 8. Thunder and Lightning	9. Whip The Cat 10. Willow Tree Wand 11. Jan's Courtship 12. Jan Tregeagle 13. Three Masts 14. John Polrudden 15. The Soldier On The Battlefield 16. Remember Me
<u>12. Carillon LP</u> Produced by Nigel Pegrum for Plant Life Productions, all the songs were written by friends of Brenda's, including Richard Gendall, Ewen Carruthers, John Bidwell and Mike Silver. (A promo single is sometimes seen, featuring the tracks 'Apple Wine' and 'Silver Net' - Transatlantic BIG568).	**Carillon LP** LP 33rpm	Transatlantic Records TRA360
	Brenda Wootton & Dave Penhale - 1979	
	1. Cornwall the Land I Love 2. Carillon 3. Rape of the Mackerel Shoals 4. In Love Again 5. Kenavo Dew Genoughwhy 6. Apple Wine	7. Paris 8. Silver Net 9. The Reed-Beds of Erygh 10. Love's Old Sweet Refrain 11. Eles (She Angel) 12. Country Style
<u>13. Boy Jan, Cornishman LP</u> Produced by Burlington Records of Hitchin in Hertfordshire in 1980, with guitarist Dave Penhale and Richard Gendall (10 of the 13 songs on the album were written by Richard). The front cover has a photo for every track in a checkerboard: I am bottom left, and my son Davy is bottom right!	**Boy Jan Cornishman LP** LP 33rpm	Burlington Records BURL005
	Brenda Wootton, Dave Penhale, Richard Gendall - 1980	
	1. Boy Jan 2. Humphry Davy 3. The Mermaid 4. Abel George 5. Tishomingo Blues 6. Kerra Kernow	7. Five Threes 8. Allan Apple 9. Loving Eyes 10. James Ruse 11. Charlie Bate 12. I Wish That I Were Crossing Now 13. Pensevyk Byghan
<u>14. La Grande Cornouaillaise LP</u> La Grande Cornouaillaise was recorded by Brenda for the French	**La Grande Cornouaillaise LP** LP 33rpm	Burlington Records BURL007
	Brenda Wootton & Dave Penhale - 1980	

<table>
<tr><td>market in 1980, as her career on the continent was going stellar. It was produced by Burlington Records in Hitchin in Hertfordshire under their Plant Life label. The guitarist was Dave Penhale - still playing and living in Cornwall. The cover photograph was taken on the roof of the Palais de Congress in Paris.</td><td>1. Ma Chere Cornouaille
2. Le Chouchenn
3. Tamar
4. An Duren
5. Plougastel
6. Little Eyes</td><td>7. Les Demoiselles de Guilvinec
8. Hello, How Do You Do?
9. Can Yffarn
10. Chere Patrie
11. Kernow Ha Breizh
12. Mon Dieu/La Belle Histoire d'Amour</td></tr>
<tr><td rowspan="3"><u>15. Gwavas Lake LP</u>

So many of the songs written for Brenda by Richard Gendall were about boats, the sea and fishing, and the fishing industry is such an important one in Cornwall, that Brenda decided to produce an album exclusively with 'Cornish Songs of the Sea'. Four Lanes Male Voice Choir feature on this album, together with Richard Gendall and Dave Penhale.</td><td>Gwavas Lake LP
LP 33rpm</td><td>Burlington Records
BURL008</td></tr>
<tr><td colspan="2">Brenda Wootton, Dave Penhale, Richard Gendall - 1980</td></tr>
<tr><td>1. Gwavas Lake
2. Francis Drake
3. Fish to Find
4. The Anson
5. The Bristol Christ
6. Balaena (The Whale)
7. Waiting for the Tide</td><td>8. That Jolly Jack Tar
9. Fearing for You
10. Towl Ros! (Cast Net!)
11. The Lifeboat
12. Home To Scilly
13. Lullaby for an Island Child</td></tr>
<tr><td rowspan="3"><u>16. Un Jour de Fête au Feminin Présent</u>

Produced from a live recording at a large festival for women in the Paris Hippodrome, March 8th 1980. Brenda sings 2 tracks.</td><td>Un Jour de Fête au Feminin Présent LP 33rpm</td><td>Ecoute s'il Pleut
AT 26 006</td></tr>
<tr><td colspan="2">Brenda Wootton & Dave Penhale, Various artists - 1980</td></tr>
<tr><td colspan="2">House of the Rising Sun
Brown Sugar</td></tr>
<tr><td rowspan="3"><u>17. Berceuses Celtes des Iles Britanniques</u>

The EP has 2 lullabies on each side, each one taken from a different Celtic country, including Cornwall, Wales, Isle of Man, and Scotland. The EP was recorded at John Knight's Studio at Coverack in Cornwall.</td><td>Berceuses Celtes des Iles Britanniques - EP</td><td>La Chante du Monde, France; CDM 100133</td></tr>
<tr><td colspan="2">Brenda Wootton, David King – 1981</td></tr>
<tr><td>1. Lul Hay Lay [Lullaby]
2. Suo Gan (Cradle Song)</td><td>1. Cadul Gu Lo (Sleep Until Day)
2. O Can Ye Sew Cushions</td></tr>
<tr><td rowspan="3"><u>18. Lyonesse LP</u>

Lyonesse was the first album produced in France by RCA - it has a wonderfully eclectic mix of material, from songs by Richard Gendall, blues numbers, popular standards and a Beatles number. The cover photo is taken at Land's End in Cornwall.</td><td>Lyonesse LP
LP 33rpm</td><td>RCA France; 37656
PL 70299</td></tr>
<tr><td colspan="2">Brenda Wootton & Dave Penhale - 1982</td></tr>
<tr><td>1. Lyonesse
2. Here, There and Everywhere
3. Doro
4. Port Quin
5. De Sul Vyttyn
6. House of the Rising Sun</td><td>7. In Love Again
8. Come On In
9. The Room Nobody Lives In
10. September Song/ Autumn Leaves
11. Cornwall, the Land I Love
12. Honky Tonk Woman</td></tr>
</table>

19. My Land LP My Land was produced by RCA Germany in 1983, with a lovely selection of tracks - lots of bluesy numbers, some gentle and lyrical, and the best version of Summertime ever. It is usually seen as an LP, and was also available as a cassette. It features a host of musicians including guitarist Chris Newman, the Phil King Trio, Rog & Gill Butler, John Knight and Treviscoe M V Choir.	**My Land LP** LP 33rpm *Brenda Wootton & Chris Newman - 1983* 1. Country Style 2. What's in a Name? 3. My Land 4. Silver Net 5. Dus Tre 6. All of Me/Ain't She Sweet? Medley/Sweet Georgia Brown	RCA Germany PL 70234 7. Baby Doll Blues 8. Friend Love 9. Paris 10. Summertime 11. Hold Your Head Up Jan Boy 12. The Eternal Year
20. Deux Noels Cornouaillais (Two Cornish Carols) Single Produced by RCA France for the Christmas market in 1983.	**Deux Noels Cornouaillais** Single 45 rpm *Brenda Wootton, Mousehole Male Voice Choir, Camborne Town Band* Hark the Glad Sound	RCA 61264 Softly, Sweetly, Through the Air
21. Way Down to Lamorna LP 'Way Down to Lamorna' was a compilation of favourite tracks from Brenda's Cornish Sentinel albums. Produced in 1984, the album includes tracks from SENS 1006, 1016, 1021, 1031 & 1036.	**Way Down to Lamorna LP** LP 33 rpm *Brenda Wootton, Robert Bartlett, Richard Gendall - 1984* 1. Lamorna 2. Mordonnow 3. Soldier on the Battlefield 4. Stratton Carol 5. Pasties and Cream 6. Delyo Syvy 7. Whip the Cat 8. Old Time Religion	Sentinel Records SENS1056 9. Camborne Hill 10. Tryphena Trenary 11. Comish Alphabet 12. Well of St. Keyne 13. Opie Davy Foote Trevithick & Bone 14. Ringers of Egloshayle 15. Tom Bawcock's Eve 16. Jan Knuckey
22. Cornish Australian Single Privately produced by Brenda for her trip to the Kernewek Lowender Festival in 1985. Both tracks were written by Richard Gendall.	**Cornish Australian Single** Single 45 rpm *Brenda Wootton, Chris Newman, Perran Hill Singers, the children of Ludgvan School - 1984* Cornish Australian (Just Like Me...)	BW001 Do You Come From Moonta, Wallaroo, Kadina?
23. 'B' Comme Brenda LP Recorded in John Knight's studio on the Lizard, it was produced by DiskAZ in France. The name of each track is prefaced with an appropriate French word beginning with B – 'B' Like Brenda...	**'B' Comme Brenda LP** LP 33 rpm *Brenda Wootton, Chris Newman, Ray Roberts Trio, Camborne Town Band -* 1. **Benediction**: Durzona 2. **Brel**: Song for Old Lovers 3. **Ballade**: Once in a While 4. **Beautemps**: Over the Rainbow	DiskAZ LP: AZ494; Cassette: C494 6. **Bascule**: O Holy Lord 7. **Belle Grâce**: Amazing Grace 8. **Belmondo**?: Oh Daddy! 9. **Bistrôt**: Baby Won't

	5. **Bientôt**: Soon I'll Be Home (Telephone Song)	You Please Come Home? 10. **Burlesque**: Nobody Loves a Fat Girl 11. **Bœuf**: The Last Performance
24. Tamar LP Tamar is a compilation album with selected tracks from earlier LPs, produced in 1986 in France by DiskAZ, with producer John Knight from the Lizard (who also took the back sleeve photo). Featured musicians and accompanists are Chris Newman, Dave Penhale and Four Lanes Male Voice Choir.	**Tamar LP** LP 33 rp	DiskAZ LP: AZ505; Cassette: C505
	Brenda Wootton, Chris Newman, Ray Roberts Trio, Camborne Town Band - 1986	
	1. Tamar 2. Towl Rus! 3. Balena 4. Tishomingo Blues 5. I Wish That I Were Crossing Now 6. Lullaby to an Island Child 7. Little Eyes	8. Gwavas Lake 9. Ma Chere Cornouaille 10. Home To Scilly 11. Boy Jan 12. Kerra Kernow 13. Waiting for the Tide 14. Kenavo Dewgenoughwy
25. Everybody Knows Maxi Single A Maxi Single, 2 tracks on a 33rpm LP sized album. Produced as a special promotion for a global charity initiative called Walk Across the World. Lyrics to 'Everybody Knows' are by Brenda, music by Francis Lai. Made number 1 in the pop charts in Japan for several weeks.	**Everybody Knows** Maxi Single 45 rpm	Edition23 France EDM039
	Brenda Wootton, Francis Lai - 1987	
	Everybody Knows	Walk Across the World
26. 'So Long' Audio Cassette Recorded at a special concert staged to raise funds for the SIDS Charity (Foundation for the Study of Infant Deaths), and held at the Penventon Hotel, Redruth in the late 1980s. The material performed represented a real 'blast from the past' for those who remember the early years of the Count House and Pipers' Folk Club. Proceeds from sales of the cassette go to SIDS - now renamed The Lullaby Trust. The cassette was produced by Chris Blount of Chough Tapes (and Radio Cornwall fame).	**'So Long'** Audio Cassette	Chough Tapes
	Brenda Wootton, John the Fish – 1988?	
	1. Old Time Religion 2. She Moves Through the Fair 3. Chickens 4. Careless Love Blues 5. Harp Song of the Dane Women 6. Been on this road... So Long 7. Copper Kettle 8. Winter Winds of Sorrow 9. Lamorna	1. The White Rose 2. The Little Husband 3. The First Time Ever 4. Down and Out Blues 5. Far Side of the Hill 6. Ain't No More Cane on the Brazos 7. Just a Closer Walk With Thee 8. Green Eyes 9. The Coming of the Roads 10. Wild Mountain Thyme
27. Seagull LP Brenda's last record – never properly	**Seagull** LP 33 rpm	Vogue France; VG406 506223 MC706223 CD600260

released, as Brenda had a stroke before the final mixing was complete. All the tracks were laid down in John Knight's recording studio on the Lizard.	*Brenda Wootton, Chris Newman, Praze MVC - 1990*	
	1. Clayports 2. Hills of Penwith 3. Saturday Night in the Country 4. Eughelvar (Mistletoe) 5. Everybody Knows 6. An Tour Dantelezet 7. Muddy Waters	8. Cornwall 9. Trevaylor 10. Jan Knuckey 11. Pew A Ore? (Who Knows?) 12. Birth of the Ain't Misbehavin' Blues 13. The Shadow of Your Smile 14. Kenavo
<u>28. Berceuses du Monde Entier LP</u> Following on from the Berceuses Celtes des Iles Britanniques, Le Chante du Monde made a full LP of Lullabies of the World, featuring artists from different countries. Brenda's four Celtic lullabies from the British Isles were reprised, and there were also contributions from Colette Magny, Naomi Moody, Talila, and Marina Vlady - singing songs in various different languages.	**Berceuses du Monde Entier LP** LP 33 rpm	Le Chant du Monde LDX 100312
	Brenda Wootton + David King, Colette Magny, Talila, Marina Vlady, Naomi Moody - 1990	
	Berceuses Francais (Colette Magny) 1. Toutouic 2. Le grand Lustukru (Theodor Botrel) 3. Le p'tit Quinquin (Desrousseaux) 4. La petite poule grisse Berceuses Yiddish (Talila) 5. A mol is gueven a mayse (Il etait une fois une histoire) 6. Chlof mein kinde (Dors mon enfant)	Berceuses Russe (Marina Vlady) 1. Berceuse cosaque 2. La jeune fille se promenait dans les bois 3. Berceuse pour endormir l'orage Berceuses Celtes des Iles Britanniques (Brenda Wootton) 4. Lul ha lay,(Cornouaille) 5. Suo Gan (Pays de Galles) 6. Cadul gu lo (Ile de Man) Berceuses Noires (Naomi Moody) 7. Who dat? 8. Put on the skillet 9. Go to sleep
<u>29. The Voice of Cornwall CD</u> The Voice of Cornwall was released by Keltia Music of Quimper in Brittany in 1996, with the assistance of Bob Brimley of Brio Music in St Just, Cornwall. It consists of compilation tracks from SENS1056, SENS1006, and SENS1021. The CD contained a bilingual booklet - reverse-printed on one side, in French with the title 'La Grande Cornouaillaise, and on the other in	**The Voice of Cornwall** CD	Keltia Music Brittany KMCD67
	Brenda Wootton, Robert Bartlett, Richard Gendall - 1996	
	1. Lamorna 2. Mordonnow 3. The Soldier on the Battlefield 4. The Stratton Carol 5. Pasties and Cream 6. Delyo Syvy 7. Whip the Cat 8. Old Time Religion 9. Camborne Hill	1. Well of St. Keyne 2. Opie, Davy, Foote, Trevithick & Bone 3. The Ringers of Egloshayle 4. Tom Bawcock's Eve 5. Jan Knuckey 6. An Tour Dantelezet 7. Tamar

English with the title 'The Voice of Cornwall'.	10. Tryphena Trenerry	8. To the Sea 9. Betsy Watson
<u>30. All of Me CD</u> The discovery of the master tapes of this concert, recorded in 1984, has provided the material for the first new album by Brenda in fifteen years and marks a significant time when she was at the peak of her musical career.	**All of Me** CD	Knight Design
	Brenda Wootton, Chris Newman, Camborne Town Band, Ray Roberts Jazz Trio – recorded 1984, produced 2010	
	1. The Land I Love 2. Farewell Shanty 3. The Mystery 4. Pyu a Wor 5. My Land 6. What's In a Name 7. Paris 8. Tishomingo Blues 9. Silver Net 10. Jan Knuckey 11. Friend Love	12. All of Me/Aint She Sweet/Sweet Georgia Brown Medley 13. Lyonesse 14. Summertime 15. Country Style 16. The Can Can (instrumental, CTB) 17. Little Eyes 18. Over the Rainbow 19. Trelawney
<u>31. Brenda at Buryan CD</u> A performance by Brenda and John the Fish at a typical Pipers club night at St Buryan Village Hall, recorded in 1968 by Mike Gluyas.	**Brenda at Buryan 1968 CD** Live recording CD	Sue Ellery BWCD1
	Brenda Wootton, John the Fish – recorded 1968, produced 2013	
	1. I'm Counting Stars 2. Marta, Marta 3. Lady Mary 4. Port Mahon 5. The Old Grey Duck 6. Harp Song of the Dane Women 7. The First Time Ever	8. Old Maid's Song 9. Two Brothers 10. Going to the Zoo 11. Cockleshells/ Waley Waley 12. I'm Troubled 13. Stay Not Late 14. A Good Man is Hard to Find 15. Mingulay Boat Song 16. Old Time Religion
<u>32. Brenda at Christmas CD</u> A compilation of much-loved seasonal tracks & newly discovered old recordings. Get into the seasonal mood with some favourite tracks of Brenda Wootton – together with some never-before-published Christmassy recordings from Pipers' Folk Club in the late 1970s. This compilation of previously published tracks, together with additional archive material recently discovered on old private recordings, we hope will give you a flavour of Brenda's enjoyment of music at Christmas, one of her favourite times of the year. These are vintage recordings,	**Brenda at Christmas CD** Compilation CD + new tracks	Sue Ellery-Hill BWCD2
	Brenda Wootton, John the Fish, Robert Bartlett, Al Fenn, Richard Gendall, Dave Penhale, Four Lanes Male Choir, Chris Newman, John Knight, Ray Roberts Trio, Donald Jarvis, Mousehole Male Voice Choir, Camborne Town Band - 2017	
	1. Old Time Religion (Pasties & Cream LP, 1971) 2. Three Masts (Children Singing LP, 1978) 3. Cornish Alphabet (Pasties & Cream LP, 1971) 4. Stratton Carol (Starry Gazey Pie LP, 1975) 5. Eughelvar (Mistletoe) (Seagull LP, 1990) 6. Allan Apple (Boy Jan LP,	9. Five Threes (Boy Jan LP, 1980) 10. Evening Prayer (Children Singing LP, 1976) 11. Amazing Grace ("B" Comme Brenda LP, 1985) 12. Hark the Glad (Xmas Single, 1983) 13. Steren Yn Nos (Archive

many available for the first time on CD, and Mic has done sterling work to bring them up to suitable quality. (A scanned copy of the original music and lyrics of 'Softly Sweetly' are included with the CD.)	1980) 7. Softly Sweetly (Xmas single, 1983) 8. Tom Bawcock's Eve (Pipers' Folk LP, 1968)	recording, 1978) 14. Bristol Christ (Gwavas Lake LP, 1980) 15. Christmas Medley (Archive recording, 1978)

Amateur Dramatic Productions Brenda was involved in 1957-1965

Year	Play	Author	Players	Venue	Brenda's involvement
1956	The Emperor's Nightingale	?	Lands End WI	Sennen Church Hall	Singing – the Real Nightingale
March 1957	Ring of Roses/A Shot in the Dark/The Rocks Won't Tell (3 One-Act Plays)	Marcel Achard/?	Sennen Drama Group	Sennen Church Hall	Acting, Scenery
Jan 1958	The Golden Goose (Pantomime)	Brenda (from Hans Christian Anderson)	Sennen Drama Group	Sennen, St Just Town Hall (British Legion)	Author, Acted, Producer, Scenery
Jan 1958	Keeper of the Keys (One-Act Play)	Vera I Arlett	Sennen Drama Group	Sennen Church Hall (Maundy Thursday)	Producer
Apr 1958	None So Blind (One-Act Play)	Armitage Owen	Sennen Drama Group	Sennen Church Hall	Stage Manager, make-up; John, electrician
July 1958	The Marvellous History of St Bernard (Three-Act Play)	Henri Gheon - trans. Sir Barry Jackson	Cornwall Religious Drama Fellowship CRDF	Minack Theatre & Treloyhan Manor, St Ives	Costumes
Jan 1959	Abou Hassan (Pantomime)	Brenda (from Arabian Nights)	Sennen Drama Group	Sennen Church Hall Paul, St Buryan, St Just	Author; Acted John performed
May 1959	Haul for the Shore (Three Act Comedy)	Jean McConnell	Sennen Drama Group	Madron, Landithy Hall	Stage Manager, scenery; John: electrics
June 1959	Noah (Play)	André Obey	Cornwall Religious Drama Fellowship	Minack Theatre	Costume?
Jan 1960	Grisleybeard (Pantomime)	Brenda (from Brothers Grimm)	Sennen Drama Group (in aid of World Refugee Year)	Sennen Church Hall, St Buryan, St Just, Cheshire Homes	Author; scenery
May 1960	Comedy, Mime & Minstrel Show	Brenda & Martin Scrase	Playgoers Theatre Club	Little Theatre, Morrab Road, Penzance	Performer
June 1960	The Comedian	Henri Gheon - trans. Alan Bland	Cornwall Religious Drama Fellowship	Minack Theatre	Acted

Nov/Dec 1960	Power Without Glory (Three-Act Play)	Michael C Hutton	Playgoers Theatre Club	Little Theatre, Morrab Road	Producer
Jan 1961	Rumpelstiltskin (Pantomime)	Ann Havelock Davies (from Brother's Grimm)	Sennen Drama Group	Sennen Church Hall	?
Feb 1961	The Smugglers of Sennen (Play)	Molly Bartlett (for WI competition)	Madron Players	Madron, Landithy Hall	Producer, scenery
Feb 1961	The Golden Goose – (Pantomime)	Brenda (from Hans C Anderson)	Playgoers Theatre Club	Little Theatre, Morrab Road	Author
Feb 1961	The Night of the Fox + The Wreckers of Auburnswyck – Plays	Joan Forman Robert Horspool	Madron Players + Madron Young Farmers Club	Madron, Landithy Hall	Producer Producer
March, April 1961	The Night of the Fox – Play	Chosen for National Festival of Community Drama	Madron Players + MYFC Certificate by Howard Spring, Pres of Cornwall Drama Soc.	Penzance County Grammar School for Girls; County Hall, Truro	Producer
1961?	Frying Tonight	?	Penzance Players	Penzance Players Theatre Club?	?
Jan 1962?	The Shoes that were Danced to Pieces (Pantomime)	Brenda (ad. from Brothers Grimm)	Playgoers Theatre Club	Little Theatre, Morrab Road	Producer
May 1962	Breath of Spring (Full-length comedy play)	Peter Coke	Playgoers Theatre Club	Little Theatre, Morrab Road (2 nights)	Producer
June 1962	Salad Days – Musical ...and The Boy Friend – Musical	Julian Slade Sandy Wilson	Fabian Theatrical Productions (Repertory theatre)	Pavilion Theatre, Promenade, Penzance	??
July 1962	Dry Rot (Full length Farce)	John Chapman	Fabian Theatrical Productions (+ guest actor Arthur English)	Pavilion Theatre, Promenade, Penzance	Acting: Sergeant Fire policewoman
Dec 1962	Badgers Green (3 Act play)	R C Sheriff	?	?	Producer?

Dec 1962?	Carpet Slippers (Play)	W A Darlington	Madron Players	Madron, Landithy Hall	Producer
Feb 1963	The False Prince (Pantomime)	Brenda (adapt. from Wilhelm Hauff)	Playgoers Theatre Club	Little Theatre, Morrab Road	Producer
April 1963	An Air For Murder (Three-Act Play)	Falkland L Cary & Philip King	Madron Players	Madron Landithy Hall	Producer
Nov 1963	The White Sheep of the Family (Full-length play)	L Du Garde Peach & Ian Hay	Madron Players	Madron Landithy Hall	Set design + Peter Winchester
Jan 1964	The Rolling Stones or The Stones of Plouhinec (Pantomime)	Brenda, from a Breton legend	Sennen Drama Group	Sennen, Little Theatre, Morrab Road?	Author, Producer, Acted, Scenery
May 1964	The Mayor of Torontal (Full-length play)	Gwenyth Jones	Madron Players, Cwall 14th BDL Drama Festival entry	Truro City Hall, Leamington Spa Finals	Produced and acted
May 1964	Blithe Spirit (Full-length Comedy)	Noel Coward	Playgoers Theatre Club	Little Theatre, Morrab Road	Produced, John played Dr Bradman
Jan 1965	The Royal Sturgeon (Pantomime)	Brenda	Sennen Drama Group	St Just Town Hall	Author
May 1965	CFWI Golden Jubilee Pageant	Kathleen Mackenzie	Madron WI	?	Produced, backstage, acted
Nov 1965	And So To Bed (Play)	J B Fagan	Madron Players	Madron Landithy Hall	Producer

Count House FM Club & Pipers Folk Club, Guests

(Roughly in date order, resident singers listed at the end; not necessarily complete, and some guests returned a few times during the year; after 1974 Brenda was no longer doing the Club bookings)

1966 Count House	1968 Pipers, St Buryan	1969 Pipers, St Buryan
Martin Windsor	Martin Wyndham-Read	Jug Trust
Gerry Lockran	Tim Hart & Maddy Prior	Johnny Silvo
Joy Hyman	Derek Brimstone	Gary Peterson
Worman Jeffs	Gerry Lockran	Cliff Aungier
The Haverim	Noel Murphy	Noel Murphy
1967 Count House	Cliff Aungier	Leesiders
Cliff Aungier	Jon Betmead	Mike Silver
Johnny Silvo	Clive Palmer	The Yetties
The Haverim	Wizz Jones	Michael Chapman
1967 Pipers, St Buryan	Ron Geesin	Wizz Jones
Cliff Aungier	Country Wake	Ralph McTell
Derek Brimstone	Michael Chapman	
Ralph McTell	Ralph McTell	**1969 Pipers, Count House**
Pete Stanley & Wizz Jones	Stefan Grossman	Keith Chetwin
Noel Murphy	The Yetties	Alex Atterson
Mervyn Whiddon	Terry Gould	Gerry Lockran
Michael Chapman	Ian McCann	Martin Windsor
Steve Benbow	The Strawbs	Pongo Flossie
Alex Atterson	John Renbourn	Packi Byrne
Terry Masterson	Alex Atterson	Mike Cooper
Martin Windsor	Steve Benbow	Derek Brimstone
Ron Geesin	Colin Scott	Roger & Eileen Knowles
Terry Gould	Mike Silver	Morgan
Jon Betmead	Cornish All Stars Trad Jazz Band	Barry Skinner
Jug Trust		Mike Absalom
Johnny Silvo	Martin Windsor	Noel Murphy & Shaggis
Gerry Lockran	Mike Cooper	Jon Betmead
Rod Wilmott	Contrasts	Martin Wyndham-Read
Joanne Kelly	Alex Campbell	Strawbs
Redd Sullivan	Studio 4	Pete Ryder
Stefan Grossman	Johnny Silvo	Malcolm Price
1970 Pipers, Count House	**1971 Western Hotel, Pz**	Diz Disley
Michael Chapman	John James	Allan Taylor
Cliff Aungier	Tony Rose	Barrie Beattie
John Foreman	Mudge & Clutterbuck	Colin Scott
Jon Betmead	Ian Hunt	Studio 4
Jug Trust	Noel Murphy	Cliff Aungier

Martyn Wyndham Reade	Jack Hudson	Ralph McTell
Ralph McTell	Derek Brimstone	Johnny Sillvo
Stefan Grossman	Barry Skinner	Mike Silver
Alex Atterson	Harvey Andrews	The Yetties
Derek Brimstone	Pete Stanley	
Steve Benbow	Pete Ryder	**1972 Western Hotel, Pz**
Noel Murphy	Paul Weaving	Martin Carthy
Wizz Jones	Dave & Dave	Harvey Andrews
Colin Scott (Scottie)	The Yetties	1812
Mike Silver	Martin Carthy	Barry Skinner
Cornish All Stars Trad Jazz	Songwainers	Bonded Boots
Tim Hart and Maddy Prior	Sean Cannon	Allan Taylor
Gerry Lockran	Tony Capstick	Totem
Country Wake (Duo)	Shelagh McDonald	Tony Capstick
Martin Windsor	Singing Tradition	Alex Atterson
Mike Cooper	Allan Taylor	Jon Betmead
Contrasts (Duo)	Strange Fruit	Decameron
Alex Campbell	Wizz Jones	Jack Hudson
	Gerry Lockran	Noel Murphy
1971 St Johns Hall	Jon Betmead	Cyril Tawney
Decameron	Black on White	Bill Clifton
Ralph McTell	1812	Hunter Muskett
Michael Chapman	Johnny Collins	Gordon Giltrap
Magna Carta	Diz Disley	Pete Atkin
Diz Disley + Pigsty Hill L.O	Alex Atterson	Jon Raven
Steeleye Span	Martin Wyndham-Read	Agincourt
1973 Western Hotel, Pz	Jasper Carrot	Mike Boreham (Silver)
John St Field	Tim Hart & Maddy Prior	Tony Rose
Pat Woods	Kelston Roundhill	Sarah Grey
Bob Davenport	Lonesome Travellers	
Friedeman	Nic Jones	**1972/73 The Garden, Promenade, Penzance**
Bob Williamson	Gothic Horizon	
Nic Jones	Dave Cartwright	Plainsong
Bill Clifton	Johnny Silvo	Diz Disley + John James
Barry Dransfield		The Yetties
Hunter Muskett		Michael Chapman
Gerry Lockran		Ralph McTell
Jack Hudson	**1974 Western Hotel, Penzance**	Martin Carthy + Jeremy Taylor
Allan Taylor		
Mike Boreham (Silver)	Tony Capstick	Celtic Concert: Margaret McCleod (Scotl) Brenda + Charlie Bate (Cornwall) The Henneseys (Wales)
Dave Burland	Dave Burland	
Roy Bailey	Jon Betmead	
Alex Atterson	Ian Anderson	
Sara Grey	Noel Murphy	

Strange Fruit	Jack Hudson	Mick Maloney/Dave Doherty (Ireland) The Henneseys (Wales)
Diz Disley	Martin Wyndham-Read	
Decameron	Rosie Hardman	
White on Black	Jon Betmead	Albion Country Band: Sue Draheim, Ashley Hutchings, Steve Ashley, Dave Mattacks, Simon Nicol, Royston Wood, Al Stewart
Tony Capstick	Tony Rose	
Bandersnatch	Robin Dransfield	
Canton Trig	Vin Garbutt	
Mask	Sara Grey	
Jasper Carrott	Geoff & Penny Harris	
Rosemary Hardman	Crowdy Crawn (Brenda Rob)	Bert Jansch
Jon Betmead	Pete Atkin	The J.S.D.Band
Ian Hunt & Graham Davies	Alex Atterson	Michael Chapman
Noel Murphy	Mike Silver	John Renbourn, Jacqui McShee
Burgundy	Chris Rohman	
Pete Atkin	White on Black	Julie Felix
Sandy & Hanks	Stained Glass	Bridget St John
Michael Chapman	Sadie	Andy Roberts
John James	Barbara Dickson	John James
Martin Carthy	Roy Bailey	Richard & Linda Thompson
Stained Glass	Joe Stead	**Itinerants & Residents**
Tim Greenwood	John Goulding	John the Fish
Sean Cannon	Magic Lantern	Brenda Wootton
Odd Folk	Gordon Giltrap	Mel & Miles
1975 Western Hotel, Pz	Richard Digance	Tell Mann
Dave Paskett	Odd Folk	Des Hannigan
Steve Tilston	White on Black	Ronald Handfield Jones Alan Robinson
The Farewell Band	Hoddesdon Morris Men	
Decameron in Concert	Decameron	Mike Sagar-Fenton
Ian Anderson	Cottage Pie	Steve Hall
Celebrated Ratcliffe Stout Band	Dave Peabody & Hugh McNulty	Ralph McTell
Crowdy Crawn (Brenda Rob)	Steve Tilston	Terry Kemp
Jon Betmead	Meniscus	Alec Shaw
George Deacon & Marion Rose	Dave Paskett	Mic McCreadie
	Nic Jones	Dave Semmens
Alex Atterson	Porl Reynolds	Creepin' Jane
Tony Capstick	Strange Fruit	Dick Reynolds
Derek Brimstone	George Norris	Adrian O'Reilly
Stained Glass	Allan Taylor	Roger Brookes
Noel Murphy		Niall Timmins
Chris Foster		Four-Fifths Jug Band
Chris Rohmann		Terry Broad
Dave Peabody & Hugh McNulty		Mike Smith + The Other Band
Pete Finch & Andy Legatt		Clive Palmer

		Keith Hills
		Bert Biscoe
		Bob Devereux
		Philip Knight
		Guy Chalker-Howells

Acknowledgements

Such a prodigious book for a larger-than-life character was never going to be the work of just one person. My mentor throughout has been Mike Sagar-Fenton, who knew Brenda for as long as just about anybody, apart from me. He has been lavish with his enthusiasm, encouragement and praise, but has also spent much time sorting through the ton of boxes of memorabilia for useful material, helping, advising, critiquing and selecting photos. Mike had hoped to be able to write it himself, but Brenda, as ever, was too demanding on his time. Anne Bellingham, sent from the Hypatia Trust and Jameson Library, was the first to step up for the task. She also did fantastic work sorting and cataloguing the material, but was unable to continue for personal reasons. I am grateful to them both for breaking the ice so effectively.

To all of Brenda's long-suffering accompanists, particularly those I have been able to interview – thank you for everything you did for her, and for me, and for everything you put up with. I must mention in particular John Langford, and Michael Chapman – friends for life in my book – which this is – and there are too many more to detail. Apologies to those I wasn't able to reach for comment.

So many friends, and relatives of course, have had words and support to offer, and I am grateful to all who have contributed their memories, comments and anecdotes.

The book was written largely from the memories within my own head (an imperfect place at best), but much research has been done in interviewing people, referencing books and online sources, at Cornwall Record Office, and burying myself knee-deep, literally at times, in Brenda's memorabilia (hold my glass – I'm going in...) – a veritable mountain of assorted boxes that have been following me around ever since Brenda died. The significant elements of all that memorabilia will, in due course, be housed in the new Kresen Kernow archive centre in Redruth.

This book would not have happened at all without the light of my life, my husband, Chris Ellery-Hill. Thank you for ever, my lovely, for your unflinching support, forbearance, good humour, invaluable insights and endless patience.

Bibliography

- 'Eighty From the Eighties', edited by Martin Val Baker; (*1993*)
- 'Folk in Cornwall', by Rupert White; *Antenna Publications* (*2015*)
- 'Girls Not Allowed: A History of Bedminster Down Boys Club', by Andy Lewis; *SilverWood Books Ltd* (*2014*)
- 'Pantomime Stew', a compilation of Brenda's poems by Sue Ellery-Hill; *from the Brenda website* (*1994*)
- 'Ten Years of Folk', by Ken Woollard & Elizabeth Twinnem; *Grand Ole Opry* (*England*) *Ltd*
- 'The Human Spring', by Gladys Tranter; *publ. by Penzance Girls' Grammar School* (*1980*)
- 'The Importance of Being Cornish in Cornwall', by Professor Charles Thomas; *Inaugural Lecture, Institute of Cornish Studies* (*1973*)
- 'The Lorient Interceltic Festival', by Alain Cabon; *Editions Ouest-France* (*2010*)
- The Story of Our WI, by Land's End WI; *Cornwall Record Office*
- 'Thirty Years of the Cambridge Folk Festival', by Dave Laing & Richard Newman; *Music Maker Books (1994)*
- 'Thirty Years at the Pump', by John Alderslade, Trevor Porter, John Whitcombe; *Village Pump Publishing* (*2000*)

Websites:

- Brenda Wootton website: www.brendawootton.org
- Kernow Beat website: www.kernowbeat.co.uk
- Tremaen Pottery website: www.tremaen.com

Subscribers

The following people have kindly contributed to the book's publication:

We love you all!!

Andrew Bolton
Andy & Sheila Gill
Anne & Tony Frost
Barbara Tresidder Ryan
Beatrice Kerno
Brian Dunn
Bunty Davies
Chris Ellery-Hill
David G Tubby
Des Hannigan
Dik Cadbury
Elizabeth Trenary
Geoff & Frankie March
Geoffrey Rogers
Guy Chant
H M James Music Shop, Penzance
Jack King
Jane Trenary Mutch
John Alderslade
John Trewhella & Brian Ivory
Johnny Coppin
Linda Collins
Loveday Jenkin
Martin Woods
Merv Davey
Michael Sagar Fenton
Phil Saward
Philip Rush
Richard Reynolds
Sue Eddy
Theodore Mendenhall Rodriguez
Tom Richards
Will Coleman

Index